**1 YEAR UPGRADE**
BUYER PROTECTION PLAN

# C# for Java Programmers

**Brian Bagnall**

**Philip Chen**

**Stephen Goldberg**

**Jeremy Faircloth**  Technical Reviewer

**Harold Cabrera**  Technical Editor

| KEY | SERIAL NUMBER |
|-----|---------------|
| 001 | JA9CK8HUM2 |
| 002 | 7YQA4FT7MZ |
| 003 | PE5ET3K8N6 |
| 004 | 8YG6FTX54A |
| 005 | 7TBJ45S3KQ |
| 006 | SH7T3W2NAR |
| 007 | UBT46NEA2P |
| 008 | VC29KLBG5R |
| 009 | JKR34SDH78 |
| 010 | TG7BH34WSX |

PUBLISHED BY
Syngress Publishing, Inc.
800 Hingham Street
Rockland, MA 02370

**C# for Java Programmers**

Printed in the United States of America

1 2 3 4 5 6 7 8 9 0

ISBN: 1-931836-54-X

Technical Editor: Harold Cabrera
Technical Reviewer: Jeremy Faircloth
Acquisitions Editor: Jonathan Babcock
Indexer: J. Edmund Rush

Cover Designer: Michael Kavish
Page Layout and Art by: Shannon Tozier
Copy Editor: Mike McGee, Jesse Corbeil

Distributed by Publishers Group West in the United States and Jaguar Book Group in Canada.

# Acknowledgments

We would like to acknowledge the following people for their kindness and support in making this book possible.

Ralph Troupe, Rhonda St. John, Emlyn Rhodes and the team at Callisma for their invaluable insight into the challenges of designing, deploying and supporting world-class enterprise networks.

Karen Cross, Lance Tilford, Meaghan Cunningham, Kim Wylie, Harry Kirchner, Kevin Votel, Kent Anderson, Frida Yara, Jon Mayes, John Mesjak, Peg O'Donnell, Sandra Patterson, Betty Redmond, Roy Remer, Ron Shapiro, Patricia Kelly, Andrea Tetrick, Jennifer Pascal, Doug Reil, David Dahl, Janis Carpenter, and Susan Fryer of Publishers Group West for sharing their incredible marketing experience and expertise.

Jacquie Shanahan, AnnHelen Lindeholm, David Burton, Febea Marinetti, and Rosie Moss of Elsevier Science for making certain that our vision remains worldwide in scope.

Annabel Dent and Paul Barry of Elsevier Science/Harcourt Australia for all their help.

David Buckland, Wendi Wong, Marie Chieng, Lucy Chong, Leslie Lim, Audrey Gan, and Joseph Chan of Transquest Publishers for the enthusiasm with which they receive our books. And welcome back to Daniel Loh—glad to have you back Daniel!

Kwon Sung June at Acorn Publishing for his support.

Ethan Atkin at Cranbury International for his help in expanding the Syngress program.

Jackie Gross, Gayle Voycey, Alexia Penny, Anik Robitaille, Craig Siddall, Darlene Morrow, Iolanda Miller, Jane Mackay, and Marie Skelly at Jackie Gross & Associates for all their help and enthusiasm representing our product in Canada.

Lois Fraser, Connie McMenemy, Shannon Russell and the rest of the great folks at Jaguar Book Group for their help with distribution of Syngress books in Canada.

Thank you to our hard-working colleagues at New England Fulfillment & Distribution who manage to get all our books sent pretty much everywhere in the world. Thank you to Debbie "DJ" Ricardo, Sally Greene, Janet Honaker, and Peter Finch.

# Contributors

**Philip Chen** (MCP, JCP) is an independent consultant in enterprise Web infrastructure and distributed application architecture. Philip's specialties include J2EE and .NET based server-client application development, database integration, and technology migration. Philip's background includes positions as a senior member of technical staff at SUN Microsystems and as CTO/VP of Engineering at OnVest.com, an online financial analysis and investment planning firm. Philip holds a bachelor's degree from UC Berkeley and a master's degree from Stanford. Philip would like to thank his parents for their motivation and support throughout his life, and Dr. Si-En Chang and Dr. Liu-Xi Yang for their tremendous mentorship throughout his technical tenure.

**Chris Peiris** currently lectures on Distributed Object Technology and Software Component Technologies subjects at Monash University, Caulfield, Victoria, Australia. He has been designing and developing MS Web solutions since 1995. His expertise lies in developing scalable, high-performance Web solutions for financial institutions and media groups. He has written many articles, reviews and columns for various online publications including *Developer Exchange* (www.devx.com) and Wrox Press. Recently he co-authored the book *C# Web Service with .NET Remoting and ASP.NET*. Chris also presents at seminars at professional developer conferences including Microsoft Tech Ed 2002 in Brisbane, Australia. He is at work on his third book on Web Services. Chris's core skills are C++, Java, .NET, DNA, MTS, Site Server, Data Warehousing, WAP, and SQL Server. Chris has a bachelor's of Computing, bachelor's of Business, and a master's of Information Technology. Currently he is undertaking a Ph.D. on Web Service Trust Agents. Chris lives in Flemington, Melbourne, Australia with his family. He would like to thank his friends Sanjeev, Nilantha, Sumedha, Brumoon, Janik, Rowie, Andy, Natalie, Ben Loke, Mark Holmes, Ben Morrell, and Tommy. This is a measure of gratitude for the support, patience, guidance, and their friendship over the years.

**Stephen Goldberg** (CCNP, MCP, MCP+I, MCSE) is a Senior Developer with AT&T Labs. He currently works on the development team for the AT&T Netclient family of products. Stephen has developed client applications with several programming languages, including C/C++, Java, and C#. He is also a Founder and Development Lead for Absolute IT Solutions LLC, a .NET solutions provider.

**Brian Bagnall** (Sun Certified Java Programmer and Developer) is the author of the popular book *Core LEGO MINDSTORMS Programming* and co-author of the *Sun Certified Programmer for Java 2 Study Guide*. Brian has worked for IBM and other leading computer companies. He is a key programmer of leJOS, a Java SDK for LEGO MINDSTORMS. Brian has bridged the world of LEGO MINDSTORMS and .NET by figuring out how to program the LEGO RCX brick or Cybermaster using C#.

**David Chung** (MCP, MCT, Sun Certified Java Programmer, WebLogic Certified Programmer, WebLogic Certified Trainer) is a Senior Consultant with LearningVoyage. He provides training and consulting services in Java and distributed object technologies to enterprise clients across the United States and Canada. David is a frequent conference speaker and author and is founder of the 380 Java Users group. David holds bachelor's degrees in Mathematics and Computer Science from the University of Northern Iowa. He is the co-author of several Java programming books and training materials in C and C++. His development experience spans embedded systems, enterprise systems, and consumer software. David and his wife, Janice, have eight children whose names begin with 'J'.

**Ed Lee** (MCSD, MCSE, Sun Certified Java Programmer) is a consultant with the professional services division of a leading technology company, where he provides expert assistance on distributed system architecture and implementation. He has developed systems for many large enterprises using various technologies, including Java and C#. Prior to his current engagement, Ed worked as Vice President of Technology for Netexe, Inc., a provider of solutions for handheld and wireless devices, and a pioneer in using Java and the .NET Framework on mobile devices. Ed holds a bachelor's of Science and a master's of Business Administration from Brigham Young University.

**Dreamtech Software Inc.** is a software solution and service provider that provides a broad range of services and offers a dynamic blend of consultancy and system integration to help corporations build and implement innovative e-business strategies. A futuristic vision motivates the globally acclaimed software products of Dreamtech Software. Dreamtech has already distinguished itself with an excellent track record of publishing books on advanced technologies including XML and XSLT, WAP, Bluetooth, 3G, peer-to-peer networking, C#, and Java. The success of Dreamtech's endeavors to provide world-class software products can be gauged by the fact that its clientele includes some of the most distinguished names in IT-related publishing and solutions.

# Technical Reviewer and Contributor

**Jeremy Faircloth** (CCNA, MCSE, MCP+I, A+) is a Systems Analyst for Gateway, Inc., where he develops and maintains enterprise-wide client/server and Web-based technologies. He also acts as a technical resource for other IT professionals, using his expertise to help others expand their knowledge. As a Systems Analyst with over 10 years of real-world IT experience, he has become an expert in many areas of IT including Web development, database administration, programming, enterprise security, network design, and project management. Jeremy currently resides in Dakota City, NE and wishes to thank Christina Williams for her support in his various technical endeavors.

# Technical Editor and Contributor

**Harold Cabrera** (Sun Certified Java Programmer) was the Technical Editor of the *Sun Certified Programmer for Java 2 Study Guide 2nd Edition* and is a Software Engineer and Co-Founder of IdleWorks Inc. Harold is the Lead Architect for the software development team at IdleWorks, which develops distributed processing solutions for large- and medium-sized businesses with supercomputing needs. Harold holds a bachelor's degree in Computer Engineering from the University of Manitoba and is a recipient of the IEEE Best Thesis Award for his undergraduate thesis entitled *A Distributed Computing System: An Application Written in Java for Distributed Computing*. Harold's other interests include developing for mobile devices and Web Services development with J2EE and C#. He would like to thank his family and friends for their constant support and encouragement.

# Contents

**Java Code Cycle**

## Chapter 3 Language Fundamentals    63

**Mathematical Operators**

| Operator | Definition |
|---|---|
| + | Addition |
| – | Subtraction |
| * | Multiplication |
| / | Division |
| % | Modulus |

**Arrays**

- Standard C# arrays are identical to their Java counterparts.

- C# provides two different kinds of multidimensional arrays, rectangular and jagged.

- A rectangular array has equal dimensions, a jagged array does not.

- The *params* keyword can be used to specify that an array of unknown dimensions will be passed to a method.

## Chapter 5 Objects and Classes                       **179**

**NOTE**

Only nested classes permit the use of the *new* keyword. The *new* modifier specifies that the class hides an inherited member by the same name. Inner classes and Inheritance will be discussed in Chapter 6.

**Frequently Asked
Questions**

**Q:** Does C# support
multiple inheritance?

**A:** Yes and no—just like
Java, C# allows single
inheritance of classes
and multiple
inheritance of
interfaces.

**Q:** Does Java support
inner classes?

**A:** Yes. C# supports only
one kind of inner class
compared to Java's
four.

## Unboxing

⟨≈⟩ ————————— ⟨≈⟩

Unboxing is the act of converting an object back into a value type. The syntax for this process looks very similar to explicit casting in Java, as the following C# code demonstrates:

```
int x = 29;

object xObj = x; //
Boxing

int x1 = (int)xObj;
// Unboxing
```

## Delegates

⟨≈⟩ ————————— ⟨≈⟩

■ Delegates are similar to C/C++ function pointers.

■ Delegates reference a method.

■ Delegates are object-oriented, type-safe, and secure.

**Creating Assemblies**

■ Assemblies are the C#
equivalent to Java's
packages and are used
to segment
namespaces.

■ Assemblies in the .NET
architecture can be
written and compiled
in different languages,
and still work together.

■ All information about
an assembly is stored
in the assembly
manifest.

**Developing &
Deploying...**

**Monitor.Wait()
Parameters**

The *Wait()* method can
take on a variety of
parameters, including an
integer specifying the
number of milliseconds to
wait as well as a *TimeSpan*
structure. In the event that
the specified time expires
before it is notified by a
corresponding *Pulse()*,
*Wait()* returns a *boolean*
value of *false*.

**Debugging...**

**The Directory Separator**

One of the most frequent bugs when programming with the file system is the backslash used to identify directory structures. Notice the need to use two backslashes in the preceding example. This is because the backslash is an escape character, so it is necessary to nullify the first by using two backslashes. An even better solution is to indicate a verbatim string literal by placing the @ symbol in front of the string, as follows:

```
String filename =
@"c:\Program Files";
```

**Financial Calculator**

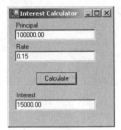

## Chapter 13 Web Development with C#     479

**Creating Proxy Objects**

To interact with a Web service you will need to create a proxy object that will act as the middleman between your application and the service. The proxy object can be generated from the WSDL file in two ways:

- Using the *wsdl.exe* command line utility

- Using Visual Studio.NET

## Chapter 14 Working with ActiveX, COM, and Unmanaged Code      527

**Unmanaged Code**

The interoperability services in .NET could be categorized into the following scenarios:

- .NET assembly (managed) calling a single COM DLL (unmanaged)

- .NET assembly (managed) calling a COM object or an ActiveX control (unmanaged)

- COM DLL (unmanaged) calling a .NET assembly (managed)

**What Is J#?**

J# is a complete implementation of the Java language specification. J# allows the majority of existing Java applications to run after recompilation or after binary conversion.

# Foreword

Welcome to *C# for Java Programmers*. I think you'll find that this book will be both enjoyable and challenging at the same time. It will cover Microsoft's new platform called .NET and the exciting new language for the platform called C#. According to Microsoft, the C# language is a simple, modern, object-oriented, and type-safe programming language derived from C and C++. But looking closely, you can see that C# also has a lot of similarities with Java. Our main goal here is to teach you the C# language by leveraging your existing Java skills.

I know, I know, you're probably wondering why you should learn another language when you already know Java and are reasonably comfortable with it. Well, here are several reasons:

- First, it's from Microsoft. When a big company like Microsoft puts most of their resources into a new technology it's hard for developers not to take notice. This new technology will certainly make an impact in the industry.

- As a programmer, C# is a language that will benefit you if it's add to your repertoire. With your Java skills, it'll be a relatively small leap to learn this new language. Therefore, learning C# will increase your marketability in the workplace relatively painlessly.

- By learning C# and .NET, you'll have several choices when implementing a solution for a specific project. For example, you can choose between .NET and J2EE when it comes to developing XML-based Web services.

- It's arguable that Java lacks the performance needed when it comes to Windows applications development. C# enables you to develop fast

Windows applications without having to resort to learning the more complicated C++ language. Not only that, Web Services development is a breeze, and integration with COM and the Win32 API makes this new language very appealing.

With the same ease of use as Java, and the raw power of C++, I think that you'll definitely like what you'll get from C#.

For those of you who are not expert with Java, I assure you that there is no need to worry. Knowing Java is not a pre-requisite for this book. Most of the explanations will be easy enough to follow. However, since we will be drawing a lot of comparisons with Java, you might find the going a little tough at times. If you have a programming background in other languages such as C, or C++, then you have nothing to worry about. At the end of the book, you'll probably even learn how to program Java! Two books for the price of one!

All right, having said all of that, I'm sure that you're all excited and ready to get started learning C#. Here are the topics we'll be covering in the book: First, we'll learn Microsoft's .NET strategy and its significance in the IT industry in Chapter 1. Then, Chapter 2 will provide an overview of the C# language and all of its features. This chapter will also teach you how to set up all the different tools you'll need for developing C# applications.

We'll then dive into more specifics. Chapter 3 will focus on the language fundamentals. You'll learn the basics of the language starting from the *Main()* method, to the common type system, and up to expressions and statements. Chapter 4 will go into the rest of the C# language. It will discuss strings, arrays, and the different types of program flow controls. Chapter 5 will introduce objects and classes in C#. The more advanced object-oriented topics such as inheritance and polymorphism will be covered in Chapter 6. You will also get to see the use of interfaces and inner classes in this chapter.

In Chapter 7, we'll learn the rest of the C# features that aren't available in Java. In this chapter you'll find out about structs, enumerators, and some of the syntactical sugar that C# provides such as properties and indexers. You'll also get to see operator overloading and the concept of automatic *boxing* and *unboxing*. Chapter 8 will discuss delegates and events, which is C#'s way of dealing with event handling. You'll also get to see how you can use delegates for callback functions in this chapter. In Chapter 9 you will discover C#'s method of application packaging with assemblies. This chapter will also cover how to add metadata information to your program by using attributes.

Next we'll look into some of the classes available in the .NET Framework Class Library. Chapter 10 will look at the classes available in .NET for multithreading programming. Then, in Chapter 11, you'll learn how to work with I/O streams in .NET. This chapter will show you all the classes offered for handling input and output.

The next three chapters will go into creating different types of applications you can develop with C#. Chapter 12 will show you how to create a graphical user interface using Windows Forms. In this chapter you will gain knowledge of how to create Windows applications by using some of the objects and components available in Windows Forms. Chapter 13 will cover Web development with C#. It will demonstrate how to create Web Services and how to build Web applications with Web Forms. Chapter 14 will illustrate C#'s support for COM, ActiveX, and pointers. In this chapter you'll discover all the necessary tools for interfacing with applications not written for the .NET Framework.

Finally, Chapter 15 will discuss Microsoft's JUMP (Java User Migration Path) strategy. It will give you a preview of J#, which is another tool available for Java programmers who wish to work with the .NET platform using the same Java syntax. The book concludes with an appendix of C# keywords and their Java equivalents.

You might think that this is a lot to cover, but don't loose sleep over it; after all, you can go at your own pace. There are also some exercises you can do; one of the main features of this book is that it provides you with extensive code examples. These code examples will be very useful for enhancing your understanding of how to build C# applications. Therefore, I highly suggest that you go through them. You can obtain the source code for each chapter by registering at the Syngress Web site (www.syngress.com/solutions).

All the source files are packaged in one Zip file. The code files for each chapter will be located in their own directory. Any further directory structure depends on the projects that are presented within the chapter.

The filenames for each example will be the same as the program class name. In some cases where the same class name is used several times in the chapter, the filename will be appended with the *-ex#*. For example, if a class named *Point* is used in three different examples, the examples will be named *Point-ex1.cs*, *Point-ex2.cs*, and *Point-ex3.cs*.

I hope that you enjoy this book and experience the same pleasure I had in discovering the C# language. I hope that you'll use this book not only as a teaching tool, but also as a valuable resource when developing. Okay, enough with the preamble—we have a lot of learning to do. Have fun learning C#, and please turn your books to Chapter 1.

*Harold Cabrera, Technical Editor and Contributing Author*
*B.Sc. Comp. Eng., Sun Certified Java Programmer*
*Software Engineer, IdleWorks Inc.*

# The .NET Philosophy

## Solutions in this chapter:

- Overview of the .NET Platform
- Examining the .NET Framework Features
- Understanding the .NET Architecture
- Following .NET Code from Source to Binary

☑ Summary

☑ Solutions Fast Track

☑ Frequently Asked Questions

# Introduction

Before we start our journey into the C# language, let's step back and look at the bigger picture. C# is a key part of Microsoft's new .NET initiative. The Redmond view of .NET is that is provides a development platform for the Internet, while at the same time providing new application programming interfaces (API) to the Windows operating system. Internet development can come in many forms, but the key components of the .NET platform are Web Services, which will be discussed in this chapter.

The .NET platform is much more than a new language, a software development kit (SDK), or even an operating system. It offers powerful new services, a new processor-independent binary format, new managed languages, managed language extensions to existing languages, and more. These new tools will empower you to create amazing Internet applications, but effective use of these tools requires a firm background knowledge of the .NET platform.

According to Microsoft, they are devoting 80 percent of the company's resources to the development of .NET. This results in a platform that encompasses and touches almost all segments of the computer industry. For the programmer segment of the industry, C# is the most important tool. C# is designed specifically to create .NET applications; therefore it is essential that we learn the relevant aspects of .NET before we get started. This chapter discusses the overall .NET platform and its importance to application development. It introduces not only technological concepts, but also the terminology used to describe them. It provides a strong understanding of the internal workings of .NET so you can understand concepts described in the remainder of the book. Let's take our first few steps.

# Overview of the .NET Platform

The philosophy behind the .NET platform is that the world of computing is changing from one of PCs connected to servers through networks such as the Internet, to one where all manner of smart devices, computers, and services work together to provide a richer user experience. The .NET platform is Microsoft's answer to the challenges imposed by this new paradigm. The .NET platform has several broad components. The reality of the .NET platform is that it is not a small, focussed product; rather, it includes many different components, all thrown into the .NET category. This can make things confusing, especially when the word .NET is bandied about so much on the Internet.

The core of the .NET platform includes programming languages, the .NET *[handwritten: C#, VB.NET]* Common Language Runtime (CLR), and the .NET Framework Class Libraries. *[handwritten: CLR, class Libraries]* The other components may be required by specific applications, but they are not a necessary part of all .NET applications. Looking at the overall picture, .NET can be broken down to the following different product groups:

- *The .NET Framework infrastructure for the overall .NET platform.* The Common Language Runtime (CLR) and the Framework Class Library (including Windows Forms, ADO.NET, and ASP.NET) are used to create Web services, Web applications, and Windows applications. The framework supports a wide set of languages including C#, J#, and Visual Basic.NET.

- *A commercial Web services initiative called .NET My Services* (previously called Project Hailstorm), which supplies developers with the necessary building blocks to create user-centric Web applications. My Services also includes Passport, which is a way for users to consolidate their identities and other information in data repositories on the Internet. This project is actually an attempt to package some of the most crucial Web Services under the Microsoft brand name.

## NOTE

As of this writing, Microsoft has announced that it will discontinue a large part of the .NET My Services project due to lack of industry support (Passport will continue). According to Gartner Group, it turns out companies were not very enthusiastic about a large centralized customer database controlled by Microsoft.

- *The .NET Compact Framework*, which is a scaled-down version for devices running the upcoming Windows CE.NET operating system. This includes cell phones, PDAs, set-top boxes, and game boxes.

- *The Microsoft.NET Enterprise Servers*, which is a range of products from messaging and collaboration to database management, and for e-commerce and mobile information access. These applications are based on the .NET Framework, including new versions of SQL Server, Exchange, and Mobile Information Server among others. They are all XML-enabled and integrated into the .NET platform.

Most of the product groups that make up the .NET platform have a Java counterpart. Although it is not exactly a one-to-one comparison, the Java platform also provides a rich set of products that match the .NET offering. For example, you can compare the .NET Compact Framework to J2ME (Java 2 Micro Edition). Similarly you can compare .NET to J2EE (Java 2 Enterprise Edition), as a tool for building XML-based Web services. It is clear the scope of .NET is huge, but this book will focus on the .NET Framework and its similarity to the Java platform.

When we talk about Java, we use it to refer to three distinct things that make up the Java platform. First, you can think of Java as an object-oriented programming language. Second, there are the Java Foundation Classes that make up a comprehensive set of class libraries. Finally, the Java Virtual Machine (JVM) is used to run and execute Java byte-code. If you compare the .NET Framework to Java, there is one major difference that stands out. The .NET Framework offers a wide set of languages, whereas the Java platform only supports one, though as you will soon learn other languages can develop Java-compliant byte-code too. Let's proceed by looking at the different features that make up the framework.

# Examining the .NET Framework Features

The .NET Framework contains many features common to the JVM, and offers all the benefits of a modern object-oriented programming language. This framework acts as a layer below each of the .NET languages (C#, C++, VB.NET). The .NET Framework Class Library exposes the features of the Common Language Runtime in much the same way that the Java Foundation Classes utilize the features of the Java Virtual Machine.

This architecture gives a great number of benefits, not the least of which is a consistent API. By writing to the Common Language Runtime and using the .NET Framework Class library, all application services are available via a common object-oriented programming model. One advantage of this is that it provides the ease of use that you're familiar with in Java and brings it to the Windows platform. For example, today some Windows functions are accessed via DLL calls using the C-based API and other facilities are accessed via COM objects, making the developer do the necessary legwork to make everything work together smoothly. The .NET Framework greatly simplifies the efforts that were required when writing Windows applications, or for that matter, almost any Win32 and COM project. Developers no longer need to be a Windows or COM architecture guru with an in-depth understanding of GUIDs, IUnknown, AddRef,

Release, HRESULTS, and so on. .NET doesn't just hide these from the developer; in the new .NET Framework, these concepts simply do not exist at all. This means that by using methods and design philosophies you're familiar with in Java, you'll be able to create Windows applications without having to learn the more complicated Microsoft Foundation Classes (MFC).

Of course being able to create Windows application more easily is not all that .NET has to offer. In fact Windows is not the only platform that .NET is targeting. There are projects in the works for porting .NET to several other platforms such as UNIX. Other features also offered by the .NET Framework include shorter development cycles (code reuse, fewer programming surprises, support for multiple programming languages), easier deployment, fewer data type–related bugs due to integral type safety, reduced memory leaks thanks to the garbage collector, and, in general more scalable, reliable applications. The following sections will outline these features in more detail.

## Multilanguage Development

One feature that separates .NET from Java is its support for multiple languages. Not only does it support multiple languages, it allows these languages to be integrated together. For example, you can easily sub-class a VB.NET class from C# and then use the resulting class in managed C++. Since many languages target the .NET Common Language Runtime, it is now much easier to implement portions of your application using the language that's best suited for it.

Although there are projects out there that allow other languages to compile to Java byte-code (see the Note sidebar in this section), most of them are merely interpreters or scripts written in Java, which don't allow them to use any Java features. The .NET Framework allows languages to be integrated with one another through the use of the *Microsoft Intermediate Language* (MSIL). All languages designed for .NET are compiled to MSIL, which is then executed by the CLR—a process that is analogous to Java source code being compiled to byte-code that is then executed by the JVM. The MSIL, or IL for short, contains instructions that appear similar to assembly code, such as pushing and popping values and moving variables in and out of registers, and it also contains instructions for managing objects and invoking their methods, manipulating arrays, and raising and catching exceptions. This gives the framework a very flexible ability to mix and match the languages being used in an application that doesn't exist in Java. We'll discuss compilation in more detail later on in this chapter.

> **NOTE**
>
> For a list of languages for the Java Virtual Machine please visit
> http://grunge.cs.tu-berlin.de/~tolk/vmlanguages.html.

Microsoft is also providing the *Common Language Specification* (CLS), which describes how other compilers must behave in order to output IL code that will allow them to integrate well with other .NET languages. Microsoft currently provides several compilers that produce IL code targeting the .NET CLR: C++ with managed extensions, C#, J#, JScript, and Visual Basic. In addition, several companies other than Microsoft are producing compilers for languages that also target the .NET CLR. Currently there is support for COBOL, Eiffle, Fortran, Perl, Python, and Scheme with more in the pipeline. For a current list check http://msdn.microsoft.com/vstudio/partners/language/default.asp.

# Platform and Processor Independence

Since the MSIL is targeted for the Common Language Runtime, it means that it is processor- and platform-independent. Like Java byte-code, the MSIL is much higher-level than most machine languages. The CLR is analogous to the JVM, so a managed .NET application can execute on any platform that supports the .NET CLR. The .NET Framework also provide something called as the *Common Type System* (CTS) that defines the size of the base data types that are available to .NET applications run within the CLR. This means that the application developer is insulated from the specifics of any hardware or operating system that supports the .NET platform.

At the time of this writing a full version of the .NET Framework is only available on the Windows platform. However, Microsoft is also involved in several projects that are trying to port .NET to several other operating systems. Currently Microsoft has an agreement with Corel to develop a shared-source implementation of a C# compiler and the .NET Framework infrastructure components for the FreeBSD version of UNIX.

Also, Microsoft has given the go-ahead to an open source version of .NET being planned by Ximian, the developer of the popular GNOME user interface for Linux. You can find the project, called Mono, at www.go-mono.net. The group is developing a C# language compiler, along with the .NET Common Language Runtime. Work has also begun on the Base Class Library.

It is therefore safe to say that the .NET Framework is designed to equal Java's *write once, run anywhere* philosophy and has the potential to rival Java's platform independence.

## Automatic Memory Management

Java programmers have always enjoyed not having to worry about memory management. To some, however, the mere mention of a memory leak problem brings forth images of endless hours of debugging if you've come from a development environment that did not offer automatic memory management. Even those fortunate enough to work within a "garbage collector" environment have likely spent some time trying to hunt down obscure bugs caused by tricky code that circumvented the resource management methodology. The .NET Framework has brought to the table automatic memory management, which will alleviate most of the headaches associated with manual memory allocation and de-allocation from the programmers.

If you have some Visual Basic or COM background, you are familiar with the reference counting technique. This technique recovers the memory used by an object when no other object has a reference to it, essentially when it's no longer needed. Although this sounds perfect in theory, in practice it has a few problems. One of the most common is a circular reference problem where one object contains a reference to another object which itself contains a reference back to the first object. When the memory manager looks for objects that are not in use, these objects will always have a reference count greater than zero, so unless they are implicitly deconstructed, their memory may never be recovered.

For a C or C++ programmer—accustomed to ensuring that objects are properly destroyed, essentially managing memory on their own—this sounds perfectly normal, and a good reason for not trusting anyone else to take care of managing resources. However, in the .NET environment, Microsoft is striving to make developing software easier. Much like Java, the CLR employs a garbage collector to collect objects and free up memory that is no longer in use. In Chapter 5 you will see how garbage collection works in .NET, and the improvements that have been made over strict reference counting or manual memory management approaches.

## Versioning Support

A common problem with Windows development occurs when applications conflict with each other because of a shared Dynamic Link Library (DLL). This common dilemma has been coined "DLL Hell". This scenario doesn't really apply when you're developing in Java but if you have some experience in Windows development chances are that you've encountered this problem before. For the uninitiated, you'll find yourself in DLL Hell someday when a customer installs a software package that uses one of the same DLLs as your application. However, your application used version 1.0 of this DLL, and the new software replaces it with version 1.1. We developers all always make sure everything is 100 percent backwards compatible, right? The new DLL makes your application exhibit some strange problem or perhaps just stop working altogether. After a lot of investigation, you figure out what the offending DLL is and have the customer replace the new one with the version that works with your software. Now their new software doesn't work… welcome to DLL Hell. When DLLs where invented, disk space was scarce and reusing DLLs seems like a good idea. So now many developers resort to simply installing every DLL their application requires in the application directory so that it will be found first when the application loads the libraries. This defeats the purpose of shared libraries, but it is one way around the problem.

The .NET architecture now separates application components so that an application always loads the components with which it was built and tested. If the application runs after installation, the application should always run. This is done with *assemblies*, which are .NET-packaged components that are similar to Java's JAR files. Although current DLLs and COM objects do contain version information, the OS does not use this information for any real purpose. Assemblies contain version information that the .NET Common Language Runtime uses to ensure that an application will load the components it was built with. You'll get to learn more about assemblies and versioning in Chapter 9.

## Support for Open Standards

In today's world, not every device you may want to work with is going to be running a Microsoft OS or using an Intel CPU. Realizing this, the architects of .NET are relying on XML and its most visible descendant, Simple Object Access Protocol (SOAP), an emerging standard for sending messages across the Internet that activates programs or applications regardless of their underlying infrastructure. SOAP will provide the means for disparate systems to exchange information easily, but even more, SOAP allows you to invoke methods on remote systems and return the results. Because SOAP is a simple text-based protocol that uses HTTP for transport, it can easily pass through firewalls, unlike Java RMI, DCOM or CORBA objects. This makes .NET as a very suitable platform for creating distributed applications and Web services.

Other standards employed by the .NET platform include Universal Description, Discovery and Integration (UDDI), a directory of companies and their XML interfaces and the Web Services Description Language (WSDL), which describes what a piece of application code can do. By basing much of .NET on open standards and by submitting the proposed draft standards for C# and the .NET Common Language Infrastructure to ECMA (an international standards organization), Microsoft hopes to see its version of the future of software adopted beyond its own domain.

# Easy Deployment

Today, developing installations for Windows-based applications can be incredibly difficult, to the point that most companies use third-party tools for developing their installation programs, and even then it's not pleasant. There are usually a large number of files to be installed in several directories, various Registry settings, installation of required COM components, and shortcuts that need to be created, and so on. Completely uninstalling an application is nearly impossible, most leave bits and pieces of themselves around even if they provide an uninstall feature. With the release of Windows 2000, Microsoft introduced a new installation engine that helps with some of these issues, but it is still possible that the author of a Microsoft Installer Package may fail to do everything correctly. Even with those third party tools specifically designed to make developing installation programs easier, it is still frequently a monumental task to correctly install a retrieval application.

## Developing & Deploying…

### Using the Visual Studio.NET Setup Tools

Realizing that deploying applications and authoring installation packages is frequently a monumental task, the Visual Studio.NET team integrated a number of setup tools into the Visual Studio.NET environment.

After you have completed your Visual Studio.NET project development, start a new project from the File menu. Choose **Setup and Deployment Projects** from the selection list.

You'll see a number of setup project options listed:

**Continued**

- Cab Project
- Deploy Wizard
- Merge Module Project
- Setup Project
- Setup Wizard
- Web Setup Project

Using the wizards, you can select the Visual Studio project you want to use and have a setup or deployment project created automatically. If the defaults are not sufficient for your needs, you can use the new setup project as a basis for creating your custom setup or deployment.

The .NET design team must have felt the same way about this problem, because .NET plans to do away with these issues for good. For Java developers this is not an issue but if you've ever been intimidated about writing to the System Registry then this is great news. Your .NET components are neatly packaged and are not referenced in the Registry, thanks to the use of metadata and reflection, components are self-describing. In fact, installing many .NET applications will require no more than copying their files to a directory, and uninstalling an application will be as easy as deleting those files.

## Interoperability with Unmanaged Code

Since Windows is still the primary platform for .NET, Microsoft has bundled several tools that will allow you to support legacy COM applications. As you can probably guess, *unmanaged code* is code that isn't managed by the .NET Common Language Runtime. This means that this code is run outside of the CLR and therefore doesn't receive certain advantages, such as the Common Type System and Automatic Memory Management. Similar functionality can be found in Java through the Java Native Interface (JNI), which allows you to extend the functionality of your application by calling native code. The .NET Framework comes with a set of tools that makes this very easy when it comes to dealing with COM components. You will probably end up using unmanaged code in a couple of different situations:

- **Calling DLL functions** There is a lot of functionality locked inside DLLs today. Not every company is going to rush to deliver a .NET component version of their products, so if you need to interface with them, you'll be calling unmanaged code.

- **Using COM components** This is likely to be for pretty much the same reasons you might be required to call DLL functions.

- **Calling .NET services from COM components** Although this sounds a little odd, it is possible. A COM client can be made to call a .NET component as though it was a COM server.

Here's a little more information on the COM interoperability issue. When a new piece of technology is introduced, legacy support is one of the main things it needs in order to gain acceptance and adoption in the industry. Microsoft didn't want to force companies to abandon their existing COM components; especially because many of Microsoft's own products are COM-based today. COM components interoperate with the .NET runtime through an *interop* layer that handles all the work required when translating messages that pass back and forth between the managed runtime and the COM components operating as unmanaged code.

On the other side of the coin, companies with a vested interest in COM technology might want to use a few bits and pieces from the .NET platform, sticking a toe in before taking the plunge. COM clients can easily interface with .NET components through the COM *interop* layer.

## Providing Security

Distributed component-based applications require security, and thus far Microsoft hasn't had a lot of positive feedback about its products' security features. Fortunately, the .NET designers decided to take a new approach, different than traditional OS security, which provides isolation and access control based on user accounts. Like the model used by Java, where code that is not trusted is run in a "sandbox" with no access to critical resources, the .NET Framework provides a fine-grained control of application security.

Security for .NET applications starts as soon as a class is loaded by the CLR. Before the class loader instantiates a class, security information—such as accessibility rules and self-consistency requirements—are checked. Calls to class methods are checked for type safety. If you've ever heard of a security vulnerability caused by a "buffer overrun," you can understand why this is important. With verified code, a method that is declared as taking a 4-byte integer parameter will reject an attempt to call it with an 8-byte integer parameter. Verification also prevents applications from executing code at a random location in memory, a common tactic in buffer overflow exploits.

Additionally, as code requests access to certain resources, the class credentials are verified. .NET security crosses process boundaries and even machine boundaries to prevent access to sensitive data or resources in a distributed application environment. The following are some of the basic elements of the .NET security system:

- **Evidence-based security is a new concept introduced by the .NET Framework.** An assembly contains several important pieces of information that can be used to decide what level of access to grant the component. Some of the information used includes what site the component was downloaded from, what *zone* that site was in, (Internet, intranet, local machine, and so on) and the *strong name* of the assembly. The strong name refers to an encrypted identifier that uniquely defines the assembly and ensures that it has not been tampered with.

- **The .NET Common Language Runtime further provides security using a Policy-Driven Trust Model Using Code Evidence.** It sounds worse than it really is. Essentially this is a system of security policies that can be set by an administrator to allow certain levels of access based on the component's assembly information. The policies are set at three levels: the enterprise, the individual machine, and the user.

- **Calling .NET Framework methods from the Base Class Library get the benefits of built in security.** That is, the developer doesn't have to make explicit security calls to access system resources. However, if your components expose interfaces to protected resources, you will be expected to take the appropriate security measures.

- **Role-based security plays a part in the .NET security scheme.** Many applications need to restrict access to certain functions or resources based on the user, and .NET introduces the concepts of identities and principals to incorporate these functions.

- **Authentication and authorization functions are accessed through a single API.** These functions can easily be extended to incorporate application-specific logic as required. Authentication methods include basic operating system user identification, basic HTTP, ASP.NET forms, Digest and Kerberos, as well as the new .NET service, Microsoft .NET Passport.

- **Isolated storage is a special area on disk assigned to a specific assembly by the security system.** No access to other files or data is allowed, and each assembly using isolated storage is separated from each other. Isolated storage can be used for saving a components state, or saving settings, and can be used by components that do not have access to read and write files on the system.

- **A robust set of cryptographic functions that support encryption, digital signatures, hashing, and random-number generation are included in the .NET Framework.** These are implemented using well-known algorithms, such as RSA, DSA, Rijndael/AES, Triple DES, DES, and RC2, as well as the MD5, SHA1, SHA-256, SHA-384, and SHA-512 hash algorithms. Additionally, the XML Digital Signature specification, under development by the Internet Engineering Task Force (IETF) and the World Wide Web Consortium (W3C), is also available. The .NET Framework uses these cryptographic functions to support various internal services. The cryptographic objects are also available in the Base Class Library for developers who require this functionality.

# Understanding the .NET Architecture

Let's take a closer look at the inner workings of .NET Framework. The diagram in Figure 1.1 shows the .NET Framework architecture. Essentially, the .NET families of languages are each compiled into the Microsoft Intermediate Language according to the Common Language Specification. These languages are supported by a rich set of class libraries intended for Web Services, Web Forms, and Windows Forms application development. Plus another layer of data and XML classes for communication and for designing applications with n-tier architectures. Finally, the Base class library layer is also provided for lower level functions such as IO, threading, string, net, etc. Collectively these classes are called the .NET *Framework Class Library*, which is very extensive and facilitates rapid development of applications. Lastly, the most important layer of the .NET Framework is the Common Language Runtime, which is responsible for the execution of each program. Visual Studio.NET is not required in order to develop .NET Framework applications, however it does offer an extensible architecture that makes it an ideal choice for developing .NET software.

**Figure 1.1** The .NET Platform Architecture

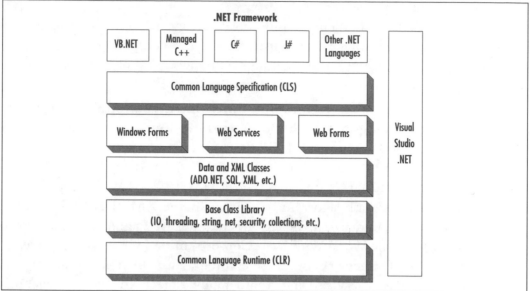

# The Common Language Runtime

The heart of the .NET Framework is the CLR. Similar in concept to the Java Virtual Machine, it is a runtime environment that executes MSIL code. The following is a list of the most important features the CLR has to offer.

- Conversion of MSIL code into native code for the platform in which the application is executing

- Automatic memory management including garbage collection

- Providing security restrictions on applications being executed

- Version control when applications are being loaded and executed

- Integration of code written in various languages

Unlike the Java environment, which is the concept of one language for all purposes, the .NET platform supports multiple programming languages through the use of the CLS, which defines the output required of compilers that want to target the CLR. The CLS provides the minimum requirements for being a .NET language by outlining a series of basic rules.

Along with language independence, the .NET Framework also supports language integration. Compilers that conform to the CLS can create objects that can interoperate with one another. All .NET applications, regardless of their source languages all share a Common Type System. What this means is that you no longer have to worry when doing development in multiple languages about how a data type declared in one language needs to be declared in another. Any .NET type has the same attributes regardless of the language it is used in. Furthermore, all .NET data types are objects, derived from *System.Object*. Since all data types derive from a common base class, they all share some basic functionality, for example the ability to be converted to a string, serialized, or stored in a collection.

When you set your compiler to generate the .NET code, it runs through the CTS and inserts the appropriate data within the application for the CLR to read. Once the CLR finds the data, it proceeds to run through it and lay out everything it needs within memory, declaring any objects when they are called (but not before). Any application interaction, such as passing values from classes, is also mapped within the special data and handled by the CLR.

## The .NET Framework Class Library

The .NET *Framework Class Library* (FCL) provides access to the system functionality through a set of classes, interfaces, and value types, which are designed to be the foundation on which .NET applications are built. The very extensive library will allow you to focus on building applications very rapidly without having to worry about some lower level functions that are already provided by the Base Class Library (BCL) such as IO, threading, network communication, string manipulation, security management, etc. This Base Class Library, which is the lowest lever of the FCL, provides similar sets of classes as its Java counterpart. For the most part the class names only differ in capitalization and that means it will be very familiar for Java programmers.

Above the BCL layer are a set of classes for data management and XML manipulations. This is essential for creating distributed applications and designing n-tier architectures. With a set of classes using the Structured Query Language (SQL) standard and ADO.NET for data management, you can easily manipulate persistent data and interface with databases. Also, the FCL has classes that support the open standard of the Extensible Markup Language (XML). It has a rich set of classes for parsing, manipulating XML data and providing translations.

The Framework Class Library also has a separate layer for technologies specifically geared towards creating Windows Forms, Web Forms, and Web Services. With a set of class libraries having a hierarchy similar to Java's AWT or Swing, .NET offers the same Rapid Application Development techniques to building Web and Windows applications that Java programmers are used to. There are also several tools and classes that will help you create Web services, which allow you to expose your object's functionality over the Internet with the use of HTTP and SOAP as the underlying communications protocols.

Since all .NET languages share the same common set of libraries, the code being executed by your C# program when it uses one of these classes is the same code being executed by a program written in another language. This means that all languages that target the .NET environment essentially share the same capabilities, except that they have different syntax.

Some people will wonder why we even have different languages if they all have the same capabilities. A few reasons immediately spring to mind:

- Programmers don't like change.

- Programmers usually have a favorite language.

- Programmers don't like change…

Imagine if Microsoft had come out with all the good things in .NET, but said that in order to use it, we all had to learn a new language. Lots of people might have never even given it an honest look unless forced by their employers. Making it available for all languages makes it seem less like the chore of learning a new language and more like the excitement of receiving a new library with tens of thousands of functions that will make your life as a developer easier. This also gives you the flexibility to choose a language that might be better suited for a specific application.

### Developing & Deploying…

### Using the Framework Class Library APIs

I don't know a single Java programmer that programs without having the Java APIs open in another window. With the massive volume of classes available (and not to mention all the different methods) it is impossible to have all of them committed to memory. Therefore, when you're developing in C#, it is very useful to have the .NET Framework Class Library at your disposal. You can find the APIs for the FCL by searching the Microsoft Developer's Network (http://msdn.microsoft.com) or by following this link: http://msdn.microsoft.com/library/default.asp?url=/library/en-us/cpref/html/cpref_start.asp

# The Microsoft Intermediate Language (MSIL)

When you build your C# application, it is compiled to the Microsoft Intermediate Language. Similar to Java's byte-code, the IL provides portability to the .NET Framework and is also the key to the framework's language interoperability. However, this means that the IL code is not a portable executable file and needs the CLR in order for it to run. The IL is defined in the Common Language Specification. It is an amalgam of a low-level language similar in many ways to a machine language and a higher object language. You can even make a claim of being some sort of .NET wizard by writing your applications directly in IL, much as you can write directly in assembly language. Thankfully, this is not necessary for most purposes.

The .NET Framework manages many of its cross-language features through the IL. Cross-language functionality is enabled because the IL provides metadata information that handles the entire translation. For instance, with an Exception object defined by IL, the same object can be caught regardless of the .NET language used. Your component written in C# can raise an exception that can be caught by the VB.NET application using it. No more worries about different calling conventions or data types, just seamless interoperability.

## NOTE

Metadata is information describing the data associated with it. You'll get to learn more about metadata in later chapters.

Cross-language inheritance is another feature made possible by the use of IL. You can now create new classes based on components written in other languages, without needing the source code to the base component. For example, you can create a class in C# that derives from a class implemented in C++.

# Just-In-Time Compilation

After compiling your program, the IL code is saved in a file on disk. Before the application gets executed, the CLR performs another compilation known as Just-In-Time (JIT) compilation. The CLR utilizes a JIT compiler to compile the IL code again, which can then be executed. Each method will get compiled once as it gets called within a program. Subsequent calls to the same method will not have to undergo the same compilation; therefore there is only one overhead in this process. In .NET, you currently have three types of JIT compilers:

- **Pre-JIT** This JIT compiles an assembly's entire code into native code at one stretch. You would normally use this at installation time.

- **Econo-JIT** You would use this JIT on devices with limited resources. It compiles the IL code bit-by-bit, freeing resources used by the cached native code when required.

- **Normal JIT** The default JIT compiles code only as it is called and places the resulting native code in the cache.

In essence, the purpose of a JIT compiler is to bring higher performance to interpreted code by placing the compiled native code in a cache, so that when the next call is made to the same method, the cached code is executed, resulting in an increase in application speed.

# Following .NET Code from Source to Binary

Let's take a look at what's really going on with a .NET application from code to execution. We've already covered that the compiler is going to transform your source code into MSIL, now we'll take a look at the whole code cycle from compilation all the way to execution.

As mentioned before, MSIL is not native code and cannot be executed without the CLR. What actually gets generated is a small wrapper around three blocks of data. This wrapper is called a *Portable Executable* (PE), which is the binary format used to contain Windows applications.

The PE wrapper is an .exe file that has a standard Win32 executable header. It contains a stub that specifies it needs the CLR to run the program, or if the CLR is not available it will say something like "This program requires .NET". This is similar to the old MS-DOS days, when you tried to run a Windows application from DOS and got the message saying, "This program requires Microsoft Windows".

Within the PE wrapper, you'll find the CLR header followed by the MSIL itself. It also contains the metadata information describing the contents of the assembly such as method names, parameters, return types, etc. A manifest is also included that describes the other necessary components or files the executable requires in order to run. Figure 1.2 shows the entire process of compiling and executing your .NET programs.

**Figure 1.2** .NET Code Cycle

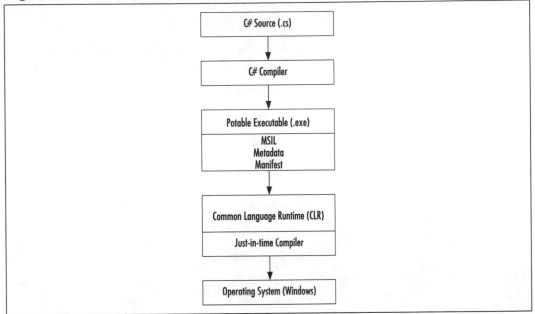

A C# application (or any other .NET language) goes through the following process before being executed on the Windows platform.

1. The application is developed using C# or any other .NET language.

2. The source is compiled by the C# compiler (or any other CLS-compliant compiler) into an executable (.exe) file.

3. The .exe file produced by the compiler has a standard PE (portable executable) header and contains the MSIL code, metadata, and manifest.

4. When the compiler creates the output, it also imports a function called _CorExeMain from *mscoree.dll,* which is the main .NET execution engine, or basically the CLR.

5. Upon execution, the operating system loads the PE as well as any other DLL the application needs, such us the *mscoree.dll* that exports the _CorExeMain function.

6. The operating system loader then jumps to the entry-point inside the PE. And since the OS can't execute MSIL code, the entry-point is a small stub that points to the _CorExeMain function.

7. The _CorExeMain_ will then begin execution of the MSIL code. However, since the MSIL cannot be executed directly, it uses a Just-in-Time compiler to compile the code into native code as it processes the MSIL. This compilation only happens the first time a function gets called.

8. The native code is then executed by the system.

In Java this process is a little different. The Java code is either interpreted by the Java Virtual Machine or gets compiled to native code by a JIT compiler. To illustrate the difference Figure 1.3 shows the Java code cycle.

**Figure 1.3** Java Code Cycle

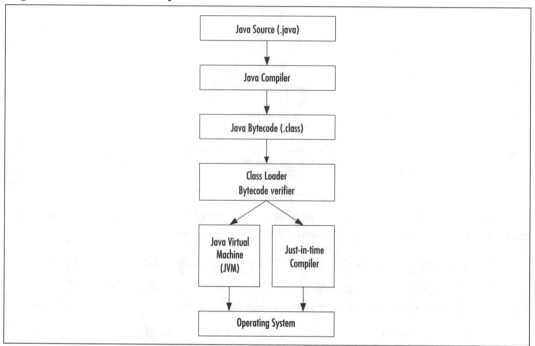

This is slightly different from .NET code, which is never interpreted; it is always JIT compiled to native code before execution. The overhead of the JIT compilation is only incurred as the function is called for the first time. This means that as .NET applications run, they tend to get faster as the already compiled code is reused.

# Summary

The .NET platform is a great leap forward in the evolution of computing. It has evolved from PCs connected to servers through networks such as the Internet, to one where all manner of smart devices, computers, and services work together to provide a richer user experience. The .NET philosophy is Microsoft's vision of how the developers of this new breed of software will approach the challenges of this latest form of computing.

Automatic resource management—a feature that Java programmers have always enjoyed—is one of the most discussed features of the .NET platform, and for good reason. Countless man-hours have been spent chasing problems introduced by poor memory management. Thanks to automatic garbage collection, the developer is now relieved of this tedious task and can concentrate on the problem to be solved, rather than on housekeeping. When the program no longer needs an allocated object, it is automatically cleaned up and the memory is reclaimed for later use.

Once written and built, a managed .NET application can execute on any platform that supports the .NET Common Language Runtime (CLR). Because the .NET Common Type System (CTS) defines the size of the base data types that are available to .NET applications, and applications run within the CLR environment, the application developer is insulated from the specifics of any hardware or operating system that supports the .NET platform. Although currently this means only Microsoft Windows family of operating systems, work is underway to make the .NET core components available on FreeBSD and Linux.

The .NET architecture now separates application components so that a program always loads the components with which it was built and tested. If the application runs after installation, the application should always run. This is done with assemblies, which are .NET-packaged components. Assemblies contain version information that the CLR uses to ensure that an application will load the components it was built with

Given the massive amount of legacy code in use, it is necessary to allow .NET applications to interact with unmanaged code. Unmanaged code is code that isn't managed by the .NET Common Language Runtime. However, this code is still run by the CLR, it just doesn't get the advantages that it offers, such as the Common Type System and Automatic Memory Management. There may be times when you will end up using unmanaged code, such as when using APIs or other DLL calls, interfacing with COM components or allowing COM components to utilize .NET components. However, it is important to realize that by calling unmanaged code, you may be giving up portability.

The components at the heart of the .NET Framework are the Common Language Runtime, the Framework Class Library (FCL), and the Common Language Specification (CLS). The .NET Base Class Library exposes the features of the CLR in much the same way the Java Foundation Classes allow you to utilize the features of the JVM. However, it also provides many higher-level features that facilitate code reuse. The CLS gives language vendors and compiler developers the base requirements for creating code that targets the .NET CLR, making it much easier to implement portions of your application using the language that's best suited for it. The .NET Framework allows languages to be integrated with one another by specifying the use of the Microsoft Intermediate Language (MSIL, or just IL) as the output for all programming languages targeting the platform. This intermediate language is CPU-independent, and much higher level than most machine languages.

Developing software using .NET technology is a big change. The technology adds a lot of pieces to the puzzle and more than a few new ideas. With a solid understanding of the underlying framework that C# is designed for, you now have the foundation needed to start learning the language.

# Solutions Fast Track

## Overview of the .NET Platform

☑ Software design is changing from a closed to a connected world, much like personal computers themselves are. The .NET platform is designed to make it easier to create distributed applications that leverage this new paradigm.

☑ There are multiple pieces to the .NET platform, starting from the .NET Framework, and extending to various Microsoft servers and commercial Web Services.

☑ The .NET Framework is designed as a single, consistent development environment offering shorter development cycles, improved scalability, and better behaved programs.

# Examining the .NET Framework Features

☑ The .NET platform hides the gory details of interfacing with the underlying operating system functions and lets you concentrate on the solution at hand.

☑ Multilanguage development is greatly simplified thanks to the use of the Microsoft Intermediate Language and the Common Language Runtime.

☑ Automatic memory management reduces the level of effort required to manage resources; you can simply let the garbage collector take care of cleaning up and preventing memory leaks.

☑ .NET includes a new versioning system designed to end "DLL Hell."

☑ Much of the platform is built on open standards, such as XML and SOAP.

☑ Existing code does not have to be rewritten to use .NET— interoperability with existing code and components is maintained.

☑ .NET includes an improved security model, which allows fine-grained control as well as integrated safety from security flaws caused by problems related to buffer overruns.

# Understanding the .NET Architecture

☑ The Common Language Runtime is a managed execution environment offering many advantages over the traditional native code development methods.

☑ The Common Type System allows all languages to share data types without requiring the developer to interpret different language conventions.

☑ .NET includes a large Framework Class Library shared by all .NET languages, offering a wide range of functionality intended to speed up development.

☑ All .NET languages compile to the same Intermediate Language. The IL is platform and processor independent, potentially allowing .NET applications to run on non-Windows operating systems.

☑ Several kinds of Just-in-Time compilers are available for executing your IL code to the native platform.

## Following .NET Code from Source to Binary

  ☑    Compiling source code, regardless of the language used, results in IL code output.

  ☑    The IL code is wrapped in a Portable Executable (PE) .exe file, which also contains the metadata and manifest.

  ☑    Behind the scenes, the compiler inserts a stub function to load the CLR, which then runs the Just-in-Time compiler to transform the IL code into native code.

# Frequently Asked Questions

The following Frequently Asked Questions, answered by the authors of this book, are designed to both measure your understanding of the concepts presented in this chapter and to assist you with real-life implementation of these concepts. To have your questions about this chapter answered by the author, browse to **www.syngress.com/solutions** and click on the **"Ask the Author"** form.

**Q:** If all .NET languages have access to everything in the Framework Class Library, why is there so much talk about C#?

**A:** Although in theory all .NET languages have equal access to the FCL, in reality it is left up to the language teams to determine the level of support to offer, at least beyond the minimum requirements for basic compliance. C# is ideal for .NET development because it was developed as a new language specifically for the .NET platform.

**Q:** Is everything in the Win32 API exposed through the FCL?

**A:** Not through the FCL, but you can make API calls directly through most languages.

**Q:** What is the key difference with the Java platform?

**A:** Java as a platform requires the developer to buy into the idea of a single language for all things, which goes against the philosophy of "use the right tool for the job." The .NET design allows and encourages cross-language development, letting programmers make use of existing language skills, as well as leveraging the various strengths of each .NET language.

**Q:** Do I have to use Visual Studio.NET to create .NET applications?

**A:** Although Visual Studio.NET is a nice IDE that provides rapid application development and an integrated debugger tool, it is not part of the .NET Framework and not necessary to develop .NET applications. With the .NET Framework SDK available, you can develop your application in any text editor and use the supplied compilers to compile and run it.

# Chapter 2

# Introducing C#

## Solutions in this chapter:

- **The C# Language**
- **Getting Started**
- **Using Different IDEs**
- **A Stroll through C#**

☑ **Summary**

☑ **Solutions Fast Track**

☑ **Frequently Asked Questions**

# Introduction

C# is a new generation language designed to work within the .NET framework. It's a strongly typed, object-oriented language that is a direct descendent of other languages including C, C++, and Java. C# was developed by a small team led by Microsoft researcher Anders Hejlsberg, who is known for creating the popular Turbo Pascal programming language and for his work on Borland Delphi, an integrated development environment (IDE) for client-server programming. C# is designed to give the optimum blend of simplicity, expressiveness, and performance.

This chapter will provide you with a whirlwind tour of the new C# programming language. You will be introduced to the basic language features and learn about the many similarities and differences it has compared with Java. This chapter also covers installing and using the tools you'll need to program your very first C# application.

# The C# Language

The C# language is highly expressive in implementing all the features of a modern object-oriented programming language. It provides support for encapsulation, inheritance, and polymorphism—the three pillars of object-oriented programming. At its core, C# has about 80 keywords and a dozen built-in data types (Java has 51 reserved words and 8 data types). It includes language features such as single inheritance, multiple interfaces, and compilation to an intermediate format. It is designed with the Internet and component architecture in mind, making it the ideal language to use with .NET.

Java and C# have a lot in common. With the properties mentioned earlier, plus a syntax that is almost identical to Java, it is hard to deny the similarities between these two languages. Both languages aim for a simple language derived from C++. By eliminating some of the complexities of C++, Java was able to achieve significant gains in programmer productivity. This is the same case with C#, and you'll find that the language is just as friendly as Java.

However, C# is broader than Java in what its designers chose to derive from C++, while offering new features of its own. Since C# is a language that is geared for programming on the .NET Framework, the two technologies work together hand in hand. There are some C# features that exist primarily to work within the .NET Framework, and it could even be argued that some features of .NET exist because of C#. This symbiotic relationship results in some impressive features, such as versioning, COM support, and multilanguage development, which can't be found in Java.

# Similarities with Java

Microsoft claims that the C# language definition has been derived primarily from C++ and offers the same raw power. There has been some industry rivalry between Microsoft and Sun, so it makes sense that they would diminish the perceived impact Java had on the development of C#. For anyone who has studied both languages, however, the similarities are quite apparent. Following is a list of features that C# and Java share in common, which are intended to improve on C++.

- Both languages compile to an intermediate format that is run in a managed environment.

- Each runtime environment provides support for automatic garbage collection.

- All classes in both languages descend from *Object* and are allocated on the heap when they are created.

- Everything must belong to a class, which means that there are no global functions or constants.

- Both languages abandoned multiple inheritances, although implementing multiple interfaces is allowed.

- Both C# and Java use exceptions for error handling.

- Arrays are bound checked.

- Inline code comments are used to produce API documentation.

- They both use packages/namespaces to avoid type collision.

In addition to sharing a number of features with Java, most keywords in C# have their Java counterpart. For the most part these keywords are descendant from C++, such as *class*, *new*, *this*, *static*, *throw*, *break*, and *null*. However, it is interesting to note that Java keywords that do not have a C++ equivalent have different names in C#. For example, the Java keywords *super*, *import*, *package*, and *final* are called *base*, *using*, *namespace*, and *sealed* in C#.

## Developing & Deploying…

### Similarities between Class and Method Names

It's a good idea to keep in mind that a lot of classes and method names are similar in C# and Java. In most cases the class names are identical and the method names differ only in their capitalization (in C# all methods start with a capital letter). Therefore, when looking for a C# counterpart to a Java class or method that you're familiar with, start by using the same class name and capitalizing the method name. For example, the *System.Object* class in C# has similar methods as its Java counterpart, the *java.lang.Object* class. The following list shows some similar method names in both classes:

- C# has Object.Equals(), whereas Java has Object.equals().
- C# has Object.Finalize(), whereas Java has Object.finalize().
- C# has Object.ToString(), whereas Java has Object.toString().

By keeping this in mind, you'll be able to leverage your Java knowledge to help learn the class libraries available in C# and make the transition a lot smoother.

As you can see, there are a lot of cosmetic similarities between the two languages. This would be a great advantage, as it will greatly ease the transition in learning the language. However, C# also brings some significant changes and features that aren't found in Java, as described in the next section.

## Differences with Java

As expected, C# offers features that can't be found in Java. The following list briefly outlines some of the main differences and new features, which will be addressed later in the book.

- C# has a new iteration statement called the *foreach* statement. The *foreach* statement in C# allows you to enumerate over classes that support the *Enumerable* interface. This makes for easier array and collection handling.

- C# has a cleaner and more concise syntax for encapsulating data using *Properties*. A property is essentially a pair of *get* and *set* accessor methods that provide access to a field. Properties provide syntax like you're accessing a member field, while actually implementing that access through a class method.

- C# also implements the use of enumerations with the *enum* keyword. Enumerations provide a powerful alternative to constants. *Enums* are a distinct value type, consisting of a set of named constants.

- C# has chosen to adopt the concept of *structs* from C++, but altered its use significantly. In C#, a *struct* is a lightweight alternative to classes that is a value type as opposed to a reference type. It has a lower impact on memory and can be used to define types that behave similarly to built-in types.

- C# methods are nonvirtual by default and must be explicitly declared as *virtual* to be overridden. In Java, all methods are virtual by default and can be overridden by a derived class. C# provides some versioning control for the language by preventing accidental overriding of a method.

- C# implements delegates as a replacement for the old function pointer of C++. Delegates are an object-oriented function pointer that can reference *static* or *instance* methods. It provides a type-safe mechanism for implementing callback functions and events.

- C# allows operator overloading. Operator overloading allows you to redefine the semantics of operators for your classes. In Java this is not allowed, and only the built-in *String* class has used this feature by overloading the + operator for concatenating strings. In C# you can overload most operators (+, −, +=, ++, etc.) for any given type to provide an intuitive syntax for handling your classes like a primitive type.

- C# also provides support for cast operators that allow you to define cast operations for your classes. This allows you to specifically define how you can convert your class to another class. For example, you can define a cast operator for a *Fraction* class to be converted to a *double*.

- C# provides XML style documentation for inline documentation that is more flexible than Javadocs. This greatly simplifies the creation of online and print reference documentation for an application.

- C# provides support for directly accessing memory using pointers. Although seen as potentially dangerous, pointers can provide programmers with an extra level of control that isn't available in Java. It uses the *unsafe* keyword to warn the garbage collector not to collect or move

objects in memory that are referenced by the pointer until they are
released.

■  C# incorporates built-in support for the Component Object Model
(COM) and the Windows API. This is great news for Windows programmers because integration with COM and Win32 in C# is very painless,
unlike J/Direct or the Java Native Interface (JNI).

This list should give you an idea that C# does offer some new features and
improvements that clearly distinguish it from Java. These features will be covered
in more detailed throughout the book, but for now let's stop with the theory and
start writing our first program.

# Getting Started

Microsoft has several commercial products available for developing C# applications, such as Visual C# or the full blown Visual Studio.NET, which also includes
VB.NET and Visual C++. However, you don't need to buy anything to get
started with C# programming. The Microsoft .NET Framework software development kit (SDK) is freely available for download from the Microsoft Web site.

Most of the programs in this book can be run by using the SDK and a text
editor such as Notepad. However, we highly recommend that you use an integrated development environment (IDE) such as Visual Studio.NET to be as pro-
ductive as possible. Later in this chapter, we'll go over some basic features of
Visual Studio.NET and list some other IDEs that are freely available on the
Internet. But to get the ball rolling, first let's look at setting up the .NET
Framework SDK and testing it by writing a simple C# program.

**NOTE**

If you're planning on using Visual Studio.NET you may skip the following
section.

## Installing the .NET Framework SDK

The .NET Framework SDK has all the tools you need to compile, test, run, and
deploy your C# application. You can write your application in any text editor
and use the command line compiler that comes with the SDK to compile the

program. Not only that, it also comes with a debugger tool to help you find and fix bugs, plus a slew of other utilities to help in application development.

To install the .NET Framework SDK:

1. Go to http://msdn.microsoft.com/.

2. Go to the Software Development Kit Section, or you can type **.NET Framework SDK** in the search box and you should be able to reach the download site.

3. Download and install the **.NET Framework SDK** and **.NET Framework** on your computer. Note that the download is 131 MB big, which you can download as one file or in parts.

4. To make sure that the SDK has been installed properly open a command line window (*cmd.exe*) and type **csc.exe /help** on the command prompt. If the program has been installed properly, you should see something similar to Figure 2.1.

**Figure 2.1** The C# Compiler Options

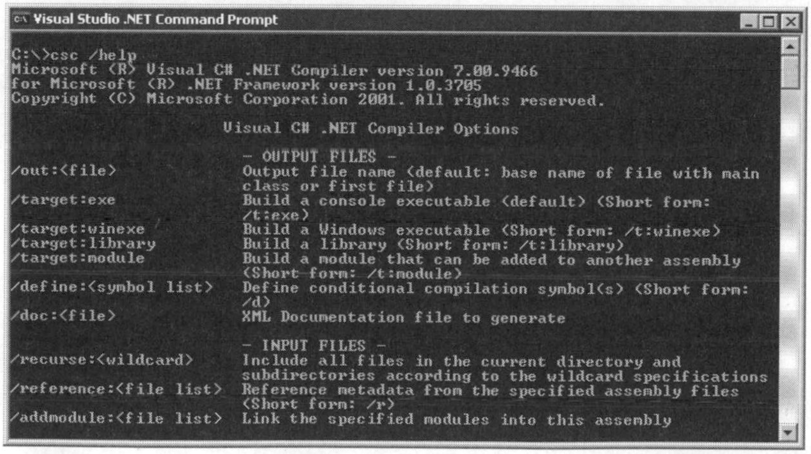

The *csc.exe* program is the main C# compiler for the .NET SDK. It has several switches that allow you to specify compiler options. By typing **/help**, the program will list all the different compiler options available as shown in Figure 2.1. Once everything is up and running we can begin writing our first test program.

## Creating Your First C# Program

The sample C# program is a very simple program that writes a couple of lines of text to the console. This example program is used simply to demonstrate how to use the .NET SDK tools to develop C# applications. Don't worry too much about the details of how this program works; all the inner workings of this program will be explained to you in greater detail throughout the book (although with your Java knowledge you'll have a pretty good idea of how the program works).

Open up your favorite text editor and type the following code, then save the file as **Hello.cs**. If you don't have a favorite text editor, Notepad will do.

```
using System;
class Hello
{
  static void Main( string[] args )
  {
    DateTime today = DateTime.Now;
    Console.WriteLine( "I wrote my first C# program at: " +
        today.ToString() );

    string msg = "You wanted to say hello to ";

    if(args.Length > 0)
    {
      for(int i=0; i<=args.Length; i++)
      {
        msg += args[i] + " ";
      }
      Console.WriteLine(msg);
    }
  }
}
```

This program will print a message on the console followed by the current time. You can also add some command line arguments to the program that will be printed on the screen. For now, let's look at compiling and executing our little program.

## Compiling and Running the Program

As mentioned previously, the command line compiler included in the Microsoft .NET Framework SDK is called *csc.exe*. To compile the application, simply type the following on the command prompt:

```
csc /out:Hello.exe Hello.cs
```

In this case, we're supplying the compiler with two arguments. The first is the */out* switch, which specifies the output for our compiled file. This is optional and if you don't supply one, the compiler will create the output filename the same as the input filename followed by an *.exe* extension. The last argument is the name of our source file to be compiled. If everything has been entered correctly, you should see something similar to Figure 2.2.

**Figure 2.2** C# Compiler Output

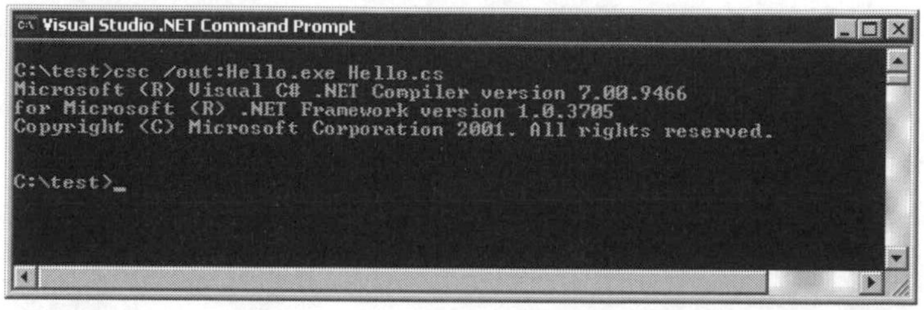

As discussed in Chapter 1, all C# programs are JIT compiled, unlike Java where it is interpreted at most times by a Java runtime. Therefore, after compiling the program, all you have to do is type the output filename at the command prompt to execute it. In our case, type **Hello** at the prompt and you should see the following output.

## *Output*

```
I wrote my first C# program at: 5/14/2002 2:24:37 PM
```

The same program can also accept some command line arguments. For example you can execute the program with the following arguments:

```
C:\test>Hello Rosie Andrea Karen
```

If you execute this same program with some arguments an error dialogue box will pop up similar to Figure 2.3.

**NOTE**

You might get a different window such as the Just-In-Time debugger depending on what's installed on your machine. If you do, just click on **No** or **Cancel**.

**Figure 2.3** Runtime Error Dialogue Box

Just click on **Cancel** and you should see the following:

```
C:\test>Hello Rosie Andrea Karen
I wrote my first C# program at: 5/15/2002 2:27:01 AM


Unhandled Exception: System.IndexOutOfRangeException: Index was outside
    the bounds of the array.
    at Hello.Main(String[] args)
```

You might ask yourself what happened there. Well, don't be too alarmed because this is done deliberately, and if you typed the code exactly as shown then you should have the same output. Obviously, something is not right with our code. However, the error message doesn't really tell us where the problem is. To solve this, we can recompile the **Hello.cs** with the */debug* switch.

```
csc /debug Hello.cs
```

By adding this debug switch the compiler will generate an extra file with the *.pdb* extension, which contains debugging information. After running the program again, it should display more information, as shown:

```
C:\test>Hello Rosie Andrea Karen
I wrote my first C# program at: 5/15/2002 2:48:33 AM


Unhandled Exception: System.IndexOutOfRangeException: Index was outside
    the bounds of the array.
    at Hello.Main(String[] args) in C:\test\Hello.cs:line 15
```

By compiling the program with the */debug* switch, we can now tell where exactly the error is occurring. Here's the block of code where the error is happening:

```
    for(int i=0; i<=args.Length; i++)
    {
```

```
msg += args[i] + " ";   //line 15
}
```

At first glance, this code block is perfectly legitimate. This *for* loop is perfectly valid and the line itself where the error is occurring seems fine. As with most bugs, some are trivial to fix and others can take days of debugging. The next section will look at how we can use the debugger tool that comes with .NET so that we can find and fix the bug in our program.

## Using the Debugger Tool

At the time of this writing, the current version of the .NET SDK is 1.30705, and it offers two debugging tools. There's a command line tool called *cordbg.exe* and a version with a graphical user interface called *dbgclr.exe* that can be found in the **GUIDebug** subdirectory of the Framework SDK. When it comes to programming, the majority of your time is probably spent debugging. Therefore, it makes sense to learn how to use the debugger to greatly decrease your development time.

Since it is much more convenient to use the *dbgclr.exe* because of its graphical user interface, we'll try to debug our program using this tool. To debug your application follow these steps:

1.  In Explorer, launch the debugger, which can be found in <InstalledDirectory>/Microsoft.NET/FrameworkSDK/GuiDebug/ dbgclr.exe. Figure 2.4 shows the CLR Debugger window.

**Figure 2.4** Debugger Window

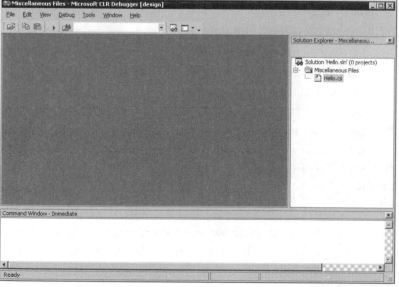

2. Click on **Debug | Program To Debug.** This will let you specify the program you wish to debug and enter in any arguments the program needs. You can enter **Hello.exe** under **Program**, and type some names under the **Arguments** field. After doing so, you should see something similar to Figure 2.5.

**Figure 2.5** Program to Debug Selection Window

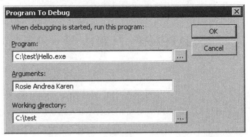

3. Click on **OK.** Once that's done, you can start debugging the program by clicking on **Debug | Start F5**, or by simply pressing the **F5** key. This will start the debugging process and the program will halt once it encounters an error.

4. Click on **Break.** The program will pause and highlight the piece of code that caused the error.

5. We can visibly see where the problem is occurring. Now we can set a breakpoint at this location in the code so that we can watch what's causing it. To do this, right-click on the line and select **Insert Breakpoint** from the menu, as shown in Figure 2.6.

6. Now we can start the debugging process again, and as soon as the debugger encounters the breakpoint it will automatically stop the program. The debugger provides the **Locals** window to display all the values of all the local variables. This is extremely useful because you get a glimpse of the variable states at a specific time of code execution. This is the key in analyzing and solving the bug. The Locals Window is located in the lower right corner of the window, and it should display something similar to Figure 2.7.

7. As you can see, at this point the **Locals** window shows all the different variables that our program is using. The next step is to watch what's happening to the variables when the program continues executing. To do this we can step through the program line by line and see what's happening

to each variable. To step into the program, click on **Debug | Step Into** or just press **F11.** Once you start stepping through the program you can see the results of each line of the code by observing changes to the variables. You'll notice the *msg* and *i* variables are changing after each iteration of the loop. After going through the loop three times (or however many arguments you entered) you'll notice that the problem occurs because the loop doesn't stop even though there are no more arguments. If you look closely, it seems that I've introduce an "off-by-one error" by using the <= operator instead of the < operator in the *for* loop. Problem solved!

**Figure 2.6** Inserting a Breakpoint

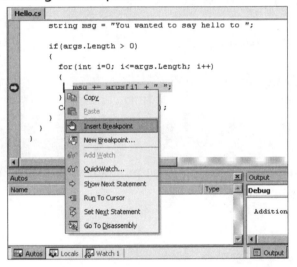

**Figure 2.7** The Locals Window

Now, that we're able to find the bug in our program we can easily change the offending code and recompile the program. The new code should be as follows:

```
using System;
class Hello
```

```
{
  static void Main( string[] args )
  {
    DateTime today = DateTime.Now;
    Console.WriteLine( "I wrote my first C# program at: " +
        today.ToString() );

    string msg = "You wanted to say hello to ";

    if(args.Length > 0)
    {
      for(int i=0; i<args.Length; i++)
      {
        msg += args[i] + " ";
      }
      Console.WriteLine(msg);
    }
  }
}
```

After compiling and running the program with several arguments, you should get the following output.

*Output*

```
C:\test>Hello Rosie Andrea Karen
I wrote my first C# program at: 5/15/2002 4:24:11 AM
You wanted to say hello to Rosie Andrea Karen
```

These are just rough steps you can follow when debugging your program. You might have other techniques when it comes to debugging, but you will definitely want to invest some time in learning how to use the debugger effectively. This tool will save you a lot of headaches down the road, and you can thank me for it later!

# Using Different IDEs

As you can see, with just a simple text editor and the .NET Framework SDK, we were able to write, run, and debug our first program. The SDK has all the basic tools needed for developing C# applications. However, an integrated development environment (IDE) is highly recommended in order to gain full productivity.

Although this book assumes that you'll be using Visual Studio.NET, the examples focus more on the language and not on the tools you're developing with. Therefore, all examples in this book can be tested by copying the code to any text editor and using the basic .NET Framework SDK. However, since most programmers don't limit themselves to using Notepad as the main development tool, it's worth becoming familiar with some of the IDEs available.

---

**NOTE**

In later chapters some examples will use Visual Studio.NET for developing Windows Forms and Web Forms. However, even these examples can be created manually using a text editor, if you are really hardcore and want to do things the hard way.

---

## Visual Studio.NET

Visual Studio.NET is Microsoft's next step in the evolution to the popular Visual Studio IDE. It's designed as a rapid application development (RAD) tool for creating Windows applications, Web applications, and XML Web services. It has several nice features such as indentation support, color-coding, integration with help files, and *Intellisense* word completion. Plus it has a powerful built-in debugger and a wealth of other tools for end-to-end application development.

Let's start familiarizing ourselves with the IDE by developing the previous *console* application. A *console* application is an application that has no user interface and typically uses the command prompt for input and output. This is a good place to start, since most of the examples in this book are console applications, to help simplify things and focus on the main concepts.

To create a console application in Visual Studio.NET, click on **New Project** on the **Start Page**, or you can click on **File | New | Project**. This will display the **New Project** window where you can select the type of project you want to develop. Scroll down and select **Console Application**, then name the project **Hello Project** and click on **OK** as shown in Figure 2.8.

**Figure 2.8** The New Project Selection Window

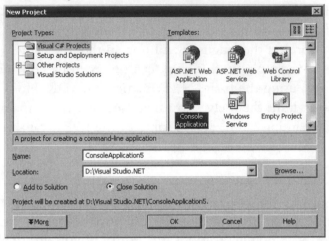

After clicking **OK**, Visual Studio.NET will take you to the source view page where you can start entering code. You'll notice that the helpful IDE automatically generates some skeleton code for you to get your application started. The skeleton code provides the basic structure for your console applications. It even starts the documentation for you because, as computer science professors like to remind us, "*Always document your code!*" Don't worry too much about what all this skeleton code means, as you'll learn all about it in the following chapters. For now, let's duplicate the previous example using the IDE. All we need to do is copy our previous code into the *Main()* method as shown.

```
using System;

namespace Hello_Project
{
  /// <summary>
  /// Summary description for Class1.
  /// </summary>
  class Class1
  {
    /// <summary>
    /// The main entry point for the application.
    /// </summary>
    [STAThread]
    static void Main(string[] args)
```

```
    {
      //
      // TODO: Add code to start application here
      //
      DateTime today = DateTime.Now;
      Console.WriteLine( "I wrote my first C# program at: " +
          today.ToString() );

      string msg = "You wanted to say hello to ";

      if(args.Length > 0)
      {
        for(int i=0; i<args.Length; i++)
        {
          msg += args[i] + " ";
        }
        Console.WriteLine(msg);
      }
    }
  }
}
```

Now that our source code is complete, all that's left to do is compile and run our code. To do this, all you need is to do is click on **Debug | Start**, or just press **F5**. This automatically will compile and start running the application. Also, if you just want to compile your application without running it, you can do so by clicking on **Build | Build Solution**. This will compile your application and show the output of the compilation in the **Output** window, which is located at the bottom of the screen. If there are any errors during compilation they will be displayed here. Once you run the program, you should get the expected output as shown in Figure 2.9.

But wait, you probably noticed that the console output window quickly disappears before you get a chance to view the result. You can easily work around this by adding the *Console.Read()* to the end of the program. This method waits for a keyboard input. In effect, it will pause the program until you press the Enter key before exiting.

The last thing to point out is the built-in Debugger that comes with Visual Studio.NET. You'll notice that this debugger is very similar to the one that comes with the .NET Framework SDK. Because of these similarities, you can follow the same steps that were outlined previously in order to debug your programs.

**Figure 2.9** Console Application Output

### Debugging…

## Finally, a Complete Debugging Solution

Some old-school programmers eschew today's fancy integrated development environments (IDEs) as mere toys for the weak. However, the debugging capabilities offered by the new Visual Studio.NET IDE may finally change their minds. The new IDE provides end-to-end debugging of applications across languages, projects, processes, and stored procedures. This is a monumental achievement on the part of the Visual Studio development team.

Using the integrated debugger, developers can step between HTML, script, and code written in any of the .NET supported languages, complete with integrated call stacks offering a total solution for end-to-end development.

# Other IDEs

If you're learning C# for work and your company is willing to shell out the cash to purchase the development tools you need (or if you just have a couple of hundred bucks lying around) then I suggest purchasing Visual Studio.NET. If not, don't worry because you don't have to be stuck using Notepad when developing your C# applications. If you're just starting out and want to learn the language for your own benefit but don't have the money to buy Visual Studio.NET there are options. The Internet (bless its kind soul) has several IDEs freely available that are more than capable of doing the job.

One of the more popular IDEs for C# at the moment is an open-source package called SharpDevelop. It's a full-fledged editor that contains most of the features you need to get started. It even has support for other languages, including VB.NET and even Java. Since the package is open-source you can start hacking the SharpDevelop code to include your own features. Plus the best feature of open-source is that it's free! SharpDevelop can be downloaded at http://www.icsharpcode.net/OpenSource/SD/default.asp.

# A Stroll through C#

Now that we have our development environment all set up, we can actually start learning the language. To get things started, let's try creating a more powerful C# application to whet your appetite. The following example highlights some of the power of C# by creating a full-blown application with just a few lines of code. Since one of the major features of C# is the ease of developing Windows applications and the ease of COM integration, we'll create an application that will utilize this technology. This section will demonstrate how to create a media player that can play most media file types including MP3, WAV, AVI, and MPG by using the Windows Media Control.

First we'll code the example by hand and then cover some of the rapid application development features that Visual Studio.NET has to offer. The explanations for the code will be brief since each subject area will be discussed in more detail throughout the book.

## Creating the Media Player Application

The first thing we need to do is create an eye-catching graphical user interface for our media player. The GUI for our application will be fairly simple: it will contain only a menu where a user can open a file dialog and select a song or movie. To do this, we need to create a Windows Form that will anchor the rest of our components. The process is similar to creating a Swing or AWT application in Java, where first you create a *JFrame* and then add components to it. The code for creating the interface for the media player application is shown as follows.

```
using System;
using System.Windows.Forms;

public class MediaPlayerApp : Form
{
    private MainMenu mainMenu;
    private MenuItem fileMenu;
```

```csharp
private MenuItem fileOpen;
private MenuItem fileExit;
private OpenFileDialog openFileDialog;

//Constructor
public MediaPlayerApp()
{
  //Creates the File Menu
  mainMenu = new MainMenu();
  fileMenu = new MenuItem();
  fileOpen = new MenuItem();
  fileExit = new MenuItem();
  openFileDialog = new OpenFileDialog();

 //Sets the file filters for the file dialog
  openFileDialog.Filter = "MP3 files (*.mp3)|*.mp3|AVI files (*.avi)
     |*.avi |All files (*.*)|*.*";
 openFileDialog.FileOk += new System.ComponentModel.CancelEventHandler
     (this.openFileDialog_FileOk);

  //fileOpen
  fileOpen.Text = "Open";
  fileOpen.Index = 0;
  fileOpen.Click += new
     System.EventHandler(this.fileOpen_Click);

  //fileExit
  fileExit.Text = "Exit";
  fileExit.Index = 0;
  fileExit.Click += new
     System.EventHandler(this.fileExit_Click);

  //fileMenu
  fileMenu.Text = "File";
  fileMenu.Index = 0;

  //Adds the Menu Items
```

```
        fileMenu.MenuItems.Add(fileOpen);

        fileMenu.MenuItems.Add(fileExit);

        mainMenu.MenuItems.Add(fileMenu);


        //Creating the Form Window

        this.Text = "Media Player App";

        this.AutoScaleBaseSize = new System.Drawing.Size(5,10);

        this.ClientSize = new System.Drawing.Size(305,230);

        this.Menu = mainMenu; //Sets the main menu for the form

    }


    //Handle the file open event

    private void fileOpen_Click(object sender, System.EventArgs e)

    {

        openFileDialog.ShowDialog();

    }


    //Handle the file exit event

    private void fileExit_Click(object sender, System.EventArgs e)

    {

      Application.Exit();

    }


    //Handles the file selection event

    private void openFileDialog_FileOk(object sender,

                        System.ComponentModel.CancelEventArgs e)

    {

      //Do nothing for now

    }


    public static void Main()

    {

      Application.Run(new MediaPlayerApp());

    }

}
```

The first two lines import some libraries that our program needs by declaring it with the *using* statement. Think of this as similar to the *import* statement in Java,

but with some differences you'll see later. The next line of code declares the
*MediaPlayerApp* class, which is extended from the *Form* class.

```
using System;
using System.Windows.Forms;


public class MediaPlayerApp : Form
```

C# doesn't use the *extend* keyword, but instead uses the colon (:) when
extending another class. After this, the code declares some components that make
up the file menu for our application. These are all declared as *private,* following
proper object-oriented design. The code then enters the constructor where each
component is instantiated using the *new* keyword.

```
mainMenu = new MainMenu();

fileMenu = new MenuItem();

fileOpen = new MenuItem();

fileExit = new MenuItem();
```

Once each component has been instantiated, the program sets some *properties*
and introduces an event handler for each *MenuItem.* For example, we set the
*fileOpen. Text* property to "*Open*" and its *Index* property to 0. Remember, these
are properties, not public fields, even though on the surface it appears as though
they are. By using properties in C#, you can set private fields as if they were
declared as *public.* In reality they are being accessed through *get* and *set* accessor
methods, which makes for a more intuitive syntax:

```
fileOpen.Text = "Open";

fileOpen.Index = 0;

fileOpen.Click += new System.EventHandler(this.fileOpen_Click);
```

C# uses *delegates* for event handling, which is similar to a function pointer in
C++. A delegate specifies a callback method to be called when an event occurs.
To define an event handler for a component, we simply pass the method to be
called to the *System.EventHandler* delegate. For the *fileOpen* menu item, the callback method is *fileOpen.Click()* for the click event. The declaration for this
method is as follows:

```
//Handle the file open event
private void fileOpen_Click(object sender, System.EventArgs e)
{
  openFileDialog.ShowDialog();
}
```

Since we want to show the open file dialog when we click on the *fileOpen* menu item, this method simply calls the *openFileDialog.ShowDialog()* method.

Once each component has been instantiated and initialized they are added to the *mainMenu* component, which is then added to the main form:

```
//Adds the Menu Items
fileMenu.MenuItems.Add(fileOpen);
fileMenu.MenuItems.Add(fileExit);
mainMenu.MenuItems.Add(fileMenu);
```

This is all very similar to Java. Finally, the application is started in the *Main()* method by creating an instance of *MediaPlayerApp* and passing it through the *Application.Run()* method. The *Application* class is used for managing Windows Form applications.

```
public static void Main()
{
    Application.Run(new MediaPlayerApp());
}
```

Save the file as **MediaPlayerApp.cs** and then compile it using the following command:

```
csc /target:winexe MediaPlayerApp.cs
```

The */target* switch tells the compiler that we're developing a Windows application. After compiling and executing the program and you should see something similar to Figure 2.10.

**Figure 2.10** The Eye-Catching Media Player GUI

When you click on **File | Open,** the open file dialog box should come up as shown in Figure 2.11. Notice the file dialog will display only MP3 files first because we set the *openFileDialog.Filter* property to show MP3 files.

**Figure 2.11** Open File Dialog Box

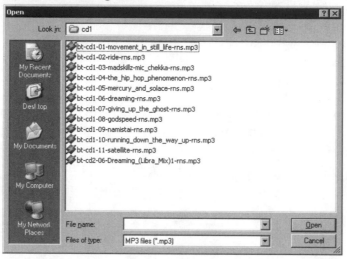

There you have it; you've just created your first graphical Windows application. Okay, it's pretty boring and doesn't even do anything. Well, don't worry because the next thing we'll do is add some functionality to it.

To add the actual media player functionality to our program, we'll use the Windows Media Player ActiveX control. This ActiveX control is called *msdxm.ocx*, and should be located in the *c:/windows/System32* directory. In C# you can easily import ActiveX controls by using the *aximp.exe* utility that comes with the .NET Framework SDK. To import the ActiveX control into C#, type the following command in the directory where your program is saved.

```
aximp c:\winnt\system32\msdxm.ocx
```

The *AxImp* utility creates a .NET assembly that acts as a proxy for the actual ActiveX control. For now, you can think of an assembly as a JAR file in Java. You can then use this assembly in your application just like any other .NET assembly. Figure 2.12 shows the output of the *AxImp* utility.

**Figure 2.12** Importing an ActiveX Control Using AxImp.exe

After generating the assemblies we can use the ActiveX control and add it to our application. The following is the modified code (in bold) with the addition of this new component.

```
using System;
using System.Windows.Forms;
using AxMediaPlayer;


public class MediaPlayerApp : Form
{
    private MainMenu mainMenu;
    private MenuItem fileMenu;
    private MenuItem fileOpen;
    private MenuItem fileExit;
    private OpenFileDialog openFileDialog;
    private AxMediaPlayer.AxMediaPlayer mediaPlayerControl;


    //Constructor
    public MediaPlayerApp()
    {
        //Adds media player control and sets some properties
        mediaPlayerControl = new AxMediaPlayer.AxMediaPlayer();
        mediaPlayerControl.Location = new
                            System.Drawing.Point(8, 0);
        mediaPlayerControl.Size = new
                            System.Drawing.Size(285,305);


        //Instantiate the open file dialog box.
        openFileDialog = new OpenFileDialog();
        openFileDialog.Filter = "MP3 files (*.mp3)|*.mp3|AVI files (*.avi)
```

```
                |*.avi |All files (*.*)|*.*";
     openFileDialog.FileOk += new System.ComponentModel.CancelEventHandler
          (this.openFileDialog_FileOk);


     //Creates the File Menu
     mainMenu = new MainMenu();
     fileMenu = new MenuItem();
     fileOpen = new MenuItem();
     fileExit = new MenuItem();


     //fileOpen
     fileOpen.Text = "Open";
     fileOpen.Index = 0;
     fileOpen.Click += new
            System.EventHandler(this.fileOpen_Click);


     //fileExit
     fileExit.Text = "Exit";
     fileExit.Index = 0;
     fileExit.Click += new
            System.EventHandler(this.fileExit_Click);


     //fileMenu
     fileMenu.Text = "File";
     fileMenu.Index = 0;


     //Adds the Menu Items
     fileMenu.MenuItems.Add(fileOpen);
     fileMenu.MenuItems.Add(fileExit);
     mainMenu.MenuItems.Add(fileMenu);



     //Creating the Form Window
     this.Text = "Media Player App";
     this.AutoScaleBaseSize = new System.Drawing.Size(5,10);
     this.ClientSize = new System.Drawing.Size(305,230);
     this.Menu = mainMenu; //Sets the main menu for the form
```

```
   //Adds the media player control to the form
   this.Controls.Add(mediaPlayerControl);
}


//Handle the file open event
private void fileOpen_Click(object sender, System.EventArgs e)
{
   openFileDialog.ShowDialog();
}


//Handle the file exit event
private void fileExit_Click(object sender, System.EventArgs e)
{
   Application.Exit();
}


//Handles the file selection event
private void openFileDialog_FileOk(object sender,
            System.ComponentModel.CancelEventArgs e)
{
   //Sets the filename to be played
   //by the media player control
   mediaPlayerControl.FileName = openFileDialog.FileName;
}

public static void Main()
{
   Application.Run(new MediaPlayerApp());
}
}
```

The first change to the new code is the *using AxMediaPlayer* statement, which declares that we're going to be using the *AxMediaPlayer.dll* assembly that was previously generated. The code then creates an instance of the *AxMediaPlayer* control and sets some of its properties, just like a regular component:

```
   //Adds media player control and sets some properties
```

```
mediaPlayerControl = new AxMediaPlayer.AxMediaPlayer();
mediaPlayerControl.Location = new
                       System.Drawing.Point(8, 0);
mediaPlayerControl.Size = new
                       System.Drawing.Size(285,305);
```

Then we add our component to our main Windows form, as follows:

```
//Adds the media player control to the form
this.Controls.Add(mediaPlayerControl);
```

Finally, the last bit of code is the event handler for the open file dialog. This sets the *FileName* property of *mediaPlayerControl* to the file selected from the open file dialog. The file name is selected via the *FileName* property of the *openFileDialog* object. The complete event handler for the *openFileDialog* is as follows:

```
//Handles the file selection event
private void openFileDialog_FileOk(object sender,
         System.ComponentModel.CancelEventArgs e)
{
   //Sets the filename to be played
   //by the media player control
   mediaPlayerControl.FileName = openFileDialog.FileName;
}
```

Now all that's left to do is compile and run the application. Since our program is using a separate library, you'll have to specify this when you compile it by using the */reference* switch. This indicates to the compiler the libraries that your program needs, which is similar to specifying the classpath for the JAR file in Java. To compile the program type the following command:

```
csc /target:winexe /reference:AxMediaPlayer.dll MediaPlayerApp.cs
```

That's it! We've just created our own media player application that can play any MP3 file and other media types. The final application is shown in Figure 2.13.

# Rapid Application Development with Visual Studio.NET

Rapid application development is where Visual Studio.NET really shines. Designing windows applications is a breeze by simply dragging and dropping components onto your form. Not only that, Visual Studio provides an easy way for configuring the properties of each component. The end result is that all the GUI code is generated for you. About the only thing you'll have to write is the event handling code.

**Figure 2.13** The Completed Media Player Application

Let's go through the Media Player example and see how we can create the same application using Visual Studio.NET. For this example, we'll take advantage of the properties window in VS.NET to display the relevant information for the ActiveX control. To create the application, follow these steps:

1.  Start by creating a new Windows Application project. Click on **File | New | Project** and then select **Windows Application**. Name your project as **MediaPlayerProject** and then click on **OK**. This will bring you to the design environment as shown in Figure 2.14. The design window displays a blank Windows Form where you can drag and drop components onto it.

2.  You'll notice that in the bottom right-hand corner is the **Properties** window. This window displays all the properties for the component that is currently selected. For example, to change the text label of the window form, just go change the **Text** property from **Form1** to **Media Player App** as shown in Figure 2.15.

3.  The next step is to create the file menu. We can use the **Toolbox** window, which contains a selection of Windows widgets and controls. Look for the **MainMenu** control and drag it onto the form. Then type **File**, **Open**, and **Exit** for the menu items as shown in Figure 2.16. This will create three menu item components and name them *menuItem1*,

*menuItem2*, and *menuItem3*, respectively. Go to the **Properties** window for each one and change the **(Name)** property to **file**, **fileOpen**, and **fileExit**, respectively.

**Figure 2.14** The Design Environment

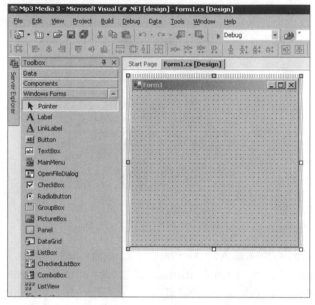

**Figure 2.15** The Properties Window

**Figure 2.16** Creating the Main Menu

4. Now look for the **OpenFileDialog** component in the **Toolbox** and add it to the form. This will add the OpenFileDialog component and name it *openFileDialog1*. With the OpenFileDialog component selected, go to the **Properties** window and look for the **Filter** property. Change this to **MP3 files (\*.mp3)|\*.mp3|AVI files (\*.avi)|\*.avi |All files (\*.\*)|\*.\***. This will set the file filter of the open file dialog box.

5. It's now time to add the Windows Media Player ActiveX control. In Visual Studio.NET you don't have to use the *AxImp.exe* utility because the IDE will import it automatically for you. To do this, click on **Tools | Customize Toolbox**. In the **COM Components** tab, scroll down until you find the **Window Media Player** control and put a check beside it as shown in Figure 2.17.

**Figure 2.17** Customize Toolbox Window

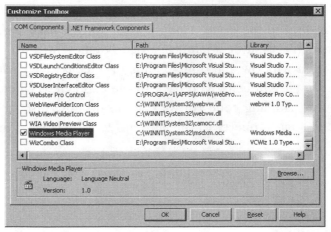

6. After clicking on **OK**, Visual Studio will add the **MediaPlayer** to the **Toolbox** window. Now you can visually add the component to the form. The component is named *axMediaPlayer1* by default. Next, go to the **Properties** window and set the **ShowDisplay** property to **True**. At this point it would be a good idea to adjust the Media Player control to make sure that everything fits nicely in the window.

7. Now we'll add some code. All we need to do is add the event handling code for each component. Let's do the *fileOpen* event first. To do this, just double-click on the component in the form. This will automatically bring you to the code view for your application. All we need to do is call the *openFileDialog1.ShowDialog()* method, as follows:

```
private void fileOpen_Click(object sender, System.EventArgs e)

{

    openFileDialog1.ShowDialog();

}
```

8. Next, we'll add the event handling code for the *fileExit* menu item. Go back to the design window by clicking on the **Form1.cs [Design]** tab. Again, double-click on the **fileExit** menu item. This brings you back to the code view where you can enter the event handling code for the component. For this event, we want to close the application so we'll call the *Application.Exit()* method, as follows:

```
private void fileExit_Click(object sender, System.EventArgs e)

{

    Application.Exit();

}
```

9. Finally, add the event handling code for the *openFileDialog1* component (which should be a familiar process by now). To do this, go back to the design window and double-click on the *openFileDialog1* component. Again, it will bring you back to the code view where you can enter the event handling code. All we need to do now is set the *axMediaPlayer1 .FileName* property to the *openFileDialogl.FileName* property:

```
private void openFileDialog1_FileOk(object sender,
            System.ComponentModel.CancelEventArgs e)

    {
```

```
        axMediaPlayer1.FileName = openFileDialog1.FileName;
    }
```

10. Now all that's left for us to do is compile and run the program. Click on **Debug | Start** or just press **F5**. The final output is shown in Figure 2.18.

**Figure 2.18** Using the Media Player Application designed in Visual Studio.NET

There you have it, the same media player application designed in Visual Studio. As you can see, designing the application with Visual Studio is much simpler and much faster. With the help of the *Properties* window, you can easily configure each component as opposed to coding it by hand. This allows you to design your programs, especially the graphical user interface, more rapidly. Visual Studio also combines all the tools you need in one easy-to-use development environment.

# Summary

This chapter has introduced the C# language and highlighted some basic features. C# is a modern object-oriented programming language descending from other languages including C, C++, and Java. It shares many features with Java, which are intended to eliminate some of the complexities of C++. The shared features of C# and Java include both compiling to an intermediate language and support for automatic garbage collection.

C# supports the notion of classes and the object-oriented nature of classes, including inheritance and polymorphism. Like Java, it supports only single-inheritance but can implement multiple interfaces. Other similar features include single rooted inheritance, which means that all classes are derived from *Object*.

C# also adds some new features, not available in Java. It has properties and indexers, which provide intuitive syntax for accessing data members while promoting data encapsulation. It also carries over support for other C++ constructs such as e*nums*, *structs*, operator overloading, and allowing the use of pointers for direct memory access. It has XML style documentation, which is more flexible than using Javadocs. C# also incorporates built-in support for COM and the Windows API, which is great news for Windows developers. Overall, C# brings together the raw power of C++ and the simplicity of the Java language.

This chapter also demonstrated the tools you need for developing C# applications. With the use of the .NET Framework SDK, you should be able to compile, test, and run programs. The .NET SDK provides two debuggers, which are essential to learn when it comes to application development. Perhaps the easiest debugger is the *dbgclr.exe* tool, which contains an easy-to-use graphical interface.

Visual Studio.NET is not necessary for developing C# applications. However, using an integrated development environment makes application development much faster. By developing a Media Player application, you were able to get a glimpse at some of C# features plus the advantages of using a rapid application development tool such as VS.NET.

# Solutions Fast Track

## The C# Language

☑  C# has all the features you would expect in a modern object-oriented language.

☑ It has about 80 keywords and a dozen primitive data types.

☑ It contains features similar to Java, such as compilation to an intermediate language and a runtime that supports automatic garbage collection.

☑ The C# syntax is similar to Java, but provides other features such as properties and indexers, which make it more intuitive.

☑ Other advanced features include operator overloading, cast operators, and pointer support.

☑ C# incorporates built-in support for COM and the Windows API.

# Getting Started

☑ The .NET Framework SDK is all you need for developing C# applications.

☑ The *csc.exe* is the main C# compiler in the .NET SDK.

☑ The .NET SDK provides two tools for debugging, a command line debugger called *cordbg.exe* and *dbgclr.exe*, which has a graphical user interface.

# Using Different IDEs

☑ Using an integrated development environment (IDE) increases programmer productivity.

☑ Visual Studio.NET is a feature-rich development environment available from Microsoft.

☑ SharpDevelop is an open-source IDE that is freely available on the Internet that can be used to develop C# and Java applications.

# A Stroll through C#

☑ The .NET SDK provides tools for integrating COM and ActiveX components into your application, such as the *aximp.exe* utility.

☑ You can use Visual Studio.NET for rapid application development, especially when creating graphical Windows applications.

☑  Visual Studio.NET allows you to easily drag and drop components and
modify properties when developing a user interface for you program.

# Frequently Asked Questions

The following Frequently Asked Questions, answered by the authors of this book,
are designed to both measure your understanding of the concepts presented in
this chapter and to assist you with real-life implementation of these concepts. To
have your questions about this chapter answered by the author, browse to
**www.syngress.com/solutions** and click on the **"Ask the Author"** form.

**Q:** What debugging tools can I use when developing my programs?

**A:** The .NET Framework SDK provides several tools for debugging your application. You can use *cordbg.exe,* which is command line debugger, or you can
use the *dbgclr.exe* debugger utility, which has a graphical user interface.

**Q:** Do C# and Java have the same class and method names?

**A:** Although a lot of C# classes have a Java counterpart, they don't all have the
same class names and method names. However, the most common classes
have similar names. For the most part, the class methods are also the same and
differ only by the capitalization of the first letter.

**Q:** Does C# support global functions or constants?

**A:** No, C# is similar to Java in this respect. Everything must belong to a class,
which means that there are no global functions or constants. This is an
improvement over C++ and makes code maintenance easier.

**Q:** Can I use my old COM and ActiveX components with C#?

**A:** Yes, you can. C# provides built-in support for COM and ActiveX integration.
You can use the *aximp.exe* utility to import your ActiveX component. This
utility will create a .NET assembly that you can use in your C# application.

**Q:** Is Visual Studio.NET the only IDE available for developing C# applications?

**A:** There are other freely available IDEs on the Internet, such as SharpDevelop.
Although Visual Studio.NET provides a rich set of features for end-to-end
application development, it is not necessary for developing in C#. If you like to
do things the hard way, you can even just use a text editor such as Notepad.

# Chapter 3

# Language Fundamentals

## Solutions in this chapter:

- **Main() Method**
- **Single-Line and Multiline Comments**
- **Data Types and the Common Type System**
- **Variables**
- **Constants**
- **Assignment Statements**
- **Operators**
- **Preprocessor Directives**
- **Namespaces**

☑ **Summary**
☑ **Solutions Fast Track**
☑ **Frequently Asked Questions**

# Introduction

After familiarizing ourselves with the C# programming environment, it's time to move forward and get to work. You're probably eager to get started and dive right into programming your first full-blown C# enterprise application. Before we can continue, however, we need to learn some subtle differences between C# and Java.

This chapter will go over the basic building blocks of writing a C# application. It will explain all of the language fundamentals such as data types, variables, expressions, and operators. We will learn the difference between *namespaces* and *packages,* as well as C# language features not found Java. This includes XML type comments and the preprocessor directives.

As most of you already have some Java programming experience under your belts, this stuff will be a piece of cake. But read it carefully—you will want to know the exact differences between Java and C#.

# Main() Method

We'll start our overview of C# fundamentals in the same manner that our applications start, with the *Main()* method. Similar to Java, C# uses the *Main()* method as the starting point for every application. When an application is executed, it starts by calling the *Main()* method of the application's controlling class. Additional methods from the same or other classes are then called as needed by the *Main()* method. Chapter 5 will cover encapsulation and classes in more detail.

Let's examine a quick example of a C# application using the *Main()* method. Following an ancient tradition, this "Hello World" program illustrates the use of the *Main()* method.

```
class SayHello
{
  public static void Main()
  {
    System.Console.WriteLine("Hello "+"World!");
  }
}
```

Let's go through this example and see how it works. As with Java, C# uses the class as the basic unit of encapsulation; therefore, the *Main()* method must be located within a class. In this example we are using the *SayHello* class to encapsulate the *Main()* method. The name of this class is unimportant as long as it contains a *Main()* method. The compiler will start the application execution within any class that holds the *Main()* method; however if more than one class contains a *Main()* method, a compiler error will occur stating that you have more than one entry point defined. There is an exception to this: If you have multiple instances of a *Main()* method defined for testing purposes, you can specify which *Main()* method to use by specifying the compiler command line argument:

```
/main:<class>
```

One final word about classes at this point: As with Java, it is considered good programming practice to use Pascal-case for your class names. Pascal-case means that the first letter is uppercase and the first letter of any additional concatenated words is uppercase. Your application will still compile if you don't follow this rule, but it really does make your code easier for you or others to follow later.

After declaring the class, we use a pair of curly braces to contain the class definition. This is done in the same way as Java, C, and C++ so we're not going to focus on this too much. Just remember that all opening curly braces must have a corresponding closing curly brace and that all contents of a program entity such as a class or method must be located within this curly brace pair.

In examining the declaration of the *Main()* method, you've no doubt noticed some major differences between this declaration and the way a similar declaration would be done in Java. One of the first things that you learned in Java was that the *main()* method must always be defined as:

## *Java*

```
public static void main(String[] args)
```

The differences between C# and Java really start here. The first thing that should be mentioned is that in C#, the method name *must* be capitalized. As you probably learned with Java, case-sensitivity is the first issue you'll run up against in C#. As with Java, if you attempt to compile with the *Main()* method capitalized incorrectly, you will receive a compile error stating that you have no entry point defined. This basically means that your compiler has no idea where to begin execution because it cannot find its starting point.

Also, in the declaration of the *Main()* method in C#, you've probably noticed that no parameters have been specified for the method. In Java you must specify the *String[] args* parameter for the *main()* method even if you are not passing any command line arguments to the method. C# has changed this by removing this requirement. C# can still accept the same argument; we'll discuss this in the next section, "Command Line Arguments."

One additional requirement when defining a *main()* method in Java is that the method must be *public* due to the fact that it is started from code outside its class. C# does not have this requirement, therefore the *Main()* method can also be declared as either of the following:

```
static void Main()
static void Main(String[] args)
```

After the *Main()* method has been defined, we can begin our program code, again encapsulating it within a pair of curly braces. In our example here, we are making a call to the *System.Console* namespace, and executing the *WriteLine* function. The process as to how this works is described in the section, "Namespaces," later in this chapter. For our purposes here, it is sufficient to know that this call can be performed by either the method shown in our first example, or the following:

```
using System;
class SayHello
{
  public static void Main()
  {
    Console.WriteLine("Hello "+"World!");
  }
}
```

In this example, we are using the *using* keyword to specify that we are using the *System* namespace. The *using* keyword basically creates a shortcut allowing us to specify the *Console.Writeline* function without using the complete fully qualified name.

Following our program code, we have our closing curly braces for the method and the class. That's it for our little sample application. By this point, you should have a fairly good understanding of the differences between Java's use of the *main()* method and C#'s use of the *Main()* method. The differences and similarities between these are really your stepping stones for understanding the differences and similarities between all aspects of the two languages.

## Command Line Arguments

You now know how the *Main()* method works and how to write a very basic program. Our next step will be to expand on the functionality of our application by allowing it to accept command line arguments or parameters.

In Java, command line arguments are passed to the *main()* method by way of a single argument, *String[] args*. To refresh your memory, basically this declares an array of instances of the *String* class. Based on this declaration, an array called *args* receives all of the command line arguments passed to the program when it is executed.

C# functions in a similar manner. The *Main()* method accepts a parameter of *string[] args*, which declares that an array of string values is to be stored in the variable *args*. Just as in Java, this allows you to accept command line arguments and to process them within your application. Let's take a look at a quick example:

```
using System;
class SayHello
{
  public static void Main(string[] args)
  {
    foreach (string arg in args)
      Console.WriteLine("Hello "+"{0}", arg);
  }
}
```

In this example, we are taking each command line argument passed to the executable and placing those arguments into our "Hello" message. When this is used, the *args* array is filled with all of the strings following the executable name on the command line. We then execute the *Console.Writeline* statement against each string in the array. You probably noticed the *foreach* statement, which is new in C#. This will be discussed later in Chapter 4, but for now think of it as a *for* loop that iterates through the array. When this is executed, the following output results:

```
C:\chapt3-code\c#>sayhello Austin Bobby Christina
Hello Austin
Hello Bobby
Hello Christina


C:\chapt3-code\c#>
```

Although this is good for a sample application, what you're probably interested in is how to make this feature truly functional in your application. In many applications, program flow or program options can be set via command line arguments. The following code illustrates how this can be done in C#.

```
using System;
class SayHello
{
  public static void Main(string[] args)
  {
    if (args.Length >0)
    {
      foreach (string arg in args)
      {
        if (arg.Equals("/help"))
          Console.WriteLine("Run this program as follows:"+
              "sayhello.exe [name1] ...");
        else
          Console.WriteLine("Hello "+"{0}", arg);
      }
    }
    else
      Console.WriteLine("For help, run sayhello.exe /help");


  }
}
```

In this sample, we are taking the command line arguments and performing a few actions against them. First, we check to see if there actually are any command line parameters by using the *Length* method of the *args* object. If there are no command line arguments, we output the string "For help, run sayhello.exe /help". If there are command line arguments, we first check each one to determine if it is "/help" by using the *Equals* method of the *arg* object. If the string stored in *arg* is "/help", we send output to the console explaining how to properly use our program. If the command line argument is something other than "/help" we use it as the string to append to "Hello". Running this application results in the following display:

```
C:\chapt3-code\c#>sayhello
For help, run sayhello.exe /help


C:\chapt3-code\c#>sayhello /help
Run this program as follows:sayhello.exe [name1] ...
```

```
C:\chapt3-code\c#>sayhello Mike Chad Dave Sajan
Hello Mike
Hello Chad
Hello Dave
Hello Sajan
```

# Return Values

Another feature in C# that differs from Java is the fact that the *Main()* method can actually return a value. In Java, this was not possible due to the fact that the *main()* method had to be declared using the keyword *void*, which specifies that no value is returned from the method. In order for a method to return a value, the variable type for the returned value must be defined when calling the method. C# supports returning an *int* value from the *Main()* method. In order to do this, declare the *Main()* method and your return values as demonstrated in the following code.

```
using System;
class SayHello
{
public static int Main(string[] args)
{
  if (args.Length >0)
  {
    foreach (string arg in args)
    {
      if (arg.Equals("/help"))
      {
        Console.WriteLine(  "Run this program as follows:" +
                            "sayhello.exe [name1] ...");
        return(1);
      }
      else
        Console.WriteLine("Hello "+"{0}", arg);
      }
     return(0);
  }
```

```
  else
    Console.WriteLine("For help, run sayhello.exe /help");
  return(2);
}
}
```

As you can see in this example, the program returns a different value depending on how it is executed. You'll also notice that even if the *Main()* method has been defined to return a value, it can still accept the *string[] args* parameter.

So how do you make use of this feature? By returning an integer value from the *Main()* method, you are able to make use of the command interpreter's error level conditions. This allows you to enable your program to function within batch processes and control the flow of the batch process depending on the outcome of your program's execution. This is best explained by an example. The following DOS batch file calls the program created by our previous C# source code example:

## HI.BAT

```
@echo off
sayhello %1 %2 %3 %4 %5
IF ERRORLEVEL 2 GOTO NOARG
IF ERRORLEVEL 1 GOTO HELPMENU
IF ERRORLEVEL 0 GOTO NORMAL


:HELPMENU
ECHO Help menu has been accessed during this run.
GOTO END


:NOARG
ECHO Program was called with no arguments.
GOTO END


:NORMAL
ECHO Program executed standard greeting.
GOTO END


:END
```

When this batch file (called hi.bat) is executed, we are presented with the following output depending on how the batch file was called.

```
C:\chapt3-code\c#>hi
For help, run sayhello.exe /help
Program was called with no arguments.


C:\chapt3-code\c#>hi /help
Run this program as follows:sayhello.exe [name1] ...
Help menu has been accessed during this run.


C:\chapt3-code\c#>hi Austin
Hello Austin
Program executed standard greeting.


C:\chapt3-code\c#>hi Austin Mark
Hello Austin
Hello Mark
Program executed standard greeting.


C:\chapt3-code\c#>
```

As you can see, returning a value from the *Main()* method can be a very useful feature. Whenever you are writing a console application, it is a good idea to return a value from your *Main()* method. This will make your application useful within batch executions and also helps automate success or failure reporting.

## Debugging...

### Return Statement

There is something very important to keep in mind when using the *return* statement. When this statement is encountered during program execution, the method containing the *return* statement is terminated and passes the return value to the calling routine. In the case of the *Main()* method, execution of the entire program terminates and returns the specified return value. Always verify that you wish for your application

**Continued**

> to terminate at the position where you place the *return* statement if you
> are using this statement within the *Main()* method. For example, if you
> place the *return* statement within a loop in your *Main()* method, the
> loop will exit immediately without any further processing when it
> encounters the *return* statement.

# Single-Line and Multiline Comments

Regardless of what kind of program you are writing, there is always one portion
of the code that should be considered as the most important: programmer comments. As you well know, without adding appropriate comments into your code,
neither you nor anyone else can understand or remember why a program was
coded the way it was. By using comments extensively in your code, you can go
back to it a week, a month, or years after and within a few moments understand
exactly what the program does and how it works.

Java supports three main commenting styles; single-line, multiline, and documentation comments (*javadoc*). In this section, we will cover single-line and multiline comments. The following code shows examples of these comments as they
are implemented in Java:

*Java*

```
//This is a single line comment.

/* This is a
 * multiline comment.
 */
```

In C#, single-line and multiline comments are done in the exact same way.
Single-line comments are prefaced with // and multiline comments are encapsulated between /* and */. Let's go ahead and add some comments to our *SayHello*
sample program. For brevity, I'll list just one small section of code:

```
//There are args, parse through them.
foreach (string arg in args)
{
        //Check for /help arg.
        if (arg.Equals("/help"))
        {
```

```
//Requested help, display prog info.
        Console.WriteLine(
                "Run this program as follows:" +
                "sayhello.exe [name1] ...");
        return(1);
    }
    /* This arg wasn't /help, assume it's a
     * name and greet it.
     */
    else
        Console.WriteLine(
                "Hello "+"{0}", arg);
}
return(0);
```

As you can see from this example, adding comments in your code helps greatly with readability and can help in understanding how the program works. When adding comments to your code, it is best to follow these standard practices to help make your code more understandable to others:

- When commenting out just a few lines of code, use multiple single-line comments.

- When commenting out a lot of code, use multiline comments, but preface each line included in the segment with a ★. This will make each line more easily identifiable as a comment.

- Comment your program flow, explaining what you are doing and why.

- Use single-line comments to mark off sections of code for debugging purposes.

- Over-commenting is better by far than under-commenting.

One final word on single-line and multiline comments: These comments are not included with your compiled executable; therefore the additional space taken up by comments in your source files will not increase the size of your executable. Also, any proprietary or confidential information that you include in your comments will not be able to be disassembled from your executable later. This gives you a safe and effective way to include necessary information within your source files without worrying about who will be able to read it when the program is compiled.

# XML Documentation Comments

As mentioned in the previous section, Java includes a style of commenting called *documentation comments*. These comments are encapsulated between /** and */ and are used by the *javadoc* utility to provide documentation for your code. The *javadoc* utility takes these comments and generates a series of HTML files containing this information. *Javadoc* creates a separate HTML file for each class and also creates an index for the documentation.

C# supports a similar documentation style, but its use is almost completely different from the Java documentation comments. These comments are called "XML documentation comments" and, similar to Java's documentation comments, allow you to create dynamic documentation based on your source code. This documentation is generated by the C# compiler when your program is compiled, and is stored in the XML format. XML documentation can be used to easily document each class, member, and method while you are coding. As you know, going through your code after it is complete and documenting how each method is called and what every class is used for is a very long and tedious job. Using XML documentation as you are coding allows you to simply export an XML file when your project is complete and have all your documentation complete as well.

You can create this XML file when your application is complete, or create it on every compile. The choice is completely yours. In order to tell the compiler to create this documentation, you must include an additional command-line parameter, */doc:filename.xml*, when calling the compiler. The following example calls the compiler with this parameter:

```
csc SayHello.cs /doc:SayHello.xml
```

This will take our *SayHello.cs* file and create an XML file containing the XML documentation comments included in the file. Of course, at this point we have no XML documentation comments in our source file, so the compiler generates an XML file that looks like this:

```
<?xml version="1.0"?>
<doc>
    <assembly>
        <name>SayHello</name>
```

```
    </assembly>
    <members>
    </members>
</doc>
```

Before we start adding in XML documentation comments to our source file, let's take a look at what XML documentation tags we have available. XML documentation tags are used in the XML documentation comments to specify what our comment is about as well as provide some special functions when the XML file is generated. Table 3.1 is a list of standard XML documentation tags and what they mean or do.

**Table 3.1** XML Documentation Tags

| Tag | Subtag | Attribute | Values | Description |
| --- | --- | --- | --- | --- |
| <c> | | | | Indicates that the text within the tags should be marked as code. This is used for small segments of code on a single line. |
| <code> | | | | Indicates that the text within the tags should be marked as code. This is used for code that takes up multiple lines. |
| <example> | | | | Indicates that the text within the tags is an example. Generally this is used to show how to use a method or member. |
| <exception> | | | | This allows you to specify which exceptions a class can throw. |
| | | cref | exception | Any valid exception. |
| <include> | | | | This allows you to include documentation from external files in your generated XML file rather than including them in your source file |

**Continued**

**Table 3.1** Continued

| Tag | Subtag | Attribute | Values | Description |
|---|---|---|---|---|
| | | | | itself. This is useful in a team environment where some members are writing code and others are providing the documentation. |
| | | file path | filename tagpath [@name ="id"] | Filename to include. *tagpath* is the XML path to the tag containing the XML documentation comments and includes *id*, which matches the *name* attribute of the tag containing the XML documentation comments. |
| <list> | | | | Indicates that the data within the tags is part of a list. |
| | | type | bullet, number, or table | This specifies what type of list this is. |
| | <listheader> | | | This indicates that the subtags contained within this tag are the heading row of a table or list. |
| | <item> | | | This indicates that the subtags contained within this tag are items to include in the list. |
| | <term> | | | Indicates that the text within the tag is a term to define. |
| | <description> | | | Indicates that the text within the tag is the description of a term. |
| <para> | | | | This formats the text contained within the tag as a paragraph. |

*Continued*

**Table 3.1** Continued

| Tag | Subtag | Attribute | Values | Description |
|---|---|---|---|---|
| <param> | | | | Indicates that the text within the tag describes the parameter specified by the *name* attribute. |
| | | name | method parameter name | Specifies the name of a parameter to be described. |
| <paramref> | | | | References a parameter specified by the *name* attribute. |
| | | name | valid parameter name | Specifies the name of a parameter to reference. |
| <permission> | | | | Indicates that the text within the tag is the description of the security access to a member. |
| | | cref | valid member or field | Specifies the member to be described. |
| <remarks> | | | | Indicates that the text within the tag contains an overview description. |
| <returns> | | | | Indicates that the text within the tag describes the return value. |
| <see> | | | | Specifies a link from within some text. |
| | | cref | valid member or field | Specifies the member to be linked to. |
| <seealso> | | | | Specifies a link to be included in a "see also" section. |
| | | cref | valid member or field | Specifies the member to be linked to. |

**Continued**

**Table 3.1** Continued

| Tag | Subtag | Attribute | Values | Description |
|-----|--------|-----------|--------|-------------|
| &lt;summary&gt; | | | | Indicates that the text within the tag is the description of a member. |
| &lt;value&gt; | | | | Indicates that the text within the tag describes a property. |

Let's focus for a moment on how XML tags work. Every tag has an opening, has a closing, and can contain one or more parameters. Specifying the tag name and encapsulating it within a <> opens a tag. For example, *<summary>* opens the *summary* tag.

A tag can be closed either within the same tag definition or by specifying a closing tag. An example of closing a tag within the same definition would be *<seealso cref="member"/>*. The */>* at the end of the tag specifies that it closes itself. This is used for tags that just specify parameters. A normal closing tag would be in the format of *</tagname>*.

Parameters (known as attributes) are specified within the opening of the tag. They are specified in the format *attribute=value*, where *attribute* is the name of the attribute and *value* is the value to which the attribute refers. An example of this is *<seealso cref="member"/>*. In this example, *cref* is the attribute and *"member"* is the value.

Putting all this together, you can end up with tags that look like the following:

```
<tagname attrib1=value1 attrib2=value2>text</tagname>
<tagname2 attrib1=value1/>
```

Why would you need to know exactly how the XML tags work? There are two main reasons for this. First, the XML documentation comments are completely extensible due to the fact that you can add in your own tags. I mentioned before that the preceding tag list contained standard tags. These are the current standard XML documentation comment tags, but the format is extensible, so you can add as many tags as you like. Additional tags, when preceded by ///, will be included in the generated XML file.

The second reason for understanding XML is that you can customize the display of your XML documentation by creating or modifying XML stylesheets. To do this, you need to have a good understanding of XML tags and how they work.

Now let's take our *SayHello* sample code and add XML documentation comments to it. Then we'll compile it from the command line and see what we end up with. Please note that the indentations in this example don't follow standard programming practice due to page width limitations, and further note that the body of the method has been removed for simplicity.

```
using System;

/// <summary>
/// The SayHello class is a container for a simple
/// Main method.
/// <para>This sample is pretty useless.</para>
/// </summary>
class SayHello
{
/// <summary>
/// This is the Main method for the class and is
/// the execution starting point for our application.
/// Please note that <paramref name="args">args</paramref>
/// is a array of strings.
/// </summary>
/// <param name="args">People to say "Hello" to</param>
/// <returns>Returns a value depending on how the program
/// was called.</returns>
//We want Main to return an integer.
public static int Main(string[] args)
{
  //Check to see if there are any cmdline args.
  if (args.Length >0)
{
  //Method body removed for simplicity
  return(0);
  }
  return(1);
 }
}
```

When this is compiled with the command-line syntax *"csc SayHello.cs /doc:SayHello.xml"*, we end up with the following XML file.

```xml
<?xml version="1.0"?>
<doc>
    <assembly>
        <name>SayHello</name>
    </assembly>
    <members>
        <member name="T:SayHello">
            <summary>
            The SayHello class is a container for a simple
            Main method.
            <para>This sample is pretty useless.</para>
            </summary>
        </member>
        <member name="M:SayHello.Main(System.String[])">
            <summary>
            This is the Main method for the class and is
            the execution starting point for our application.
            Please note that <paramref name="args">args</paramref>
            is a array of strings.
            </summary>
            <param name="args">People to say "Hello" to</param>
            <returns>Returns a value depending on how the program
            was called.</returns>
        </member>
    </members>
</doc>
```

After our *SayHello.XML* file has been generated, we can simply open Internet Explorer and view it. This will result in a screen that shows us our XML tags in a format that can either be collapsed or expanded by clicking on the + or − signs. This output is shown in Figure 3.1.

So we now have our *SayHello.XML* file and we can see that it does include all of our XML documentation comments. The problem at this point is that the format that it is displayed in is cryptic and difficult to read. That's where XML stylesheets fit in. XML stylesheets take this XML output and format it in the manner specified in the stylesheets. They use the XSL extension and basically are used just for making XML files more readable. A complete explanation of XML stylesheets and how to use them is beyond the scope of this book; however, we will cover how to use them with our XML file. Full information on XML stylesheets currently can be found at www.w3.org/TR/xsl/. In addition, the XSL file we will use in our example was obtained from Microsoft MSDN and can be found by searching for doc.xsl at http://msdn.microsoft.com.

**Figure 3.1** XML Documentation—Standard Format

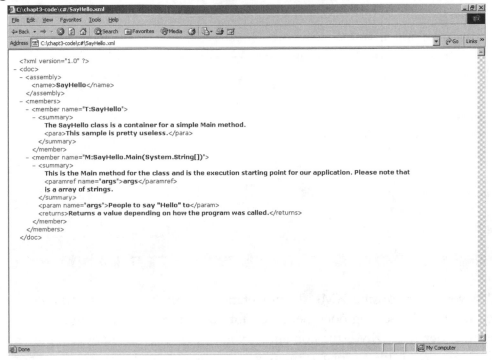

To cause an XML file to be formatted by an XSL file, you must specify which XSL file to use in the header of the XML file. This process is best shown by an example. Currently, the top line of our *SayHello.XML* file is:

```
<?xml version="1.0"?>
```

In order to cause this XML file to be processed by our *doc.xsl* file, add a line immediately after this that references the *doc.xsl* file. The syntax for this is as follows:

```
<?xml-stylesheet href="doc.xsl" type="text/xsl"?>
```

By adding this line and saving the *doc.xsl* file in the same directory as the *SayHello.XML* file, we can now view this file using the formatting specified in the XSL file. Opening the *SayHello.XML* file in Internet Explorer now results in the screen shown in Figure 3.2.

**Figure 3.2** XML Documentation—Stylesheet Format

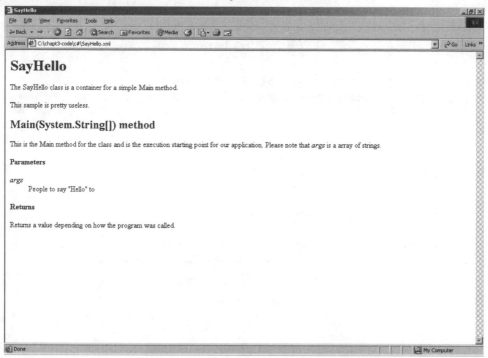

As you can see, using XML documentation comments is a fast and convenient method of creating documentation for your program. By using the compiler to generate an XML file containing your XML documentation comments and using an XSL file to format them, you can quickly generate excellent documentation in an easy-to-read format.

# Data Types and the Common Type System

C# is, of course, based on the Microsoft .NET framework. One of the fundamental parts of this framework is a shared *Common Type System* (CTS). The CTS defines how types are declared and used throughout the .NET framework and provides the cross-platform type support for which .NET was designed.

In Java, you are provided with the following eight built-in, primitive data types: *boolean, byte, char, double, float, int, long,* and *short.* C# provides the equivalent of these as well as several new data types. Table 3.2 outlines the C# data types and their Java equivalents.

**Table 3.2** C# Data Types

| C# Data Type | Java Data Type | Runtime Type | Size (bytes) | Range | Description |
|---|---|---|---|---|---|
| bool | boolean | Boolean | n/a | True or false | Boolean Value |
| byte | | Byte | 1 | 0 to 255 | Unsigned Integer |
| char | char | Char | 2 | 0x0000 to 0xFFFF | Unicode Character |
| decimal | | Decimal | 8 | −79,228,162,514,264,337,593,543,950,335 to 79,228,162,514,264,337,593,543,950,335 | Decimal Number |
| double | double | Double | 8 | −1.79769313486232e308 to 1.79769313486232e308 | Double-Precision 64-Bit Number |
| float | float | Single | 4 | −3.402823e38 to 3.402823e38 | Single-Precision 32-Bit Number |
| int | int | Int32 | 4 | −2,147,483,648 to 2,147,483,647 | Signed Integer |
| long | long | Int64 | 8 | −9,223,372,036,854,775,808 to 9,223,372,036,854,775,807 | Signed Integer |
| sbyte | byte | SByte | 1 | −128 to 127 | Signed Integer |
| short | short | Int16 | 2 | −32768 to 32767 | Signed Integer |
| uint | | UInt32 | 4 | 0 to 4,294,967,295 | Unsigned Integer |
| ulong | | UInt64 | 8 | 0 to 184,467,440,737,095,551,615 | Unsigned Integer |
| ushort | | UInt16 | 2 | 0 to 65535 | Unsigned Integer |

In this table, there is a column that deserve special note. In the Runtime Type column, a value is listed for each data type. In C#, all data types are part of the *System* namespace and can be referenced through there. For example, the *bool* data type can be referenced as *System.Boolean*.

C# supports two kinds of types: *value* types and *reference* types, which are both based on the *object* (*System.Object*) type. *Value* types hold actual data in the form of variables. They are stored in the *stack* by C#, which is a temporary memory space. With *value* types, every stored value is stored separately from all of the other stored values, and changing one will not affect another.

*Reference* types hold objects, which refer to actual data. They are stored in the *heap*, which is a more permanent and larger memory space. Since an object can be referred to by multiple variables, operations using one of the variables can affect operations by the other. This is something to keep in mind when referring to the same object through different variables.

These basic data types are, by default, value types and are stored in the stack. You can, however, store any data type in the heap and reference it as an object if necessary. This process is called *boxing* and basically creates a wrapper that makes the value type look like a reference object containing the value that was stored in the value type. This process can also be reversed. An example would be as follows:

```
using System;
class ShowNumber
{
  public static void Main()
  {
    Console.WriteLine("Your number is: {0}", 8);
  }
}
```

In this example, the 8 is boxed and can be referenced as an object. The *Int32.ToString()* function is called to transform this object to a string, and our number is displayed. *Unboxing* works in the same way; simply assign a converted object to a variable. Boxing and unboxing will be covered in more detail in Chapter 7. Conversions and assignments to variables are covered in the next few sections.

# Variables

C# works with variables in a manner similar to Java. All variables must be declared prior to use and are declared with a statement of what data type the variable is. Also similar to Java, variables can be initialized with a default value when declared and multiple variables of the same type can be declared at the same time. The following example shows the declaration of a few variables:

```
using System;

/// <summary>
/// This class declares and initializes a few
/// variables.
/// </summary>
class UseVars
{
  static void Main()
  {
    //Initialize a few integers.
    int a, b, c, d, e;
    object o = d;
  }
}
```

In this example, we are creating several integer variables (*a*, *b*, *c*, *d* and *e*) and one object variable (*o*). As you can see in this code, we have declared three of the integer variables at the same time.

For the .NET architecture, Microsoft recommends using PascalCasing for variable names, and naming them in relation to what they are used for. In the past, many programmers used *Hungarian Notation* for variable names (e.g., strMyString, intMyInteger, etc.) in which the type of variable being used can be determined by the first few characters of the variable's name. Microsoft has recommended against this practice in .NET and instead recommends simply referring to the variable's use. For example, in our code, we would rename *a* to *BoxHeight*, *b* to *BoxWidth*, *c* to *BoxDepth*, *d* to *BoxVolume*, *o* to *Box*, and *e* to *ValueOfBox*.

All of the variables we've declared in this example are within the *Main()* method. Although we haven't explicitly declared it, their visibility is limited to within the *Main()* method and they cannot be seen from outside that method. Therefore, they are considered local. In C#, there are four primary access modifiers for variables, and one combination access modifier. They are outlined with their visibility in Table 3.3.

**Table 3.3** Access Modifiers

| Access Modifier | Definition |
| --- | --- |
| internal | Access to the variable is limited to the local project. |
| private | Access to the variable is limited to the containing type (i.e., class or method). |
| protected | Access to the variable is limited to the class. |
| protected internal | Access to the variable is limited to the class *or* the local project. |
| public | Access to the variable is unrestricted. |

There are three main types of variables: class variables, instance variables, and local variables. Class variables are prefaced with the term *static* and are initialized only once, when the class is initialized. Instance variables are initialized every time an instance of the class is created. The last variable type is local, and these are initialized every time the variable is declared.

In the following code sample, these variable types are demonstrated. We'll create a class variable called *a*, an instance variable called *b*, and a local variable called *c*. We'll also see how these variables are initialized.

When the *SetVars* class is first initialized, the *a* and *b* variables are both initialized. When a second instance of the *SetVars* class is initialized, only the *b* variable is initialized because the *class* variable *a* has already been initialized. The following code sample illustrates this:

```
using System;

class SetVars
{
  public static int a;
  public int b;
}

class WorkVars
{
```

```
   static void Main()
   {
      int c;
      SetVars MyVars = new SetVars();
      SetVars MyOtherVars = new SetVars();
   }
}
```

# Constants

Constants in C# are basically variables that are read-only. A similar functionality exists in Java and is called by using the *final* keyword. By specifying a variable as a constant, you can be sure that the value of the variable will not be changed from its original assignment. In C#, a constant is declared by using the keyword *const* prior to the data type in your declaration. Also, you can use access modifiers with a constant just as you would with a normal variable. Note that in Java there is a *const* keyword, but it is reserved and does not perform the same function. The following code illustrates the declaration and use of a constant:

```
class SetVars
{
  public static int a;
  public int b;
  public const string IniFileName = "SETVARS.INI";
}
```

In this example, we have declared a class variable named *a*, which is only initialized the first time the class is initialized. We've also declared an instance variable named *b*, which is initialized each time an instance of the class is created. Finally, we've declared a constant named *IniFileName*. This constant is a string and is an instance variable, therefore it is recreated for each instance of the *SetVars* class. Due to the fact that it is a constant, it is static and cannot be changed after it has been declared.

# Assignment Statements

The process of assigning a value to a variable in C# is very similar to the same process in Java. Value assignments can be performed either when the variable is declared or any time thereafter. The only prerequisite to assigning a value to a variable is that the variable be declared. Also, when working with constants, the value of a variable must be assigned at the time the variable itself is declared. This is due to the fact that constants are read-only and cannot be changed after they are initially declared.

When assigning values to variables, we use the = symbol to show that the variable should be set to whatever follows the = symbol. It is important to keep in mind that in C# as in Java, this symbol should be considered to mean "set value to" instead of "is value equal to." That function will be covered later in the chapter in the "Operators" section.

The following code sample shows the declaration of several variables, the assignment of values to those variables, and their subsequent use.

```
using System;


class BoxTest
{
  static void Main()
  {
    //Declare and set our length,
    //width and height variables.
    int Length = 10, Width = 5;
    int Height;
    Height = 2;
    //Create a box.
    Box MyBox = new Box(Length, Width, Height);
    //Show the box's volume.
    MyBox.DisplayBoxVolume();
  }
}
```

You can see from this example the process for assigning values to your variables. If you look in the *Main()* method, you will notice that the values for the integers *Length* and *Width* have been set as they were declared. The value for the integer *Height* has been set after it has been declared. You can use either of these methods for setting values for your variables as necessary.

In addition to setting values to variables directly as we have seen in the previous example, you can set the values of variables based on other variables. This is done just as it is in Java and is illustrated in the following modification to our previous example:

```
using System;

class BoxTest
{
  static void Main()
  {
    //Declare and set our length,
    //width and height variables.
    int ProductLength = 10, ProductWidth = 5;
    int ProductHeight;
    ProductHeight = 2;

    //When designing the box for our product,
    //we will need additional space for packing
    //material.
    const int PackingMaterialSize = 3;

    int PackedBoxLength = ProductLength +
                          PackingMaterialSize;
    int PackedBoxWidth = ProductWidth +
                          PackingMaterialSize;
    int PackedBoxHeight = ProductHeight +
                          PackingMaterialSize;
    //Create a box.
    Box MyBox = new Box(PackedBoxLength, PackedBoxWidth,
                        PackedBoxHeight);
    //Show the box's volume.
    MyBox.DisplayBoxVolume();
  }
}
```

In this example, we have taken the dimensions of a product, and then added additional space for the product packing material by using both the variables containing the product dimensions and a constant containing the packing material size. As you can see in this example, C# works just like Java in manipulating the values stored in variables.

# Conversions between Data Types

One of the more common functions that is necessary to perform on variables is that of conversion. This is necessary when a value has been stored in a variable of a specific data type and you need to move the value into a variable with a different data type. Several examples of this would be:

- Changing an *int* to a *decimal* to support currency
- Changing a *byte* into a *short* so you have room for a larger value
- Changing a *char* into an *int* so it can be worked as a number

There are two types of conversions possible: *implicit* and *explicit*. Another term for this would be *automatic* and *casted* conversions. Implicit conversions are used in the following situations:

- The two data types are identical
- The two data types are compatible
- The destination data type is larger than the source data type

Implicit conversions are very easy to define and are performed automatically as they are needed. By simply assigning a variable of the source type as the value of a variable of the destination type, the conversion is performed. The following code shows examples of some implicit conversions:

```
using System;
class ImplicitConversion
{
  public static void Main()
  {
    byte a=1;
    int b=1234;
    int c=a;   //Implicit cast
    double d=b; //Implicit cast
    Console.WriteLine("{0}", c);
    Console.WriteLine("{0}", d);
  }
}
```

In this example, we have taken a *byte* value and used an implicit conversion to convert it to an *integer* value. We've also taken an *integer* and converted it to a *double*. Both of these are implicit conversions and suffer no data loss in the conversion.

When using implicit conversions, keep in mind that the precision of some variables may be changed after conversion. For example, converting from an *int, long,* or *uint* to a *float* or from a *long* to a *double* will result in this effect.

Explicit conversions will attempt to convert the value stored in your source variable into the data type of your destination variable. A couple things should be noted about explicit conversions before attempting to use them. First of all, not all conversions will be successful so you should plan your code around this eventuality. Second, some data may be lost in the conversion. This may be in the form of truncated data following a decimal point, or modified numeric values. Keep in mind also that all valid implicit conversions can be performed as an explicit conversion.

To perform an explicit conversion, we simply perform a standard value-to-variable assignment and include a statement specifying what type of conversion to perform. The following code example illustrates this technique:

```
using System;

class ExplicitConv
{
  static void Main()
  {
    double a = 5.654321;
    int b;

    b = (int) a;
    Console.WriteLine("The value is {0}", b);
  }
}
```

When this code is compiled and run, the output appears as follows:

```
The value is 5
```

Depending on your needs, explicit conversions may or may not always result in the values you are looking for. To account for this, C# also provides the ability to create your own user-defined *implicit* or *explicit* conversions. This will be discussed in more detail in Chapter 7.

# Operators

C#, much like Java, makes available a large number of operators for us to use. In C#, these are broken up into six major groups: mathematical, assignment, increment and decrement, relational, logical, and bitwise. In the following sections, we'll go into detail on each of these operators and see how they function.

We'll also examine the differences between the functionality of these operators in C# and in Java. Some operators in Java do not have a C# equivalent, but there are also several new operators available that did not exist in Java. In the final part of this section, we'll examine operator precedence and see how this differs between C# and Java. Table 3.4 lists the available operators in C# as well as the operator group of which they belong.

**Table 3.4** Operator Groups

| Operators | Group |
| --- | --- |
| + – * / % | Mathematical operators |
| =  +=  -=  *=  /=  %=<br>&=  \|=  ^=  <<=  >>= | Assignment operators |
| ++ -- | Increment and decrement operators |
| ==  !=  <  >  <=  >= | Relational operators |
| &  \|  ^  !  ~  &&  \|\| | Logical operators |
| << >> | Bitwise operators |

# Mathematical Operators

In C#, mathematical operators perform in the same way as arithmetic operators do in Java. Table 3.5 lists the C# mathematical operators and their definitions. This is mainly for review as they are the same as in Java.

**Table 3.5** Mathematical Operators

| Operator | Definition |
| --- | --- |
| + | Addition |
| – | Subtraction |
| * | Multiplication |
| / | Division |
| % | Modulus |

Any of these operators can be used between multiple numeric data types, but not with other data types such as *boolean*. You can perform mathematical operations on variables, or directly on values. These operations can be performed either after a variable has been defined, or within its definition. The following code example shows how this works:

```
using System;
class Operators
{
  static void Main()
  {
    int a = 5, b = 10, c = 15;
    int d = a + b;
    int e = c - b;
    int f = a * e;
    int g = f / a;
    Console.WriteLine("{0}", g);
    Console.WriteLine("{0}", g % 2);
  }
}
```

The operations shown in this code sample are all pretty simple. However, it is worth noting just for review that the % operator does perform a modulus operation. Basically, this returns the resulting remainder after dividing the first value by the second.

## Assignment Operators

In the previous section on variable assignments, we made use of the = symbol to assign a value to a variable. This symbol is actually one of several assignment operators. With = being the most basic of the assignment operators, it assigns the designated value to a variable. This assignment operator is considered a *simple* assignment operator. There are, however, many other assignment operators that perform more complex functions. These operators are referred to as *complex* assignment operators. They are the same as those in Java, so we won't spend too much time on them. Table 3.6 shows the C# assignment operators and their definitions.

**Table 3.6** Assignment Operators

| Operator | Definition |
|----------|------------|
| = | Simple assignment |
| += | Addition assignment |
| -= | Subtraction assignment |
| *= | Multiplication assignment |
| /= | Division assignment |
| %= | Modulus assignment |
| &= | AND assignment |
| \|= | OR assignment |
| ^= | Exclusive OR assignment |
| <<= | Shift Left assignment |
| >>= | Shift Right assignment |

Basically, these assignment operators perform an operation, and then assign the result of the operation to a variable. For example, the %= assignment operator performs a modulus operation upon the destination variable and the source value, then assigns that result to the destination variable. Note that the >>>= assignment operator that you may have used in Java is not available in C#.

The following code sample illustrates the use of some of these assignment operators in C#. Before we go on, one final thing should be mentioned: with assignment operators, unlike mathematical operators, you cannot perform a complex assignment with a variable that is undefined.

```
using System;

class Operators
{
  static void Main()
  {
    int a, b, c, d, e;
    a = 14;
    b = 15;
    c = 20;
    d = a + b - c;   //d=9
    c += d;          //c=29
```

```
    e = c + d;        //e=38
    e /= 2;           //e=19
    Console.WriteLine("{0}", e);
  }
}
```

# Increment and Decrement Operators

In C# (just as in Java) there are increment and decrement operators, which function exactly as they do in Java. The ++ operator increases a value by 1, and the −− operator decreases the value by 1.

Again, identical to Java, these operators can be placed ahead of or behind the value that is the object of the operation. Where the operator is placed does modify the resulting value of the operation. This is referred to as a *prefix* or *postfix* operation.

By placing the increment or decrement operator ahead of the value, a prefix operation is performed. This means that the result of the operation will actually be the value of the object prior to the operation being performed.

If you place the increment or decrement operator behind the value, a postfix operation is performed. By performing a postfix operation, the result of the operation is returned as the value after the operation has been performed. The following code sample illustrates the use of these two operators in both the postfix and prefix forms:

```
using System;

class Operators
{
  static void Main()
  {
    int a=10, b, c;
    b = a++; //Postfix operation
    c = ++a; //Prefix operation
    Console.WriteLine("{0}", b);
    Console.WriteLine("{0}", c);
    b = b--; //Postfix operation
    c = --c; //Prefix operation
    Console.WriteLine("{0}", b);
```

```
      Console.WriteLine("{0}", c);
   }
}
```

## Output

```
10
12
10
11
```

# Relational Operators

Relational operators basically take two values and evaluate the relationship between them. Again, these are identical to the same functions in Java. Relational operators return a *boolean* value after the operation has been performed. You can think of relational operators as asking the question, "Is *x operation y*?" where *x* is your first value, *y* is your second, and *operation* refers to what relationship the values have to each other. For example, the question, "Is 4 greater than 5?" could be programmatically written in C# as:

```
using System;

class Operators
{
   static void Main()
   {
      bool a = 4 > 5;
      Console.WriteLine("{0}", a);
   }
}
```

This results in the variable *a* having a value of *false*. Table 3.7 shows the available relational operators and their definitions.

**Table 3.7** Relational Operators

| Operator | Definition |
| --- | --- |
| == | Equal to |
| != | Not equal to |
| < | Less than |
| <= | Less than or equal to |
| > | Greater than |
| >= | Greater than or equal to |

# Logical Operators

C#'s logical operators are identical in functionality to Java's logical operators, although you may not be familiar with grouping all of them as logical operators. Table 3.8 shows the logical operators available in C# and their definitions.

**Table 3.8** Relational Operators

| Operator | Definition |
| --- | --- |
| & | Bitwise AND |
| \| | Bitwise OR |
| ^ | Bitwise XOR (exclusive OR) |
| ! | Logical negation |
| ~ | Bitwise complement (NOT) |
| && | Logical AND |
| \|\| | Logical OR |

The &, |, and ^ operators can be used on both numeric and *boolean* data types. The ! , &&, and || operators are used exclusively with *boolean* values. The ~ operator is used on numeric data types and returns the bitwise opposite or compliment of the value similar to the way the ! operator performs on *boolean* values. The following sample code illustrates the use of these operators and shows the result of the operation.

```
using System;
class Operators
{
```

```
static void Main()
{
    int a=10, b=15, c=20, d, e, h, i;
    bool f, g, j = (a==b), k;
    d = (a&b);
    e = (a|b);
    f = (j&&(b==c));
    g = (j||(b==c));
    h = (a^b);
    i = ~b;
    k = !j;
    Console.WriteLine("{0}", d); //10
    Console.WriteLine("{0}", e); //15
    Console.WriteLine("{0}", f); //False
    Console.WriteLine("{0}", g); //False
    Console.WriteLine("{0}", h); //5
    Console.WriteLine("{0}", i); //-16
    Console.WriteLine("{0}", j); //False
    Console.WriteLine("{0}", k); //True
}
}
```

## Output

```
10
15
False
False
5
-16
False
True
```

# Bitwise Operators

In relation to bitwise operators, C# differs from Java somewhat. Both Java and C# have the << and >> operators, but Java also has the >>> operator whereas

C# does not. This is very important to note when attempting to port code over from Java to C#.

Just as in Java, the << and >> operators are defined as a bitwise shift to the left or the right, respectively. This bitwise shift is performed in the same manner as most other operators in C# and can be performed either during or after a variable declaration. The << operator basically shifts all of the bits in a value the specified number to the left. The >> does the same, but to the right. An example of this is shown in the following code:

```
using System;

class Operators
{
  static void Main()
  {
    int a=256, b=128, c, d;
    c = a >> 1;
    d = b << 1;
    Console.WriteLine("{0}", c); //128
    Console.WriteLine("{0}", d); //256
  }
}
```

## Output

```
128
256
```

# Ternary Operator

The ternary operator, also called the conditional operator, is very unique. It effectively provides you with an "if...then" statement to use with operations. This same functionality is also available in Java and it works the same way in both languages.

Like most operators in C#, this can be used on variables either after or while they are defined. It is called in the form of: *expression1 ? expression2 : expression3*. Using this syntax, *expression1* is the expression that is being evaluated, *expression2* is evaluated if *expression1* is true, and *expression3* is evaluated if *expression1* is false.

There are a couple of restrictions on the use of this operator. The first expression in the operator must result in a *boolean* value. Also, the second and third expressions must evaluate to the same data type. The following code shows an example of how this operator could be used:

```
using System;

class Operators
{
  static void Main()
  {
    int a=10, b=5;
    int c = a==b ? a : b;
    Console.WriteLine("{0}", c); //5
  }
}
```

*Output*

5

# Operator Precedence

Operators always perform their functions in a specific order. This order of operations is referred to as *operator precedence*. There are specific rules that are followed in order to make the execution of multiple operations logical and consistent.

All operations have a specific association that determines in what direction operations are read. When dealing with any operators except for assignment operators, this order is from left to right, or left-associative. Assignment operators process from right to left and are therefore right-associative.

There is also a hierarchical order of precedence that is followed when working with operators. At the top of the hierarchy are parentheses and square brackets. Anything encapsulated within these will be processed first. This hierarchy is shown in Figure 3.3.

# Preprocessor Directives

C# has a feature called Preprocessor Directives that does not exist in Java. These directives allow you to do conditional compilation, output code-specific warnings, or perform other functions as the program is being compiled. This functions in a similar manner to C or C++ where there is a preprocessor, but C# has no actual preprocessor. These directives are simply taken into account by the compiler when the program compilation occurs.

**Figure 3.3** Operator Precedence Hierarchy

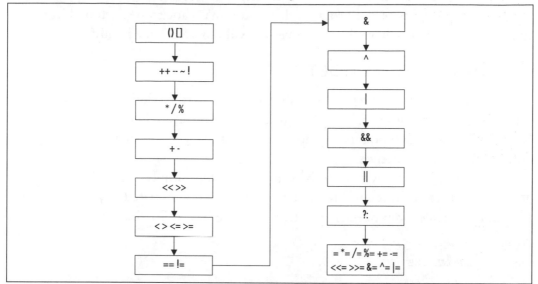

There are several preprocessor directives available in C#, which are listed and defined in Table 3.9.

**Table 3.9** Preprocessor Directives

| Preprocessor Directive | Definition |
| --- | --- |
| #define | Defines a symbol |
| #undef | Undefines a symbol |
| #if | Begins a conditional directive |
| #elif | Creates a compound conditional directive |
| #else | Creates a compound conditional directive |
| #endif | Specifies the end of a conditional directive |
| #error | Generates an error at a specific place in your code |
| #warning | Generates a warning at a specific place in your code |
| #region | Specifies a block of code for outlining |
| #endregion | Specifies the end of an outlining region |
| #line | Modifies the line number shown for errors and warnings |

By using these directives, changes in the way your application compiles can be made at compile time. This is a very useful feature and can be used in many ways to improve both the way your application is compiled and the way the compiler itself performs. For example, when you're debugging you might want to compile certain parts of the program that you don't want to be included in the final version. This is where the preprocessor will come in very handy.

# #define and #undef

The *#define* and *#undef* preprocessor directives are used to define or undefine symbols for use by other preprocessor directives. Basically, when other directives need to evaluate a symbol, that symbol will be either defined or undefined by the *#define* or *#undef* directives.

If you wish for the symbol to be evaluated as *true*, simply define it with the *#define* preprocessor directive. If the symbol should be evaluated as *false*, undefine it with the *#undef* preprocessor directive. Consider the following two statements:

```
#define DEBUG
#undef PERSONALIZE
```

In the previous statements, if a *#if* or *#elif* preprocessor directive evaluates these two symbols, they will evaluate to *true* and *false*, respectively. Note that the *#define* and *#undef* preprocessor directives must appear in your code prior to any other instruction that is not another preprocessor directive.

In addition to the *#define* statement, you can also specify symbols to be defined at the command line when compiling, using the following syntax:

```
csc MySource.cs /define:SYMBOL1, SYMBOL2
```

# #if, #elif, #else, and #endif

The *#if, #elif, #else*, and *#endif* preprocessor directives are all used for conditional processing when your program is compiled. The *#if* and *#elif* both evaluate the symbols to determine whether they are defined or undefined. The *#else* preprocessor directive allows for a compound conditional directive to be created. And finally, the *#endif* preprocessor directive specifies the end of a conditional directive.

Now for a little more detail on how these work. You can think of these directives as a typical *if/else* statement. The *#if* preprocessor directive evaluates the symbols it is given and determines whether the end result is *true* or *false*. If the result is *true*, the code between the *#if* preprocessor directive and the *#endif* preprocessor directive is executed. If the result is *false*, the code between the *#if* preprocessor directive and a subsequent *#endif*, *#elif*, or *#else* preprocessor directive is skipped.

If, after a *#if* preprocessor directive has evaluated to false, a *#else* preprocessor directive is found, the code between the *#else* preprocessor directive and the *#endif* preprocessor directive is executed. However, if a *#elif* preprocessor directive is found after the *#if* preprocessor directive has evaluated to *false*, the symbols given to the *#elif* preprocessor directive are evaluated. This is effectively the equivalent of performing a *#else* preprocessor directive followed by another *#if* preprocessor directive, which is not allowed. The *#elif* preprocessor directive is then processed in the same way as an *#if* preprocessor directive.

When a *#if* or *#elif* preprocessor directive is evaluating the symbols it is given, there are some specific *preprocessor expressions* allowed that let you control the way this evaluation is performed. These preprocessor expressions are very similar to operators and perform in much the same way. Table 3.10 outlines the preprocessor expressions allowed and how they are evaluated.

**Table 3.10** Preprocessor Expressions

| Preprocessor Expression | Evaluation |
| --- | --- |
| == | Evaluates as true if both symbols are equal |
| != | Evaluates as true if both symbols are not equal |
| ! | Evaluates as true if symbol is false |
| && | Evaluates as true if both symbols are true |
| \|\| | Evaluates as true if either symbol is true |

In addition, parentheses can be used to group expressions, and expressions located within parentheses are evaluated first. These concepts are a little easier to understand when an example is present; so examine the following code and its subsequent output.

```
#define PERSONALIZE
#define DEBUG
#undef VERBOSE

using System;
class Operators
{
  static void Main()
  {
```

```
#if PERSONALIZE
   Console.WriteLine("Hi Author!");
#elif VERBOSE
   Console.WriteLine("Program Starting...");
#endif
   int a=10, b=5;
#if DEBUG
   Console.WriteLine("a={0}, b={1}", a, b);
#endif
#if PERSONALIZE && (VERBOSE || DEBUG)
   Console.WriteLine("Continuing, Author...");
#elif !PERSONALIZE && (VERBOSE || DEBUG)
   Console.WriteLine("Continuing...");
#endif
   }
}
```

Compiling and executing this code results in the following output.

## Output

```
Hi Author!
a=10, b=5
Continuing, Author...
```

In the preceding example, there are several preprocessor directives in use, so let's examine the logic here and see why we get this output. First of all, we have defined two symbols (*PERSONALIZE* and *DEBUG)* and undefined another (*VERBOSE).* When a symbol is undefined, it's easier to think of it as commented out. If we wanted to make use of this symbol, we'd simply change the *#undef* statement to a *#define* statement.

Following this, we have some preprocessor directives evaluating our symbols. The first directive evaluates whether the *PERSONALIZE* symbol has been defined. If it has, then the program personalizes the output. Second, we follow this with a *#elif* statement to evaluate the *VERBOSE* symbol. This will only be evaluated if the *PERSONALIZE* symbol evaluates to *false*. If *VERBOSE* has been defined, which in our case it has not, the program outputs additional information. This is followed by a *#endif* directive to specify that we're done evaluating for the moment.

Shortly after this, we use another preprocessor directive to evaluate the *DEBUG* symbol. This is very useful when performing debugging of an application. If the *DEBUG* symbol evaluates to *true*, which it does in our example, the values of our variables are written to the console. This is followed by another *#endif* to specify that we're done evaluating.

The directives that follow this are a little more complex. In the first, the directive must evaluate to *true* on the *PERSONALIZE* symbol as well as *true* on either the *VERBOSE* or *DEBUG* symbols in order to process the command that follows. In our example, both *PERSONALIZE* and *DEBUG* evaluate to *true*, so this statement is executed.

This is followed by a *#elif* directive, which is only processed if the previous statement evaluated to *false*. Since this is not the case in our example, it is not evaluated. However, if it were, it would require that the *PERSONALIZE* symbol evaluate to *false* and either the *VERBOSE* or *DEBUG* symbol evaluate to *true* before running the command that follows. This is followed by a *#endif* directive as we are done with the evaluations.

Keep in mind that if code encapsulated within a preprocessor directive is not used due to the directive evaluating to *false*, this code is not even compiled and is not included with your final application. This is very useful for including debug code within your source code, but keeping the size of your final executable down. This can also be used to personalize the compiled code for specific uses, but still have the complete application in your source code.

## Debugging...

### Using Preprocessor Directives

A great feature of the *#define* and *#undef* preprocessor directives is that they provide a simple yet effective method to control debugging. When writing your code, you can make "debug points" where you output additional information to the console or log files when debugging is enabled. These debug points simply use the #if preprocessor directive to determine whether a specific symbol (such as *DEBUG*) is defined. If it is, the additional information is output or additional functions are performed. This can be incredibly useful when you are in the development stages of a program.

# #error and #warning

The *#error* and *#warning* preprocessor directives allow you to specify errors and warnings to appear when the program is compiled. This is very useful if someone else will be compiling your source code in the future and you wish to make them aware of certain problems or conditions at compile time.

Both of these preprocessor directives are executed in the same way. Simply insert the preprocessor directive into your code and follow it with the specific text to display when the preprocessor directive is executed.

Keep in mind that the *#error* preprocessor directive will generate a compiler error and will halt the compile. This is generally used within a conditional or compound conditional preprocessor directive. The following code example illustrates the usage of these preprocessor directives:

```
#define PERSONALIZE
#define DEBUG
#undef VERBOSE
#define PROGRAMMER_IS_BRIAN
#undef PROGRAMMER_IS_DAVE


using System;

class Preprocessor
{
  static void Main()
  {
    #if PERSONALIZE
      Console.WriteLine("Hi Author!");
    #elif VERBOSE
      Console.WriteLine("Program Starting...");
    #endif
      int a=10, b=5;
    #if DEBUG
      Console.WriteLine("a={0}, b={1}", a, b);
    #endif

    #if PERSONALIZE && (VERBOSE || DEBUG)
      Console.WriteLine("Continuing, Author...");
```

```
    #elif !PERSONALIZE && (VERBOSE || DEBUG)
        Console.WriteLine("Continuing...");
    #endif


    #if PROGRAMMER_IS_BRIAN || PROGRAMMER_IS_DAVE
    #warning Execution may vary depending on programmer.
    #endif


    #if PROGRAMMER_IS_DAVE
    #error Something you did broke this code.
    #endif
    }
}
```

## Output

```
C:\chapt3-code\c#>csc Preprocessor.cs
Microsoft (R) Visual C# Compiler Version 7.00.9254
      [CLR version v1.0.2914]
Copyright (C) Microsoft Corp 2000-2001. All rights reserved.


PreProcessor.cs(30,14): warning CS1030: #warning: 'Execution may vary
      depending on programmer.'


C:\chapt3-code\c#>preprocessor
Hi Author!
a=10, b=5
Continuing, Author...
```

# #region and #endregion

The *#region* and *#endregion* are preprocessor directives that are specific to the Microsoft Visual Studio.NET Code Editor. If you are using the VS.NET Code Editor, these preprocessor directives can be used to specify blocks of code for outlining. This allows you to expand or collapse the code within the Code Editor.

To do this, simply preface the block of code you wish to specify as a region with the *#region* preprocessor directive, and place a *#endregion* preprocessor directive at the end of the code block. Keep in mind that you cannot end a region

within an *#if* block if it was begun before the *#if* block was begun. In addition, if the region was started within an *#if* block, it must end within that *#if* block. Figure 3.4 shows this feature in use.

**Figure 3.4** Region Preprocessor Directives

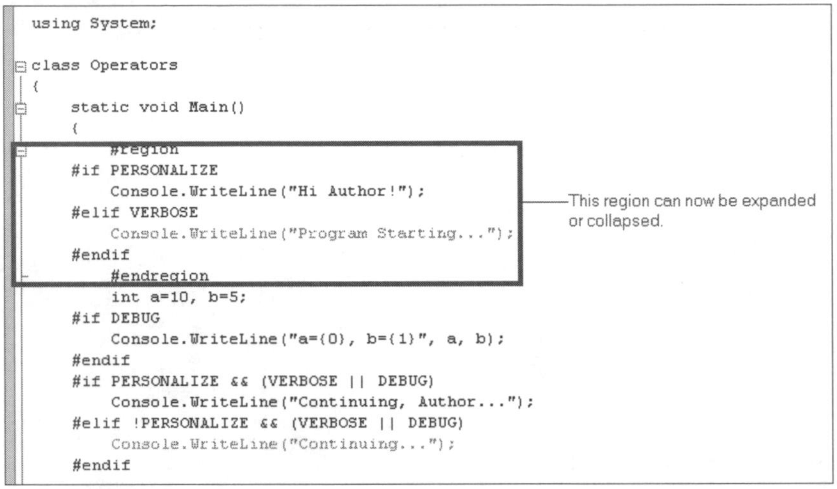

```
using System;

class Operators
{
    static void Main()
    {
        #region
        #if PERSONALIZE
            Console.WriteLine("Hi Author!");
        #elif VERBOSE
            Console.WriteLine("Program Starting...");
        #endif
        #endregion
        int a=10, b=5;
        #if DEBUG
            Console.WriteLine("a={0}, b={1}", a, b);
        #endif
        #if PERSONALIZE && (VERBOSE || DEBUG)
            Console.WriteLine("Continuing, Author...");
        #elif !PERSONALIZE && (VERBOSE || DEBUG)
            Console.WriteLine("Continuing...");
        #endif
```

This region can now be expanded or collapsed.

# #line

The *#line* preprocessor directive allows you to give the compiler a different line number or file name to use with any errors or warnings. This allows you to simulate what the error line numbers would be in the complete version of an application if you are working with only a subset of the code for the application. For example, if multiple programmers are compiling unrelated parts of an application and logging errors found during the compile, they might want to log where the error would have occurred within the context of the full application.

Specify the *#line* preprocessor directive followed by the line number where you want the compiler to start counting. Optionally, you can include an alternate source file name. With this option, the compiler will report any errors that occur and will reference this file name as the origination point for the errors. A third option is simply to specify *default*, and the line numbering will be reset to where it really is in the original source file. The following source code and compiler output demonstrate how this works:

```
using System;

class Operators
{
```

```
static void Main()
{
    #line 300
    #warning Something happened.
    #warning Something else happened.
    #line 400 "someotherfile.cs"
    #warning Something happened later.
    #line default
    #warning Nothing else will happen.
}
}
```

The following output was generated when this source was compiled at the command line:

```
C:\chapt3-code\c#>csc Operators.cs
Microsoft (R) Visual C# Compiler Version 7.00.9254
    [CLR version v1.0.2914]
Copyright (C) Microsoft Corp 2000-2001. All rights reserved.


Operators.cs(300,11): warning CS1030: #warning: 'Something happened.'
Operators.cs(301,11): warning CS1030: #warning: 'Something else
    happened.'
someotherfile.cs(400,11): warning CS1030: #warning: 'Something happened
     later.'
Operators.cs(13,11): warning CS1030: #warning: 'Nothing else will

    happen.'
```

We've gone through the entire list of C# preprocessor directives at this point and have seen their use in several code samples. There are several main points to remember about how the preprocessor directives work.

First, you can evaluate symbols defined using the *#define* directive by using the *#if* and *#elif* directives. You can also use the preprocessor expressions with these to expand on the functionality of the preprocessor directive logic.

You also have the ability to generate compile-time errors and warnings by using the *#error* or *#warning* directives. These can be used in combination with the logic provided by the *#if*, *#elif*, and *#else* directives as well as the preprocessor expressions.

There is also functionality provided by the preprocessor directives to specify specific code regions that allow you to collapse or expand code when working within the Visual Studio interface. These are the *#region* and *#endregion* directives.

Finally, you can change the line numbering used for errors reported by the compiler with the use of the *#line* preprocessor directive.

Also, remember that all of these directives are evaluated at compile time, and based on this evaluation, may or may not include specific code segments in your final application. This is a very useful feature and due to its flexibility, can be used to fulfill the needs of any number of scenarios.

# Namespaces

In Java, a new innovation in code organization was developed. Called *packages*, this innovation provided a new, unique way of organizing code and eliminating potential naming conflicts. In C#, there is a similar mechanism known as the *namespace*. This mechanism is hierarchical just like Java's packages, and allows you to nest namespaces just as you would nest packages in Java.

There are two primary advantages to using namespaces when coding applications. The first is that this technique keeps code organized. You can pull classes and methods out of multiple namespaces on an as-needed basis, which is substantially more organized than simply having all of your code in one file or including multiple files at compile time. The second advantage is that you are much less likely to end up with naming conflicts. If only one programmer in a team was allowed to use the class name *test*, imagine how many conflicts would be generated! Whereas by using namespaces, each programmer could have their own *test* class in a separate namespace and not conflict with anyone else.

In our sample code so far, we've been using the *WriteLine()* method of the *Console* class within the *System* namespace for performing program text output. This could be referenced as:

```
System.Console.WriteLine();
```

However, that sure is a lot of typing if you happen to have a deeply nested namespace. For this, C# has provided the *using* keyword. This keyword performs two functions that assist with using namespaces. The first is that it acts as a shortcut to access a nested namespace. By using the statement:

```
using System;
```

this allows us to reference the *WriteLine()* method as follows:

```
Console.WriteLine();
```

The *using* keyword allows us to do this by importing the metadata from the namespace into our program. After this is imported, the classes of the namespace can be accessed more easily.

The second function of the *using* keyword is that it allows us to assign an alias to a namespace. This is another way of dealing with potential naming conflicts. By referring to a namespace by an alias, the compiler will know which specific namespace we are attempting to use even if we actually have two namespaces that are named the same.

The following sample code demonstrates the use of the *using* keyword and how it functions when performing as a shortcut or creating an alias.

```
using System;
using MyConsole = System.Console;

class UsingExample
{
  static void Main()
  {
    Console.WriteLine("This is using the System.Console namespace.");
    MyConsole.WriteLine("So is this.");
  }
}
```

After compiling and running this code sample, we are presented with the following output:

```
C:\chapt3-code\c#>UsingExample
This is using the System.Console namespace.
So is this.
```

# Summary

In this chapter, we started with the *Main()* method in C# and examined the differences between this and the *main()* method in Java. We learned how to write a simple "Hello World" program and took this program through an evolution as we added additional capabilities such as the use of command line arguments and returning a value.

We then learned how commenting is done in C# and examined the new XML documentation comments that C# has made available. We learned how to use this powerful feature to make the documentation of our programs simple yet effective.

From there, we started working with data and exploring the different data types that C# has made available to us. We learned about variables and constants and how to assign values to them. We also learned how to convert data between different data types and perform various operations on our data ranging from mathematical operations to the powerful ternary operation.

Building on our growing knowledge of the fundamentals of the C# language, we learned a little more about how the compiler works and how we can control its operation to a limited degree through preprocessor directives.

To top everything off, we learned about C# namespaces and how they can help us to organize code and prevent naming conflicts. We also learned about some shortcuts to use when dealing with namespaces to make them a little more user-friendly.

# Solutions Fast Track

## *Main()* Method

☑ In C#, the *Main()* method is capitalized, whereas in Java it is lowercase.

☑ The *Main()* method supports command line arguments as well as having the ability to return a value.

☑ There are eight ways of using the *Main()* method:

1. public static void Main(string[] args)
2. public static void Main()
3. public static int Main(string[] args)

4. public static int Main()

5. static void Main(string[] args)

6. static void Main()

7. static int Main(string[] args)

8. static int Main()

# Single-Line and Multiline Comments

☑  // designates a single-line comment.

☑  A multiline comment can be placed between /* and */.

☑  /// designates XML documentation comments.

# Data Types and the Common Type System

☑  C# supports the same data types as Java as well as providing a few additional data types.

☑  All data types are based on the *object* data type.

☑  Data types can be referred to as objects by using a method called boxing.

# Variables

☑  In C#, variables must be defined before they can be used.

☑  Variables can be initialized with a value when they are defined.

☑  Microsoft recommends using PascalCasing for variables.

# Constants

☑  Constants are basically read-only variables.

☑  Constants must be initialized with a value when they are defined.

☑  Attempting to modify a constant will result in a compile error.

# Assignment Statements

☑ Values can be directly assigned to variables of the same data type as the value.

☑ Values can also be assigned to variables of different data types by using implicit or explicit conversions.

☑ The scope of a variable is defined when it is declared.

# Operators

☑ Operators can be used to perform a variety of functions to values or variables.

☑ When using operators, always bear in mind which data types each operator supports.

☑ Operators are evaluated in a specific order known as *operator precedence*.

# Preprocessor Directives

☑ Preprocessor directives are used at compile time even though C# does not have a preprocessor.

☑ Using preprocessor directives allows you to control compilation activities for your application depending on defined symbols.

☑ Preprocessor directives can also affect the way that the VS.NET Code Editor displays your code.

# Namespaces

☑ Namespaces are used in C# to organize code and prevent naming conflicts.

☑ The *using* keyword allows you to create a shortcut to a nested namespace.

☑ The *using* keyword also allows you to create aliases for namespaces to prevent naming conflicts or to refer to a namespace by a more friendly name.

# Frequently Asked Questions

The following Frequently Asked Questions, answered by the authors of this book, are designed to both measure your understanding of the concepts presented in this chapter and to assist you with real-life implementation of these concepts. To have your questions about this chapter answered by the author, browse to **www.syngress.com/solutions** and click on the **"Ask the Author"** form.

**Q:** Do I have to have a *Main()* method?

**A:** No. When you are compiling an assembly for use as a library or DLL file, you don't necessarily need a starting point for execution within your code. This is due to the fact that you'll simply be making use of the code within the classes, not executing an application.

**Q:** Is it better to use code comments or XML documentation comments?

**A:** A combination of both is best. The code comments allow you or other programmers to come back at a later time and easily understand why your code was written the way it was. If your code is going to be released as part of a library or DLL, XML documentation comments certainly make using the methods you include much easier.

**Q:** When dealing with data type conversions, should I try and use implicit conversions or use explicit conversions since explicit conversions can perform the same function?

**A:** Using implicit conversions in your code is best whenever it is possible. This is due to the fact that a compiler error will be generated if you try to use an implicit conversion incorrectly. An explicit conversion will usually just go ahead and do the conversion, which could possibly lead to unexpected behavior or bugs. However, there are certainly times that explicit conversions are necessary. Simply use implicit conversions wherever possible and explicit conversions when absolutely necessary.

**Q:** Why would I want to use preprocessor directives? Can't I just comment out code instead?

**A:** Commenting out sections of code or having code that requires the evaluation of constants within the application to perform the same function is certainly possible, but not recommended. There are a few reasons for this. First, using preprocessor directives are much easier than commenting or uncommenting code for each compile. Second, if evaluations are being performed during runtime to determine which sections of code to run, additional system resources are unnecessarily used. And last, when using preprocessor directives, unneeded code is not even compiled into your final application, cutting down on the executable size.

**Q:** All your sample code uses a single .cs file. Is this a recommended practice?

**A:** Not for larger projects or full applications. C# provides the namespaces capability to allow you to use multiple files and organize your code. The sample code provided in this chapter is very simple and really needs only the single file.

**Q:** What learning process would you recommend to me, as a Java programmer, to transition my skills to C#?

**A:** My best recommendation would be to take one of your current Java applications and port it over to C#. This will provide an excellent learning experience and give you real problems and issues from which you can research and learn more about how C# works.

**Q:** When writing a new C# program, I got stuck in a couple of places and need help. Where can I turn?

**A:** There are many resources available to you. The first is books like this one, which offer information and practical examples of how code works. On the Internet, you can turn to Microsoft's Web site for help as well as many other independent Web sites. Usenet newsgroups are another excellent resource. These put you in touch with many other programmers, some of which may have experienced the same problem you're having.

# Chapter 4

# Programming Structures

Solutions in this chapter:

- **Strings**
- **Flow Control**
- **Arrays**
- **The foreach Statement**
- **Indexers**
- **Collections**
- **Exceptions**

☑ **Summary**

☑ **Solutions Fast Track**

☑ **Frequently Asked Questions**

# Introduction

Chapter 3 discussed the basic building blocks of the C# programming language; this chapter will highlight more advanced programming structures necessary for building C# applications.

In this chapter you will learn about the *String* class in C#. Just like in Java, strings are special objects with special support of the language. We will introduce the basic flow controls of the C# language, and introduce the *foreach* statement (which is not available in Java). We then will examine some of the collection classes provided by the .NET Framework. We will talk about *Arrays* and a new feature not found in Java, called *Indexers*. Finally, we will look at exception handling in C#, which is very similar to Java.

# Strings

The Java and C# string classes are very similar. In many instances the only difference between a member of the Java string class *java.lang.string* and the C# class *System.String* is in the capitalization of the method name. Another interesting tidbit is that both *System.String* and the *datatype* string can be used interchangeably. The reason for this is that Microsoft has aliased the *string* datatype to the *System.String* class. Most of the Java string methods are included in the C# string class, as well as some other methods, courtesy of Perl and Visual Basic. We will go over *String* creation, and then proceed into the *StringBuilder* class, which is very much like Java's *StringBuffer*. We will then discuss the *RegEx* class, which permits use of *Regular Expressions*, a very powerful feature that was Perl's claim to fame. Regular Expressions are not yet available in the Java SDK 1.3. However, Sun is planning to include it in the next release of the Java SDK.

## The WriteLine Method

C#'s *System.WriteLine* method is the counterpart to Java's console output method *System.out.println()* . Here is a simple application that prints to the console in both languages so you can observe the similarities.

*Java*

```java
public class PrintExample
{
  public static void main(String[] args)
  {
```

```
    System.out.println("Hello Bruce!");
  }
}
```

## C#

```
class PrintExample
{
  public static void Main(string[] args)
  {
    System.Console.WriteLine("Hello Bruce!");
  }
}
```

This function has numerous overloads to permit calling it with any parameter including basic numeric data types and any object. For example, note the following syntax, which takes parameters of numeric and string types, and outputs them all as strings:

```
System.Console.WriteLine(1 + " + 2 = " + 3 );
```

This outputs 1 + 2 = 3. The *toString* method is called on the parameter to convert it to a string internally prior to output. You can also use a formatting string to get the same results, for example:

```
int x = 3;
System.Console.WriteLine("{0} + 2 = {1}",1,x);
```

The {0} and {1} are placeholders for the values or variables that follow the first parameter. There are several formatting specifications, which can be found in the MSDN Library.

An important thing to remember is that this method appends a line terminator to the end of the output; you may use *System.Console.Write();* to write to the console without appending the line terminator character to the output.

## Creating Strings

In C#, there are several methods of creating a *String* object. The first and most common method of creating a *String* is to use a literal. The following code snippet creates a string with the value "A String Literal".

```
String s1 = "A String Literal";
```

As in Java, once a C# string has been created it cannot be changed; therefore we say they are immutable. There are methods that appear to modify the string, such as *ToUpper()*, but under the covers they are creating a new string.

## Developing & Deploying...

## What Are the Implications of Immutable Strings?

It is important to remember that in C#, strings are immutable. This means that they cannot be modified after they are created. You must be careful when using functions that would modify the string; if you do not reassign the return value to the string you are doing nothing. For instance, the following code has no effect on the string.

```
String s2 = "This is a string!";

s2.ToUpper();
```

   You must reassign the return value as follows:

```
String s2 = "This is a string!";

s2 = s2.ToUpper();
```

At our disposal are several C# string constructors. Although there are eight constructors in the C# *String* class, all but three of these use pointers and create a noncompliant, "unsafe" instance. The constructors you want to get familiar with are the following:

```
String( char Ch, int Count)
String( char[] CharArray)
String( char[], int Start, int Count) —substring
```

The first of these constructors takes a character and an integer argument. This constructor will simply repeat the first *char* parameter the length of the second integer argument. For example, the following code will construct the string "cccc":

```
String repeatedCharacterString = new String( 'c', 4 );
```

The second constructor takes a character array as its argument and will convert it to a string. The following code will create the string "hello":

```
Char[] charArray = { 'h','e','l','l','o' };
String stringFromCharArray = new String( charArray );
```

The third and final constructor takes three parameters: a character array, and two integers. It will create a string from a substring in the character array, starting at the index value of the second parameter, until it has reached the number of *chars* equal to the value of the third parameter. The following code will create the string "defg" from a character array:

```
Char[] charArray = { 'a','b','c','d','e','f','g','h' };
String subString = new String( charArray, 3 , 4 );
```

Unlike in Java, there is not a *String(String s)* constructor. Since we previously mentioned that *Strings* are immutable, this would only serve to copy the *String*. Instead you may use the *Copy()* method of the string class to get the same results.

Just as in Java, you may use the + operator to concatenate strings, as well as perform implicit conversion of other objects into strings. As we see in the next example, you do not have to make an explicit call to the *ToString()* method to convert another object into a *String* when concatenating. This code will create the string "1 is a lonely number."

```
int numberOne = 1;
String lonelyString = numberOne + " is a lonely number.";
```

Table 4.1 lists several handy C# *String* methods, as well as their Java counterparts.

**Table 4.1** C# String Class Members

| C# | Java | Function | Notes |
|---|---|---|---|
| Length | length() | Returns the length of the string | In Java you call a method to get the length of a string; in C# you just access its public property. |
| [int index] | charAt(int index) | Retrieves a character at the specified index | In C# the *String* class is implemented with an indexer, so characters can be retrieved as if the string were an |

**Continued**

**Table 4.1** Continued

| C# | Java | Function | Notes |
|---|---|---|---|
| | | | array of characters. In Java you must call *charAt()* to obtain a character at a specific index into the string. |
| Concat(String str) | concat(String str) | Concatenates two strings | In most cases you would use the overloaded con-catenation oper-ator +, as opposed to calling either of these two methods. |
| Compare( string strA, string strB, bool ingoreCase); | CompareToIgnore Case (String str) | Compares *Strings*, ignoring case. | In Java, case-sensitive, and insensitive com-pare operations utilize two dif-ferent method calls. In C# it is the same method call, but the third parameter specifies the case sensitivity. |
| Split(char[] sep) | split(String regex) | Splits a string into an array of sub-strings around matches of the split parameter | This method per-forms the same way in Java and C#. |
| Join | Not Available | Joins an array of substrings, with an inserted delimiting character, into one string—the exact opposite of a Split | Java does not offer this function; to simulate it you would have to iterate through an array of substrings appending a delimiting char-acter and a sub-string to another string. |

*Continued*

**Table 4.1** Continued

| C# | Java | Function | Notes |
|---|---|---|---|
| ToLower() | toLowerCase() | Converts the string to lowercase | This method performs the same way in Java and C#. |
| ToUpper() | toUpperCase() | Converts the string to uppercase | This method performs the same way in Java and C#. |
| Trim() | trim() | Removes leading and trailing white-space from a string | This method performs the same way in Java and C#. |

# Verbatim String Literal

C# also adds a new form of literal, dubbed the Verbatim String Literal, which permits creating string literals exactly as written. Rather than interpreting the \ character as the start of an escape sequence, it interprets it verbatim. To indicate that a string literal is a Verbatim String Literal, precede it with the @ character. Keep in mind that to represent a double quote you must use two double quote characters. The following two declarations are equivalent:

```
String stringLiteral = "C:\\C# programs";
String verbatimStringLiteral = @"C:\C# programs";
```

Verbatim String Literals are very useful for situations in which you want to specify a path, either to a registry key or file, and when you are parsing data that may contain characters that normally would require an escape character to specify; for example, parsing XML, or HTML documents.

# The *StringBuilder* Class

Due to the fact that strings are immutable, and that methods that appear to modify strings such as *ToUpper()* in fact create new strings, you may have concerns about the efficiency of C#. Java provided the *StringBuffer* class to remedy such a problem. C# has its own flavor of Java's *StringBuffer* class in its *System.TextStringBuilder* class. The *StringBuilder* class creates strings that are not immutable and can be modified. It sets an initial storage size for the string, and whenever this size is about to exceed its limits, the buffer is reallocated at double the size. For example, examine the following code:

```
using System;
using System.Text;

class PrintExample
{
 public static void Main()
 {
  String NormalString = "String";
  StringBuilder StringBuilderString = new StringBuilder("String");
  NormalString.ToUpper();
  String StringBuilderTempString = StringBuilderString.ToString();
  StringBuilderString.Replace(StringBuilderTempString,
StringBuilderTempString.ToUpper());

  Console.WriteLine(NormalString);
  Console.WriteLine(StringBuilderString.ToString());
 }
}
```

When the preceding code has completed execution, the *normalString* will still contain the value *String*, as it is an immutable string. The *stringBuilderString* will contain the value *STRING*, as it is not immutable. Table 4.2 list some of the useful methods of the C# *StringBuilder* class and their Java equivalents.

**Table 4.2** C# *StringBuilder* Class Members

| C# | Java | Function | Notes |
|---|---|---|---|
| Capacity | capacity() | Retrieves the current capacity of the *StringBuilder* object | C# uses a public property to expose this value, as opposed to an accessor method. |
| [int index] | charAt(int index) | Retrieves a character at the specified index | In C# the *StringBuilder* class is implemented with an indexer, so characters can be retrieved as if the |

**Table 4.2** Continued

| C# | Java | Function | Notes |
|---|---|---|---|
| | | | string was an array of characters. In Java you must call *charAt()* to obtain a character at a specific index into the *StringBuffer*. |
| Length | length() | Returns the length of the *StringBuilder* object | C# uses a public property to expose this value, as opposed to an accessor method. |
| Append (String str) | append(String str) | Appends the specified string to the end of this instance | This method performs the same way in Java and C#. |
| Insert(int offset, String str) | insert(int offset, String str) | Inserts the string into the *StringBuilder* object at the specified offset | This method performs the same way in Java and C#. |
| Remove(int startindex, int length) | delete(int start, int end) | Removes characters from the *StringBuilder* | The C# implementation of this function requires a starting offset within a *StringBuilder* object, and then the number of characters to remove. The Java implementation requires a starting offset within the *StringBuffer* object, and an ending offset for the delete operation. The ending offset is not included as a deleted character. |

**Continued**

**Table 4.2** Continued

| C# | Java | Function | Notes |
|---|---|---|---|
| Replace (String substring, String Replacement) | replace(int start, int end, String str) | Replaces a substring in the *StringBuilder* object, with the specified replacement string | The C# implementation of this function requires a string argument specifying the substring to replace, and the string to replace it with. The Java implementation requires a starting and ending index for the substring to replace, and the string to replace it with. |
| ToString() | toString() | Converts data in the *StringBuilder* object, into an immutable *String* object | This method performs the same way in Java and C#. |

# Using Regular Expressions

One feature that is not yet in Java, yet is present in C#, is support for regular expressions. This support is provided via the *System.Text.RegularExpressions* classes, and is based on the Perl 5 syntax for Regular Expressions. Regular Expressions are sets of characters and syntactic elements used to match patterns of text. They can be used in advanced search and replace operations, such as locating all repeated words in a document, or parsing strings between two values. They encompass a language within themselves; a detailed discussion of this is outside the scope of this book. I recommend reading the Regular Expressions reference in the MSDN library on Microsoft's Web site for more information on how to write Regular Expressions. The following is an example of a program that utilizes regular expressions to parse an HTML file for links.

```
using System;
using System.Text.RegularExpressions;
using System.IO;
using System.Text;
```

```
public class HTMLParser
{
  public static void Main(String[] args)
  {
    FileInfo MyFile = new FileInfo(args[0].ToString());
    if(MyFile.Exists)
    {
      StreamReader sr = MyFile.OpenText();
      string text = sr.ReadToEnd();
      sr.Close();

      string pattern = @"<a\shref\S*/a>";
      MatchCollection patternMatches = Regex.Matches(text, pattern,
          RegexOptions.IgnoreCase);

      foreach (Match nextMatch in patternMatches)
      {
        Console.WriteLine(nextMatch.ToString());
      }
    }
    else
      Console.WriteLine("The input file does not exist");
  }
}
```

We want to focus on the following portion of code:

```
string pattern = @"<a\shref\S*/a>";

MatchCollection patternMatches = Regex.Matches(text, pattern,
    RegexOptions.IgnoreCase);

foreach (Match nextMatch in Matches)
{
  Console.WriteLine(nextMatch.ToString());
}
```

Regular Expressions require that you pass a string containing the Regular Expression to the static method *Matches()* of the *Regex* class. The Regular

Expression in this example uses \s to denote any whitespace character, and \S*
to denote any string of nonwhitespace characters. Since regular expressions make
extensive use of the \ character, this is a good opportunity to use Verbatim String
Literals, so that your \'s are not mistaken for escape characters. The *Matches()*
method returns an object of the *MatchCollection* class; *MatchCollection* is a collection
of *Matches*. We will discuss collections later in this chapter. The first parameter of
this function is the text string to search using the regular expression. The second
parameter is the string containing the actual regular expression, and the third and
final parameter is any one or more of the *RegexOptions* enumeration flags. The
most commonly used of these options would be *RegexOptions.Ignorecase*, which
tells the search to ignore case when doing a criteria check against the regular
expression. For a list of the remaining flags please check the .NET Framework
class reference library available at the MSDN Web site.

The final section of this code utilizes a *foreach* statement to iterate through the
matches, and writes them out to the console window. (We will cover the *foreach*
statement later in this chapter.)

Let's see this code in action. For our example run, we will feed the following
HTML file, *HTMLParse.html*, into our program. The file contains the following
code:

```
<HTML>
<BODY>
Click <a href="http://www.syngress.com">here</a>,
or <a href="http://www.google.com">here<a> if you prefer.
</BODY>
</HTML>
```

After compiling the code, we can run *HTMLParser* as follows:

```
c:\HTMLParser HTMLParse.html
```

This gives the following output:

```
C:\csharp>HTMLParser HTMLParse.html
<a href="http:\\www.syngress.com">here</a>
<a href="http:\\www.google.com">here</a>
```

As you can see our program parsed all the URL links out of the HTML file,
and displayed them as console output. Try this on your own HTML files, or on
an HTML file you downloaded from the Internet.

# Flow Control

All languages would have a hard time doing their jobs without some form of flow control—this was true in Java, and it still holds true in C#. It is likely that you have used the following flow control constructs in your Java programming, so we will discuss them briefly. We will spend more time on statements that did not exist in Java, such as the *foreach* iteration statement, and the infamous *goto*.

## Branch Statements

Branch statements, also known as Conditional statements, permit us to branch our code in a different direction based on a condition. Branch statements in both C# and Java consist of *if/else* and *switch* statements.

## The *if/else* Statement

The *if/else* construct is the most frequently used flow control statement. It tests a condition and if that condition is true, it executes either the next code statement or several code statements if they are enclosed in curly braces. If the condition does not evaluate to true, then it either skips the code segment, or executes code in an *else* statement. It is used in C# the same way as it is used in Java. For example:

```
if(x == 1)
     System.Console.WriteLine("X is equal to 1.");
else
     System.Console.WriteLine("X is not equal to 1.");
```

It is often common to nest *if/else* statements as in the following example.

```
if(x == 1)
  if(y == 2)
    System.Console.WriteLine("x = 1,  y = 2");
  else
    System.Console.WriteLine("x = 1, y != 2");
else
  System.Console.WriteLine("x != 1");
```

As you can see, nested *if/else* statements can easily begin to get cumbersome. Complex nested *if/else* statements can be better-written using *switch* statements.

## Debugging...

### The Dangling else Problem

Since every *else* in an *if/else* statement complements the immediately preceding *if* statement, if you are not careful you can run into what has been dubbed The Dangling Else problem.

```
if( x == 1)

    if( y == 2)

        System.Console.WriteLine("X = 1, Y = 2");

else

    System.Console.WriteLine("X != 1 ");
```

In this example the programmer intended that the *else* statement be for the *if(x ==1)* statement, but since there is another *if* statement preceding it in the same code block, it belongs to the *if( y==2)* statement. This can be corrected by using the curly braces {} to clearly define the limits of each *if* statement.

```
if( x == 1)

{

    if(y == 2)

        System.Console.WriteLine("X = 1, Y = 2");

}

else

    System.Console.WriteLine("X = 1, Y =2");
```

# The *switch* Statement

A *switch* statement will evaluate an expression and execute the corresponding *case* statement. *Switch* statements are a common alternative to using nested *if/else* constructs for testing multiple conditions. The specifics of the *case* and *break* statements will be discussed later in this chapter. *Switch* statements in C# have some differences from their counterparts in Java. Their syntax and usage are still primarily the same. They are the best approach towards multidecision logic, as opposed to extensive nested *if/else* statements. Unlike Java, C# *switch* statements do not require integers. C# *switch* statements can use any of the following data types: *sbyte, byte, short, ushort, int, uint, long, ulong, char, string,* or *enum*. Note that C# strings are included in this list. The ability to switch on a *string* expression is a welcome feature. In Java, making decisions based on *string* values would require a multi *if/else* statement. The following is an example of a C# *switch* statement using a *string* as its switch value. All case labels must be constants.

```
String testString = "Test";

switch(testString)
{
    case "Hello":
        System.Console.WriteLine("The string says Hello.");
        break;

    case "Test":
        System.Console.WriteLine("The string says Test");
        break;

    default:
        System.Console.WriteLine("The string is unknown");
        break;
}
```

Another diversion C# *switch* statements take from Java is in the fall-through mechanism. In Java and in C/C++, if a *case* is listed without a *break* statement, it will fall through to the next *case* statement. This feature, although sometimes intended, was a common source of bugs. In C# you have to specify that you want one case to fall-through to the next one using the *goto* statement. There is one exception to this, and that is empty cases. If a *case* label is empty, then it will fall-through to the next *case*. The following code comparison between Java and C# *switch* statements highlights these differences. In the Java example, because we left the *break* out of *case* 2, it will print both "x = 1" and "x = 2". In the C# example, this will not occur unless we specifically state *goto case 3* in *case* 2. As a matter of fact, the C# example will not even compile because it is lacking the *break* statement.

## Java

```
int x = 2;
switch(x)
```

```
{
case 1:
    System.out.println("x = 0.");
    break;
case 2:
    System.out.println("x = 1.");
case 3:
    System.out.println("x = 2.");
    break;
}
```

## C#

```
int x = 2;
switch(x)
{
case 1:
    System.Console.WriteLine("x = 0.");
    break;
case 2:
    //Will not compile without the goto line
    System.Console.WriteLine("x = 1.");
    //goto case 3;
case 3:
    System.Console.WriteLine("x = 2.");
    break;
}
```

To have the C# example perform the fall-through, uncomment the *goto case 3* line and you'll notice that the program will behave exactly as its Java counterpart.

# Iteration Statements

C# shares the same Iteration statements as Java, the pretest *while* and *for* loop, and the posttest *do-while* loop. C# also adds a new Iteration statement, the *foreach* loop, which will be discussed in more detail in the sections "Arrays" and "Collections."

# The *while* Loop

The *while* loop executes a segment of code 0 or more times, based on the outcome of a *boolean* control expression. The while *loop* is called an indeterminate loop and is usually used when the program will be unaware of the number of iterations of the loop until it has been entered. The following code demonstrates the *while* loop.

```
bool noMoreRecords = false;
while(!noMoreRecords)
{
  noMoreRecords = ReadRecord();
}
```

The use of the *while* loop in C# is very similar to Java.

# The *do-while* Loop

The *do-while* loop executes a segment of code 1 or more times. It is similar to the *while* loop, except that the control condition is evaluated after the loop body had run once.

```
bool noMoreRecords;
do
{
  noMoreRecords = ReadRecord();
} while(!noMoreRecords);
```

Again there are no surprises here. The *do-while* loop behaves identically to its Java counterpart.

# The *for* Loop

The *for* loop is a pretest determinate loop. This means that the program knows how many times it's going to execute the loop code prior to entering the loop. The *for* loop is handy for situations in which you need to repeat something a predetermined number of times, or need to iterate through an array. In C# a new flow control loop is provided, called the *foreach* loop, which is described later. This loop is specifically designed to iterate through arrays and collections so is therefore preferred over the *for* loop for this purpose. The following code presents a sample *for* loop that will execute 31 times and print out the days in the month of January.

```
for (int x = 0; x < 31; x++)
{
    System.Console.WriteLine("January {0}", x + 1);
}
```

As you can see, the three major flow control statements in C# are very similar to Java, so you should be familiar with them. Later on we'll discuss the *foreach* loop construct, which is new in C#.

# Jump Statements

A Jump statement transfers control of the program to another block; they are used to exit the current block of code. These statements are identical to their Java counterparts, the one exception being the *goto* statement.

## The *goto* Statement

Although the *goto* statement is declared a keyword in Java, its function is not implemented. The *goto* statement transfers control to a code segment marked with a label. For example the following code will print 4 as opposed to 5. The reason for this is that when the execution flow of the program encounters the *goto* statement, it will move execution to the label indicator, which is *Print* in this example.

```
int x = 4;
goto Print;
x = 5;
Print:
    System.Console.WriteLine(x);
```

As you can see, extensive use of the *goto* command can make the execution flow of code difficult to follow. Code that abuses the *goto* command is often termed "Spaghetti Code" because the flow of execution is so convoluted it is like looking at a bowl of spaghetti and trying to find out which noodle goes where. In C# there is one place where it will be more common to use the *goto* command, and that is in *switch* statements. Remember, C# *switch* statements do not support case fall-through. You can use the *goto* command to move from one case to another, to get the same effect as case fall-through. Since this takes active coding on your part, it solves the problem of accidentally omitting the *break* statement, yet still permits fall-through if you deem you need it. When using *goto*'s in this manner, you do not have to define a new label within each *case*. You can use the *case* label in the *goto* statement.

# The *break* Statement

As you may have noticed in the *switch* example, the *break* statement will transfer control of the program to the first line outside the current block of code. It may also be used to exit any loop (Iteration statement). If the *break* is within a nested loop, it will only exit the innermost loop in which it occurs. This functionality is identical to the *break* statement in Java. Contrary to Java, however is that C#'s *break* statement does not permit use of labels. This capability is not required due to C#'s support of the *goto* statement. The following code uses a *break* statement to exit a *for* loop early.

```
for( int i=0; i < 10; i++ )
{
    int x = DoSomething();
    if(x == 0)
      break;
}
```

The preceding code would execute the for loop 10 times, unless the imaginary method *DoSomething()* returned a 0, if such an event occurred, the *break* statement would execute and program flow would pick up immediately following the *for* loop.

# The *continue* Statement

The *continue* statement performs in the same way as the *break* statement, but rather than exit the loop entirely, it returns control to the start of the loop. You can think of it as only exiting the current iteration of the loop, whereas the *break* statement would have exited the loop completely. Again, this is the same functionality as the *continue* statement in Java. The following code uses a *continue* statement to exit one iteration of a *for* loop.

```
for( int i =0; i < 10; i ++ )
{
    int x = DoSomething();
    if(x == 0)
      continue;
    System.Console.WriteLine("loop iteration " + i);
}
```

The preceding code will execute the *for* loop 10 times, and output the loop iteration each time. If the *DoSomething()* function returns a 0, we will not print the loop iteration, and will return to the start of the loop. This is because the *continue* statement does not exit the loop entirely, it merely exits the current iteration of the loop.

## The *return* Statement

When a program calls a method, the program flow moves to the start of that function. For the flow to return to the code that called the method, it must encounter a *return* statement. Once this is encountered, the flow returns to the code that called the method. This is pretty much standard behavior for programming languages—Java and C# are no exception. If a method returns a value, then you must include a value of the same type in the *return* statement. We will discuss methods in Chapter 5.

The following example shows a program that calls a function, and traces the program flow.

```
using System;

class ProgramFlow
{
    public static void Main(String[] args)
    {
      Console.WriteLine("Main Line 1");
      MethodSample();
      Console.WriteLine("Main Line 2");
    }

    static void MethodSample()
    {
      Console.WriteLine("MethodSample line 1");
      return;
    }
}
```

## *Output*

```
Main Line 1
MethodSample line 1
Main Line 2
```

As you can see, once the *return* statement was encountered, program flow returned to the line immediately after the *method* call. Please note that in our example we're returning *void* and therefore the *return* statement is not completely necessary. You would want to use the *return* statement if a method returns a value; then you must use the same data type in the *return statement* as you specified in the method initialization. For example:

```
public static int MethodSample()
{
    int x = 10;
    //Perform method function here
    return x;
}
```

# Arrays

As was the case with strings, C#'s *Array* class shares many similarities with its Java counterpart. You are most likely familiar with the concept of an array; an array is a series of objects consisting of the same data types. Individual objects in the series, called *elements*, are referenced by their index into the array.

This concept of an array holds true for most programming languages. The similarities specifically between Java and C# arrays deal with the methods and properties of their classes. Both C# and Java provide a *length* property, which provides the number of elements in an array. They also provide similar methods for sorting or searching arrays. We will discuss these similarities in more detail after we go over how to declare and initialize arrays in the next section.

## Declaring and Initializing Arrays

Arrays are declared using the same syntax as in Java:

```
// data_type[] arrayname;
int[] IntegerArray;
```

Arrays can be initialized in several different ways. The most common way is by using the new operator, which will initialize an array, but not assign any values to it. The following code will create an integer array with four elements:

```
int[] integerArray = new int[4];
```

If you knew the values you wished to assign the array elements at the time you created the array, you can also use the following syntax. This method will create an integer array with four elements, and assign the values 1, 2, 3, and 4 to the elements, respectively.

```
int[] integerArray = {1,2,3,4};
```

To access an individual element of an array you specify the index of that element. The following code reassigns the value of the third element in the previously created array. Note the third element is accessed via [2]. This is because all arrays in C# are 0 indexed. This means the first element of the array is accessed via [0], not [1].

```
integerArray[2] = 7;
```

As we mentioned in the introduction to the Array section, C# provides methods for searching and sorting arrays similar to the methods provided in the *java.util.Arrays* package. In Java you can use *Arrays.sort()* to sort an array, in C# sharp you use *Array.Sort()*. The C# counterpart to Java's *Arrays.binarySearch()* method is *Array.BinarySearch()*. As you can see from these similarities, a Java programmer familiar with the Java *Array* implementation should not have much trouble using C#'s approach.

Table 4.3 shows some common *Array* methods and properties.

**Table 4.3** C# *Array* Methods and Properties

| C# | Java | Function | Notes |
|---|---|---|---|
| [int index] | get(Object array, int index) | Gets an element of the array | C# arrays utilize the standard indexer for individual element access. |
| Length | length | In C#, this property gets the total number of elements in all the dimensions of the array. In Java, this property gets the number of elements in a single dimensional array. | In Java, this property will cause a compile error when used on a multidimensional array, however C# simply returns the total number of elements in the multidimensional array. |

**Continued**

**Table 4.3** Continued

| C# | Java | Function | Notes |
|---|---|---|---|
| Rank | Not Available | Gets the number of dimensions of the array | This public property returns the number of dimensions in a multidimensional C# array object. This is not possible in Java. |
| BinarySearch(Array array, Object value) | binarySearch(Object[] array, Object value) | Searches a one-dimensional sorted array for a value, using a binary search algorithm | This method performs the same in Java and C#. |
| GetLength(int Dimension) | getLength(Object array) | Gets the number of elements in the specified dimension of the array | The C# implementation of this method requires that the programmer pass in an integer value that represents the dimension of the array from which to get the number of elements. The Java implementation assumes the array is one-dimensional. |
| GetLowerBound() | Not Available | Gets the lower bound of the specified dimension in the array | In Java, arrays are always 0 based, in C# this is the recommend and default approach; however there are methods that permit you to create nonzero based arrays. |

**Continued**

**Table 4.3** Continued

| C# | Java | Function | Notes |
|---|---|---|---|
| GetUpperBound() | Not Available | Gets the upper bound of the specified dimension in the array | |
| Sort(Array array) | sort(Object[] Array) | Sorts the elements of a one-dimensional array | This method performs the same in Java and C#. |

# Using the *params* Keyword

The *params* keyword is a new C# language construct that permits us to pass a variable number of parameters to a method. A method can have only one *params* argument, and it must be the rightmost argument. This makes sense, as the size of the argument is variable; if it is not the rightmost, it would be impossible for the method to determine where one argument ends and the next begins. The following sample shows how to declare a method that makes use of the *params* keyword, and demonstrates multiple calls to the method.

```
using System;

class ParamsSample
{
  static void PrintStrings(params String[] StringArray)
  {
    for (int i = 0; i < StringArray.Length; i++)
      Console.Write("{0} ", StringArray[i]);

    Console.WriteLine();
  }

  static void Main(String[] args)
  {
    String names = "Kyle";
```

```
        PrintStrings("Andrew");
        PrintStrings(names,"Roz", "Slater");
        PrintStrings("Rosie","Eileen","Conrad","Susan");
    }
}
```

Notice that because we used the *params* keyword we were able to pass a variable number of strings to the *PrintStrings* method, and it still worked. Because all array elements must be of the same data type, the *params* keyword does require that all *params* passed as part of the *params* array must be of the same data type. The *System.Console.Writeline()* method we discussed at the beginning of this chapter utilizes the *params* keyword to permit a variable number of arguments to support the use of placeholders. The output of the program is as follows.

## Output

```
Andrew
Kyle Roz Slater
Rosie Eileen Conrad Susan
```

As you can see, the program appended each of the strings we passed into the *PrintStrings* method into one line of output. This in itself is not remarkable—what makes this interesting is that we were able to pass a variable number of strings into the same function, and had to write only one implementation for this function. In Java this would have required other techniques such as multiple method overrides, or specifically passing the arguments as a string array. In either event, both would have required foreknowledge on the number of strings that would be passed in, so neither solution would be as dynamic as C#'s *params* keyword.

# Multidimensional Arrays

So far we have looked at single-dimension arrays. C#, like Java, also provides support for multidimensional arrays. A multidimensional array, sometimes called a *matrix,* provides multiple levels of indexing. Each level of indexing is referred to as a *range*. In C# there are two varieties of multidimensional arrays, rectangular and jagged. In Java, jagged arrays were referred to as ragged arrays.

## Rectangular Arrays

Rectangular arrays are multidimensional arrays in which the number of rows and columns is the same. The first dimension in a two-dimensional array can be thought of as the row, and the second as the column. This kind of array is excellent for representing a two-dimensional axis or a graph. It can be initialized in two different ways, depending on whether you wish to assign values to each element at initialization time.

To initialize a rectangular array we use the following syntax. This notation is not found in Java so pay close attention. This code declares and initializes a 2 x 2 dimensional array.

```
int[,] Integers = new int[2,2];
```

If we wanted to initialize each element of the array at the same time that we initialize the array itself, we would use the following syntax. This code will declare and initialize a 2 x 2 dimensional array, and also assign values to the elements.

```
int[,] Integers = {{ 1,2 }, { 3,4 }};
```

After the preceding code, Integers[0][0] equals 1, Integers[0][1] equals 2, Integers[1][0] equals 3, and Integers[1][1] equals 4. To illustrate this further, let's look at an example. The following program creates a class to represent a chessboard, a common two-dimensional grid we are all familiar with. At this stage we will simply draw the chessboard, using the letter B to represent a black square and the letter W to represent a white square.

```
using System;

class ChessBoard
{
    public Char[,] SquareColor = new Char[8,8];

    public ChessBoard()
    {
        for(int i = 0; i < SquareColor.GetLength(0); i++ )
        {
            for(int x = 0; x < SquareColor.GetLength(1); x++ )
            {
                if((x % 2) == 0)
                    if((i % 2) == 0)
                        SquareColor[i,x] = 'W';
                    else
```

```
                            SquareColor[i,x] = 'B';
                else
                    if((i % 2) == 0)
                            SquareColor[i,x] = 'B';
                    else
                            SquareColor[i,x] = 'W';
            }
        }
    }


    void DrawBoard()
    {
      for(int i =0; i < SquareColor.GetLength(0); i++ )
      {
        for(int x = 0; x < SquareColor.GetLength(1); x++)
        {
          Console.Write(SquareColor[i,x]);
        }
        Console.WriteLine();
      }
    }


    static void Main(String[] args)
    {
      ChessBoard MyChessBoard = new ChessBoard();
      MyChessBoard.DrawBoard();
    }
}
```

## Output

```
WBWBWBWB
BWBWBWBW
WBWBWBWB
BWBWBWBW
WBWBWBWB
BWBWBWBW
```

```
WBWBWBWB
BWBWBWBW
```

Nothing too spectacular, but as you can see we output eight rows and eight columns, with alternating black and white squares. The two-dimensional array that held this information was declared as an 8 x 8 array of characters. We simply used a *for* loop to iterate through the rows, and then used another *for* loop to iterate through the columns. What you want to focus on is how we indexed the array. Notice how we can use *SquareColor[i,x]* for indexing an array, which you can't do in Java. As you can see, array iteration in this manner is somewhat cumbersome—a better solution is to use the *foreach* statement, which we will discuss shortly.

## Jagged Arrays

Jagged arrays, called ragged arrays in Java, are multidimensional arrays in which the numbers of rows and columns can be different. They are actually arrays of arrays. This kind of array is useful when you know the length of one element but not another. For example, if we knew the number of columns, but not rows in a chart, we could initialize the columns, and initialize the rows at a later time. The syntax for declaring jagged arrays is different than rectangular arrays. To declare a jagged array you must use additional braces [].

The following code segment declares an integer array with two rows, but an unspecified number of columns.

```
int[][] Integers = new int[2][];
```

Now if we want to initialize the second dimension of this array we can write the following code. This code creates an array where the first row has two columns, and the second row has three columns.

```
Integers[0] = new int[2];
Integers[1] = new int[3];
```

After these initialization statements have executed the following elements would all be valid: Integers[0][0], Integers[0][1], Integers[1][0], Integers[1][1], and Integers[1][2]. Note that Integers[0][2] is not valid, as the first row if this Jagged Array has only two columns.

Let's look at an example where we'll create a jagged array of chess pieces and then print them to the console. To create the chess pieces we can utilize a jagged array since the quantity of each piece is different. We can use the first dimension to represent the type of piece and the second dimension can represent which piece it is. For example, we can designate the Knight as the fifth piece and we'll use a *for* loop to create two knights:

```
ChessPiece[4] = new String[2];
for (int i = 0; i < ChessPiece[4].Length; i++)
{
   ChessPiece[4][i] = "Knight";
}
```

To access one of the Knights, you can use the following syntax:

```
ChessPiece[4][0];
```

As you can see, this is very similar to how you would access multidimensional arrays in Java. The following is the full code listing for our example:

```
using System;

class ChessPieces
{
  private String[][] ChessPiece = new String[6][];

  public ChessPieces()
  {
    ChessPiece[0] = new String[1];
    // Create one King.
    ChessPiece[0][0] = "King";

    ChessPiece[1] = new String[1];
    // Create one Queen.
    ChessPiece[1][0] = "Queen";

    ChessPiece[2] = new String[2];
    // Create two Rooks.
    for (int i = 0; i < ChessPiece[2].Length; i++)
    {
      ChessPiece[2][i] = "Rook";
    }
```

```
    ChessPiece[3] = new String[2];
    // Create two Bishops.
    for (int i = 0; i < ChessPiece[3].Length; i++)
    {
      ChessPiece[3][i] = "Bishop";
    }


    ChessPiece[4] = new String[2];
    // Create two Knights.
    for (int i = 0; i < ChessPiece[4].Length; i++)
    {
      ChessPiece[4][i] = "Knight";
    }


    ChessPiece[5] = new String[8];
    // Create eight Pawns.
    for (int i = 0; i < ChessPiece[5].Length; i++)
    {
      ChessPiece[5][i] = "Pawn";
    }
  }


void PrintChessPieces()
{
  for(int i = 0; i < ChessPiece.Length; i++ )
  {
    for(int x = 0; x < ChessPiece[i].Length; x++)
    {
      // Write out each chess piece on its own line.
      Console.Write(ChessPiece[i][x] + " ");
    }
    Console.WriteLine();
  }
}


static void Main(String[] args)
{
```

```
      ChessPieces MyChessPieces = new ChessPieces();
      MyChessPieces.PrintChessPieces();
   }
}
```

## Output

```
C:\csharp>ChessPieces
King
Queen
Rook Rook
Bishop Bishop
Knight Knight
Pawn Pawn Pawn Pawn Pawn Pawn Pawn Pawn
```

The preceding code created a jagged array of chess pieces. In chess each side has six different types of pieces, and the quantity of each piece is different: eight Pawns, two Rooks, two Knights, two Bishops, one Queen, and one King. This made it easy to represent the pieces as a jagged array. The first dimension of the jagged array represents what type the piece is. The second dimension identifies the individual piece. For example, the first Pawn can be accessed via the following syntax.

```
ChessPiece[5][0];
```

This code would have benefited further from use of the *foreach* loop and enumerations. Fortunately, we discuss the *foreach* loop in the next section. Enumerations will be discussed later in this book.

# The foreach Statement

The *foreach* statement is a language construct that is very useful and is currently not available in the Java language; in fact its origins can be traced back to Visual Basic. It is an iteration statement, but was not mentioned earlier as it is used on arrays and other container classes. *Container* classes include *Arrays*, preexisting container classes in the *System.Collection* namespace, as well as collections created by you that support the *IEnumerable* interface. We will provide more detail on the container classes later in this chapter.

In the last two sections I mentioned how use of the *foreach* statement would have been superior to *for* loops. If you recall, a *for* loop has several elements—a counter, a control condition, and an increment operation on the counter. In the *for* loop you need to keep in mind the number of elements in the array you are iterating through, or you will end up throwing an index out of range exception. It is very easy to miscalculate the number of iterations a *for* loop will go through before meeting its control condition. Even experienced programmers make that mistake every now and then, myself included. The *foreach* statement takes away many of the opportunities where we might shoot ourselves in the foot, yet leaves us with the functionality we wanted.

The following code snippet demonstrates iteration through an integer array using the *for* loop.

```
int[] IntArray = new int[6];
for(int i = 0; i < 6; i++ )
   System.Console.WriteLine(IntArray[i]);
```

Here is the same code snippet, but utilizing the *foreach* loop.

```
int[] IntArray = new int[6];
foreach (int i in IntArray)
   System.Console.WriteLine(i);
```

As you can see, with the *foreach* statement we don't need prior knowledge of the array size. This should help eliminate indexing problems when iterating through an array or any type of collection. The syntax for the *foreach* statement is

```
foreach(type identifier in expression) statement
```

Make note of the *in* keyword, which is used only in a *foreach* statement. One key thing to remember is that the elements accessed in a *foreach* statement (*int x in* the preceding code sample), are read-only. This means their contents cannot be modified within the *foreach* statement. For example, the following code will not compile:

```
int[] integerArray = new int[6];
foreach (int x in integerArray)
{
   x = 5; //will not compile
   System.Console.WriteLine(x);
}
```

If you try compiling this code the Visual Studio compiler will give the error message: error CS1604: Cannot assign to 'x' because it is read-only.

Let's rewrite the *PrintChessPieces()* method in our previous jagged array example, but this time we will use the *foreach* statement instead of the nested *for* loops, to illustrate how it is more natural when iterating through a collection.

```
using System;

class ChessPieces
{
  private String[][] ChessPiece = new String[6][];

  public ChessPieces()
  {
    ChessPiece[0] = new String[1];
    // Create one King.
    ChessPiece[0][0] = "King";

    ChessPiece[1] = new String[1];
    // Create one Queen.
    ChessPiece[1][0] = "Queen";

    ChessPiece[2] = new String[2];
    // Create two Rooks.
    for (int i = 0; i < ChessPiece[2].Length; i++)
    {
      ChessPiece[2][i] = "Rook";
    }

    ChessPiece[3] = new String[2];
    // Create two Bishops.
    for (int i = 0; i < ChessPiece[3].Length; i++)
    {
      ChessPiece[3][i] = "Bishop";
    }

    ChessPiece[4] = new String[2];
    // Create two Knights.
    for (int i = 0; i < ChessPiece[4].Length; i++)
```

```
      {
        ChessPiece[4][i] = "Knight";
      }


      ChessPiece[5] = new String[8];
      // Create eight Pawns.
      for (int i = 0; i < ChessPiece[5].Length; i++)
      {
        ChessPiece[5][i] = "Pawn";
      }
    }


    void PrintChessPieces()
    {
      foreach(String[] x in ChessPiece )
      {
        foreach(String y in x)
          Console.Write(y + " ");
        Console.WriteLine();
      }
    }


    static void Main(String[] args)
    {
      ChessPieces MyChessPieces = new ChessPieces();
      MyChessPieces.PrintChessPieces();
    }
  }
```

The output of the code is the same as before. Notice that we could not use the *foreach* statement when we were iterating the array to assign the names of the pieces, due to the previously mentioned fact that the elements we access via the *foreach* statement are read–only.

# Indexers

Indexers are an interesting technique in C# that permits your classes to be treated as arrays. This feature is not found in Java. It is a very handy technique if you have an object that can reasonably be thought of as an array. However, it is not recommended that you give every object this capability. For example, if we were going to make a class to represent a deck of cards, it would make sense to use indexers for the cards themselves, but there would not be a need to use indexers for the whole deck. We will actually expound on this example in the upcoming sections.

## Implementing an Indexer

Although this is a powerful ability, it is not difficult to implement. Internally it uses a special kind of property with *get* and *set* accessor methods to specify its behavior. Properties will be discussed in Chapter 7.

Imagine we had a class to represent a playing card deck. It would make sense that we should be able to treat this deck as an array of 52 playing cards. To define an indexer we need to add the *this []* property to our class, as well as its return type. The following code snippet does this.

```
private String[] Cards = new String[52];
public String this [int index]
{
    get
    {
        return Cards[index];
    }
    set
    {
        Cards[index] = value;
    }
}
```

The preceding code declared a private *String* array called *Cards*. This is the private data that we will return via the indexer. The next code segment is the declaration of the *Indexer:*

```
public String this [int index]
```

This declaration states that the indexer [] will return a *String* data type, and that it is indexed by integer values, just like an array is. The *get* property is called when someone tries to read from the class, and the *set* property is called when someone tries to assign to the class. Please note the use of the *value* keyword in the *set* accessor. When you define a *set* accessor you must use the *value* keyword to represent the argument whose value is passed to and stored by the property. In our example, when someone tries to read an element of the class, we return the corresponding element in our private array *Cards*. If they try to assign a value to an element of the class, we assign the value to its corresponding element in the private array.

Now that we have added an indexer to our class, we can treat instances of it like an array. The following driver code snippet illustrates this.

```
CardDeck PokerDeck = new CardDeck();

//Write each card's value out to the console.

for(int i =0; i < 52; i++)

{

   Console.WriteLine( PokerDeck[i] );

}
```

This code snippet uses a *for* loop to iterate through the class as if it were an array, and outputs the card's name and value to the console. Notice that we did not use a *foreach* loop. This is because *foreach* loops will not work on indexers. The following is the complete code sample.

```
using System;

class CardDeck
{
   private String[] Cards = new String[52];
   public String this [int index]
   {
      get
      {
        return Cards[index];
      }
      set
      {
        Cards[index] = value;
      }
   }
}
```

```
   public CardDeck()
  {
    int y = 0;
    int i = 0;
    while(i < 52)
    {
     for(int x = 0; x < 13; x++ )
     {
       switch(y)
       {
         case 0:
           Cards[i] = (x+1) + " of Hearts";
         break;
         case 1:
           Cards[i] = (x+1) + " of Clubs";
         break;
         case 2:
           Cards[i] = (x+1) + " of Spades";
         break;
         case 3:
           Cards[i] = (x+1) + " of Diamonds";
         break;
       }
       if(y == 3)
         y = 0;
       else
         y++;
       i++;
     }
    }
  }
}


class CardDeckClient

{
```

```
public static void Main()

{

  CardDeck PokerDeck = new CardDeck();

  // Write each card value to the console.

  for(int i =0; i < 52; i++) {

    Console.WriteLine( PokerDeck[i] );

  }

  }

}
```

## Output

```
1 of Hearts

2 of Clubs

3 of Spades

4 of Diamonds

5 of Hearts

6 of Clubs

7 of Spades

8 of Diamonds

9 of Hearts

10 of Clubs

11 of Spades

12 of Diamonds

13 of Hearts

1 of Clubs

2 of Spades
```

They may not be in order, but we have all 52 cards here. As you can see in the example, using indexers permitted us to access the individual cards in the *CardDeck* as if they were elements of a 52-element array. In Java we would have to call an accessor such as *getCard()* to return a specific card from the deck.

One thing to keep in mind is that although *Indexers* permit you to use your classes as if they were arrays, they are not in fact actual arrays. Due to this you may not use the *foreach* loop to iterate through the elements.

# Multiple Indexers

C# permits you to have multiple indexer types for the same class. This means you that you're not limited to just using integer values as the index. For example if we wanted to be able to extend our previous *CardDeck* example so that we could draw a card, not just based on its index into the deck, but also by its name, we can overload the *Indexer* to accept *String* indexes as well. Here is the implementation for this.

```
using System;

class CardDeck
{
  private String[] Cards = new String[52];
  public String this [int index]
  {
    get
    {
      return Cards[index];
    }
    set
    {
      Cards[index] = value;
    }
  }

  public String this [String CardName]
  {
    get
    {
      for(int i = 0; i < 52; i++) {
        if(Cards[i] == CardName)
          return Cards[i];
      }
      return Cards[0];
    }
    set
    {
```

```
      for(int i = 0; i < 52; i++) {
        if(Cards[i]== CardName)
          Cards[i] = value;

      }

    }

  }

public CardDeck()
{
  int y = 0;
  int i = 0;
  while(i < 52)
  {
   for(int x = 0; x < 13; x++ )
    {
      switch(y)
      {
        case 0:
          Cards[i] = (x+1) + " of Hearts";
        break;
        case 1:
          Cards[i] = (x+1) + " of Clubs";
        break;
        case 2:
          Cards[i] = (x+1) + " of Spades";
        break;
        case 3:
          Cards[i] = (x+1) + " of Diamonds";
        break;
      }
      if(y == 3)
        y = 0;
      else
        y++;
      i++;
    }
  }
}
```

```
}

class CardDeckClient

{

  public static void Main()

  {

    CardDeck PokerDeck = new CardDeck();

    String FourOfHearts = PokerDeck["4 of Hearts"];
    Console.WriteLine(FourOfHearts);

  }
}
```

The output of this program is simply the name of the card:

```
4 of Hearts
```

Thanks to *Indexer* overloading we were able to overload the indexer to accept a string value—in this case it was the name of the card. A class can have as many overloaded indexcrs as it wants provided that they are all of different types, or numbers of index parameters.

# Multiparameter Indexers

Multiparameter indexcrs are useful when you are dealing with an object that you feel should be treated as a multidimensional array. For instance if you had a class representing a lookup table, it would make sense to permit people to access it as if it was a two-dimensional array with rows and columns. The following code illustrates this by simulating a multiplication table.

```
using System;

class MultiplicationTable
{
  private int[,] MultiplicationArray = new int[10,10];

  public int this[int x, int y]
  {
    get
    {
```

```
            return MultiplicationArray[x,y];
        }
        set
        {
            MultiplicationArray[x,y] = value;
        }
    }
    public MultiplicationTable()
    {
        for(int i = 0; i < 10; i++)
        {
            for(int y = 0; y < 10; y++)
            {
                MultiplicationArray[i,y] = i * y;
            }
        }
    }
}


class MultiplicationTableClient
{
    public static void Main(String[] args)
    {
        MultiplicationTable MyTable = new MultiplicationTable();
        Console.Write("3 x 9 is " + MyTable[3,9] );
    }
}
```

## Output

```
3 x 9 is 27
```

We simply created a table of multiplication results, and used the row and column to look up the result of multiplying the row with the column. This, of course, is a lot of overkill since finding the result of a multiplication is very easy, but it is a simplified example of how you could use multiparameter indexers to look up data in a table. Now that you can see the power of indexers, don't use them as liberally as I have done in this last example. Indexers should never be used where a simple method would make more sense.

# Collections

Collections are a means of grouping objects of the same type into a structure. You may be thinking: Isn't that what arrays are? In fact, you would be correct. Arrays are a type of Collection object; the simplest type, in fact. Some disadvantages of arrays are that they do not permit us to dynamically resize them when needed. When they are initialized we specify their dimensions, and the only way we can change this is to actually reinitialize them. With Collections we can add elements to our collection object, without worrying that the collection cannot hold any more, as we would with arrays.

You have most likely used collection classes in Java such as the *Vector* class, and the *ArrayList* class. C# has its own *ArrayList*, which contains the capabilities of these Java classes. Both Java and C# store the items in the collection as objects, so the responsibility is on you to cast it back to its type. An advantage C# has over Java is the use of indexers to access items in a collection, as opposed to Java, which requires use of the *get* method. Here is a side-by-side comparison of identical code in Java and C# to create, initialize, and use an *ArrayList*. This code keeps track of players at our poker game.

## *Java*

```
import java.io.IOException;
import java.util.*;


class CollectionsDemo
{
  public static void main(String[] args)
  {
    ArrayList PokerPlayers = new ArrayList(3);
    PokerPlayers.add(new String("Joe Bob"));
    PokerPlayers.add(new String("Mike Smith"));
    PokerPlayers.add(new String("Al Capone"));
    PokerPlayers.add(new String("Johnny Come Lately"));

    for(int i = 0; i < PokerPlayers.size(); i++)
```

```
    {
      String Player = (String)PokerPlayers.get(i);
      System.out.println(Player);
    }


    PokerPlayers.set(0, "Alice McShark");
    System.out.println(PokerPlayers.get(0));
  }
}
```

## C#

```
using System;
using System.Collections;

class CollectionsDemo
{
  public static void Main(String[] args)
  {

    ArrayList PokerPlayers = new ArrayList(3);
    PokerPlayers.Add("Joe Bob");
    PokerPlayers.Add("Mike Smith");
    PokerPlayers.Add("Al Capone");
    PokerPlayers.Add("Johnny Come Lately");

    foreach(String Player in PokerPlayers)
    {
      Console.WriteLine(Player);
    }

    PokerPlayers[0] = "Alice McShark";
    System.Console.WriteLine(PokerPlayers[0]);
  }
}
```

The output for both of these programs is a listing of the players.

## *Output*

```
Joe Bob
Mike Smith
Al Capone
Johnny Come Lately
Alice McShark
```

The thing that stands out is that *ArrayList* was created with room for only three elements, but we added four. This occurred without any exceptions, because under the cover the *ArrayList* class was able to resize itself. Also note the use of the indexer in C#, which makes accessing the *ArrayList* a little easier, as opposed to using the *get()* and *set()* methods in Java. Table 4.4 shows some frequently used *ArrayList* methods and members.

**Table 4.4** Common *ArrayList* Methods and Members

| C# | Java | Function | Notes |
| --- | --- | --- | --- |
| Capacity | capacity() | Gets or sets the number of elements the *ArrayList* can contain | In Java, the *ArrayList* class does not have this method, it is available as part of the *Vector* class. |
| Count | size() | Gets the number of elements that are actually in the *ArrayList* | In Java, the *ArrayList* class does not have this method, it is available as part of the *Vector* class. |
| [int Index] | get(int index) | Gets an individual element | C# *ArrayList*s utilize the standard indexer for individual element access. |
| Add(Object obj) | add(Object o) | Adds an element to the *ArrayList* | This method performs the same in Java and C#. |

**Continued**

**Table 4.4** Continued

| C# | Java | Function | Notes |
| --- | --- | --- | --- |
| AddRange (Icollectionc ) | addAll(Collection c) | Adds a range of elements to the *ArrayList* | This method performs the same in Java and C#. |
| BinarySearch(Object obj) | binarySearch(Object[] objArray) | Searches an *ArrayList* for a value, using a binary search algorithm | In C# this is a member of the *ArrayList* class; in Java you must use the *Arrays* utility class. |
| Clear() | clear() | Clears the contents of the *ArrayList*. | This method performs the same in Java and C#. |
| Contains(Object obj) | contains(Object obj) | Determine if an element is in the *ArrayList* | This method performs the same in Java and C#. |
| GetRange(int Index, int Count) | Not Available | Gets a range of elements from the *ArrayList* | In Java you would have to implement this as a *for* loop, repeatedly calling *get(int Index)*. |
| Insert(int Index, Object obj) | set(int Index, Object obj) | Inserts an element into the *ArrayList* | This method performs the same in Java and C#. |
| InsertRange(int Index, Icollection c) | Not Available | Inserts a range of elements into the *ArrayList* | In Java you would have to implement this as a *for* loop repeatedly calling *set(int Index, Object obj)*. |

**Continued**

**Table 4.4** Continued

| C# | Java | Function | Notes |
|---|---|---|---|
| Remove(Object obj) | Not Available | Removes an element from the *ArrayList* | |
| RemoveAt(int Index) | remove(int Index) | Removes an element at a specific position from the *ArrayList* | This method performs the same in Java and C#. |
| RemoveRange(int Index, int Count) | removeRange(int FromIndex, int ToIndex) | Removes a range of elements from the *ArrayList* | This method performs the same in Java and C#. |
| Sort() | sort(A) | Sorts the elements in the *ArrayList* | In C# this is a member of the *ArrayList* class. In Java you must use the *Arrays* utility class. |
| ToArray() | toArray() | Converts the *ArrayList* to an Array object | This method performs the same in Java and C#. |
| TrimToSize() | trimToSize() | Trims *ArrayList* so that capacity and count are the same | This method performs the same in Java and C#. |

# Collection Interfaces

Previously we mentioned that if you use indexers, you couldn't use the *foreach* statement. That is because although they permit your class to be treated as an array, in fact, it is not one. If you would like to use this functionality with your class, you can implement the collection interfaces. The base collection interface is called *Ienumerable*, and implementing it makes your class a collection. This is similar to implementing the *Iterator* class in Java, but a good deal easier. Implementing an interface will be discussed in more detail in Chapter 6. Table 4.5 discusses the different collection interfaces, and provides a brief description of what they provide.

**Table 4.5** Key Collection Interfaces

| Interface | Purpose |
| --- | --- |
| IEnumerable | Provides Iteration (*foreach*) capabilities to the class |
| ICollection | Provides ability to get the count (number of elements) of a collection via a public property |
| IList | Provides ability to treat the collection like a Linked List— adding and removing elements for example |
| IDictionary | Provides Hash Table/Dictionary support to a collection |

# Exceptions

Exception handling permits you to execute code and handle error conditions prior to the program exiting. In many cases if you catch the exception you may be able to correct the problem and resume execution. In C# exception handling requires three code blocks: *try*, *catch*, and *finally*. It is very similar to exception handling in Java, except C# doesn't use the *throws* keyword.

As mentioned, among the most noticeable differences is the lack of the *throws* keyword. In Java, if a class throws an exception you indicate this with the *throws* keyword. If someone uses this class, then they have to handle the exceptions specified by the *throws* keyword. C# does not require this, which means that you're not forced to handle the exception.

## Catching Exceptions

To catch an exception you would execute the code you want to execute in a *try* block, and follow this block with a *catch* block. The following section will give examples of how to catch exceptions.

### The *try*, *catch*, *finally* Blocks

The core mechanism of exception handling in C# is use of the *try*, *catch*, and *finally* blocks. The code in which the exception is likely to occur must be encased in a *try* block followed by a *catch* block. Typically you would end with a *finally* block to perform any cleanup code that must occur regardless if an exception was thrown or not. This usually includes closing files and sockets. Although a *try* block only requires that you provide at least one *catch* or *finally* block, it is good practice to always have a *finally* block for cleanup. The *catch* block specifies the exception it is designed to catch. Since these blocks are executed sequentially, you must

catch the more specific exception first. The *finally* block executes at the end of
the routine, regardless if an exception had been thrown or not. This is the place
that you would put clean-up code. The following example demonstrates proper
use of the *try*, *catch*, and *finally* blocks. Let's say a user of our *PlayingCardDeck* from
the previous section tried to access card 53—perhaps they are cheating and
brought extra cards!

```
using System;

public class PlayingCard
{
  public String Name;
}


class CardDeck
{
  private PlayingCard[] Cards = new PlayingCard[52];
  public PlayingCard this [int index]
  {
    get
    {
      return Cards[index];
    }
    set
    {
    Cards[index] = value;
    }
  }

  public static void Main(String[] args)
  {
    try
    {
      CardDeck PokerDeck = new CardDeck();
      PlayingCard HiddenAce = PokerDeck[53];
    }
    catch( IndexOutOfRangeException e)
    {
```

```
        Console.WriteLine(e.Message);
    }
    finally
    {
      // Cleanup code
    }
  }
}
```

Because this program tries to access the fifty-third element of an array that has only 52 elements, the application throws an exception. In this situation it throws an *IndexOutOfRangeException*, which is caught by the application. When the application catches the exception, it writes the Message member out to the console. The output appears as follows.

```
Index was outside the bounds of the array.
```

Since the *catch* statements are checked in sequential order, it is imperative that you try and catch more specific exceptions first; otherwise a more general *catch* statement may qualify and handle the exception, albeit not as optimaly as one that was written specifically for it. All C# exceptions are derived from *System.Exception*. From this the Framework library provides quite a few other exceptions that are more specific. The two major ones are *SystemException*, which is usually thrown by the Framework.SDK, and *ApplicationException*, which is the base class for any exception classes you create.

In our example you saw that we were able to use a member of the *Exception* class to output a descriptive message to the console. Table 4.6 lists other properties of the *Exception* class that may be useful for handling or reporting error information.

**Table 4.6** *Exception* Class Properties

| Property | Description |
| --- | --- |
| HelpLink | Gets or sets a link to the help file associated with this exception |
| InnerException | Gets the exception instance that caused the current exception |
| Message | Gets a message that describes the current exception |
| Source | Gets or sets the name of the application or the object that causes the error |

**Continued**

**Table 4.6** Continued

| Property | Description |
| --- | --- |
| StackTrace | Gets a string representation of the frames on the call stack at the time the current exception was thrown |
| TargetSite | Gets the method that throws the current exception |

# Throwing Exceptions

Exceptions are not just thrown by the Framework libraries. In fact, you can, and should, throw exceptions yourself if the situation requires. Every method you provide should verify your assumptions about the data passed in, and if they are violated, throw an appropriate exception. Throwing an exception is as easy as returning from a method. It simply requires the *throw* keyword, followed by the exception you wish to throw. An exception is a class, so you must actually create an instance of the exception using the *new* keyword and the exceptions constructor. Let's modify the *CardDeck* class by adding a new method for getting cards, the *GetCard* method. We will, of course, remove our *Iterator* code, as it would be redundant. If someone tries to ask for a card with an index not in the range 0 to 51, we will throw an exception.

```
using System;

public class PlayingCard
{
  public String Name;
}


class CardDeck
{
  private PlayingCard[] Cards = new PlayingCard[52];

  public PlayingCard GetCard(int idx)
  {
    if((idx >= 0) && (idx <= 51))
      return Cards[idx];
    else
      throw new IndexOutOfRangeException("Invalid Card");
```

```
      }

   public static void Main(String[] args)
   {
     try
     {
       CardDeck PokerDeck = new CardDeck();
       PlayingCard HiddenAce = PokerDeck.GetCard(53);
     }
     catch( IndexOutOfRangeException e)
     {
       Console.WriteLine(e.Message);
     }
     catch( Exception e)
     {
       Console.WriteLine(e.Message);
     }
     finally
     {
       // Cleanup code
     }
   }
}
```

In the preceding code, when the programmer called the *GetCard()* method, the method validated the input data, and because it was outside the range of the accepted values, 0 to 52, it threw an *IndexOutOfRangeException*. The *catch* block in the main function caught this exception.

To understand what happens when you throw an exception, you must understand the concept of a call stack. A call stack is a way to view the layers of methods that have been called. The first method on a call stack is typically the entry point method; *Main*, in the case of C#. When a method is called from within *Main*, it is added to the top of the call stack, and when it returns it is removed from the call stack. Since most methods call other methods in turn, the call stack can get rather large. When an exception is thrown, it is passed up the call stack looking for a catch block that handles this sort of exception. If by the time it reaches the *Main* method, it still cannot find a proper handler for the exception, the program is terminated and an error is displayed to the user. The following code will illustrate the call stack, and how an exception traverses up the call stack.

```
using System;

class ExceptionThrower
{
  static void MethodOne()
  {
    try
    {
      MethodTwo();
    }
    finally {}
  }

  static void MethodTwo()
  {
    throw new Exception("Exception Thrown in Method Two");
  }

  public static void Main(String[] args)
  {
    try
    {
      ExceptionThrower FooBar = new ExceptionThrower();
      MethodOne();
    }
    catch( Exception e)
    {
      Console.WriteLine(e.Message);
    }
    finally
    {
      // Cleanup code
    }
  }
}
```

At the time the exception was thrown in the preceding code, the call stack looked like this:

```
MethodTwo()
MethodOne()
Main()
```

*MethodTwo* threw the exception, but as you can see, *MethodOne* did not have a catch block suitable for handling the exception, so it was passed up the call stack to *Main*, which did contain a catch block for the exception. Imagine if your call stack was 20 levels deep when an error occurs. Thanks to exception handling, the error will be passed up the stack until someone handles it.

In the preceding code samples we threw a predefined exception type. C# permits you to create your own exception classes, just as you could in Java. Actually, how to do this is our next topic. For your reference some commonly used exceptions are included in Table 4.7.

**Table 4.7** Common Exceptions

| Exception | Description |
| --- | --- |
| System.Exception | Base class of all exceptions |
| System.ApplicationException | Recommended base class for all user-defined exceptions |
| System.SystemException | Base class for most exceptions thrown by the Framework SDK |
| System.IndexOutOfRangeException | An attempt was made to access an element that was outside the range of an array |
| System.IO.FileNotFoundException | The file was not found |
| ArgumentException | An argument passed to a method was not valid |
| ArgumentNullException | An argument passed to the method was NULL |

# Creating New Exceptions

The standard exception classes are quite handy and fit many scenarios, but often you will want to make your own custom exceptions. In the preceding example we threw an *IndexOutOfRangeException*; however it might have been more appropriate to throw a custom exception that fit more with the *CardDeck* class. The user doesn't know that the internal implementation is an indexed array. To create your own exception class you need to create a class that is derived from *ApplicationException*. Once this is done, you simply implement your constructors. In our example we will just call the base class constructors from our custom exception class constructors. Let's revise the first exception example to use our new custom exception class.

```csharp
using System;

public class PlayingCard
{
  public String Name;

}

class InvalidCardException: ApplicationException
{
    public InvalidCardException()
        : base("An invalid card has been requested!") {
    }
}

class CardDeck
{
  private PlayingCard[] Cards = new PlayingCard[52];

  public PlayingCard GetCard(int idx)
  {
    if((idx >= 0) && (idx <= 51))
      return Cards[idx];
    else
      throw new InvalidCardException();
  }

  public static void Main(String[] args)
  {
    try
    {
      CardDeck PokerDeck = new CardDeck();
```

```
      PlayingCard HiddenAce = PokerDeck.GetCard(53);
   }
   catch( InvalidCardException e)
   {
      Console.WriteLine(e.Message);
   }
   catch( Exception e)
   {
      Console.WriteLine(e.Message);
   }
   finally
   {
      // Cleanup code
   }
  }
}
```

## Output

```
An invalid card has been requested!
```

The changes we had to implement to use our own exception were rather small. The following snippet from the code sample is all that was required to create a new exception type.

```
class InvalidCardException: ApplicationException
{
    public InvalidCardException()
        : base("An invalid card has been requested!") {
    }
}
```

It merely creates a new subclass of *ApplicationException*, and to simplify things our exception will call the base class constructor in its constructor. Don't worry too much about the syntax of this declaration—it will be discussed in the next two chapters when we talk about object-oriented programming.

# Rethrowing Exceptions

Sometimes, after doing all your error handling in a routine it is necessary to rethrow the error back up to the calling block. Doing this is simple—we just call *throw* without any arguments in the *catch* block for the exception. Previously when we discussed throwing exceptions, we mentioned the call stack, and that when an exception is thrown, it is passed up the call stack until it is handled. What if a method catches the exception and does everything it can, but still thinks it is better to pass the exception up to the next method in the call stack rather than continue on as if nothing occurred. To demonstrate we will revise our previous example to rethrow the exception.

```
using System;

class ExceptionThrower
{
  public static void Main(String[] args)
  {
    try
    {
      ExceptionThrower FooBar = new ExceptionThrower();
      MethodOne();
    }
    catch( Exception e)
    {
      Console.WriteLine(e.Message);
    }
    finally
    {
      // Cleanup code
    }
  }

  static void MethodOne()
  {
    try
    {
      MethodTwo();
```

```
      }
      catch( Exception e )
      {
        Console.WriteLine("Exception caught in Method One.");
        throw e;
      }
   }

   static void MethodTwo()
   {
      throw new Exception("Exception Thrown in Method Two");
   }
}
```

As is evident from the output,

```
Exception caught in Method One.
Exception Thrown in Method Two
```

Even though the exception was caught in Method One, because *MethodOne* rethrew the exception, it was also caught by the *catch* block in the *Main* method.

# Summary

As we have seen, the fundamental building blocks of C# are very similar if not identical to their Java counterparts. *Strings* in both languages are immutable, but a nonimmutable version of the class is also provided. Flow control is identical, with the lack of fall-through in *switch* statements being the exception. Arrays are the same as in Java, except for the introduction of two ways of declaring multidimensional arrays, as opposed to one in Java. The *foreach* statement is a handy new construct brought in from Visual Basic, which makes iterating through collections and arrays simple and natural. Indexers are another new concept not found in Java. They permit you to treat your classes as if they were arrays. The C# collection classes share many of the capabilities of the Java collection classes, and as in Java you can make your own classes into collection classes by implementing an interface. Exception handling is also the same as in Java, except for the lack of the *throws* keyword. Since C# does not require that you catch exceptions, the *throws* keyword was not implemented. We also discussed how to make a custom exception class using an interface.

# Solutions Fast Track

## Strings

- ☑ Strings can be created either by supply or a literal, or via a constructor.
- ☑ Strings are immutable, meaning once they are created they cannot be modified.
- ☑ If a mutable string is required, use the *stringBuilder* class.
- ☑ The + sign is the concatenation operator.
- ☑ You may precede a string literal with the @ character to specify that its contents are verbatim (this means escape characters are not used).

## Flow Control

- ☑ Most flow control statements are identical to their Java counterparts.
- ☑ C# includes the familiar *if/else* and *switch* construct, as well as the *while*, *do-while*, and *for* loops.

- ☑ C# also provides the new *foreach* loop for iteration through arrays and collections.

- ☑ The C# *switch* statements do not have implicit fall-through; use of the *goto* keyword is required to move to another *case* statement.

## Arrays

- ☑ Standard C# arrays are identical to their Java counterparts.

- ☑ C# provides two different kinds of multidimensional arrays, rectangular and jagged.

- ☑ A rectangular array has equal dimensions, a jagged array does not.

- ☑ The *params* keyword can be used to specify that an unknown number of parameters will be passed to a method.

## The *foreach* Statement

- ☑ The *foreach* statement is a gift from the VB language that helps to iterate through arrays and collections.

- ☑ The elements accessed within the *foreach* statement are read-only, and cannot be modified.

- ☑ The *foreach* statement does not work on classes that implemented iterators, only on true arrays and collections.

## Indexers

- ☑ Indexers permit you to treat your class as if it were an array.

- ☑ Indexers should not be abused; they should be used only if it is logical or natural for your class to be thought of as an array.

- ☑ A class can have as many overloaded indexers as it wants, provided the index types or numbers of indexes are different.

## Collections

- ☑ C#'s collection classes include the *ArrayList* class, which is C#'s counterpart to Java's *ArrayList* and *Vector* classes.

☑ The *ArrayList* class permits you to have dynamic arrays.

☑ Collection classes store data as objects; the data must be cast back to its original type once it is retrieved from a collection.

☑ You can make your class a collection by implementing the *Ienumerator* interface.

# Exceptions

☑ C# exception handling is very similar to Java exception handling.

☑ The core of C# exception handling is use of the *try*, *catch*, and *finally* blocks.

☑ You must catch more specific exceptions first, as the *catch* blocks are evaluated sequentially.

☑ Your class can throw an exception using the *throw* keyword.

☑ There is not a *throws* keyword, as in Java.

☑ You may make your own custom exceptions by implementing the *IapplicationError* interface.

# Frequently Asked Questions

The following Frequently Asked Questions, answered by the authors of this book, are designed to both measure your understanding of the concepts presented in this chapter and to assist you with real-life implementation of these concepts. To have your questions about this chapter answered by the author, browse to **www.syngress.com/solutions** and click on the **"Ask the Author"** form.

**Q:** In Java, I used the *Stringbuffer* class for strings that were not immutable. Does C# offer a similar class?

**A:** Yes, C# offers the *StringBuilder* class. This class is the counterpart to the *Stringbuffer* class in Java, and has similar methods.

**Q:** Why do my fall-through cases not fall through in my *switch* statement?

**A:** C# does not support implicit fall-through. You must use the *goto* command to switch to another case.

**Q:** In Java, we would put a *throws* specifier on a class if it threw an exception. Is this required in C#?

**A:** No, C# does not support the *throws* specifier.

**Q:** When should I make my class a collection, and when should I use indexers?

**A:** If your class can be considered logically, or might be used by someone else as an array, then you might want to use indexers. If you wish to support the *foreach* iterator, you must make your class a collection.

# Chapter 5

# Objects and Classes

## Solutions in this chapter:

- **Using Classes**
- **Using Methods**
- **Creating Objects**
- **Destroying Objects**

☑ **Summary**

☑ **Solutions Fast Track**

☑ **Frequently Asked Questions**

# Introduction

C# is a modern object-oriented programming language (OOPL) just like Java. This means that it upholds the three pillars of object-oriented programming—encapsulation, inheritance, and polymorphism. This chapter will review the concepts of objects and classes, which is the heart and soul of any OOPL. Most of this will be very familiar to you, but pay attention—there are some differences between the two languages.

This chapter will look at C# classes and objects. Just like Java, all code in C# runs as part of a class that has a group of methods that act upon common data. Each instance of a class is called an object and has its own copy of the data. This is the main difference between an object and a class. C# has introduced new keywords (*ref* and *out)* for declaring and handling method parameters, which will be highlighted in the method parameters section.

The last section of this chapter will discuss how to create and destroy objects. You will learn how to create constructors and destructors for your class. A constructor is the very first method called when you instantiate your object. A destructor is a method you can use to free up unmanaged resources for you object. However, the Common Language Runtime (CLR) provides a garbage collector for cleaning up your objects after they are used, so you don't need to explicitly declare a destructor. Let's now proceed and see how these are all done.

# Using Classes

C# and Java both use classes to combine data and the methods that operate on that data. This combining of data and methods is called encapsulation. Encapsulation is an important part of object-oriented programming. Encapsulation, however, is neither new nor unique to OOPLs. Before object orientation, programmers designed their code in "black boxes" and used information hiding.

If you are a Java developer, you will find C#'s class structure familiar. C# classes may specialize other classes just like Java classes. In C# however, the syntax uses a colon (:) in place of Java's *extends* keyword, which will be discussed in more detail in Chapter 6. C# classes also require access-modifiers, but C# supports five instead of Java's four.

In C# there are no global functions or constants, and all methods and all variables are members of some class. Classes in C# define new data types, which are the templates or patterns from which objects are created. To use a baking metaphor, classes are the cookie cutters and objects are the cookies. Objects are instances of a class; the process of creating an object from a class is called instantiation.

# Access Control

As mentioned, encapsulation is an important part of object-oriented programming. Encapsulation means that you control the access to a class, method, or variable. Access to a class means that another class can do one of three things:

- Create an instance of that class
- Extend that class
- Access certain methods and variables within the class

Access control is important because it provides encapsulation by controlling the visibility of a class, a method, or a variable. Table 5.1 is a list of all C# access modifiers for classes, methods, and variables.

**Table 5.1** C# Access Modifiers and Java Equivalents

| C# | Java | Access |
| --- | --- | --- |
| public | public | C# and Java classes, methods, and variables marked *public* are accessible by everyone. |
| protected | N/A | C# classes, methods, and variables marked *protected* are accessible by any member of a class or its derived classes. The same keyword in Java behaves differently. |
| internal | default or package | C# classes, methods, and variables marked *internal* are accessible to any member of any class in the same assembly. Java classes, methods, and variables marked with *default* access are accessible within the same package. |
| protected internal | protected | C# classes, methods, and variables marked *protected internal* are accessible in the same assembly or by derived classes. Java classes, methods, and variables marked *protected* are accessible in the same package or by derived classes. |
| private | private | C# and Java classes, methods, and variables marked *private* are accessible by the class itself. |

> **NOTE**
>
> An assembly has a lot in common with Java's JAR files. It is the main form of code packaging in the .NET environment (a logical DLL). Typically, it contains the intermediate code from the compiled class, and any other resources required by the packaged code to perform its task. Chapter 9 will go into more detail on assemblies.

## Class Modifiers

Class modifiers in C# control access to classes or define some characteristic of a class. Table 5.2 shows the class modifiers supported by C# and their Java equivalents (where appropriate).

**Table 5.2** C# Class Modifiers and Java Equivalents

| C# | Java | Function | Note |
|---|---|---|---|
| public | public | C# classes marked *public* are available to everyone. | Similar to Java. |
| internal | N/A | C# classes marked *internal* are available only within the assembly. | In Java the default class access means that the class is available only within their package. This is the same in C#. However, in C# you can explicitly mark a class as *internal* for the same functionality. |
| protected | N/A | Nested C# classes marked *protected* are available to the containing class or from types derived from the containing class. | Can be used only on inner classes. |
| protected internal | protected | Nested C# classes marked as *protected internal* are available to the assembly or types derived from the containing class. | Similar to Java, it can be used on only inner classes. Nested Java classes marked *protected* are available to both derived classes and |

*Continued*

**Table 5.2** Continued

| C# | Java | Function | Note |
|---|---|---|---|
| | | | classes in the same package. |
| private | private | Nested C# classes marked *private* are available to the containing class only. | Similar to Java, it can be used only on inner classes. |
| sealed | final | C# and Java classes marked sealed cannot be subclassed. | Similar to Java, this key-word can't be used in conjunction with the *abstract* keyword. |
| abstract | abstract | C# classes marked *abstract* cannot be instantiated. Subclasses may be instantiated if they implement all the abstract methods (if any). | Similar to Java, this key-word can't be used in conjunction with the C# *sealed* modifier. |

**NOTE**

Only nested classes permit the use of the *new* keyword. The *new* modifier specifies that the class hides an inherited member by the same name. Inner classes and Inheritance will be discussed in Chapter 6.

The C# class modifiers *public*, *protected*, *internal*, *protected internal*, and *private* all control access to classes. Let us examine these access modifiers and compare them with their Java equivalents.

Top–level classes (classes not contained in other classes) may use either the *public* or *internal* modifier. The *public* modifier in C# is the same as its Java counterpart. This class modifier indicates that the class (or type) is available to every other class. The following class declaration uses the C# *public* modifier to illustrate that the class is accessible from another class in a different namespace.

```
namespace Mapping
{
  public class MercatorProjection
  {
```

```
    // Methods and member variables go here.
    . . .
  }
}


using Mapping;
namespace Routing
{
  class MinimumFuelRoute
  {
    MercatorProjection mercatorProjection;

    // Other methods and member variables go here.
    . . .
  }
}
```

The *internal* modifier is unique to C# and indicates that a class is accessible only within the assembly that contains it. The following class declaration uses the C# *internal* modifier:

```
internal class AnotherCoolClass
{
  # methods and member variables go here
  . . .
}
```

In addition to the *public* and *internal* access modifiers, inner classes (classes contained in other classes) may use the *protected* and *private* modifiers. Nested classes may also use the *protected* and *internal* modifiers together. Chapter 6 will cover nested classes in greater detail. The following class declarations show the possible access modifiers for inner classes of a public class:

```
public class Artists
{

  protected class VanGogh
  {
  // Methods and member variables go here.
  . . .
```

```
        }

        private class Picasso
        {
        // Methods and member variables go here.
        . . .
        }

        protected internal class Lautrec
        {
        // Methods and member variables go here.
        . . .
        }

    }
```

This example declared a *public* class with three inner classes, each having a different access level. Table 5.3 shows the classes and their respective access.

**Table 5.3** C# Access Level for Inner Classes Contained in a *public* Class

| Class | Access |
| --- | --- |
| Artists | Accessible by everyone. |
| Artists.VanGogh | Accessible only within the Artists class and derived classes. |
| Artists.Picasso | Accessible only within the Artists class. |
| Artists.Lautrec | Accessible by classes within the same assembly and derived classes. |

The following class declarations show the possible access modifiers for inner classes of an *internal* class:

```
internal class Mathematicians
{

    protected class Hardy
    {
    # Methods and member variables go here.
    . . .
    }
```

```
private class Cantor

{

# Methods and member variables go here.

. . .

}


protected internal Gauss

{

# Methods and member variables go here.

. . .

}


}
```

This example declared an *internal* class with three inner classes, each having a different access level. Table 5.4 shows the classes and their respective access.

**Table 5.4** C# Access Level for Inner Classes Contained in an *internal* Class

| Class | Access |
|---|---|
| Mathematicians | Accessible within the containing assembly. |
| Mathematicians.Hardy | Accessible by derived classes within the same assembly. |
| Mathematicians.Cantor | Accessible only within the Mathematicians class. |
| Mathematicians.Gauss | Accessible by classes within the same assembly and derived classes. |

# Abstract Classes

C# and Java both support abstract classes. Abstract classes are classes that are not designed to be instantiated. These classes are designed only to be subclassed. You will learn more about abstract classes in Chapter 6, "Object-Oriented Programming."

The *abstract* modifier makes a class abstract. The following declaration is for an abstract class:

```
public abstract class Einstein

{
```

```
    # methods and member variables go here
    . . .
}
```

Abstract classes in C# are similar to Java—they play an important role in designing a class hierarchy. You may use abstract classes to tie together the common features of several derived classes.

## Sealed Classes

C#'s *sealed* modifier works like the Java *final* modifier. Apply the *sealed* modifier to classes to prevent them from being subclassed. Sealed classes often are used as a security feature to prevent overriding of class methods by derived classes. The following code declares a sealed class:

```
public sealed class Newton
{
    # Methods and member variables go here.
    . . .
}
```

Sealed classes in C# are similar to Java's *final* classes. An example of a *sealed* class is C#'s *String* class, which is similar to Java's *String* class in a way such that both can't be subclassed.

## Instance Variables

C# classes may include member variables or fields. Member variables make up the data of a class. When you declare a member variable you may also provide access modifiers similar to those used in class declarations. Class members may be of any value or reference type.

There are two important types of member variables—instance members and static members. We will start by examining instance members. The following class declaration has two instance members, a *double* and a *String*:

```
public class StockPrice
{
    public double price ;
    public String symbol ;
}
```

Let's look at some code that uses the *StockPrice* class. Since both member variables and the class are *public* the member variables may be accessed anywhere. The following code creates two *StockPrice* objects and initializes their members. Finally the code prints the ticker symbol and price for our two stocks.

```
using System;
public class StockPrice
{
    public double price ;
    public String symbol ;
}


public class StockApp
{
    static void Main()
    {
        // Create two objects.
        StockPrice stock1 = new StockPrice() ;
        StockPrice stock2 = new StockPrice() ;

        // Initialize objects.
        stock1.price  = 63.08d ;
        stock1.symbol = "MSFT" ;

        stock2.price  = 32.70d ;
        stock2.symbol = "INTC" ;

        System.Console.WriteLine( stock1.symbol + " " + stock1.price ) ;
        System.Console.WriteLine( stock2.symbol + " " + stock2.price ) ;
    }
}
```

## Output

```
MSFT 63.08
INTC 32.7
```

As you can see from the output, each object or instance of type *StockPrice* has its own data. Therefore every time you instantiate a new object, it gets its own copy of the instance members *price* and *symbol*. Any time you access an instance member, you must do it through an instance of the class. If at any time there are no instances, then there are no instance variables.

## Static Variables

Instance members are not the only type of member variable allowed in C#. Both C# and Java also support class member variables. Class member variables are sometimes called static variables since they use the *static* keyword in both languages. All instance members belong to a specific class instance or object. Class members belong to the class itself. Class members are shared among all the objects of a class type and may be accessed independent of any instance. Let's revisit the *StockPrice* class, but this time making the price field *static*.

```
public class StockPrice
{
    // Now price is static
    static public double price ;
    String symbol ;
}
```

In the previous example (where *price* was an instance variable) we simply accessed it using the dot (.) operator. This was necessary because an instance variable is bound to an instance or object. So the syntax is:

```
<instance name>.<variable name>
```

When written out in code, it would look like this:

```
stock1.price
```

Static variables are not bound to any specific instance. So in C# you will need to access them through the class as shown:

```
StockPrice.price = 10.1d ;
```

This is different from the Java behavior, which supports both types of access for class or static members. In Java the following line of code would be valid:

```
StockPrice.price = 10.1d ; // Valid in Java or C#
```

The following line of code would also be valid for Java but not in C#:

```
stock1.price    = 10.1d ; // Valid only in Java
```

Modify the previous example to use the new *StockPrice* class and you get:

```
using System;
public class StockPrice
{
    // Now price is static
    static public double price ;
    public String symbol ;
}


public class StockApp
{
    static void Main()
    {
        // Create two objects
        StockPrice stock1 = new StockPrice() ;
        StockPrice stock2 = new StockPrice() ;

        // Initialize objects
        StockPrice.price  = 63.08d ;
        stock1.symbol = "MSFT" ;

        StockPrice.price  = 32.70d ;
        stock2.symbol = "INTC" ;

        System.Console.WriteLine( stock1.symbol + " " + StockPrice.price ) ;
        System.Console.WriteLine( stock2.symbol + " " + StockPrice.price ) ;
    }
}
```

## Output

```
MSFT 32.7
INTC 32.7
```

Notice that the share prices for the two stocks seem to be the same—even though they were initialized with unique values they display the same value as 32.7. Why did this happen? There is only one copy of the static variable price, and in our application we set it first to 63.08d and then *reset* it to 32.70d. Static variables exist only once and serve all instances of the class. In fact it is possible to access a static variable even if no instances of a class exist. This would be the same as the behavior of static variables in Java.

## Constants as Static Members

Use static members to provide meta-information about a class such as the number of instances that have been created. Constants are also static members. Both C# and Java use static or class members for constants. C# has a special *const* keyword; Java uses the *final* or *static* and *final* keywords in combination to indicate a constant. In Java, *final* variables do not have to be initialized as a part of their declaration. Java *static finals* and C# *const* values must be initialized. Table 5.5 illustrates some C# constants and their Java equivalents.

**Table 5.5** C# and Java Constants

| C# Constant | Java Constant |
| --- | --- |
| public const int DaysInWeek = 7 ; | public static final in DAYS_IN_WEEK = 7 ; |
| public const double Pi = 3.1459d; | public static final double PI = 3.14159 ; |
| public const String Name = "Bill" ; | public static final String NAME = "Scott" ; |

# Using Methods

Classes combine data and related functionality. The functionality part of the class is called a method. C# methods are similar to Java methods. Methods have access to the member variables and the other methods of the class. Callers that invoke methods pass data to those methods in the form of parameters. Methods may also return values to the calling methods.

Here is a simple class combining both member variables and methods.

```
public class Point
{
  public int x ;
  public int y ;


  public double DistanceFromOrigin()
  {
    return Math.Sqrt( x*x + y*y ) ;
```

```
     }

   public Point Add( Point pt2 )
   {
      Point p = new Point() ;
      p.x = x + pt2.x ;
      p.y = y + pt2.y ;
      return p ;
   }

}
```

The *Point* class represents an (x,y) point. *Point* has two public member variables, *x* and *y*. The *DistanceFromOrigin()* method calculates the distance between the point and (0,0). The following program creates two *Point* objects, puts them together to get a third *Point* object, and then finds the distance from the third point to the origin.

```
using System;
public class Test
{
   static void Main()
   {
      Point p1 = new Point() ;
      p1.x = 4 ;
      p1.y = 5 ;

      Point p2 = new Point() ;
      p2.x = -6 ;
      p2.y = 3 ;

      Point p3 = p1.Add( p2 ) ;

      System.Console.WriteLine( "p3 = ( " + p3.x + ", " + p3.y + " )" ) ;

      Double d = p3.DistanceFromOrigin() ;

      System.Console.WriteLine( "p3 is " + d + " from the origin." ) ;
```

```
    }
}
```

## Output

```
p3 = ( -2, 8 )
p3 is 8.24621125123532 from the origin.
```

Some C# methods do not need to return values to their callers. Just like Java, C# uses a special return type called *void* for methods that do not return values.

Notice that the *Main* method in this example was declared as *static*. Static methods are like static variables. Static methods are associated with the class, not with any particular object or instance. Static methods may access static variables in a class. Let's add a *static* method to the *Point* class by declaring the *DistanceFromOrigin()* as *static*. The following code shows the new version of *Point*:

```
public class Point
{
  public int x ;
  public int y ;

  public static double DistanceFromOrigin( int x, int y )
  {
    return Math.Sqrt( x*x + y*y ) ;
  }

  public double DistanceFromOrigin()
  {
    return DistanceFromOrigin( x, y ) ;
  }

  public Point Add( Point pt2 )
  {
    Point p = new Point() ;
    p.x = x + pt2.x ;
    p.y = y + pt2.y ;
    return p ;
  }
}
```

In this example we added a static version of *DistanceFromOrigin()*. In order to reuse the code the nonstatic version of the method uses the static version. The following code uses the static *DistanceFromOrigin()*.

```
using System;
public class Test
{
  static void Main()
  {
    double dist = Point.DistanceFromOrigin( 3, -7 ) ;
    System.Console.WriteLine( dist ) ;
  }
}
```

Notice that we were able to call the *DistanceFromOrigin()* without first instantiating a *Point* object. This is exactly the same as how you would call a *static* method in Java.

## Access Modifiers

C# classes control access to their methods just like Java classes. C# supports five levels of access compared to Java's four. The five access modifiers are *public*, *internal*, *protected*, *protected internal*, and *private*.

Public access is the least restrictive of all. Members declared with the *public* modifier are accessible to any class. Public access in C# is exactly like public access in Java.

Internal access is the next level. The *internal* modifier guarantees that only code within the same assembly has access to a member. This is comparable to the default or package level access in Java.

The *protected* modifier grants access only to the class and its derived classes. *Protected* access may be used to allow derived classes to extend the functionality of base classes. The *protected* modifier is not quite similar to Java's *protected* access level. *Protected* level access in Java limits the class accessibility to the same package and derived classes (even if the derived classes are in a different package).

Java's *protected* access modifier is more similar to C#'s *protected internal* modifier. This access level is a hybrid of two others; in other words it is the union of the *protected* and *internal* modifiers. Any class in the same assembly or any subclass may access *protected internal* members.

The most restrictive access level is *private*. *Private* limits access to the class itself. Not even subclasses can access *private* members. Java defines *private* access exactly the same way as C# does.

## Developing & Deploying...

### Access within Classes

Variables and methods within a class are subject to two levels of access control. The first level of access is controlled by the access modifiers for the class. The second level of access is controlled by the modifiers applied to the members within the class.

Consider a public variable of a *protected* class as shown:

```
protected class Alpha
{
    public int betaValue = 100 ;
    // Other class stuff removed
}
```

Even though *betaValue* has *public* access, it is limited by the stricter modifier of the containing class. Therefore only the class *Alpha* and any subclasses of *Alpha* can access *betaValue*.

## Method Parameters

Many methods need information from their clients in order to perform their task. In C#, methods may take parameters similar to Java methods. In Java, all parameters are passed by value, meaning they are copied into the local stack frame of the method. You may be wondering about reference types in Java—their references are also passed by value.

The following program demonstrates pass by value in C#. The class *Foo* has a single method called *modify*. *Modify* takes an *int n* and modifies it. Since *n* is passed in by value it is copied into the *Modify()* method. When *n* is set to 1000 in the method, a local copy of *n* is modified, not the value *x* that is actually passed in.

```
public class Foo
{
```

```
    public void Modify( int n )
    {
        n = 1000 ;
    }
}


public class Test
{
    static void Main()
    {
        int x = 100 ;
        Foo f = new Foo() ;
        System.Console.WriteLine( "x before modify :" + x ) ;
        f.Modify(x) ;
        System.Console.WriteLine("x after modify :" + x ) ;
    }
}
```

## Output

```
x before modify :100
x after modify :100
```

In the output we see that the method does not change the value of *x*. The
*Modify()* method gets a copy of *x* (called locally *n*) and sets *n* to 1000—not *x*.

As discussed in Chapter 4, C# methods may also take variable parameter lists
by using the *params* keyword. The *params* keyword allows an array of parameters
to be specified as the last or rightmost parameter in the list. The following is the
declaration of a method with variable parameters:

```
public class Foo
{
  public void VarParamMethod( int a, double b, params int[] vals )
  {
    System.Console.WriteLine("a :" + a ) ;
    System.Console.WriteLine("b :" + b ) ;

    int sum = 0;
    for( int i = 0; i < vals.Length; i++ )
```

```
      {
        sum += vals[i] ;
      }

      System.Console.WriteLine("sum :" + sum ) ;
    }
}
```

The *vals* parameter can be replaced by a variable number of arguments of type *int* or by an array of type *int*. The *VarParamMethod()* method can be called by any of the following:

```
public class Test
{
  static void Main()
  {
    Foo f = new Foo();
    f.VarParamMethod( 1, 2.0, 3 ) ;
    f.VarParamMethod( 1, 2.0, 1, 2, 3, 4, 5 ) ;

    int [] x = new int[5] {3,4,5,6,7} ;
    f.VarParamMethod( 1, 2.0, x ) ;
  }
}
```

As you can see, using the *params* keyword in the argument list is more flexible than not using it. The method can take any number of integers as well as array of integers.

## The *ref* and *out* Method Parameters

Pass by value is not the end of the story in C#. C# also provides the *ref* and *out* keywords for passing parameters by reference. Parameters declared with *ref* are passed by reference, which prevents the overhead of copying objects into a method. Uninitialized *ref* parameters result in a compilation error. The following code is the *Modify()* method example updated for *ref* parameters.

```
public class Foo
{
  public void Modify( ref int n )
  {
```

```
        n = 1000 ;
    }
}


public class Test
{
    static void Main()
    {
        int x = 100 ;
        Foo f = new Foo() ;
        System.Console.WriteLine( "x before modify :" + x ) ;
        f.Modify( ref x) ;
        System.Console.WriteLine("x after modify :" + x ) ;
    }
}
```

## Output

```
X before modify :100
X after modify :1000
```

Notice in the output that calling *Modify* now really changes the value of *x*. You may use *ref* parameters to allow methods to modify values. Remember that the *ref* parameters must be initialized before use.

The *out* keyword allows uninitialized references to be passed into methods. The *out* keyword is similar to *ref* with one difference: *out* parameters do not need to be initialized before passing them into a method. However, when you write a method with *out* parameters they must be initialized in the method before the method returns or you will get a compilation error. The following is an example of an *out* parameter:

```
public class Test
{
    static void GetInts( int n, out int[] rand )
    {
        rand = new int[n];
        for (int i = 0; i < n; i++ )
        {
            rand[i] = i;
```

*ref -*
*must be*
*initialized*

*out*
*—no init*
*—can wait*
*in method*

```
      }
    }

  static void Main()
  {
    int [] a ;
    GetInts( 5, out a ) ;
    for( int i = 0; i < a.Length; i++)
    {
      System.Console.WriteLine( a[i] ) ;
    }
  }
}
```

This code uses a method to get an array of integers. The caller creates an uninitialized array reference and passes it as an *out* parameter to the *GetInts()* method. This allows *GetInts()* to create the array and pass it back. This is especially useful for passing multiple parameters where you do not want to create a *struct* or *class* to wrap them.

Callers must also use the *out* keyword when calling the method as shown:

```
Point q ;
MakePoint( out q ) ;
```

In Java all method parameters are passed by value. C# gives us the flexibility of passing parameters by reference with the *ref* and *out* keywords.

## Overloaded Methods

C# and Java both allow overloaded methods. Overloaded methods are methods that have the same name. In order to prevent any ambiguities, overloaded methods must have different parameter lists. Parameters may differ in number order and type. This should be very familiar as this concept is similar to Java. To review, Table 5.6 show both valid and invalid overloaded examples.

**Table 5.6** Valid and Invalid Overloaded Examples

| Methods | Valid | Explanation |
| --- | --- | --- |
| public void foo( int a )<br>public void foo( int a, int b )<br>public void foo( int a, int b, int c ) | Yes | The parameter lists are clearly different. |
| public int bar( int a )<br>public void bar( int a )<br>public double bar( int a ) | No | Only method parameters not return values are considered when comparing overloaded methods. |
| public void foo( Fubar f )<br>public void foo( ref Fubar f )<br>public void foo( out Fubar f ) | No | There is no Java equivalent to this overloaded case. Parameters must differ by more than just *ref* and *out*. |
| public int alpha( int a, int b )<br>public int alpha( int b, int a ) | No | Even though the parameter names are different both methods still take two *ints*. |
| public void foo( int a )<br>public void foo( int a, int b )<br>public void foo( int a, int b, int c )<br>public void foo( params int[] a ) | Yes | The last method is invoked only if you have an array or more than three *ints* as parameters. |

The following example is a simple class named *Foo* with an overloaded *Bar()* method.

```
public class Foo
{
  public void Bar()
  {
    System.Console.WriteLine( "Bar()" ) ;
  }


  public void Bar( int n )
  {
    System.Console.WriteLine( "Bar( int n )" ) ;
  }


  public void Bar( ref int n )
  {
    System.Console.WriteLine( "Bar( ref int n )" ) ;
```

```
    }

    public void Bar( params int[] n )
    {
        System.Console.WriteLine( "Bar( params int[] n )" ) ;
    }
}

public class Test
{
    static void Main()
    {
        Foo b = new Foo() ;
        b.Bar() ;
        b.Bar( 1 ) ;

        int n = 10 ;

        b.Bar( ref n ) ;
        b.Bar( 1, 2 ) ;
    }
}
```

## Output

```
Bar()
Bar( int n )
Bar( ref int n )
Bar( params int[] n )
```

Each of the calls to a *Bar()* method in *main* resolves unambiguously to one of the overloaded *Bar()* methods. The first call *b.Bar()* resolves to *Bar()* because only one *Bar* method has no parameters. The second call *b.Bar( 1 )* could have been handled by either by *Bar( int n )* or *Bar( Params int[] n)*—it gets handled by *Bar( int n )* because the method with the exact match is preferred over the variable parameter list. The third call, *b.Bar( ref n )*, is resolved because of the *ref* parameter. Finally, *b.Bar( 1, 2 )* matches *Bar( params int[] n )* because there is no other version of *Bar()* with two parameters.

# Creating Objects

Similar to Java, C# primitives like *int, double, byte,* and so on are value types and are stored on the stack. And like Java, objects in C# are reference types that are stored on the heap. The heap is unstructured memory also known as the *free store.* This section will talk about creating objects in C#.

Creating objects is fairly straightforward. In C# just like Java, you use the *new* operator to create or instantiate an object. The normal process is to create a reference to an object. Then you instantiate an object and assign it to the reference. You could also do both steps at once. The following code demonstrates this process.

```
Point p ;                 // Create a reference.
p = new Point() ;         // Create the object.
Point q = new Point() ;   // Create both in one step.
```

# Constructors

Classes in C# also have special methods called constructors that are responsible for initializing objects of the class type. Constructors have the same name as the class itself and have no return type, which is similar to Java. If you do not provide a constructor, the class is instantiated using a default constructor. Earlier in this chapter we used the *Point* class in some sample code. The *Point* class represents (x,y) points. In our sample code we had to create *Point* objects in two steps. The first step was to use the *new* operator and instantiate the *Point* object. The next step was to set the initial $x$ and $y$ values.

Let us revisit the *Point* class and see whether we can simplify the construction and initialization process. Whenever we need a point we will need to give it an $x$ and a $y$ value. Therefore we will create a constructor for the *Point* class that takes and sets an $x$ and $y$ value. Consider the new and improved *Point* class:

```
public class Point
{
    public int x ;
    public int y ;

    public Point( int x, int y )
    {
        this.x = x ;
        this.y = y ;
    }
}
```

```
public double DistanceFromOrigin()
{
    return System.Math.Sqrt( x*x + y*y ) ;
}


public Point Add( Point pt2 )
{
    // This method changed to math the new constructor
    return new Point( x + pt2.x, y + pt2.y ) ;
}
}
```

**NOTE**

Both C# and Java use the *this* reference. In C#, it is a reference of a class to itself. It has its origins in Smalltalk's *this self* reference. You will most likely use the *this* reference to differentiate method parameters from instance members.

Now that the *Point* class has a constructor we can construct and initialize it on one step. In the following code we will construct some *Points*, add them together to get a third *Point*, and then calculate its distance from the origin.

```
public class Test
{
  static void Main()
  {
    Point a = new Point( 5, 3 ) ;
    Point b = new Point( -2, 1 ) ;
    Point c = a.Add( b ) ;

    System.Console.WriteLine( "c is " + c.DistanceFromOrigin() +
                        " from (0,0) " ) ;
  }
}
```

*Output*

```
c is 5 from (0,0) ;
```

As you can see, the syntax and semantics for constructors are the same in both Java and C#. Let's continue our discussion and look at how you can over-load constructors.

# Overloading Constructors

You can overload constructors in C# just like regular methods. Consider the *Point* class. It has a constructor that takes (x,y) coordinates. What if you wanted to create default points, maybe points at (0,0)? The solution is to create another overloaded constructor. Constructor overloading is subject to the same rules as method overloading. The following code shows the *Point* class with overloaded constructors:

```
public class Point
{
    public int x ;
    public int y ;

    public Point()
    {
        x = 0 ;
        y = 0 ;
    }

    public Point( int x, int y )
    {
        this.x = x ;
        this.y = y ;
    }

    // Other methods removed for simplicity
}
```

You may also implement this class with constructor chaining. Constructor chaining uses one constructor and calls another. Note that the second (or chained constructor) is invoked first. The syntax is shown in the following class:

# C#

```
public class Point
{
   public int x ;
   public int y ;

   public Point():this( 0,0 )
   {
   // This constructor does nothing; instead it calls
   // the other constructor passing in 0, 0.
   }

   public Point( int x, int y )
   {
      this.x = x ;
      this.y = y ;
   }

   // Other methods removed for simplicity
}
```

Constructor chaining in Java also uses the *this* keyword. However, it's used more like a method call, and differs from with C# only in syntax. This is the Java version of the *Point* class.

# Java

```
public class Point
{
  public int x ;
  public int y ;

  public Point()
  {
     // This constructor does nothing; instead it calls
     // the other constructor passing in 0, 0.
     this( 0,0 ) ;
  }
```

```
public Point( int x, int y )
{
    this.x = x ;
    this.y = y ;
}


// Other methods removed for simplicity
}
```

# Static Constructors

Static constructors in C# are not really constructors at all; that is, they do not instantiate objects. The function of static constructors is to initialize the class itself. Static constructors look like regular constructors and they have the same name as the class, with a *static* modifier in front. Java has a similar concept in its static initializers.

Static constructors may not access instance members of a class and they do not have access modifiers. They may not access instance methods of a class either. Their purpose is to initialize the class—especially its static variables. C# static constructors may not be called explicitly and they are not for use with the *new* operator. They are called automatically when a class is loaded, which is similar behavior to Java's static initializers. The following program has a class that uses a static constructor to initialize some static variables.

```
public class Delta
{
  static Delta()
  {
    System.Console.WriteLine(  "Static Constructor" ) ;
  }

  public Delta(int n)
  {
    System.Console.WriteLine(  "Regular Constructor" ) ;
  }
}
```

```
public class Test
{
  static void Main()
  {
    Delta a = new Delta(1);
    Delta b = new Delta(2);
    Delta c = new Delta(3);
    Delta d = new Delta(4);
  }
}
```

When you run this program you will see that the static constructor is called before any of the instance constructors. The output of this program follows.

## Output

```
Static Constructor
Regular Constructor
Regular Constructor
Regular Constructor
Regular constructor
```

C# static constructors look like constructors with a *static* modifier. Java static initializers are blocks of code outside of any method set apart with the *static* keyword. Here is the equivalent Java code:

## Java

```
class Delta
{
  static
  {
    System.out.println(  "Static Initializer" ) ;
  }

  public Delta(int n)
  {
    System.out.println(  "Regular Constructor" ) ;
  }
```

```
}

public class Test
{
 public static void main( String[] argv )
  {
    Delta a = new Delta(1);
    Delta b = new Delta(2);
    Delta c = new Delta(3);
    Delta d = new Delta(4);
  }
}
```

## Output

```
Static Initializer
Regular Constructor
Regular Constructor
Regular Constructor
Regular Constructor
```

As you can see, the Java program produced similar output. Notice that the main difference between C#'s static constructors and Java's static initializers is just syntax, but they provide the same functionality.

# Destroying Objects

One of the first things you learn to love about C# programming is that you do not have to explicitly destroy objects in memory. One of the first things you learn to hate about C# is that you can't explicitly destroy objects in memory. Both Java and C# provide automatic memory management, which generally adds to program correctness and robustness. Java offers developers very little flexibility when it comes to memory management, and programmers often complain about their inability to explicitly invoke the garbage collector. On the other hand, C# provides developers a variety of options when it comes to memory management.

## Memory Management and Garbage Collection

Similar to Java, one of the great features of C# is automatic garbage collection. Most of the C# classes you write will use the CLR's garbage collector. When objects are no longer in use and no longer referenced the CLR is free to reclaim them. This saves you a lot of time by not having to worry about writing cleanup code for their classes. The problem is that the CLR will free the objects whenever it chooses to. Like Java, C#'s garbage collection is nondeterministic. You can determine when an object is eligible for garbage collection but you cannot guarantee when it will be garbage collected.

In some situations, you may want to manually manage how your objects get cleaned up. Both languages provide support for this. In Java you can use the *finalize()* method to free up resources during garbage collection. In C# you have a couple of different methods to assist in resource management. C# classes may have destructors as well as *Finalize()*, *Dispose()*, or *Close()* methods. Let's look at how to use these methods.

# C#'s Destructor

C# classes may have a destructor as well as constructors. In C#, destructors for all objects are invoked prior to program termination. Destructors look like methods with no return type or access modifiers. They are named after their class and their names are preceded by a tilde (~) symbol. The following is a destructor for the *Point* class.

```
~Point()
{
    // Clean up here
}
```

Destructors take no parameters and return no values. You must never attempt to invoke a destructor directly. C# destructors are a syntactic shortcut for the *Object.Finalize()* method. You should generally implement the *Finalize()* method instead of destructors if you have unmanaged resources to free.

**NOTE**

*IDisposable* is an interface. It is not limited strictly to C#; it is part of Microsoft's COM technology. It provides a common mechanism for cleaning up components of all sorts, not just C#. Interfaces like *IDisposable* help C# fit into the .NET framework. *IDisposable* defines a single method, *Dispose*.

# The *Finalize*, *Dispose*, and *Close* Methods

The real work of memory management is done through the *Dispose()* method of the *IDisposable* interface and the class destructor. When the garbage collector frees an object it calls the object's destructor. The problem with the destructor is that it is called as a part of the garbage collection process. There is no way to determine exactly when the destructor is invoked. Unless we suppress finalization, the garbage collector will call the destructor on every object that needs to be cleaned up.

The destructor should be used to free shared resources in a program. There is no need to free memory resources in the destructor. One common use of the destructor is to free GUI resources like window handles or pens. The problem with this scenario is that although we may know when we are done with an object and its resources, we still have no control over *when* the destructor is called. Important resources could still be tied up even after we are through with them in our code.

The *Dispose()* method provides a callable method to clean up resources. The destructor cannot be explicitly called, whereas the *Dispose()* method *should* be called when an object's resources are no longer needed. If you have worked with the Windows API you have probably invoked a dispose method on objects.

Neither the destructor nor *Dispose* is the complete solution. If you have resources that must be freed in your class, the best practice is to provide both a destructor and a *Dispose()* method. Clients should call *Dispose* when they wish to free resources. If so, *Dispose* suppresses further *finalize* (i.e., *destructor*) calls on the object. If a client does not explicitly call *Dispose*, the garbage collector will eventually invoke the destructor and free the resources. In this example the *hwnd.Release()* method frees a Window in Win32. The following code is for a class that correctly frees a resource in both a *destructor* and a *Dispose* method.

```
public class ResourceUser : IDisposable
{

// Other methods and variables not shown

    public void Dispose ()
    {
       hwnd.Release ();
       GC.SuppressFinalization(this); // prevent Finalize
    }

    ~ResourceUser ()
```

```
    {
        hwnd.Release ();
    }
}
```

It is common in C# for some classes to provide a *Close()* method instead of *Dispose()*. Classes that represent files, sockets, or connections all sound better with close semantics. We can add a *Close()* method to our *ResourceUser* class as shown:

```
public class ResourceUser : IDisposable
{

// Other methods and variables not shown

    public void Close ()
    {
        Dispose() ;
    }

    public void Dispose ()
    {
        hwnd.Release ();
        GC.SuppressFinalization(this); // Prevent Finalize
    }

    ~ResourceUser ()
    {
        hwnd.Release ();
    }
}
```

## The *using* Statement

A well-behaved program will call *Dispose()* or *Close()* on objects that utilize resources. In C# you have the option of calling *Dispose()* explicitly after you're done with the object, or you can put the object in a *using* block. By putting an object in a *using* block, the CLR immediately will invoke the object's *Dispose()* method at the end of the block statement. The syntax is the following:

```
using( object )
```

```
{
    // Object gets used here and then Dispose
}
```

The following program demonstrates a *using* block as well as a destructor, the *Dispose* and *Close* methods.

```
using System ;

public class DeltaReport

{
 int InstanceNumber;
 public DeltaReport (int InstanceNumber)
{
   this.InstanceNumber = InstanceNumber;
   Console.WriteLine("DeltaReport {0}" , InstanceNumber);
 }
}

public class Delta : Idisposable
{
 int n ;
 public Delta( int n )
 {
  this.n = n ;
  DeltaReport MyReport = new DeltaReport(n);
 }

 public void Dispose ()
 {
  DeltaReport MyReport = new DeltaReport(this.n);
  GC.SuppressFinalize(this); // Prevent Finalize
 }


 ~Delta()
 {
  DeltaReport MyReport = new DeltaReport(this.n);
```

```
    }
}

public class Test
{
  static void Main()
  {
    Delta d1 = new Delta(1) ;
    Delta d2 = new Delta(2) ;
    Delta d3 = new Delta(3) ;
    d1 = null ;
    using ( d3 )
    {
      Delta d4 = new Delta(4) ;
    }
    d2.Dispose() ;


  }
}
```

This application creates some *Delta* objects and then calls *Dispose* or *Close* on two of them. One of the references gets set to null and another is in a using block. The output of this program follows.

## Output

```
Dispose : 3
Dispose : 2
~Delta : 4
~Delta : 1
```

You will notice that the cleanup begins with object *d3*. Object *d3* is first because it is used in a using block. The *d2* object gets cleaned up next because *Dispose* is called explicitly. Even though *d1* is set to *null* before *d4* goes out of scope, *d4* is cleaned up first. Unless you put an object in a *using* block or explicitly call *Dispose* (or *Close*), cleanup is left to the garbage collector and the behavior is not deterministic.

The *using* block guarantees that the *Dispose()* method is called at the end of the block. It's a good idea to put objects that use valuable resources in a using statement. That way you're guaranteed that the *Dispose* method will be called automatically.

# Summary

C# classes are similar to Java classes. Use them to encapsulate data and the methods that operate on that data. C# provides a rich set of access modifiers so that you can choose the appropriate level of encapsulation for your problem domain. In addition to method overloading C# provides for *ref*, *out* and variable parameters.

C# objects are automatically garbage collected just like Java objects. However C# gives you some additional options by offering *dispose, finalize,* and *destructors.*

C# provides a class model that is similar to Java's but there are some traps for the unsuspecting Java programmer. However if you take the time to learn the details you will discover that even though C# differs from Java in many ways, your Java experience can be applied to help you produce well-designed robust C# classes.

# Solutions Fast Track

## Using Classes

- ☑ Classes encapsulate data and related methods.
- ☑ Classes may have static and/or instance members.
- ☑ Static constructors are invoked before instantiating an object.
- ☑ Constructors may invoke each other (constructor chaining).

## Using Methods

- ☑ Methods may be overloaded if their parameters differ in number, order, or type.
- ☑ Static methods may not be called in the context of an object, only of the class.
- ☑ C# methods support variable argument lists.

## Creating Objects

- ☑ Similar to Java, C# primitives like *int, double, byte,* and so on are value types that are stored on the stack, and objects in C# are reference types that are stored on the heap.

☑ Classes in C# also have special methods called constructors that are responsible for initializing objects of the class type. Constructors have the same name as the class itself and have no return type, which is also similar to Java.

☑ You can overload constructors in C# just like regular methods.

☑ Static constructors in C# are not really constructors at all, in that they do not instantiate objects. The function of static constructors is to initialize the class itself.

## Destroying Objects

☑ Users may explicitly invoke *Dispose()* to free an object's resources.

☑ *Finalize()* is called only by the garbage collector.

☑ Destructors are a syntactic shortcut for *Finalize()*.

☑ A *using* block guarantees that *Dispose()* will be called immediately and should be used for shared resources.

# Frequently Asked Questions

The following Frequently Asked Questions, answered by the authors of this book, are designed to both measure your understanding of the concepts presented in this chapter and to assist you with real-life implementation of these concepts. To have your questions about this chapter answered by the author, browse to **www.syngress.com/solutions** and click on the **"Ask the Author"** form.

**Q:** How do I define global constants in C#?

**A:** It is common practice to create a class with nothing but constant members. Ideally to prevent instantiation, such a class would be sealed and would have a private constructor.

**Q:** Is it dangerous to call *Dispose* (or *Close*) more than once on the same object?

**A:** It depends on the object. For example if your *Dispose* releases a window handle, the best practice would be to test whether the handle is null, release the handle, and set the handle to null. So if the handle is already null, we won't release it twice.

**Q:** Since a static constructor has no parameters, can a class with a static constructor still have a default constructor?

**A:** Yes, static constructors are fundamentally different from normal constructors so there is no ambiguity.

**Q:** Is there any way to force garbage collection in C#?

**A:** Yes, you can use the System.GC.Collect method.

# Chapter 6

# Object-Oriented Programming

## Solutions in this chapter:

- Inheritance
- Polymorphism
- Inner Classes
- Using Interfaces

☑ Summary

☑ Solutions Fast Track

☑ Frequently Asked Questions

# Introduction

In the last chapter, you learned about C# objects and classes. As you know, there is more to object-oriented programming (OOP) than just classes and objects. This chapter will explain most of the remaining OOP concepts that you will need to know. You will learn about inheritance, polymorphism, inner classes, and interfaces.

The chapter will begin by discussing the C# inheritance model. Inheritance is the technique of deriving new classes from existing classes. Next, you will be introduced to the concept of polymorphism, which allows for method over-riding. In that section, you will learn about virtual methods and versioning with the *new* and *override* keywords, which is a feature of C# that is not found in Java.

The next part of the chapter will describe C#'s support for inner classes. The chapter will wrap up by discussing interfaces. Interfaces are a way for dealing with the common situation of wanting an object to derive behavior from two different parents, sometimes referred to as multiple inheritance.

# Inheritance

C#'s inheritance model is very similar to Java, with syntax being the only major difference. To start off, let's review the theory behind this concept.

Inheritance is a relationship between classes. In this relationship, a *child* class inherits the members and methods of a *parent* class. Inheritance is an important part of both the C# and Java object models. In both Java and C# all classes are derived from a common base class. Java classes all subclass *java.lang.Object*, and C# classes all subclass *Object*.

In object-oriented programming, inheritance is a *strong* and *fundamental* relationship. For example, I have a son who plays in a high school marching band. In the marching band, he fulfills many roles but the role that is strong and funda-mental is that he is my son. The fact that he is a trumpet player, a section leader, or a sophomore is secondary. In an object-oriented system I would model the father-son relationship using inheritance. Later in this chapter we will learn how to model the weaker relationships. From the point of view of the band director the strong relationship is membership. The choice of fundamental relationship is not always obvious—it often depends upon your point of view. When you write C# code it will be your job to identify fundamental relationships and differen-tiate between these and weaker relationships.

In either C# or Java you will often create a hierarchy of related classes. For example, a payroll system might have an *Employee* class. All companies have employees, so the *Employee* class is a reasonable abstraction. However, is this abstraction enough? Most payroll systems have more than just employees—they have many different kinds of employees. A payroll system might have salaried employees, commissioned employees and hourly employees. Some companies might even have truck drivers, lobbyists, and who knows what other kinds of employees.

---

**NOTE**

The Unified Modeling Language (UML) is a standard language for representing object-oriented code, applications, or designs. Before UML there were several competing notational systems, but today almost all developers use UML. This chapter will use UML class diagrams to show the relationships between classes.

In class diagrams the boxes represent classes and the arrows point from derived classes to base classes.

---

Even though a company may have many different types of employees, they are all employees. In code, they are all child classes derived from the base class *Employee*. Figure 6.1 is a UML diagram showing the *Employee* class and the four specialized types of employees for a mythical company called Acme Widgets Inc.

**Figure 6.1** Class Hierarchy for Acme Widgets Inc.

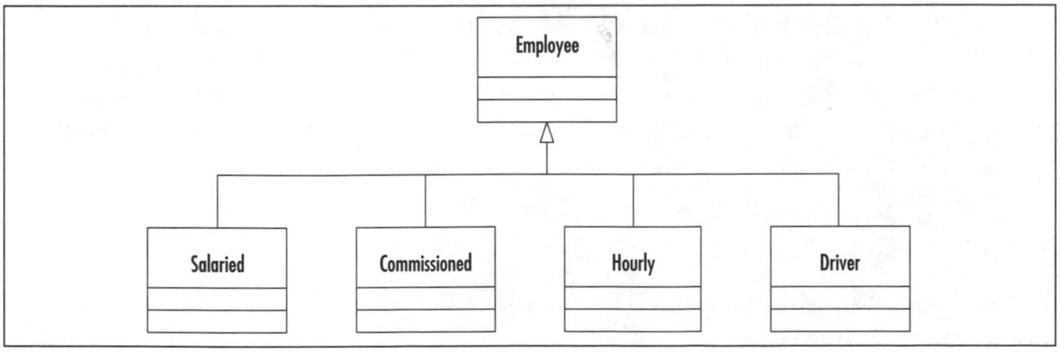

In the class hierarchy of Figure 6.1, you see that the classes *Salaried*, *Commission*, *Hourly*, and *Driver* all specialize *Employee*. The *Employee* class defines attributes common to all employees and the subclasses define those attributes unique to the specific employee type. Within a class hierarchy common attributes (and methods) are defined at the highest level at which they are common.

All employees have names and social security numbers. Salaried employees have a monthly salary. Hourly employees have a rate and hours worked. Commissioned employees have a sales and commission percentage. Truck Drivers have a base salary, miles, and rate per mile. Figure 6.2 shows the Acme Widgets class hierarchy with class attributes displayed (constructors and methods are not shown).

**Figure 6.2** Class Hierarchy for Acme Widgets Inc. with Attributes

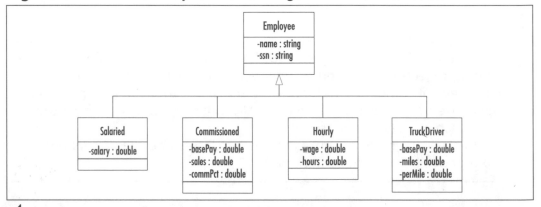

## Developing & Deploying...

### What's in a Name?

In his play, *Romeo and Juliet,* Shakespeare asks the question, "What's in a name? That which we call a Rose by any other name would smell as sweet." The terminology used to describe inheritance differs from programming language to programming language. Academic literature often uses its own set of terms. The following list defines the terms used to describe the classes in an inheritance relationship:

- *Parent* class and *Child* class
- *Super* class and *Sub* class
- *Base* class and *Derived* class

There are also a variety of terms used for the relationship itself. If a class A is a parent class and another class B is a child class of A, we use the following terminology:

**Continued**

- B subclasses A
- B derives from A
- B specializes A
- B extends A
- B is A

You are likely to see all of these terms in use by C# and other object-oriented programmers.

# Defining a Base Class

When you declare a class in C# you need to identify its base class. As we mentioned earlier, all classes in C# are derived from *Object*. If you derive a class directly from *Object*, there is no need to specify it. If you derive a class from any other class you must indicate the parent class in the class declaration.

Both Java and C# offer support for single inheritance. A C# class is allowed to have only one base class. Of course that base class may have its own base class, and so on. This limitation removes a great deal of the complexity associated with other OOPLs like C++. Later in this chapter we will see that C# classes may implement multiple *interfaces*.

In Java we use the *extends* keyword to indicate inheritance. C# uses a colon (:) to indicate a base class. Let us look at an example from the class hierarchy shown in Figure 6.2. The following is the Java version of the *Employee* and *Salaried* classes.

## *Java*

```
// Java base class
public class Employee
{
    protected String name ;
    protected String   ssn ;
}


// Java derived class
public class Salaried extends Employee
{
    protected long salary ;
```

```
    public Salaried(String name, String ssn, double salary)
    {
        this.name   = name ;
        this.ssn    = ssn ;
        this.salary = salary ;
    }
}
```

This is the C# version of the *Employee* and *Salaried* classes. As you can see, in the *Salaried* class we use the colon to indicate that *Salaried* is derived from *Employee*.

## C#

```
// C# base class
public class Employee
{
    protected string name ;
    protected string ssn ;
}


// C# derived class
public class Salaried : Employee
{
    protected double salary ;

    public Salaried(string name, string ssn, double salary)
    {
        this.name   = name ;
        this.ssn    = ssn ;
        this.salary = salary ;
    }
}
```

# Calling Base Class Constructors

In our previous code example we did not give the *Employee* class any constructors. The *Salaried* class constructor does all the work of initializing variables in both the *Employee* and *Salaried* classes. In the Acme Widgets Inc. class hierarchy (Figure 6.2) this means that we would have to initialize the *Employee* class variables in the constructors for *all* four of the derived classes. Whenever you have identical code in multiple places it is a clear sign that there is a problem with your design. In order to solve this problem we will examine the issue of base class constructors.

The following code snippet instantiates a *Salaried* object as previously defined.

```
Salaried s = new Salaried( "Albert",
                           "123456789",
                           80000.00 ) ;
```

The *Employee* class does not define any constructors so it has a *default* constructor. The system first invokes the *Employee* default constructor, then the *Salaried* constructor. Let's look at how we can improve this code. In order to prevent duplication of code, we will implement a constructor in the *Employee* class. This new constructor will initialize the *name* and *ssn* variables that are common to all *Employee* objects. We'll also add some *WriteLine()* method calls to show the order in which the object is constructed.

In many real applications you will write multiple (overloaded) constructors for your classes. As soon as you explicitly create *any* constructor(s) for a class, you must explicitly choose the constructor to invoke. When the class had no explicit constructors, the system always invoked the default constructor. Now that the *Employee* class has a constructor, the *Salaried* constructor must specify which *Employee* constructor to invoke.

We will use a *constructor initializer* in the derived class constructor to specify a base class constructor. Insert a *: base(arguments)* after the derived class constructor declaration. Make sure that the arguments match the signature of the appropriate base class constructor.

The following is a C# application that creates a *Salaried* object that uses a constructor initializer to invoke a specific *Employee* class constructor.

```
// C# base class
public class Employee
{
    protected string name ;
    protected string ssn ;

    public Employee(string name, string ssn)
    {
```

```
        System.Console.WriteLine("Employee") ;

        this.name   = name ;

        this.ssn    = ssn ;

    }

}


// C# derived class
public class Salaried : Employee
{
    protected double salary ;

    public Salaried(string name,

                    string ssn,

                    double salary) : base(name, ssn)

    {
        System.Console.WriteLine("Salaried") ;

        this.salary = salary ;

    }

}


public class Test
{
    static void Main()
    {
        new Salaried(

                "Albert",

                "123456789",

                80000.00 ) ;


    }

}
```

If you compile and run this application you will get the following output:

## *Output*

```
Employee
Salaried
```

This output clearly demonstrates that the order of construction is base class followed by derived class. Both C# and Java strictly follow this order of construction.

Calling base class constructors is very different in C# than it is in Java. C# uses the *base* keyword, and Java uses the *super* keyword. C# uses a constructor initializer, and Java uses the *super* keyword more like a method call. In Java the *super* keyword must be the first line of code in a derived class constructor. The following is the equivalent Java versions of *Employee* and *Salaried*.

## Java

```java
// Java base class
public class Employee
{
    protected String name ;
    protected String ssn ;

    public Employee(String name, String ssn)
    {
        System.out.println("Employee") ;
        this.name    = name ;
        this.ssn     = ssn ;
    }
}


// Java derived class
public class Salaried extends Employee
{
    protected double salary ;

    public Salaried(String name,
                    String ssn,
                    double salary)
    {
        super(name, ssn) ;
        System.out.println("Salaried") ;
        this.salary = salary ;
    }
}
```

# Polymorphism

Polymorphism comes from two Greek root words: *poly* means many and *morphe* means form. The idea is that something may take on many forms. In the Acme Widgets Inc. class hierarchy of Figures 6.1 and 6.2, we see a base class *Employee* and the derived classes *Salaried, Commissioned, Hourly*, and *TruckDriver*. If the chairman of Acme Widgets Inc. calls an all-employee meeting, the attendees will include managers (who are salaried), sales staff (who are commissioned), production line workers (who are hourly), and truck drivers. So for the purpose of holding an employee meeting, all employees are treated simply as employees.

If we apply our definition of polymorphism we see that the *Employee* class takes on four specialized forms (*Salaried, Commissioned, Hourly*, and *TruckDriver*). In fact, in object-oriented programming we often are more concerned with the general or common form than the specific. It is quite common that we will use base class references to refer to derived class objects. Consider the following C# code.

```
Employee [] employees = new Employee[6] ;


employees[0] = new Salaried(
                    "Becky","123456789",80000) ;
employees[1] = new Commissioned(
                    "Chuck","234567891",20000,.05) ;
employees[2] = new Hourly(
                    "Deb","345678912",19.75) ;
employees[3] = new TruckDriver(
                    "Earl","456789123",20000,0.30) ;
employees[4] = new Salaried(
                    "Fae","567891234",110000) ;
employees[5] = new Hourly(
                    "Greg","678912345",15.50) ;
```

In the previous code snippet we created two *Salaried*, one *Commissioned*, two *Hourly*, and one *TruckDriver* objects. If you look closely you see that although we created all of these different kinds of objects, we created only one kind of reference to access them—employee references. You may wonder whether this code will even compile—not only does it compile but the practice of instantiating many different types of objects and keeping a single kind of reference is common in all object-oriented programming. What we mean by this code is that all the different specialized types of *Employee* are just *Employee*s. The *Employee* class created these other forms, so polymorphically all of these objects are *Employees.*

This polymorphic relationship is directional and is based on inheritance. In UML diagrams the inheritance arrow points from derived class to base class, so we can have *Employee* references to *Commissioned* objects but not the reverse. For example the following C# code is correct:

```
Employee e = new Salaried("Harry","789123456",55000) ;
```

On the other hand the more specific (derived) cannot point to the more general (base). Therefore the following code will not compile:

```
Salaried s = new Employee("Harry","789123456") ;
```

The *Salaried* class has all the attributes and methods of the *Employee* class. However the *Employee* class does not have all of the attributes and methods of the *Salaried* class. Therefore we can say polymorphically that a *Salaried* object is an *Employee* object. Or even more strongly, that all *Salaried* objects are *Employee* objects. However the reverse is *not* true. Only some *Employee* objects are *Salaried* objects. The rule is that base class references may be used to refer to derived class objects.

# Abstract Classes

Let us revisit the class hierarchy of Figure 6.1. Acme Widgets Inc. has four kinds of employees represented by the *Salaried, Commissioned, Hourly,* and *TruckDriver* classes. But let us consider the *Employee* class itself. If all of the people who work for Acme Widgets Inc. fit into one of the four categories (derived classes), why do we need the *Employee* class in the first place?

From a design point of view, even though there are no workers at the company who are *just* employees it is still useful to have an *Employee* class in the system. The *Employee* class does not represent any particular type of employee, since it represents *all* types of employees. The *Employee* class is an abstraction that allows us to combine all attributes and methods that are common to all employees in one place. In this class hierarchy we will never actually instantiate an *Employee* but only subclass it. Therefore we would make *Employee* an *abstract* class.

In both C# and Java, abstract classes are used in class hierarchies to tie together commonalities among derived classes. You may never instantiate an abstract class. The *abstract* keyword identifies and abstracts a class in both C# and in Java. We will make the *Employee* class abstract by using the *abstract* modifier in its declaration as shown in the following code sample:

```
// C# abstract class
public abstract class Employee
{
   protected string name ;
   protected string ssn ;

   protected Employee(string name, string ssn)
   {
      System.Console.WriteLine("Employee") ;
      this.name    = name ;
      this.ssn     = ssn ;
   }
}
```

You may wonder why a class that cannot be instantiated needs a constructor. The reason is that derived classes need to have a way to initialize the base class part just like they did when the base class was not abstract. Notice also that there is no longer any need to make the constructor public. Since the class will be constructed only by derived classes we will declare it to be *protected*.

In UML notation we use italics to indicate abstract classes. Figure 6.3 shows our class hierarchy with an abstract *Employee* class.

**Figure 6.3** Class Hierarchy for Acme Widgets Inc. with Abstract Employee Class

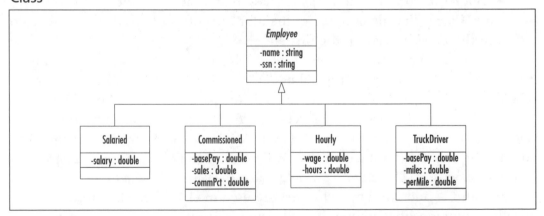

UML class diagrams are a powerful way to visualize your classes. Take a close look at the class diagram in Figure 6.3. Notice that both the *TruckDriver* and *Commissioned* classes have a *basePay* attribute. In order to prevent duplication, let's

*refactor* the classes and move the common attribute up the hierarchy. We will accomplish this by creating a new class called *BasePlus*.

*BasePlus* will be a child of *Employee* and will be the parent of both *TruckDriver* and *Commissioned*. Figure 6.4 shows the refactored Acme Widgets Inc. hierarchy.

**Figure 6.4** Refactored Class Hierarchy for Acme Widgets Inc.

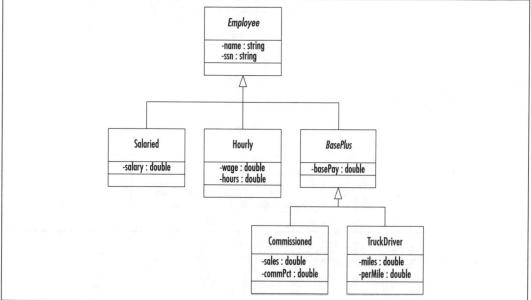

In the refactored class hierarchy of Figure 6.4, the *BasePlus* class is an abstract class. On further reflection, the *BasePlus* and *Salaried* classes look very similar. We can do one slightly more radical refactoring and replace *BasePlus* with *Salaried*.

In Figure 6.5, the *Salaried* class is not abstract since many actual employees are salaried. This hierarchy suggests that *Commissioned* and *TruckDriver* employees are specialized versions of *Salaried*. You may end up doing this sort of refactoring more than once in a single project.

Now that we've reviewed the theory behind polymorphism and abstraction, let's look at actual code. The following is the source code for the Acme Widgets Inc. class hierarchy:

**Figure 6.5** Final Class Hierarchy for Acme Widgets Inc.

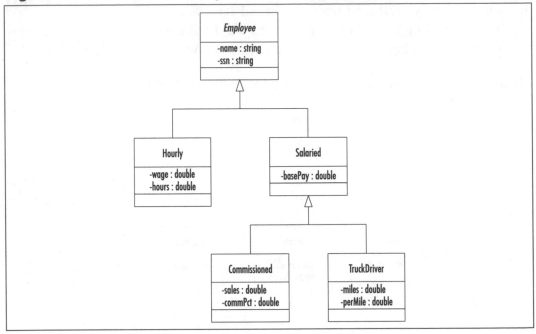

```
public abstract class Employee
{
  protected string name ;
  protected string ssn ;

  public Employee(string name, string ssn)
  {
    this.name   = name ;
    this.ssn    = ssn ;
  }
}


public class Hourly : Employee
{
  protected double wage ;
  protected double hours ;

  public Hourly(
          string name,
```

```
                    string ssn,

                    double wage,

                    double hours) : base(name,ssn)

   {

     this.wage  = wage ;

     this.hours = hours ;

   }

}


public class Salaried : Employee

{

  protected double basePay ;


  public Salaried(

                string name,

                string ssn,

                double basePay) : base(name,ssn)

   {

     this.basePay = basePay ;

   }

}


public class Commissioned : Salaried

{

  protected double sales ;

  protected double commPct ;


  public Commissioned(

                string name,

                string ssn,

                double basePay,

                double sales,

                double commPct ) : base(name,ssn,basePay)

   {

     this.sales   = sales ;

     this.commPct = commPct ;
```

```
      }
}


public class TruckDriver : Salaried
{
  protected double miles ;
  protected double perMile ;

  public TruckDriver(
            string name,
            string ssn,
            double basePay,
            double miles,
            double perMile ) : base(name,ssn,basePay)
  {
    this.miles   = miles ;
    this.perMile = perMile ;
  }
}
```

# The *abstract* Modifier

Similar to Java, C# provides support for abstract methods which are familiar to most of you. An abstract method is a method that *must* have an implementation in a derived class. This is because abstract methods have no implementation in their own class. For example, let's consider the following C# class:

```
abstract class Alpha
{
  public void Beta()
  {
    System.Console.WriteLine("Beta") ;
  }

  public abstract void Delta() ;
}
```

The *Alpha* class has two methods: *Beta()*, with no qualification, and *Delta()*, which is *abstract*. What would be the purpose of a class like this? The abstract class provides a method, *Beta*, that is inherited by all its subclasses. The *Delta* method is really a requirement that all (nonabstract) subclasses must provide a suitable *Delta* implementation.

Going back to our example, so far the Acme Widgets Inc. hierarchy consists of classes with attributes and constructors. We can now add some methods to this hierarchy. We are going to add two methods, *GetName* and *GetGrossPay*. Since the *name* attribute is at the *Employee* class level, the *GetName* method will be a method of the *Employee* class. There is no reason for any derived class to provide its own implementation of *GetName*, so it will not be *abstract*. The *GetGrossPay* method is different, and though we will want to get the gross pay for all types of employees, it is calculated differently for each type. Therefore in the base class *Employee* there is really no common implementation that can be shared. *GetGrossPay* is a perfect candidate to be an *abstract* method. Figure 6.6 shows the Acme Widgets Inc. hierarchy with these methods added.

**Figure 6.6** Acme Widgets Inc. Class Hierarchy with Methods

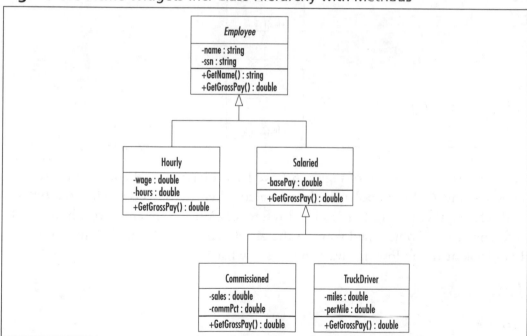

As you can see in Figure 6.6, all classes in the hierarchy inherit the *GetName* method from *Employee*. All classes also inherit the *requirement* that they either implement or inherit the implementation of a *GetGrossPay* method with the same method signature including accessibility.

# The *virtual* Modifier

When multiple classes in a hierarchy implement similar methods it can be confusing determining which method is actually invoked by any particular call. C# handles these polymorphic methods quite a bit differently than Java. Consider the Java class hierarchy in Figure 6.7.

**Figure 6.7** A Simple Java Class Hierarchy

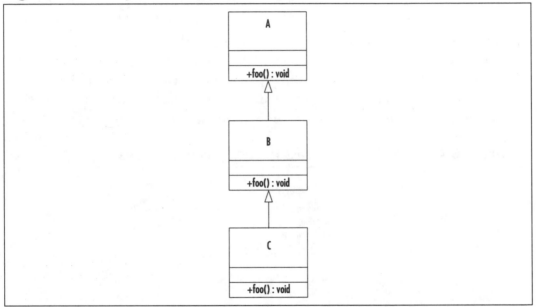

In the class hierarchy of Figure 6.7 we have a base class *A* and two derived classes *B* and *C*. Using polymorphism we could create objects of all three types and refer to them using *baseclass* or *A* references. What happens if you have an *A* reference to a *C* object and you use the *A* reference to call the *foo()* method? Let's look at the following Java code to see what happens.

## *Java*

```
class A
{
   public void foo()
   {
   System.out.println("A.foo") ;
   }
}
```

```java
class B extends A
{
  public void foo()
  {
    System.out.println("B.foo") ;
  }
}


class C extends B
{
  public void foo()
  {
    System.out.println("C.foo") ;
  }
}

public class Test
{
  public static void main(String[] args)
  {
    A[] a = new A[3] ;
    a[0] = new A() ; // A.foo
    a[1] = new B() ; // B.foo
    a[2] = new C() ; // C.foo

    for(int i=0;i<3;i++)
    {
      a[i].foo();
    }

    B b = new B() ;
    b.foo() ; // B.foo

    C c = new C() ;
    c.foo() ; // C.foo
  }
}
```

## *Output*

```
A.foo
B.foo
C.foo
B.foo
C.foo
```

When you look at the output, you see that in Java the actual class of the object determines the method called. In the *for* loop we have this code:

```
for(int i=0;i<3;i++)
{
   a[i].foo();
}
```

When *a[i]* is of type *A* we get *A.foo*. When *a[i]* is of type *B* we get *B.foo*. And *a[i]* of type *C* results in *C.foo*. Java uses the type (or class) of the object, not the type of the reference, to select which version of the method to invoke.

We could build the same program in C# as we did in Java. The difference is that this is default Java behavior whereas C# supports more choices. In C#, when you build a class hierarchy with polymorphic methods you will have to choose whether to use the *virtual*, *override*, *new* or even *abstract* modifier.

We will begin by looking at the *virtual* modifier. We use the *virtual* modifier in C# to indicate that a method may have alternate implementations in a derived class. So if we redo the preceding Java example in C#, the class *A* will have a *foo* method declared to be virtual, like this:

```
class A
{
   public virtual void Foo()
   {
      System. Console.WriteLine ("A.Foo") ;
   }
}
```

In Java there is no *virtual* keyword. All Java methods are essentially considered to be *virtual*. In C# you must use the *virtual* keyword to mark any methods that will have their implementations determined by derived classes.

# The *override* Modifier

Whenever you use the *virtual* or *abstract* modifier in a base class method, the matching methods in derived classes must use either the *override* or *new* modifier. The purpose of the *override* modifier is to indicate that the derived class version of the method overrides the base class implementation. In Java this is the default behavior. In the Acme Widgets Inc. hierarchy all of the *GetGrossPay* methods in the derived classes should be declared *override*. The declaration is as follows:

```
public override double GetGrossPay()
```

The *override* keyword tells the compiler that this class has intentionally over-ridden how the *GetGrossPay* method works. The following is the source code for the Acme Widgets Inc. hierarchy.

```
public abstract class Employee
{
  protected string name ;
  protected string ssn ;

  public Employee(string name, string ssn)
  {
    this.name = name ;
    this.ssn  = ssn ;
  }

  public string GetName() { return name ; }
  public abstract double GetGrossPay() ;

}


public class Hourly : Employee
{
  protected double wage ;
  protected double hours ;

  public Hourly(
            string name,
            string ssn,
            double wage,
```

```csharp
                    double hours) : base(name,ssn)
  {
    this.wage  = wage ;
    this.hours = hours ;
  }


  public override double GetGrossPay()
  {
    return wage * hours ;
  }
}



public class Salaried : Employee
{
  protected double basePay ;

  public Salaried(
            string name,
            string ssn,
            double basePay) : base(name,ssn)
  {
    this.basePay = basePay ;
  }


  public override double GetGrossPay()
  {
    return basePay ;
  }
}

public class Commissioned : Salaried
{
  protected double sales ;
  protected double commPct ;

  public Commissioned(
```

```
                    string name,
                    string ssn,
                    double basePay,
                    double sales,
                    double commPct ) : base(name,ssn,basePay)
    {
      this.sales   = sales ;
      this.commPct = commPct ;
    }


    public override double GetGrossPay()
    {
      return basePay + (sales * commPct) ;
    }
}


public class TruckDriver : Salaried
{
  protected double miles ;
  protected double perMile ;

  public TruckDriver(
                string name,
                string ssn,
                double basePay,
                double miles,
                double perMile ) : base(name,ssn,basePay)
    {
      this.miles   = miles ;
      this.perMile = perMile ;
    }


    public override double GetGrossPay()
    {
      return basePay + (miles * perMile) ;
    }
}
```

The *abstract* or *virtual* modifiers combined with *override* give you a powerful mechanism for customization within a class hierarchy. In the Acme Widgets Inc. hierarchy, the abstract *GetGrossPay* method requires that all the specialized employee types provide their own *GetGrossPay* method. It is a perfect fit for our hierarchy since each employee class has its own way of computing gross pay.

The *sealed* modifier is used in conjunction with the *override* modifier to indicate that a method that overrides a base class method may not be further overridden.

Derived class methods may invoke overridden base class methods by using the *base* keyword. In the following code example the *fubar* method in the *Bar* class overrides the *virtual fubar* method in *Foo*.

```
class Foo
{
  public virtual void fubar()
    {
    System.Console.WriteLine("Foo.fubar") ;
    }
}


class Bar : Foo
{
  public override void fubar()
    {
    System.Console.WriteLine("Bar.fubar") ;
    base.fubar() ;
    }
}


public class Test
{
    static void Main()
    {
    Foo a = new Foo() ;
    Foo b = new Bar() ;
    a.fubar() ;
    b.fubar() ;
    }
}
```

In this example, the *Bar* implementation of *fubar* invokes the *Foo* implementation. Here is the output of the program:

```
Foo.fubar
Bar.fubar
Foo.fubar
```

The *base* keyword allowed the overriding method, *bar.fubar()*, to access the overridden method *Foo.fubar()*.

# The *new* Modifier

The C# *new* method modifier has no equivalent in Java. The *new* modifier is used on a derived class's method in conjunction with the *abstract* or *virtual* modifier in a base class. You may use the *new* modifier to indicate that a method in a derived class that has the same signature as a *virtual* method in a base class *does not* override the base class method. It is almost as if the *new* method had a different signature.

Let's look at a simple class hierarchy in Figure 6.8.

**Figure 6.8** A Simple Class Hierarchy

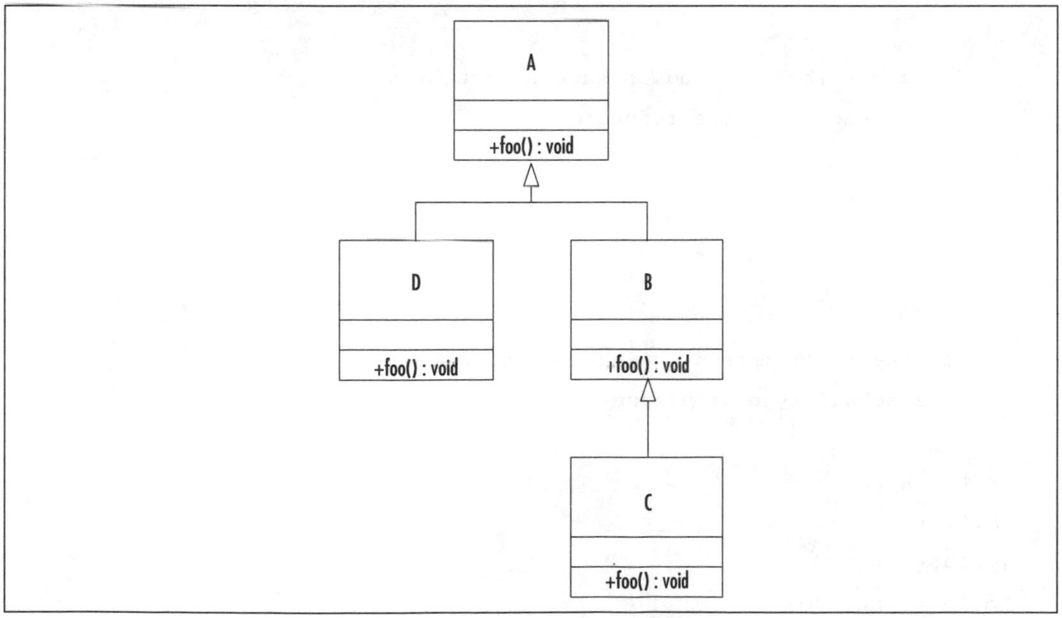

Using the hierarchy of Figure 6.8 we will experiment with the *virtual*, *override*, and *new* keywords. In addition to the four classes shown we will need the following *Test* class:

```
public class Test
{
  static void Main()
  {
    A[] x = new A[4] ;

    x[0] = new A() ;
    x[1] = new B() ;
    x[2] = new C() ;
    x[3] = new D() ;

    A a = new A() ;
    B b = new B() ;
    C c = new C() ;
    D d = new D() ;

    for(int i = 0; i < 4; i++)
      {

      // Invoke foo() method on each object using
      // A(baseclass) type reference.

      x[i].foo() ;

      }


    // Invoke foo() method on each object using
    // its actual type reference.

    a.foo() ;
    b.foo() ;
    c.foo() ;
    d.foo() ;
  }
}
```

In this code example we create objects of type $A$, $B$, $C$, and $D$. We then invoke their *foo()* methods with $A$ references and then with $A$, $B$, $C$, and $D$

references, respectively. Table 6.1 shows the results of various combinations of *virtual*, *new*, *override*, and *sealed* on the method invocations.

**Table 6.1** Use of Virtual, New, Override, and Sealed Modifiers

| Example | Output | A.foo | B.foo | C.foo | D.foo |
|---------|--------|-------|-------|-------|-------|
| 1 | A.foo<br>B.foo<br>C.foo<br>D.foo<br>A.foo<br>B.foo<br>C.foo<br>D.foo | virtual | override | override | override |
| 2 | A.foo<br>B.foo<br>B.foo<br>D.foo<br>A.foo<br>B.foo<br>C.foo<br>D.foo | virtual | override | new | override |
| 3 | A.foo<br>A.foo<br>A.foo<br>A.foo<br>A.foo<br>B.foo<br>C.foo<br>D.foo | virtual | new | new | new |
| 4 | * Compilation error since C.foo tries to override the nonvirtual method B.foo | virtual | new | override | override |
| 5 | A.foo<br>A.foo<br>A.foo<br>D.foo<br>A.foo<br>B.foo<br>C.foo<br>D.foo | virtual | virtual | override | override |

**Continued**

**Table 6.1** Continued

| Example | Output | A.foo | B.foo | C.foo | D.foo |
|---------|--------|-------|-------|-------|-------|
| | * compilation warning since B.foo replaces A.foo. | | | | |
| 6 | * Compilation error since B.foo cannot be overridden by C.foo | virtual | sealed override | override | override |

In example 1 from Table 6.1, the *A.foo()* is *virtual*. All the derived class implementations are declared override. Therefore, regardless of which type of reference you use, the version of *foo()* depends only on the type of the object. This is the same behavior as in Java where none of these modifiers apply.

In example 2, *A.foo()* is *virtual*. *B.foo()* and *D.foo()* are declared override. So like the previous example, using the base class reference results in the actual class implementation of *foo()*. *C.foo()* however is declared *new*. Therefore *C.foo()* is not in any way related to *A.foo()* or *B.foo()*. So the call to *A.foo()* on the *C* object results in *B.foo()*. But the call *C.foo()* ends up with *C.foo()*.

In example 3, all of the *foo()* methods except *A.foo()* are *new*. Therefore a call to *foo()* with an *A* reference always returns *A.foo()*. On the other hand, calling each individual object with a pointer of its own type results in the object's specific *foo()* implementation.

Examples 4 and 6 do not compile. In example 5, the compiler warns that *B.foo()* replaces *A.foo()*. It might be helpful to think of the *virtual* keyword as if it had an implied *new* associated with it.

The *new* method modifier essentially allows a child method to hide a parent's class method. This means that you can explicitly prevent polymorphism by redefining the inherited methods in the child class at the cost of hiding the parent's method.

# Inner Classes

Java supports four kinds of inner or nested classes. The four kinds are top-level nested classes, member classes, local classes, and anonymous classes. Top-level nested classes are *static* classes declared inside another class. Member classes are similar to top-level nested classes, except that they are not static. Both local and anonymous classes are declared within the body of a method, whereas anonymous classes are used and declared in the same statement. C# supports only one kind of inner class, equivalent to Java's top-level nested (or static) inner class.

You create an inner class in C# by simply declaring a class within another class's declaration. Inner classes may have either *public* or *internal* access. Let us take a look at an example of a C# inner class:

```
public class Outer
{
  public int x ;
  public int y ;

  public class Inner
  {
    public int x ;
    public int z ;

    public void InnferFoo()
    {
      // Do something here.
    }
  }

  public void OuterFoo()
  {
    // Do something here.
  }
}
```

This source code defines a class called *Outer* with an inner class named *Inner*. Like Java's static inner classes, you may create an instance of *Inner* from within *Outer*, or from anywhere else. Here is the syntax:

```
// From code within Outer
Inner i = new Inner() ;

// From all other locations in code
Outer.Inner oi = new Outer.Inner() ;
```

Notice that you can create instances of the nested class without having to create instances of the class that contains it. Therefore there is no access from the methods of an inner class to the methods or attributes of its containing class. The *InnerFoo* method cannot access *Outer.y* nor can it call *OuterFoo* unless it gets an *Outer* reference. Inner classes may access only *static* methods and data members of their containing classes.

In some ways inner classes may be thought of as *genetically engineered* classes. These classes are often not part of any hierarchy and are designed to serve a single role tightly coupled to their containing class. For example, if you build a linked list class you might create in inner class to represent the nodes.

# Using Interfaces

Interfaces are an important part of both Java and C#. Earlier in this chapter I mentioned that my son was in the marching band. From my point of view, the inheritance relationship, the *strong essential* relationship, is the father-son relationship. If I were building a management system for the band director I might choose the band-member relationship or band member-musical section relationship as the strong essential or fundamental relationship. In my case I'll stick to the father-son relationship. The problem is we are allowed to have only *one* inheritance relationship. In fact my son plays many other roles, both in the band and at school in general—he is on the tennis team, in the band he is a section leader and a trumpet player, and of course, he is a student. This combination of one essential and strong relationship with *many* weaker ones is common in all sorts of systems. We need to model these other roles without using inheritance. The best way to do this in either Java or C# is by using interfaces. Interfaces specify weaker less essential relationships that are still useful. Consider the UML class diagram in Figure 6.9.

Figure 6.9 shows the essential father-son relationship using a solid line indicating inheritance. The dashed lines point from the *Son* class to the roles that he plays. Some of the roles are subroles of *Student*; other roles are further subroles of *BandMember*. In C# and Java we model these roles using interfaces.

Interfaces are really just abstract classes whose methods are all abstract. Interfaces are often called contracts. In our class diagram these is a *SectionLeader* contract. All *SectionLeaders* (i.e., all *BandMembers* who are *SectionLeaders*) must be able to march, count, turn, straighten up their rows, and so on. As long as a *BandMember* can do these things he can be a *SectionLeader*. Of course *SectionLeaders* must also be *BandMembers* and *BandMembers* must be *Students*. *TennisPlayers*, however, do not have to be *BandMembers*, only *Students*.

**Figure 6.9** UML Representing a Busy High School Student

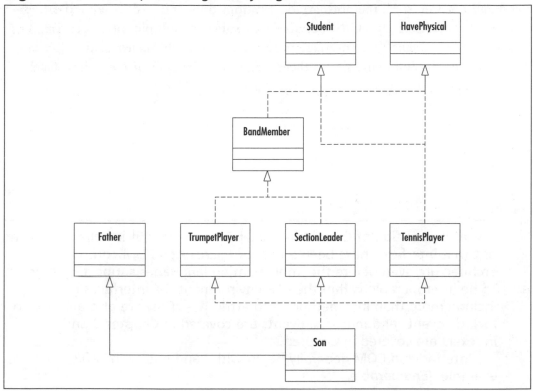

If you look closely you will see that the *Son* class has exactly one base class (Father) but it directly implements three interfaces. Also note that interfaces may specialize each other and an interface may specialize more than one interface. For example, *TennisPlayers* must be *Students* and they must *HavePhysical*.

## Creating an Interface

Interface declarations in C# look a lot like their Java counterparts. Here is a simple interface:

```
interface ILocatable
{
  Point GetLocation() ;
  void  SetLocation( Point pt ) ;
  void  Move( int xOffset, int yOffset ) ;
  double CalculateDistance( Ilocatable loc ) ;
}
```

Methods in an interface are *public* and *abstract* by default and generally do not need any modifiers. All methods are declarations only and end in semicolons (;) with no bodies. Like Java, C# interfaces may subclass multiple interfaces. In Figure 6.9, the *TennisPlayer* interface is derived from both *Student* and *HavePhysical*. The following shows the declaration of the *TennisPlayer* interface.

```
interface TennisPlayer : Student, HavePhysical
{
  // TennisPlayer methods here
}
```

**NOTE**

Given the position of C# within the .NET framework, it is helpful to point out that interfaces have been a part of Microsoft's COM component architecture even before the implementing languages supported them. To be interoperable within the CLR environment C# interfaces may include more than just methods and attributes. They are also allowed to include events and indexers. Events are covered in Chapter 8 and indexers are covered in Chapter 7.

Interfaces in COM generally begin with *I* and end with *–able*—for example, *IEnumerable.*

## Declaring Interfaces

A class or interface declares the interfaces that it implements using a colon (:). Since classes may both subclass another class and implement interfaces, any base classes must come first in the declaration list. So a class *B* that subclasses *A* and implements an interface *IQ* must declare them as shown:

```
class B : A, IQ
```

If *A* implements other interfaces, they follow *IQ* in the list. Remember that in Java you use *extends* to indicate class inheritance and *implements* to indicate interface inheritance. In C# the colon (:) is used to indicate both types of inheritance. The following Java and C# code snippets demonstrate declaring a class that inherits from another class and two interfaces. The example is based on the class diagram from Figure 6.9.

## *Java*

```
class Son extends Father implements TrumpetPlayer, SectionLeader,
    TennisPlayer
{
  // Methods and variables here
}
```

## *C#*

```
class Son : Father, TrumpetPlayer, SectionLeader, TennisPlayer
{
  // Methods and variables here
}
```

# Implementing Interfaces

When a class implements an interface it must provide an implementation of *all* the methods declared in the interface. These implementations can be declared with the *virtual* modifier. Therefore subclasses can declare methods that use *new* or *override* on these methods.

Interfaces define a set of common operations supported by all implementing classes. In the following example, *ISavable* defines *Read()* and *Write()* methods for saving an object. The *TextFile* class implements *ISavable*. *ZipFile* subclasses *TextFile* and by inheritance, *ZipFile* also implements *ISavable*. This example uses the *virtual, override*, and *new* modifiers.

```
using System;
interface ISavable
{
  void Read();
  void Write();
}

public class TextFile : ISavable
{
  public virtual void Read()
  {
    Console.WriteLine("TextFile.Read()");
```

```csharp
  }

  public void Write()
  {
    Console.WriteLine("TextFile.Write()");
  }
}

public class ZipFile : TextFile
{
  public override void Read()
  {
    Console.WriteLine("ZipFile.Read()");
  }

  public new void Write()
  {
    Console.WriteLine("ZipFile.Write()");
  }
}

public class Test
{
  static void Main()
  {

    Console.WriteLine("\nTextFile reference to ZipFile");
    TextFile textRef = new ZipFile();

    textRef.Read();
    textRef.Write();

    Console.WriteLine("\nISavable reference to ZipFile");
    ISavable savableRef = textRef as ISavable;

    if(savableRef != null)
    {
```

```
        savableRef.Read();
        savableRef.Write();
    }


    Console.WriteLine("\nZipFile reference to ZipFile");
    ZipFile zipRef = textRef as ZipFile;


    if(zipRef!= null)
    {
        zipRef.Read();
        zipRef.Write();
    }
  }
}
```

## Output

```
TextFile reference to ZipFile
ZipFile.Read()
TextFile.Write()


ISavable reference to ZipFile
ZipFile.Read()
TextFile.Write()


ZipFile reference to ZipFile
ZipFile.Read()
ZipFile.Write()
```

The sample application begins by creating a *TextFile* reference to a *ZipFile* object. Next it uses an *ISavable* reference to call *Read()* and *Write()* followed by the same method calls with a *ZipFile* reference. Regardless of the type of reference used, the results of the *Read()* calls are the same. The *Read()* method is declared in an interface—*virtual* in the derived class and *override* in the implementing class (*ZipFile*). Therefore it does not matter what sort of reference we use to call it; the runtime binding of a call to the *Read()* method for this object is *ZipFile.Read()*.

The output is a little different for the *Write()* method. Java developers may have some difficulty resolving why it is so different. In the *ZipFile* class, *Write()* is

declared *new*. This means that it is not a polymorphic implementation of
*TextFile.Write()* or *ISavable.Write()*. Therefore when you call *Write()* with either an
*ISavable* or *TextFile* reference, you get the implementation of *Write()* from
*TextFile*. It is only when you use the actual type reference (*ZipFile*) that you can
ever invoke *ZipFile.Write()*.

Let's take a look at another example. In this example we have an interface,
*ILocatable*, and a class *Point*, and another class, *GamePiece*, that implements
*ILocatable*. The *ILocatable* interface defines location in terms of *Point* objects. This
would be useful for points on a computer display.

```
class Point
{
    public int x;
    public int y;

    public Point( int x, int y )
    {
        this.x = x;
        this.y = y;
    }
}


interface ILocatable
{
    Point GetLocation();
    void  SetLocation( Point pt );
    void  Move( int xOffset, int yOffset );
    double CalculateDistance( ILocatable loc );
}

class GamePiece : ILocatable
{
    protected Point position ;

    public GamePiece( Point position )
    {
        this.position = position ;
    }
```

```
    public Point GetLocation() { return position ; }

    public void  SetLocation( Point pt ) { position = pt ; }

    public void  Move( int xOffset, int yOffset )
    {
       position.x += xOffset ;
       position.y += yOffset ;
    }


    public double CalculateDistance( ILocatable loc )
    {
       Point pt = loc.GetLocation() ;
       double xDiff = position.x - pt.x ;
       double yDiff = position.y - pt.y ;
       return Math.Abs( xDiff*xDiff - yDiff*yDiff ) ;
    }
}
```

The *GamePiece* class must provide an implementation for each method in *ILocatable*. If a class does not implement *all* the methods of an interface, the class itself must be declared *abstract*. When you create a *GamePiece* object you may use an *ILocatable* reference to it. The ILocatable interface serves to provide location support for all the classes that implement it. It is a powerful abstraction since in a graphical system it is often useful to think of objects in terms of their location only.

## The *is* Operator

The *is* operator in C# is similar to Java's *instanceof* operator. This operator takes two operands, the first being an object and the second being a class. The operator has a *bool* value. The *is* operator returns *false* where the cast operator would throw an exception. Therefore, you might use the *is* operator to test before doing a cast. The syntax of the *is* operator is:

```
a is A
```

In this example, *a* is an object reference and *A* is a class. Table 6.2 gives the possible values for the expression.

**Table 6.2** Possible Values for an Expression

| Expression | True or False |
|---|---|
| *a* is *null* | False |
| *a* is of type *A* | True |
| *a* is a subclass of *A* | True |
| There is a reference conversion from *a* to *A* | True |
| There is a boxing/unboxing conversion from *a* to *A* | True |
| All other conditions | False |

The C# *is* operator and the Java *instanceof* operator both fail at compile time if it is not possible for them to be true at runtime. The *is* operator can be used to determine the *real* class of an object at runtime. It may be used with a collection of base class or interface references to identify members of a specific derived class.

Figure 6.10 shows a class hierarchy of pets. All pets share a common abstract base class from which they override an *Eat* method. Three types of pet classes implement the interface *IAffectionate*. (Of course the *Cat* class does not since everybody knows that cats are not truly affectionate!) The *Dog, Snake,* and *Fish* classes all implement *IAffectionate*.

**Figure 6.10** A Pet Hierarchy Putting Cats in Their Place

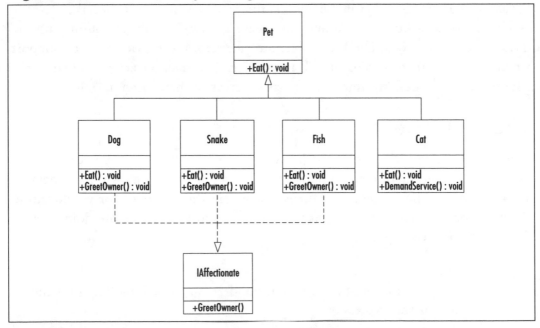

The following program uses the classes from the hierarchy in Figure 6.10:

```
using System ;

abstract class Pet
{
  public virtual void Eat()
  {
    Console.WriteLine( "Pet.Eat" ) ;
  }
}


interface IAffectionate
{
  void GreetOwner() ;
}


class Dog : Pet, IAffectionate
{
  public override void Eat()
  {
    Console.WriteLine( "Dog.Eat" ) ;
  }

  public void GreetOwner()
  {
    Console.WriteLine( "Woof!" ) ;
  }
}


class Snake : Pet, IAffectionate
{
  public override void Eat()
  {
    Console.WriteLine( "Snake.Eat" ) ;
  }
```

```csharp
    public void GreetOwner()
    {
      Console.WriteLine( "Hiss!" ) ;
    }
}

class Fish : Pet, IAffectionate
{
  public override void Eat()
  {
    Console.WriteLine( "Fish.Eat" ) ;
  }

  public void GreetOwner()
  {
    Console.WriteLine( "Splash!" ) ;
  }
}

class Cat : Pet
{
  public override void Eat()
  {
    Console.WriteLine( "Cat.Eat" ) ;
  }

  public void DemandService()
  {
    Console.WriteLine( "Waiter, ..." ) ;
  }
}

public class Menagerie
{
  static void Main()
  {
    Pet [] pets = new Pet[4] ;
```

```
      pets[0] = new Dog() ;

      pets[1] = new Snake() ;

      pets[2] = new Fish() ;

      pets[3] = new Cat() ;


      // Master comes home
      for ( int i=0; i<4; i++)
      {
        if ( pets[i] is IAffectionate )
        {
          ((IAffectionate)pets[i]).GreetOwner() ;
        }
      }


      // Master feeds pets
      for ( int i=0; i<4; i++)
      {
        pets[i].Eat() ;
      }
    }
}
```

In this example we create an array of *Pet* references and assign all four types of *Pet* to the array. When the master comes home all the affectionate pets line up to greet him. Since we did not keep an array of *IAffectionate* references, we will test each *Pet* in the array to see whether it is affectionate. The *Pet* array is very general; we used the *is* operator to extract specific information about objects in the array. The output of this program is:

```
Woof!
Hiss!
Splash!
Dog.Eat
Snake.Eat
Fish.Eat
Cat.Eat
```

## The *as* Operator

The C# *as* operator has no equivalent in Java. In a way it is like the *is* operator—it does not throw exceptions. The difference is that the *as* operator performs a cast, and the result is the object on the left side cast to the type on the right (or null if it is not possible). We could replace the *is* operator with the *as* operator in the previous code as follows:

```
// Master comes home
for ( int i=0; i<4; i++)
{
  IAffectionate cuddly = (pets[i] as IAffectionate);
  if ( cuddly != null )
  {
cuddly.GreetOwner() ;
  }
}
```

The best practice is to use the *is* operator when testing the type of an object. The *as* operator is more appropriate when actually doing a cast. Either one allows you to do a safe cast, but if you use *is*, you end up testing the type once for the *is* operator and once again for the actual cast. As a rule, if you're just testing whether an object is of a particular type then you would want to use the *is* operator. However, if you're testing whether the object is of a particular type and then would want to cast it to that type, then you would use the *as* operator to eliminate the overhead of the checking the cast twice.

## Explicit Interface Implementation

It is possible for a class to implement two interfaces with the same method signature. For example in the pet hierarchy we could introduce a new interface, *IFriendly*, which like *IAffectionate*, has a *GreetOwner* method. Figure 6.11 shows the *Dog* class in the pet hierarchy with *IFriendly*.

There are a couple of ways to implement the *Dog* class in this case. The first is simple; implement a single *GreetOwner* method in the *Dog* class to fulfill the contract of both interfaces. This is illustrated in the following example:

```
class Dog : Pet, IAffectionate, IFriendly
{
    public override void Eat()
```

```
    {
        Console.WriteLine( "Dog.Eat" ) ;
    }
    public void GreetOwner()
    {
        Console.WriteLine( "Woof!" ) ;
    }
}
```

**Figure 6.11** Dog Hierarchy with IFriendly

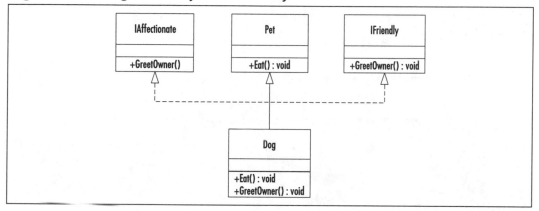

Another way is to say explicitly which interface method you're implementing. Explicit implementation is a way to provide different methods to handle the *GreetOwner* call depending on which interface is invoked. The following is an example of the *Dog* class with explicit implementation.

```
interface IFriendly
{
        void GreetOwner() ;
}


class Dog : Pet, IAffectionate, IFriendly
{
        public override void Eat()
        {
                Console.WriteLine( "Dog.Eat" ) ;
        }
        void IAffectionate.GreetOwner()
```

```
        {
                Console.WriteLine( "Woof!" ) ;
        }
        void IFriendly.GreetOwner()
        {
                Console.WriteLine( "Jump up!" ) ;
        }
}


public class Pets
{
        static void Main()
        {
                IFriendly mansBestFriend = new Dog() ;
                mansBestFriend.GreetOwner() ;
                (mansBestFriend as IAffectionate).GreetOwner() ;
        }
}
```

## Output

```
Jump up!
Woof!
```

In this example—a call to the *GreetOwner()* method using an *IFriendly* reference—the result is *"Jump up!"*. And by using the *IAffectionate* interface, the same method call will result to *"Woof!"*

# Implementation Hiding

If you need to implement an interface, you can do so without making the interface methods publicly available in your implementation class. Consider the following without implementation hiding:

```
class Dog : Pet, IFriendly
{
    public override void Eat()
    {
        Console.WriteLine( "Dog.Eat" ) ;
```

```
    }
    public void GreetOwner()
    {
        Console.WriteLine( "Jump up!"  ) ;
    }
}
```

In this example, the *GreetOwner* method is directly available as part of the *Dog* class. Implementation hiding is an explicit interface implementation. You can use implementation hiding to fully implement an interface without publicly exposing the methods in your class. The interface methods are accessible *only* if you use an interface reference.

```
class Dog : Pet, IFriendly
{
    public override void Eat()
    {
        Console.WriteLine( "Dog.Eat" ) ;
    }

    void IFriendly.GreetOwner()
    {
        Console.WriteLine( " Jump up!" ) ;
    }
}
```

Notice that *GreetOwner* is not *public* in the *Dog* class. Thus the following produces a compile error:

```
Dog fido = new Dog() ;
fido.GreetOwner() ;     // Compile error
```

In order to access the *GreetOwner* method, you must use the interface *IFriendly*:

```
Dog fido = new Dog() ;
((IFriendly)fido).GreetOwner() ;     // Jump up!
```

# Summary

C# is a modern object-oriented language. It borrows many features from previous OO languages like Java and C++. C#, however, is newer than either Java or C++ and has many features that do not exist in previous languages. In this chapter we examined the C# object model.

Three of the primary features of an object-oriented programming language are encapsulation (covered in Chapter 5), inheritance, and polymorphism. In this chapter we began by looking at inheritance. We described inheritance as an *essential* and *strong* relationship. A class may only subclass one other class, and in C# as in Java, all classes are directly or indirectly derived from a common base class. We looked at how to organize class hierarchies and examined a few UML class diagrams. Next we looked at how to specify base classes and invoke their constructors.

Our next topic was polymorphism. In this section we saw how a base class could take on many forms and how a single type could be a general representation of many derived types. We discovered along the way that many classes exist in our hierarchies simply to combine common features. Some of these classes are not even meant to be used other than as an abstraction. These classes, called abstract base classes, are extremely useful in modeling real-world systems.

Still in the realm of polymorphism we visited the topic of virtual methods. Use virtual methods when different classes in a hierarchy provide similar but different behavior. Although both Java and C# support virtual methods, C# provides a variety of nuances that have no equivalent in Java. We looked at overriding and hiding methods.

C# supports one type of inner class (compared to Java's four). We looked next at how to use inner classes and access their methods. We also noted that inner classes have only limited access to the instance members of the classes that contain them.

Whereas inheritance is a fundamental and strong relationship, our real-world systems often require other, weaker (albeit no less important) relationships. You normally will use interfaces to model these relationships. Once again both C# and Java support interfaces, but C# provides more nuances in its implementation. We looked at explicit interface implementation and implementation hiding.

C# provides a flexible robust object model. Using object-oriented methodology in C# you will be able to model both simple and complex systems and generate solutions for your business problems.

# Solutions Fast Track

## Inheritance

☑ Classes inherit the methods and attributes of their parent classes.

☑ In Java all methods are essentially virtual—in C# you must use the *virtual* keyword.

☑ C# also supports *override* and *new* modifiers to allow classes to implement methods that are not related to super class methods of the same name.

## Polymorphism

☑ Any class in a hierarchy may be referenced by using a reference of a type higher in the hierarchy.

☑ You can refer to any object that implements an interface by the interface type.

☑ The mapping of a reference to an object of a specific type is a runtime mapping.

## Inner Classes

☑ Inner classes are classes that are declared within other classes.

☑ Inner classes may implement interfaces and/or subclass another class.

☑ Classes that are *helpers* to others are often implemented as inner classes.

## Using Interfaces

☑ Interfaces are used all over C# and .NET.

☑ Classes are often required to implement a particular interface to be used in a component framework.

☑ Interfaces define the methods (including signatures) that a class supports without defining the implementation.

☑ Use explicit interface implementation when a class implements two interfaces with the same methods.

☑ Use *is* when you want to test the runtime type of an object.

☑ The *as* operator should be used to provide type-safe casts.

☑ For robust coding you must test the results of an *as* operation since it may be *null*.

# Frequently Asked Questions

The following Frequently Asked Questions, answered by the authors of this book, are designed to both measure your understanding of the concepts presented in this chapter and to assist you with real-life implementation of these concepts. To have your questions about this chapter answered by the author, browse to **www.syngress.com/solutions** and click on the **"Ask the Author"** form.

**Q:** Does C# support multiple inheritance?

**A:** Yes and no—just like Java, C# allows single inheritance of classes and multiple inheritance of interfaces.

**Q:** What is the difference between *is* and *as*?

**A:** The *is* operator tests whether an object is of a particular type and returns a Boolean (*is* does the same thing as Java's *instanceof* operator). The *as* operator both tests the validity and does the cast. If the cast is invalid, *as* returns *null*.

**Q:** What are interfaces for?

**A:** Interfaces define a standard for interaction between objects. They are essentially a contract between objects. Interfaces place requirements on the classes that implement them.

**Q:** What is *polymorphism*?

**A:** Polymorphism is the object-oriented property that allows objects to be referenced with different levels of specificity. This fits our intuitive understanding of the world where we may say that a dog is a four-legged animal, a mammal, a pet, or an animal. We choose the level of abstraction appropriate for our problem.

**Q:** Does C# support inner classes?

**A:** Yes. C# supports only one kind of inner class compared to Java's four.

**Q:** Are all C# classes derived from a common class like Java, or are classes independent like C++?

**A:** All C# classes are derived from object. C# classes do not need to explicitly declare that they subclass object.

# Chapter 7

# Other C# Features

## Solutions in this chapter:

- **Properties**
- **Read-Only Fields**
- **Enumerations**
- **Boxing and Unboxing**
- **Operator Overloading**
- **User-Defined Conversions**
- **Structs**

☑ **Summary**

☑ **Solutions Fast Track**

☑ **Frequently Asked Questions**

# Introduction

At this point you have learned most of the basic tools for object-oriented programming. This chapter will complete the tool set by introducing the rest of the new C# features that are not found in Java. Many of the concepts in this chapter will be familiar to those who also know C++, but pure Java developers will be unfamiliar with most of these.

This chapter begins by discussing some syntactic sugar that C# provides. We will discuss properties as they apply to the C# language. Properties provide data encapsulation, but allow direct access to member fields. You will then learn about enumerations, a distinct value type consisting of a set of named constants. Next, the chapter will discuss support for boxing and unboxing of data types. This is a convenient way to move from primitives to objects and back. Operator overloading is a powerful new addition to C# that allows users to define how operators behave with objects. In a similar vein, C# also supports user-defined conversions, known as casting to Java programmers. Finally, you will learn about the *struct,* which is a lightweight user-defined alternative to a class.

# Properties

Properties are an interesting addition to C# that allow the benefits of encapsulation while also allowing direct access to a field. In Java, *set* and *get* methods are the only way to provide encapsulation of data. C# allows this through the use of properties, which have *get* and *set* methods that are invisible to the programmer accessing the field. Let's examine a property within an actual class. This example uses a *Circle* class with *diameter* and *circumference* members. In this case, diameter is a regular variable but circumference is defined as a property.

```
using System;

namespace Other_Features
{
    public class Circle
    {
        private double diameter;

        //Creates the property
        public double Circumference
        {
```

```
        set
        {
            diameter = value/Math.PI;
        }
        get
        {
            return diameter * Math.PI;
        }
    }
}

public class CircleTester
{
  public static void Main()
    {
        Circle c = new Circle();
        c.Circumference = 20;
        Console.WriteLine("New Circumference = " + c.Circumference);
    }
}
}
```

This program creates a *Circle* object with only an accessible *Circumference* member. The *diameter* variable is private. The *Main* method changes the *Circumference* value, which must also change *diameter*. The inner workings of the *Circle* object are hidden in true object-oriented fashion, so from the outside it's impossible to know how the data is stored internally. In this program the *diameter* variable is a regular private field, just as it would appear in Java. The *Circumference* property, however, looks like part variable and part method. As you can see, the *Circumference* property is accessed just like a field, without the use of methods, as follows:

```
c.Circumference = 20;
```

Even though it appears we are accessing the property like a normal field, there are actually methods at work. Notice that neither of the accessors in the example have arguments or brackets. The *Circumference* property uses two accessors, *set* and *get*. The *set* and *get* accessors behave just like normal class methods. The *set* accessor is similar to a method that takes a value type and returns *void*.

The *get* accessor is similar to a method that returns an object of the same property type.

Of course, the real reason for using *get* and *set* accessors is to provide object encapsulation. Any code can be contained in these two accessors, but typically the code performs some specific functions. Some typical uses of *set* and *get* accessors in properties are as follows:

- Verify that the new data is correct.
- Recalculate values for this or other variables.
- Refresh a GUI object.

The *get* accessor code is very basic:

```
get
{
    return diameter * Math.PI;
}
```

There are no limitations to this *get* accessor, as long as it returns a double value. Keep in mind the return type must be compatible with the declared type of the property (implicit casts are fine). The set code is a little more complex, but not by much, as the following shows.

```
set
{
    diameter = value/Math.PI;
}
```

The *set* value contains a special variable called *value*. The *value* keyword represents the *value* passed to the *set* accessor when a programmer attempts to change the value of the property.

In the *Circle* class it might be useful to make the diameter field visible. In the preceding example we would use the following code, which simply shows how to access the private diameter field.

```
private double diameter;

public double Diameter
{
    get
    {
```

```
        return diameter
    }
    set
    {
        diameter = value;
    }
}
```

These are the most basic types of accessor methods possible, since there are no calculations performed. Each accessor just sets or gets a variable.

## NOTE

Properties normally are capitalized in C#.

# Read-Only Fields

In C#, fields can be declared as constants so a programmer cannot attempt to alter the value once it is initialized (Java declares it as *final*). Sometimes, however, it is necessary to allow a field to be altered in the constructor, but still keep it off limits to the programmer accessing the class. In order to prevent a field from modification, the *readonly* keyword is used.

```
using System;

namespace Other_Features
{
    public class Polyhedron
    {
        public readonly double Volume;

        public Polyhedron(int length, int width, int height)
        {
            Volume = length * width * height;
        }
```

```
        public static void Main()
        {
            Polyhedron poly = new Polyhedron(3,4,5);
            Console.WriteLine("Volume = " + poly.Volume);
        }
    }
}
```

This program creates a *Polyhedron* object and calculates *Volume* within the constructor. This field can be accessed as usual, but if a programmer tries to modify it an error will be generated. For example, if a programmer tries to change this field outside of a constructor (such as in the *Main()* method) an error will occur during build:

```
poly.Volume = 200;
```

This generates the following response from the compiler:

```
A readonly field cannot be assigned to (except in a constructor or a
    variable initializer)
```

**NOTE**

Accessible fields (nonprivate) normally are capitalized in C#.

# Enumerations

In Java, lists of constants are often stored in interfaces instead of storing them right in classes. C# provides an alternative to this in the form of enumerations. The main difference between enumerations and constants is that an enumeration may consist only of integral numbers (no *Strings, chars, doubles,* or *floats*). First, let's examine an alternative, but somewhat cumbersome, way of doing this.

```
using System;

namespace Other_Features
{
    public class PowerPlant
    {
```

```
        const int Low = 0;
        const int Medium = 1;
        const int High = 2;
        const int Emergency = 3;

        public static void Main()
        {
            int level = 3;
            if(level >= High)
                Console.WriteLine("Evacuate facility!");
        }
    }
}
```

In this example we have four levels of danger, each represented by an integer. This works out okay unless there are other parameters in the *PowerPlant* class, such as temperature level or power level. The temperature level constants might look like this:

```
const int Sub_Boiling = 0;
const int Low = 1;
const int Medium = 2;
const int High = 3;
const int Too_Hot = 4;
```

Now there is the potential for conflicts. The programmer will need to get creative to think up new variable names to distinguish them from one another. Things become less cumbersome by using enumerations to group these constants together. The following example shows an enumeration called *DangerLevel* within a class.

```
using System;

namespace Other_Features
{
    public class PowerPlant
    {
        public enum DangerLevel :int
        {
```

```
        Low = 0,
        Medium = 1,
        High = 2,
        Emergency  = 3
    }

    public static void Main()
    {
        DangerLevel level = GetDangerLevel();
        if(level >= DangerLevel.High)
            Console.WriteLine("Evacuate facility!");
    }

    public static DangerLevel GetDangerLevel()
    {
        return DangerLevel.Emergency;
    }

  }

}
```

This nicely illustrates the use of an enumeration. The keyword *enum* specifies an enumeration. Notice after the enumeration name there is a type specification of *int*. The enumerator list is within the curly braces of the enumeration, and the values within this list are separated by commas. In pseudocode, an enumeration is defined as follows (italics indicate optional statements):

[*access modifier*] enum [name] [:*type*] {}

Enumerations may be passed into methods as parameters or retrieved from methods as the method *GetDangerLevel()* demonstrated previously. Essentially, enumerations behave like objects, and they even have their own set of standard methods (see Table 7.1). These methods are stored in the *System.Enum* class, which is the base class for all enumerations.

**Table 7.1** Enum Methods

| Method Name | Description |
| --- | --- |
| CompareTo | Compares this instance to a specified object and returns an indication of their relative values |
| Equals | Returns a value indicating whether this instance is equal to a specified object |
| Format | Converts the specified value of a specified enumerated type to its equivalent string representation according to the specified format |
| GetHashCode | Returns the hash code for this instance |
| GetName | Retrieves the name of the constant in the specified enumeration that has the specified value |
| GetNames | Retrieves an array of the names of the constants in a specified enumeration |
| GetTypeCode | Returns the underlying *TypeCode* for this instance |
| GetUnderlyingType | Returns the underlying type of the specified enumeration |
| GetValues | Retrieves an array of the values of the constants in a specified enumeration |
| IsDefined | Returns an indication whether a constant with a specified value exists in a specified enumeration |
| Parse | Converts the string representation of the name or numeric value of one or more enumerated constants to an equivalent enumerated object |
| ToObject | Returns an instance of the specified enumeration type set to the specified value |
| ToString | Converts the value of this instance to its equivalent string representation |

If you want to use an enumeration value as a number (for example, in an equation) it must be cast into an *int* value. This is because *enum* is a formal type, so the *enum* must be explicitly cast into an *int*. Obviously enumerations are not meant to be used in equations or comparisons, but rather to represent abstractions.

Enumerations do not need specific values assigned to them. If you leave out literal values in the enumerator list, C# assigns values automatically:

```
enum DangerLevel :int
{
```

```
    Low,

    Medium,

    High,

    Emergency

}
```

By default, values are assigned starting with 0 and incrementing by 1. In this example, *Low* will have a value of 0 and *Emergency* will be 3. If you assigned *High* with a value of 10 then further enumerations will continue with 11, and so on.

```
enum DangerLevel :int

{

    Low,

    Medium,

    High = 10,

    Emergency // 11

}
```

Notice that the C# class library lists several enumerations that are not contained within classes. C# allows enumerations to be listed within their own class file, as follows:

```
namespace Other_Features

{

    public enum Mode

    {

        Forward,

        Reverse,

        Stop

    }

}
```

An enumeration typically is listed on its own when more than one class within the same package will use it.

# Boxing and Unboxing

Java has two main data types: objects and primitives. In Java, all objects derive from the *Object* class, and thus all objects have a set of methods such as *toString()*. Primitives, on the other hand, can represent only a data type and may not contain methods. C# is a little different since it provides a *unified type system*, in which all types (even value types) derive from the type *object*. This means methods may be called on value types, as the following example demonstrates:

```
int x = 29;
String xStr = x.ToString();
```

This code could not exist in Java for obvious reasons, but C# allows it. Boxing and unboxing are processes that allow value types (primitives) to be treated as objects. As we shall see, these processes are very similar to implicit and explicit casting.

# Boxing

The closest thing to boxing in Java is the use of wrapper classes. The *java.lang* package includes equivalent classes for all of the primitive types: *Byte, Short, Integer, Long, Float, Double, Character*, and *Boolean*. In Java if you want to obtain an object to represent a primitive, the primitive is used in the constructor of the wrapper class as follows:

```
int x = 29;
Integer xObj = new Integer(x);
```

C# is a little easier. To get an object equivalent of a value type, simply assign an object reference to the value type:

```
int x = 29;
object o = x; // Boxing
```

Because *object* is the root of all types (even *int*), this can be done implicitly. This act should seem very familiar to Java programmers because the syntax is almost identical to an implicit cast of an object to one of the parent classes. The reason it is called boxing is because when a value type (such as *int*) needs to be converted to a reference type (object), an object *box* is allocated to hold the value (see Figure 7.1).

---

**NOTE**

The keyword *object* can be boxed and unboxed just as well to the corresponding *System.Object* class. You can declare *Object o = x* or *object o = x* (note the capitalization).

---

**Figure 7.1** Copying a Value into an Object Box

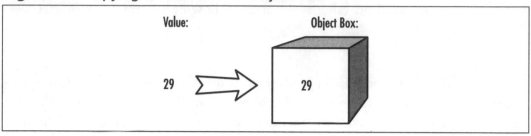

# Unboxing

Unboxing is the act of converting an object back into a value type. The syntax for this process looks very similar to explicit casting in Java, as the following C# code demonstrates:

```
int x = 29;
object xObj = x; // Boxing
int x1 = (int)xObj; // Unboxing
```

Only objects that have been boxed from a value type may be unboxed. If you attempt to cast an object that did not originate from a value type you will get an *InvalidCastException* thrown.

It is important to note that the object does not have a reference variable to the value type. In other words, if you change something with the boxed object it will not change the original value. The following example makes this clear:

```
using System;

namespace Other_Features
{
    public class Boxing
    {
        public static void Main()
        {
            int x = 29;
            object xObj = x; // Boxing
            int x1 = (int)xObj; // Unboxing
            ++x1;
            Console.WriteLine("x = " + x); //29
```

```
        Console.WriteLine("x1 = " + x1); //30
    }
  }
}
```

This program starts with an *int* value of 29. It then boxes this into an object, and then unboxes it to another value type. Now if you make a change to *x1* is it reflected in x? Of course not, as the output of this program confirms:

## Output

```
x = 29
x1 = 30
```

# Operator Overloading

Operator overloading is a useful addition to C# that is not available to Java programmers. The Java language itself overloads the + operator to work with *String*, as follows:

```
String name = "Bilbo " + "Baggins";
```

Java has overloaded the + operator with *String*, but it does not allow you as a programmer to overload other objects; however, C# does. Operator overloading is programmed slightly differently, depending on whether the operator is unary (only one operand, usually to the left of the operator) or binary (two operands, one on each side of the operator). Table 7.2 shows a complete list of the unary and binary operators that may be overloaded in C#.

**Table 7.2** Overloadable Operators in C#

| **Unary** | + | - | ! | ~ | ++ | -- | true | false | | | | | | | |
|-----------|---|---|---|---|----|----|------|-------|---|---|---|---|---|---|---|
| **Binary** | + | - | * | / | % | & | \| | ^ | << | >> | == | != | > | < | >= <= |

Several operators may not be overloaded, specifically member access, method invocation, or the =, &&, | |, ?:, *new*, *typeof*, *is*, *as*, *checked*, and *unchecked* operators.

Creating an overloaded operator is as easy as writing a method. In C# the *operator* keyword is used to create an overloaded operator. Let's try an example. New Java programmers, upon learning that the + operator is overloaded for *Strings*, try to use the − operator. This of course doesn't work, but it would seem like it could be useful to remove substrings from a string. The following example creates an enhanced *String* class called *EString* to accomplish this.

### Debugging...

## Overloading Relevant Operators

One of the best ways to keep your code error free is to make it understandable to other programmers. Operator overloading has always been available in C++ but sometimes programmers use it in a manner that is not intuitive. For example, with a *Date* object, overloading the – operator makes sense. As a programmer you would expect the – operator to subtract two *Date* values and perhaps return an integer of milliseconds.

Other operators just don't fit, however. Overloading the % operator is quite confusing because it isn't clear what function this would have. Keep in mind that just because there are 24 available operators for overloading, overloading as many as possible does not make for a better program.

Some operators are understandable for most objects to overload. The = = and ! = operators will likely be useful for all objects, and it would be rare for them not to be useful. Many objects also have a use for + or – operators, and also the + + and -- unary operators. The mathematical operators (and comparisons such as greater than) are going to be intuitive only in situations where the object represents a number. Using these with objects that contain string or other varied data types is probably a mistake. Don't use it if it is not intuitive.

### NOTE

The *String* class is *sealed* in C# and therefore cannot be extended, so the following class acts as a wrapper for *String* instead.

```
using System;

namespace Other_Features
{
```

```
public class EString
{
    public String s;

    public EString(String s)
    {
        this.s = s;
    }

    public static EString operator- (EString full, String sub)
    {
        String newStr = "";
        int pos = full.s.IndexOf(sub);
        if(pos > -1)
        {
            newStr = full.s.Substring(0,pos);
            newStr = newStr + full.s.Substring(pos + sub.Length);
        }
        else
            newStr = full.s;
        return new EString(newStr);
    }

    public static void Main()
    {
        EString test = new EString("Renowned");
        test = test - "Ren";
        Console.WriteLine(test.s);
    }
}
```

## Output

owned

This program presents an enhanced string class called *EString*. This class acts as a wrapper for the *String* class, since C# won't allow us to extend *String*. We've overloaded the − operator with the following method declaration:

```
public static EString operator- (EString full, String sub)
```

Now, when we invoke the following code in the *Main()* method:

```
EString test = new EString("Renowned");
test = test - "Ren";
```

our code removes "Ren" from the *test* string and returns a new *String* containing "owned". There are several rules that must be followed when overloading operators:

- The operator method must be both *public* and *static*.

- The method arguments must be value types (i.e., not *ref* or *out* parameters).

- The signature of the operator method must be unique within the class.

- If using the *extern* modifier a semicolon is used at the end of the definition (rather than using a body of code in brackets).

- All types referenced in the declaration must be at least as accessible as the operator definition. For example, a *public* operator may not access a *protected* type.

## Developing & Deploying…

## Supporting Other .NET Languages

Not all languages for the .NET platform support operator overloading. Some, such as VB.NET, do not contain the mechanisms that allow operator overloading. Since the languages of the .NET platform are interchangeable, it's possible for a VB class to use code written in C#. This brings to light a potential pitfall when overloading operators in a language.

If certain functionality is available only through the use of the operator then those languages will not be able to access this functionality. For this reason it is a good idea to provide an alternate method to allow

**Continued**

access. Keep in mind, however, that within the C# code (or whichever language you are using) you may use the overloaded operator freely. The inner workings of a class written in C# are completely hidden from other .NET languages accessing the members.

# Unary Operator Overloading

*Unary* operations contain one operator, normally followed by one operand, as follows:

```
++x;
```

A unary operator is defined in a class (or struct) in a manner similar to binary operator overloading. There are several specific rules that must be followed when defining a unary operator method.

When overloading the ++ or - - operators, the method must accept one argument of the same type as the class and must return a value of the same type. Let's examine how to overload a unary operator using a class that represents only prime numbers.

```
using System;

namespace Other_Features
{
    public class Prime
    {
        public int number;

        public Prime(int n)
        {
            if(isPrime(n))
                this.number = n;
            else
                throw new Exception(n + " is not a prime!");
        }

        public static bool isPrime(int number)
        {
            int max = (int)(number/2 + 1);
```

```
        for(int i = 2;i < max;++i)
            if(number % i == 0)
                return false;
        return true;
    }
  }
}
```

This simple class creates a *Prime* number object with a nifty helper method. The method *isPrime()* checks a given number to see if any other numbers evenly divide into it. If the modulo (%) operator returns a zero it means the number was evenly divisible, hence it is not a prime number.

A useful feature to add to this class would be the increment operator ++. Using this on a *Prime* object should change this object into the next prime number. This is quite easy to implement by adding the following method to the *Prime* class:

```
public static Prime operator ++ (Prime orig)
{
    bool succeeded = false;
    while(!succeeded)
        succeeded = isPrime(++orig.number);
    return orig;
}
```

Notice that the operator parameter and return type are both the same; this is required when overloading the ++ and -- operators. Now we can easily call the ++ operator on an instance of *Prime* to get the next prime number. The following example shows the complete code with our new overloaded operator and a *Main()* method.

```
using System;

namespace Other_Features
{
    public class Prime
    {
        public int number;

        public Prime(int n)
```

```
    {
        if(isPrime(n))
            this.number = n;
        else
            throw new Exception(n + " is not a prime!");
    }


    public static Prime operator ++ (Prime orig)
    {
        bool succeeded = false;
        while(!succeeded)
            succeeded = isPrime(++orig.number);
        return orig;
    }


    public static bool isPrime(int number)
    {
        int max = (int)(number/2 + 1);
        for(int i = 2;i < max;++i)
            if(number % i == 0)
                return false;
        return true;
    }


    public static void Main()
    {
        Prime p = new Prime(11);
        for(int i=0;i<10;++i)
        {
            Console.WriteLine(p.number);
            ++p;
        }
    }

    }
}
```

*Output*

```
11
13
17
19
23
29
31
37
41
43
```

---

**NOTE**

The overloaded ++ or - - operator can be used for postfix and prefix notation. In other words, p++ or ++p both work as expected, with postfix calculating the result after the operator executes and prefix calculating before the operator executes.

---

When using +, -, !, or ~ operators the method definition must take a single argument of the same type as the class, and it can return any type. For example, imagine a game with a class called *Fighter*. We could overload the ! operator so it returns an object that is the opposite of a fighter (such as a peasant). The following is a legal definition for the ! operator in this example:

```
public static Peasant operator!(Fighter f)
```

Of course, this method can return any type, including a *Fighter* object if we choose.

You might be wondering how and why you would overload the *true* or *false* operators. These operators are used in logic tests, such as *if* statements. This operator definition uses a single argument of the same type as the class and must return type *bool*, as follows:

```
public static bool operator true(GeneticComparison gc)
```

Now if you wanted to use a *GeneticComparison* object in a logic test, you just place the object in the brackets, as follows:

```
GeneticComparison gc = new GeneticComparison(fred, bill);
if(gc)
    Console.WriteLine("These two are related.");
```

The *true* and *false* operators are closely related, thus if you overload the *true* operator you are required by C# to overload *false* as well. These are called logical pairs.

# Binary Operator Overloading

*Binary operations* consist of two values and one operator, with the operator placed between the two values, as follows:

```
x != y
```

When overloading a binary operator, the first argument always represents the object to the left of the operator and the second argument represents the object to the right. At least one of the objects (it doesn't matter which) must be of the same type as the class or struct in which it is declared.

There are three logical pairs of binary operators:

- == and !=
- \> and <
- \>= and <=

If one operator of a logical pair is overloaded then the other operator must also be overloaded, otherwise the compiler will complain.

## *Equals()* Method

Java programmers are familiar with the *Object.equals()* method. C# uses an equivalent method, *Equals()* which has the same function. Programmers are encouraged to override the *Equals()* method so the object can be compared to other objects of the same type. Normally if you are overriding the == operator you would also overload *Equals()* so other languages can access the functionality.

**WARNING**

Overriding the *Equals()* method does not automatically override the functionality of the == operator.

# User-Defined Conversions

C# also allows programmers to define casting. Java programmers are probably quite familiar with the built-in casting of Java, which is identical to C#. *Implicit casts* occur when a larger type is instructed to hold the value from a smaller value type. This requires no extra syntax because it is always guaranteed that a larger data type will be able to hold the value from a smaller data type. *Explicit casts* occur when a smaller data type is instructed to hold the value from a larger data type. These types of casts require the programmer to explicitly indicate a cast is occurring in the syntax to ensure the programmer is aware of the possible loss of precision.

```
int a = 221;
double b = a; // implicit cast
a = (int)b; // explicit cast
```

Any conversion operation that might result in the loss of data should be considered an explicit cast. There are always two parts to a conversion: the *source type*, which is the original type of the value being converted, and the *target type*, which is the type it is being converted to. Defining conversion operations in C# is very similar to overloading operators. Conversion operators also use the *operator* keyword, along with the *explicit* or *implicit* keyword:

```
public static implicit operator Prime(int num)
```

> **NOTE**
>
> Conversions can occur between objects and primitive types as well as between objects and other object types.

Let's go over some general rules that must be obeyed when overloading conversions. First, you may not override an existing conversion. Implicit and explicit conversions are already defined for all objects in the same family tree. In other words, the source type may not be a base class for the target type and vice versa. As long as the two class types are in a different branch of the tree, the conversion may be overloaded. For example, let's make up a fictitious hierarchy of classes that are based on mathematical number types. In Figure 7.2 there are two separate branches of classes that inherit from *Number*. The C# language automatically defines conversions between *MersennePrimeNumber*, *PrimeNumber*, *Number*, and *Object*. It has also defined conversions between *FibonacciNumber*, *Number*, and

*Object.* Since they are already defined we may not override them. We can, however, define conversions between *FibonacciNumber* and the *PrimeNumber* types.

**Figure 7.2** Overloading Conversions

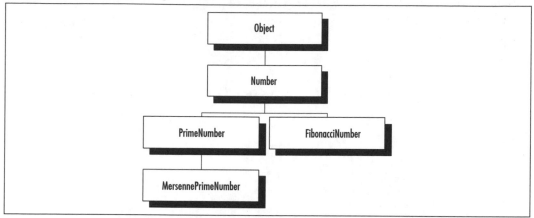

With conversions the definition can occur in either of the two classes. There are essentially two directions of conversion, *explicit* and *implicit*, so it really doesn't matter in which of the two classes it is defined. The important thing is that the conversion definition must be located in one of the classes being converted. A conversion definition may not reside in a third party class. For example, a *PrimeNumber* class could convert from *PrimeNumber* to *MersennePrimeNumber* or *MersennePrimeNumber* to *PrimeNumber*, but not *FibonacciNumber* to *MersennePrimeNumber*.

Neither the source object nor target type may be of *object* type, since it is a given that there will already be a conversion defined for this. Nor may either be an interface type, since any type may inherit the interface, hence it could create an illegal conversion. Now that we know the rules for defining conversions let's examine how they occur in code.

# The *implicit* Operator

Earlier in this chapter we created a class called *Prime* that represents a prime number. Since all prime numbers are numbers, a conversion from *Prime* to any number type should be defined as an *implicit* cast. This will allow us to assign a *Prime* object value to a variable of type *int*, as follows:

```
Prime p = new Prime(11);
int x = p; // Implicit cast
```

In order to achieve this kind of behavior we must create an *implicit* conversion definition. The following definition will allow a *Prime* instance to be treated as an *int*:

```
public static implicit operator int(Prime p)
{
    return p.number;
}
```

This is an easy conversion, but it gives our *Prime* class the impressive ability to masquerade as an *int* primitive, as follows:

```
public static void Main()
{
    Prime p = new Prime(11);
    int sum = p + 12;
    Console.Write("The sum of " + p.number);
    Console.WriteLine(" + 12 is " + sum);
}
```

## Output

```
The sum of 11 + 12 is 23
```

### Debugging...

### Integer Math vs. Floating Point Math

When performing a calculation that assigns an integer value to a *double*, an implicit conversion occurs:

```
double val = 3 / 4;
```

So what value does this return? Many novice programmers would be surprised that it returns 0. These two integers use integer division, therefore 3 divided by 4 equals 0. Once the division is complete it is assigned to the *double* variable. In order to receive a true *double* result from two integer values, you must explicitly cast one of the two values into a double so that floating point math occurs:

```
double val = (double)3 / 4;
```

**Continued**

> or by attaching the letter d beside one of the values:
>
> ```
> double val = 3 / 4d;
> ```
>
> This will assign the expected value of 0.75 to the variable *val*.

# The *explicit* Operator

The assumption with an explicit conversion is that data may be lost or altered when the conversion occurs. For example, when a *float* is converted to an *int*, all decimal places are dropped off. Using our *Prime* example, when an *int* is converted to a *Prime* the *int* may not actually be a prime number. For example, if 4 is converted to a prime number, it must somehow be metamorphosed to become prime. For our example, let's assume if the number is not prime it is converted to the next highest prime number.

```
public static explicit operator Prime(int n)
{
    while(!isPrime(n))
        ++n;
    return new Prime(n);
}
```

This gives a valid conversion from an *int* to a *Prime* object. The following class includes our new implicit and explicit definitions, as well as a *Main()* method to perform an explicit cast.

```
using System;

namespace Other_Features
{
    public class Prime
    {
        public int number;

        public Prime(int n)
        {
            if(isPrime(n))
                this.number = n;
            else
                throw new Exception(n + " is not a prime!");
```

```csharp
    }

    public static explicit operator Prime(int n)
    {
        while(!isPrime(n))
            ++n;
        return new Prime(n);
    }

    public static implicit operator int(Prime p)
    {
        return p.number;
    }

    public static Prime operator ++ (Prime orig)
    {
        bool succeeded = false;
        while(!succeeded)
            succeeded = isPrime(++orig.number);
        return orig;
    }

    public static bool isPrime(int number)
    {
        int max = (int)(number/2 + 1);
        for(int i = 2;i < max;++i)
            if(number % i == 0)
                return false;
        return true;
    }

    public static void Main()
    {
        Prime p = new Prime(11);
        int sum = p + 9;
        p = (Prime)sum;
        Console.WriteLine("p is now " + p.number);
```

```
        }
    }
}
```

*Output*

```
p is now 23
```

As you can see, the *Main()* method starts with the prime number 11. It then adds 9 to it and performs an explicit cast. The explicit cast code knows 20 is not a prime number, so it continues incrementing the number until it finds the next prime number, which is 23.

---

**NOTE**

The *implicit* and *explicit* operators are not logical pairs. You may legally define one conversion without defining the other in a class.

---

# Structs

You may have noticed a pattern to the last part of this chapter. Java has a fixed set of operators; C# allows overloading of operators. Java has a fixed set of casts allowed; C# allows you to define casting. This brings us to structs, a topic that follows this pattern. The theme for this section is that Java has a limited set of primitives, whereas C# allows you to define objects that behave like primitives.

Structs are very similar to classes; in fact there are probably more similarities than differences. Structs may define the same members as classes: methods, constructors, fields, constants, properties, events, indexers, operators, and conversions. A struct may also implement one or more interfaces, just like a class.

There are, of course, some important differences, otherwise this construct would not have been included in C#. First, structs may not inherit from classes or other structs. Structs inherit from objects automatically, just like other value types, but for all purposes they are similar to *sealed* classes. They also may not create destructor methods, since they are not instantiated in the same way as classes (more on this later).

When a class is instantiated it creates an object that is accessed by reference. The actual object is created on the *heap*. The heap is section of memory that stores long-term program data that exists even after methods returns. Structs, however, are value types and stored on the *stack*, a section of memory that holds values used and computed during program execution. It is faster for a program to access values from the stack than from the heap. Primitive values are stored on the stack. This means structs behave just like primitive values. When a struct is passed to a method, a copy of the struct is made. Normally instances are passed by reference, which results in different behavior (this will be explored later).

So what does C# gain by allowing structs? They are used primarily to represent data types such as points and number sets. Although they allow methods to be defined, a struct is generally not created for providing functionality. Something like the *Math* class, which is designed purely for functionality and not storing data, could be considered the opposite of a struct.

Using a struct instead of a class provides several benefits. Let's use the example of a *Point* class used for storing two integer values, X and Y. If we create an array to hold 200 instances of this class, the program will create an object for the array plus 200 objects to hold the points. However, if we employ a struct instead, only one object will be created for the array and the 200 *Point* structs are stored inline with the array.

Structs also have their weaknesses. When a struct is passed to a method, copies of the fields are created. If the struct contains a lot of data this can result in more memory use. Also, if the struct is used as an *object* then boxing will automatically be used (just like other primitive types). This can create some extra overhead and slow things down slightly.

# Defining Structs

The C# language defines all of its primitive types as structs. Along with operator overloading and user-defined conversions, this allows you to define very functional primitive types. In this section we will define a new primitive type, but first let's examine the basic syntax for defining a struct.

```
attributes modifiers struct identifier :interfaces {}
```

This is almost identical to a class definition. About the only difference is that inheritance of other classes is not allowed. Now let's define our own struct. C# pretty much has most useful number types defined as primitives, but there is no fraction primitive. Fractions are even more accurate than decimal numbers, since many decimal numbers are forced to round the last decimal place. Our fraction struct will store just two integral numbers: the numerator and the denominator. It will allow for conversions to and from double values, and allow fraction multiplication and addition.

```
using System;

namespace Other_Features
{
    public struct fraction
    {
        public int numerator;
        public int denominator;

        public fraction(int numerator, int denominator)
        {
            this.numerator = numerator;
            this.denominator = denominator;
            Reduce();
        }

        public static fraction operator *(fraction f1, fraction f2)
        {
            fraction f;
            f.numerator = f1.numerator * f2.numerator;
            f.denominator = f1.denominator * f2.denominator;
            f.Reduce();
            return f;
        }

        public static fraction operator +(fraction f1, fraction f2)
        {
            fraction f;
            f.numerator = f1.numerator * f2.denominator + f2.numerator *
                f1.denominator;
            f.denominator = f1.denominator * f2.denominator;
            f.Reduce();
            return f;
        }

        public static implicit operator double(fraction f)
        {
```

```csharp
        double d = (double)f.numerator/f.denominator;
        return d;
    }

    public static explicit operator fraction(double d)
    {
        fraction f;
        f.denominator = 1;
        while(d - (int)d != 0)
        {
            d *= 10;
            f.denominator *= 10;
        }
        f.numerator = (int)d;
        f.Reduce();
        return f;
    }

    public void Reduce()
    {
        int max = (int)this.denominator / 2 + 1;
        for(int i=max;i>1;--i)
        {
            if(this.numerator % i == 0 & this.denominator % i == 0)
            {
                this.numerator /= i;
                this.denominator /= i;
            }
        }
    }

    public override string ToString()
    {
        String s = this.numerator + "/" + this.denominator;
        return s;
    }
    }
}
```

In many ways this class is a summary of most of the material covered in this chapter. There is a helper method called *Reduce()*, which reduces the denominator to the lowest value possible. On the surface the methods in this struct appear to be identical to class methods, until we take a closer look. Let's examine the first two lines of the explicit operator definition:

```
fraction f;
f.denominator = 1;
```

Notice the code begins accessing *f.denominator* without calling the constructor for the struct. When creating an instance of a class it is necessary to use the keyword *new* in order to create a new object. Structs don't require this, since the data is stored right on the stack. All variables are ready for access without even using new, just like primitive types, which is why the fraction type can access denominator without a constructor.

Struct constructors behave differently from class constructors. In a regular class, when there is no constructor created, the default no-arguments constructor will initialize the variables with default values (0, null or false). The struct default constructor behaves the same way, but if you create a constructor with arguments, the variables in your struct are not automatically given default values. Try removing the lines in the constructor that assign values to numerator and denominator:

```
public fraction(int numerator, int denominator)
{
    //This.numerator = numerator;
    //This.denominator = denominator;
    //Reduce();
}
```

Now if we create a struct and attempt to access numerator or denominator we receive the following error from the compiler:

```
Field 'Other_Features.fraction.denominator' must be fully assigned before
    control leaves the constructor.
```

As you can see, the variables were not given default values of 0. The fields are not initialized with values; therefore they may not be accessed.

## Using Structs

There are two ways to obtain structs and to use them, as mentioned previously. The first is by using the *new* keyword, just like a regular class. The second is to assign it to a variable and access it right away. Try the following code to see the fraction struct in action.

```
public static void Main()
{
    fraction f1 = new fraction(10, 20);
    fraction f2;
    f2.numerator = 5;
    f2.denominator = 20;
    fraction f = f1 + f2;
    Console.WriteLine("f is " + f);
}
```

## Output

```
f is 3/4
```

> ### WARNING
>
> Obtaining a struct without calling the *new* keyword can lead to problems since it bypasses the constructor method. The programmer of a struct may have included vital initialization code in the constructor, so you are playing with fire by ignoring it.

Earlier in this section it was mentioned that when an instance of a class is passed to a method, a reference to the object is passed. In contrast, when a struct is passed to a method, a copy of the struct is made and passed to the method. Let's first see how a struct behaves when passed to a method:

```
using System;

namespace Other_Features
{
    public class Test
    {
        public static void Main()
        {
            fraction f = new fraction(10, 20);
            Console.WriteLine(" In Main() method before: " + f);
```

```
        Increment(f);
        Console.WriteLine(" In Main() method after: " + f);
    }


    public static void Increment(fraction f)
    {
        ++f.numerator;
        Console.WriteLine("In Increment method: " + f);
    }
  }
}
```

## Output

```
In Main() method before: 1/2
In Increment method: 2/2
In Main() method after: 1/2
```

As you can see, the fraction struct in the *Main()* method is not affected by changes made to the variable in the *Increment()* method. This is because a copy is passed to the *Increment()* method. Now let's make a simple *Fraction* class to demonstrate how classes behave:

```
using System;

namespace Other_Features
{
    public class Fraction
    {
        public int numerator;
        public int denominator;

        public Fraction(int numerator, int denominator)
        {
            this.numerator = numerator;
            this.denominator = denominator;
        }
    }
}
```

This is a simplified version of the fraction struct. Now let's try a similar test by passing the object to the *Increment()* method.

```
using System;

namespace Other_Features
{
    public class Test
    {
        public static void Main()
        {
            Fraction f = new Fraction(1, 2);
            Console.WriteLine(" In Main() method before: " + f);
            Increment(f);
            Console.WriteLine(" In Main() method after: " + f);
        }

        public static void Increment(Fraction f)
        {
            ++f.numerator;
            Console.WriteLine("In Increment method: " + f);
        }
    }
}
```

## Output

```
In Main() method before: 1/2
In Increment method: 2/2
In Main() method after: 2/2
```

This clearly shows a change made within a method to an object also occurs outside the method. Class instances are passed to methods using a reference variable, hence when a change occurs within the method it is reflected outside the method with other references to the same object. Most Java programmers are aware of this, but it's an important difference with *structs* that is worth reviewing.

# Summary

In this chapter we covered some important differences between Java and C#. A lot of these differences may seem revolutionary, especially for programmers who were not already familiar with C++.

Properties, read-only fields, and enumeration offer new ways of accessing variables within a class or object. A property is a great way to receive the benefits of encapsulation without needing to use accessor methods. Read-only fields allow variables to be initialized only within the constructor. Enumerations offer an alternative to the Java alternative of piggybacking constants on interfaces.

C# also offers a type of casting between primitives and objects known as boxing. This allows primitives to be passed into methods that require objects. To Java programmers, boxing appears similar to a wrapper class, only C# performs boxing automatically.

Operator overloading is yet another powerful C# feature that allows programmers to use operators such as + and % on common objects, rather than just on primitives. User-defined conversions takes polymorphism to a whole new level. With Java the only casting that can occur between objects are with objects in the same line of inheritance. Now any object not in the same inheritance line can be converted (explicitly or implicitly) to another—but it helps if the conversion makes sense.

Finally, we covered structs, a way to define primitive-like objects that exist on the stack. There are certain advantages to using structs but, depending on what the struct is used for, there can also be disadvantages. Generally they save system resources, but if they are used as objects the boxing/unboxing procedure can slow the program down.

# Solutions Fast Track

## Properties

☑ The *get* accessor must return the same type as the property.

☑ The *set* accessor uses a single parameter with the *value* keyword.

☑ Accessors can be used to

■ verify that the new data is correct.

- recalculate values for this or other variables.
- refresh a GUI object.

## Read-Only Fields

☑ Read-only fields may not be altered except for those in constructors.

☑ Fields are defined as read-only with the *readonly* keyword.

## Enumerations

☑ Enumeration lists group integer constants together.

☑ Enumerators are not integers, they are objects.

☑ Enumerators may be explicitly cast into integers.

## Boxing and Unboxing

☑ All primitives can be boxed into an object automatically.

☑ Boxed objects may be unboxed by explicitly casting them into primitives.

☑ The boxed data is in no way referenced by the original primitive.

## Operator Overloading

☑ The operator method must be both *public* and *static*.

☑ The method arguments must be value types (i.e., not *ref* or *out* parameters).

☑ The signature of the operator method must be unique within the class.

☑ If using the *extern* modifier, rather than using a body of code in brackets, a semicolon is used at the end of the definition.

☑ All types referenced in the declaration must be at least as accessible as the operator definition. For example, a public operator may not access a protected type.

# User-Defined Conversions

☑ Existing conversions may not be overridden.

☑ The conversion definition must be located in one of the classes being converted.

☑ Neither the source object nor the target type may be of *object* type.

☑ A conversion may not occur with an interface type.

# Structs

☑ Structs may not inherit from classes or other structs.

☑ Objects reside on the heap, and structs reside on the stack.

☑ Structs are generally used to represent data types such as points and number sets.

☑ Structs are passed by value, not by reference. When a struct is passed to a method, copies of the values are created.

☑ If the struct is used as an object then boxing will be used automatically.

# Frequently Asked Questions

The following Frequently Asked Questions, answered by the authors of this book, are designed to both measure your understanding of the concepts presented in this chapter and to assist you with real-life implementation of these concepts. To have your questions about this chapter answered by the author, browse to **www.syngress.com/solutions** and click on the **"Ask the Author"** form.

**Q:** Generally explicit casts return less precise data than implicit casts. Is it possible to do the opposite and make an implicit cast return less accurate data?

**A:** Yes, C# gives the programmer the freedom to determine how a cast actually operates, but a good design makes casts intuitive. When creating explicit and implicit casts between two types it is wise to analyze which type seems to have more precise data, and make those conversions implicit.

**Q:** Why would I choose to use a struct instead of a class?

**A:** When the reason for the existence of an object is mainly to store data, a struct would be a good option. Structs reside on the stack so they are slightly faster and take up less memory than an object.

**Q:** In Java, constants that are used by many different classes typically are declared in an interface. How do C# programs declare constants?

**A:** By using enumerations. An enumeration allows formal constants to be defined within a class, or as a separate entity.

**Q:** How is encapsulation of data handled in C# compared to Java?

**A:** Java uses *get()* and *set()* methods whereas C# uses properties. Properties are defined in a class by creating *get* and *set* definitions (without parameters). The *set* method accepts a single parameter by using the *value* keyword.

**Q:** How is it possible to call methods on a primitive in C#?

**A:** C# provides boxing and unboxing. This is very similar to casting in that there are implicit and explicit directives to govern this.

# Chapter 8

# Delegates
# and Events

Solutions in this chapter:

- **Delegates**

- **Using Delegates as Callbacks**

- **Using Delegates for Event Handling**

- **Multicasting**

- **Advanced Delegate Usage**

☑ **Summary**

☑ **Solutions Fast Track**

☑ **Frequently Asked Questions**

# Introduction

Interaction between the user and the computer is a fundamental part of computing. In the old days we used a procedural programming model, like a command line program that asks for user input one line (or character) at a time. Nowadays we are treated to more sophisticated programs with rich graphical user interfaces (GUI) and event-driven programming. To facilitate writing event-driven programs, a language must provide support for event handling. Java provides this by using inner class adapters in its Abstract Windowing Toolkit (AWT) event-handling model. C#, on the other hand, implements event handling through *delegates*.

A delegate is essentially a reference to some method. When it is declared, it is assigned a method signature. An application can then assign any method that matches this signature to a delegate variable. When this delegate variable is invoked, the associated method is called. If you have some C/C++ background, think of delegates as being very similar to function pointers. However, unlike function pointers, delegates are object-oriented, type-safe, and secure.

In the first part of the chapter we will look at delegates and how they can be used as callback methods. Next we'll talk about how delegates are used for events and event handling. Finally, we'll go over some more advanced delegate concepts.

# Delegates

As previously mentioned, a delegate is a reference to some method. It is much like any other variable, except that it represents a method. For instance, an integer type can hold any value that fits the description of an integer. A class reference can refer to any object, as long as that object is of the correct type. A delegate can refer to any method, as long as it has a certain signature. For example, you could specify that a delegate refer to a method that returns an integer and takes a single parameter of type *string*. It can then hold a reference to any method with that signature, and then that delegate could be used to call that method. In that sense, a delegate object is really just a variable, but instead of holding an integer or class type, it holds a method of a predetermined signature.

A delegate's ability to allow a method to be called dynamically is what makes it so powerful. The method (or methods) that is referred to by the delegate is assigned at runtime and can be added and removed at will. For this reason, delegates are especially useful for event handlers and callback functions, for which they are primarily used in the .NET Framework.

One concept that is important to remember (and somewhat confusing) with delegates is that when you initially declare a delegate, you are essentially declaring a new type, rather than declaring a reference to an object. You can then declare objects of that type, and then instantiate them. We will go into more detail on this in the next section. For the time being, just remember that a delegate declaration actually specifies a new class. This declaration can be within the current namespace, or in its own namespace.

# Using Delegates as Callbacks

Callback methods are an extremely useful programming tool. Anyone who has done good-old-fashioned Windows programming in C or C++ should be very familiar with them. For the benefit of those not familiar with callback methods, they are simply methods that are provided for another thread to call later. For example, in Windows programming, every window implements a callback function (called a *window procedure*). A reference to the window procedure is passed to Windows, so that Windows can call that procedure when a user, say, clicks the mouse when the mouse is over that window. Otherwise, our window would have to poll the mouse every few milliseconds to see if a button were clicked or not (highly inefficient, since every window would have to do its own polling).

Callbacks are useful not just for receiving notifications—they are also very handy for asynchronous processing. For example, my program may want to tell a database to do a very long re-indexing operation, but I want my program to continue normal operation in the meantime. I could start the indexing operation and provide the database engine with a reference to a callback method. The database would then do its indexing asynchronously and call my method when the operation was done to notify my program that it is finished.

Since delegates can be used to dynamically call methods, they are ideally suitable to be use for callback functions. For instance, let's look at a database-indexing example to show how we can make use of delegates. Assume that you have a database application and part of the program performs indexing on the database. When you invoke the indexing function, you don't want the main thread to have to wait for the indexing to finish. By the same token, you also don't want to have to poll the method constantly to see if it has finished. Instead, you can have the indexing method call back the main program to notify it when it has completed its task. This would be an excellent time to use delegates.

Basically, the database engine will declare a delegate type. Our program will then create an instance of that delegate type and provide it to the database engine. Finally, our database engine will use the delegate instance to call our call-back method.

# Declaration

The database indexing engine will declare the delegate type. Remember that the indexer is not declaring a variable or an instance of an object—it is actually declaring a new type. This declaration makes use of the *delegate* keyword, which means that instances of this type will be delegates. If we wanted a callback of return type *void* that takes no arguments, it would look like this:

```
class DBIndexer
{
  public delegate void DoneIndexingCallback();
}
```

Basically, this means that

- There is now a new type named *DoneIndexingCallback*.

- Instances of *DoneIndexingCallback* will contain references to methods.

- The referenced methods can be any method, as long as they have a return type of *void*, and take no arguments.

A delegate can also return a value and/or accept arguments. In this block of code, we will declare a delegate type that returns an integer, and accepts an integer and a string as arguments:

```
class DBIndexer
{
  public delegate int DoneIndexingCallback(int nNum, string
    sString);
}
```

For the purposes of our database indexer, let's say that our delegate has a return type of *void*, and takes a single integer as a parameter, namely the number of indexes that were re-indexed. Keep in mind that the indexer will be calling back our main program; thus the parameter (the number of indexes) will actually be supplied by the indexer to our main program when the callback is called. Therefore, our actual delegate declaration will look like this:

```
class DBIndexer
{
```

```
public delegate void DoneIndexingCallback(int
   nNumberOfIndexes);
}
```

## Developing & Deploying…

### Some Notes on Declaration

As mentioned earlier, a delegate does not have to be declared inside of a class namespace. This is because a delegate is not class-specific. In our previous example, all of our declarations were done within the *DBIndexer* class, but they can also be declared in their own namespace. For instance, I could create a new namespace, called *MyNamespace*, and declare a delegate in it:

```
namespace MyNamespace

{

   public delegate void MyDelegate();

}
```

Down the road, we would simply refer to the delegate as *MyNamespace.MyDelegate*, or include *MyNamespace* with the *using* keyword. Of course, if our classes were also implemented within *MyNamespace*, we wouldn't need to do anything. The .NET Framework includes many delegates that are declared outside of classes, such as the *EventHandler* delegate that is declared in the *System* namespace. We will talk more about that in the section on event handling.

Delegates do not have to be declared with any modifiers other than the *delegate* keyword, and they can have any signature. If you want to use them outside of your current class or namespace, however, (which is often the case) you must declare them as public.

## Instantiation

Once a delegate has been defined, an instance of that delegate can be instantiated and then made to reference a method. Remember that the signature of the method that the delegate will reference was determined when the delegate was declared. We can instantiate the delegate with any method that matches that signature. To take the previous example a step further, we will declare a delegate in *DBIndexer*, and then instantiate an instance of it in our main class. The instance will be constructed with a reference to the *DoneIndexing* method (a member of *DBEngine*), which is the method through which we want to get called back.

Expanding on the code we wrote before, we will now implement our *DBEngine*. Inside of the *Main()* method, we must first instantiate an instance of *DBEngine*. In this particular case, we need this instance so that we can access the nonstatic method *DoneIndexing*:

```
DBEngine dbEngine = new DBEngine();
```

Once we have an instance of *DBEngine*, we can instantiate the delegate itself. Remember that declaring a delegate declares a new type. If we were declaring a variable of type *string*, we might say:

```
string s = new string("hello");
```

In this case, however, the type is *DoneIndexingCallback*, which is the delegate type we declared earlier. The declaration will look like this:

```
DBIndexer.DoneIndexingCallback callback = new
DBIndexer.DoneIndexingCallback(DBEngine.DoneIndexing);
```

Now we have declared a new object of type *DBIndexer.DoneIndexingCallback*, and instantiated it. The constructor takes only one argument, namely the method that we want to get called (i.e., our callback). Note that *DBEngine.DoneIndexing* returns *void* and takes a single integer as a parameter, just as our *DoneIndexingCallback* declaration specified.

The final piece of *DBEngine* would be to implement the *DoneIndexing* method, which will be implemented later. For now, here is all of the code that we have thus far:

```
using System;
class DBIndexer
{
    //Declare our delegate.
    public delegate void DoneIndexingCallback(int nNumberOfIndexes);
}

class DBEngine
{
    public static void Main(string[] args)
```

```
{
   //Instantiate an instance of DBEngine.
   DBEngine dbEngine = new DBEngine();


   //Instantiate an instance of our delegate, and make it
   //reference the dbEngine.DoneIndexing method.
   DBIndexer.DoneIndexingCallback callback = new  DBIndexer.
      DoneIndexingCallback(dbEngine.DoneIndexing);
}


//The callback method
public void DoneIndexing(int nNumberOfIndexes)
{
   //We will implement later.
}
}
```

To summarize, we now have a delegate type that we declared, namely *DoneIndexingCallback*. We created the *DBEngine* class and instantiated an instance of *DoneIndexingCallback*, which we assigned to *callback*, and set it to reference the *DoneIndexing* method. Now when *callback* is invoked, it will execute the *DoneIndexing* method. In the next section, we'll take a look at actually invoking *DBEngine.DoneIndexing* from within *DBIndexer*.

## Invocation

To invoke our callback, we first provide a reference to it to the *DBIndexer* class. This can be done in various ways, but often is accomplished by passing the delegate into the method that is going to call us back. For instance, our asynchronous method will be declared like this:

```
public void Index(DoneIndexingCallback callback)
```

As you can see, we are passing an argument of type *DoneIndexingCallback* into our method. Depending on our architecture, we could either store the reference into a property so we could call it outside of this method's scope, or we could just use the argument itself to invoke the callback. In our case, we will just use the argument itself. Invoking the callback looks just like making a regular method call, like this:

```
callback(nNumberOfIndexes);
```

Now let's put it all together: the final *DBIndexer* class declaration will look like the following.

```
class DBIndexer
{
  public delegate void DoneIndexingCallback(int
  nNumberOfIndexes);

  public void Index(DoneIndexingCallback callback)
  {
    int nNumberOfIndexes=0;
    //Perfom indexing operation here.

    //Invoke the callback.
    callback(nNumberOfIndexes);
  }
}
```

Note that we invoked our callback method using the *callback* delegate that was passed in, just like we were calling any other method. In the next section, we will tie everything together and implement the entire working example.

## Implementing Callbacks

To implement the callback, the *DBEngine* will need to create an instance of the *DBIndexer* class and pass it the *callback* delegate. Here's what it will look like:

```
DBIndexer.DoneIndexingCallback callback = new
    DBIndexer.DoneIndexingCallback(dbEngine.DoneIndexing);

DBIndexer indexer = new DBIndexer();
indexer.Index(callback);
```

That's about all there is to callbacks! To summarize, in order to create a callback method, first you'll need to declare a delegate. The callback method you wish to call back must match the signature of the delegate. You then create an instance of the delegate, which references the method that you want to call back. The instance of the delegate can be passed into any method, just like any other object.

Now let's finish implementing the database indexing example. First, however, let me point out that in order to be practical and useful, callbacks really require some asynchronous processing to take place. To make a truly realistic example, we would want to spawn a new thread to perform indexing and then return to the main thread. Later, when the new thread is finished, it would call the callback to alert the main thread that it is finished. We will not be using threads for this example to make it simpler (they will be discussed later in Chapter 10). You should note, therefore, that this example is simple and single-threaded. I will point out where you would normally want to spawn another thread, but we will not actually do so.

We must add two more sections of code to our example to make it complete. The first is the complete *DBIndexer.Index* method. In our case, we will just make it waste some time by calling the *Thread.Sleep()* method, to give the appearance of hefty logic. For this exercise, we'll pass an arbitrary number (6 in this case) to the calling function. The *DB.Indexer.Index* method will look like this:

```
public void Index(DoneIndexingCallback callback)
{
   int nNumberOfIndexes=6;

   //Pretend like we are working hard.
   System.Threading.Thread.Sleep(5000);

   //Tell the calling function we are done.
   callback(nNumberOfIndexes);
}
```

The final piece of our example is the implementation of the actual method that will get called back, namely *DBEngine.DoneIndexing*. It simply will consist of a single statement that will let us know when it gets called:

```
public void DoneIndexing(int nNumberOfIndexes)
{
   Console.WriteLine("Done indexing, there are " +
   nNumberOfIndexes + " indexes in the database");
}
```

That completes our example! Now let's see the entire example, end to end:

```
using System;
namespace CallbackSample
{
```

```
class DBIndexer
{
  //This declares a delegate that we can use for
  // callbacks.
  public delegate void DoneIndexingCallback(int
   nNumberOfIndexes);

  //The indexing method, where we presumably would execute
  // complex and time-consuming logic
  public void Index(DoneIndexingCallback callback)
  {
    int nNumberOfIndexes=6;
    //Pretend like we are working hard.
    System.Threading.Thread.Sleep(5000);

    //Tell the calling function we are done.
    callback(nNumberOfIndexes);
  }
}


//This is our main class. It will be making a call to the
//DBIndexer, and will get called back when the
//indexer is done processing.
class DBEngine
{
  static void Main(string[] args)
  {
    DBEngine dbEngine = new DBEngine();

    //Assign the DoneIndexing method as the method to
    //be called back when indexing is complete.
    DBIndexer.DoneIndexingCallback callback = new
   DBIndexer.DoneIndexingCallback(dbEngine.DoneIndexing);

    DBIndexer indexer=new DBIndexer();
    Console.WriteLine("Calling the DBIndexer...");
```

```
        //Call the Index method passing the callback delegate.
        //Ideally, we would launch this method in a new thread
        //and then continue on with other logic.
        indexer.Index(callback);

        //Continue doing some work while waiting for the
        //callback, but since it's not asyncronous, it will
        //actually block before continuing.
        for(int i=0; i<100; i++)
        {
          Console.WriteLine(i);
        }
    }

    //This is the method that will get called back when
    // the Indexer is finished.
    public void DoneIndexing(int nNumberOfIndexes)
    {
      Console.WriteLine("Done indexing, there are " +
      nNumberOfIndexes + " indexes in the database");
    }
  }
}
```

If you run this example, you will see the following output:

```
Calling the DBIndexer.
Done indexing, there are 6 indexes in the database
0
1
...
99
```

Note that the callback is called *before* we write out 1 through 100. That is because, in our case, everything happens in the same thread. We call the indexer, and then the indexer calls the callback. After the callback has been called, control returns to the main thread, so it can continue. Had we added asynchronous logic to the *DBIndexer*, the results would most likely be different.

# Using Delegates for Event Handling

Events in C# follow the very common publisher-subscriber model. This model is so named because it consists of event publishers, which publish or "fire" an event, and event subscribers, which subscribe to that event (in other words, they register to receive the event). This event model is often used in GUI programs. The idea behind the event model is that some classes publish events, and consumers subscribe to the events in which they are interested. When an event fires, a method is invoked in the publisher that will cycle through each of the registered subscribers and invoke a callback method on each one. The subscribers then take some action.

When we talked about using delegates as callbacks, the delegate could represent a method with any signature—it could take any number of arguments with different types, and return any type. In the .NET Framework, there are built-in delegates defined for events. The most basic of them is the *System.EventHandler* delegate.

The *System.EventHandler* delegate specifies a return type of *void*, and it takes two arguments. The first argument is a reference to the object that published the event (the event source). The second argument consists of data about the event itself. It must be of type *System.EventArgs*, or some type derived from *System.EventArgs*. All event delegates in the .NET Framework have this same signature. For example, the *MouseEventHandlerDelegate* in the *System.Windows.Forms* namespace is used to handle mouse events, like mouse clicks. As its first argument, it takes an object type (the event source). Its second argument is of type *MouseEventArgs*, which is derived from *System.EventArgs*.

Theoretically you could create your own events and delegates that do not follow the *System.EventHandler* convention. However, there is really no need to do so. By following this convention, the Framework allows for a single known delegate signature that works for any event, no matter what kind of data needs to be supplied to the handler.

As we discuss events, keep in mind that an event handler is really just a callback method. When we discussed callbacks, we created a callback function and gave another object a reference to it so we could receive a callback notification. With events, we create an event handler, which is basically a callback function, and then provide the system with a reference to our event handler. The system will then call back our event handler when our event occurs.

# Event Handling in Java

In Java's AWT, events are usually handled through inner classes that implement the *ActionListener* interface. Let's look at an example. Figure 8.1 defines a *JPanel* object. It will use an inner class that implements *ActionListener* as an event handler. This will be added as a handler for a button click event.

**Figure 8.1** Java JPanel Object with Event Handling

```
public class MyPanel extends JPanel
{
  //Here is a button to receive click events.
  JButton myButton = new JButton("Click me");

  //And now for an inner class to listen for events
  private class ButtonClick implements ActionListener {
    public void actionPerformed(ActionEvent e) {
      //Event handler code here
      . . .
    }
  }

  public MyPanel()
  {
    //Tell ActionListener to handle button clicks.
    myButton.addActionListener(new ButtonClick());
    . . .
  }
}
```

In the example in Figure 8.1 we defined an inner class called *ButtonClick* that will act as the event subscriber for the button. In other words, it will receive the event that is published by the button. When the user clicks on the button, it invokes the *actionPerformed* method.

As you'll discover in the next section, the net effect is the same as using delegates in C#. An event handler subscribes to certain events, and then gets called when the events get fired. You could even think about the previous example in terms of delegates, and perhaps understand them better: the *ActionListener* interface (extended by *ButtonClick* in this case) is behaving as a delegate. You can think of the *actionPerformed* method as the callback method being called back when an event occurs. Events in C# behave in much the same way. Some class will delegate the handling of its events to a method (or several methods). Instead of having to implement a certain interface like *ActionListener*, it must simply have a method with the proper signature (i.e., the signature must match a certain delegate). To clearly show the analogy, let's look at how the Java code could be implemented using delegates in C#, as shown in Figure 8.2.

## Figure 8.2 C# Equivalent of Figure 8.1

```
namespace EventTest
{
public delegate void ActionListener(String actionEvent);

public class Button
{
  public void addActionListener(ActionListener actionListener)
  {
    //Generate an ActionEvent and then perform the
    //callback.
    actionListener("Button Clicked");
  }
}

public class MyPanel
{
  public MyPanel()
  {
    ActionListener buttonClick = new ActionListener(ActionPerformed);

    Button myButton = new Button();
    myButton.addActionListener(buttonClick);
  }

  public void ActionPerformed(String actionEvent)
  {
    //Event handler code here
```

**Continued**

**Figure 8.2** Continued

```
    }
}
}
```

In Figure 8.2 we named our methods and variables to match their Java equivalents. Notice that we defined the delegate within the namespace, but outside of the class definition, which is a valid declaration. The *ActionListener* delegate is behaving like its Java counterpart. However, instead of having an inner class extending an interface, we instantiate the delegate (which we called *buttonClick*) and assign a callback method which, in this case, we called *ActionPerformed*.

Note that this example is not the proper way to create buttons and event handlers in C#—it is used just to illustrate a point. You'll get to see how to handle GUI events in C# later.

> **NOTE**
>
> Microsoft first introduced delegates in their Visual J++ product, which was designed by Anders Hejlsberg (also one of the lead designers for C#). This caused a lot of legal and technical disputes between Sun and Microsoft. Sun claims that *delegates* are unnecessary and that *inner classes* provide better support for user-interface event handling requirements. Microsoft strongly disagrees with this point of view. It's hard to judge which technology is superior. The important thing is that both languages provide support for event handling. As a Java programmer you might be a little biased, but once you get the hang of delegates, you will probably find that they are extremely flexible and do tend to lead to more concise source code.
>
> For more information on Microsoft and Sun's arguments you can read the white papers at http://msdn.microsoft.com/visualj/technical/articles/delegates/truth.asp and at http://java.sun.com/docs/white/delegates.html.

# Event Handling in C#

Event handling in C# is fairly simple. As stated earlier, the *System.EventHandler* delegate specifies a return type of *void*, and takes two arguments. The first argument is a reference to the event source, and the second is the event data, which must derive from *System.EventArgs*. Any method that has the correct signature can be used as an event handler. For example, the following method might be used to handle the *Click* event for a button named *cmdClickMe*. (The *cmdClickMe_Click* is an arbitrary name for the function.)

```
private void cmdClickMe_Click(object sender,
 System.EventArgs e) {
 MessageBox.Show("cmdClickMe was clicked!");
}
```

To register our method as an event handler we must create a new *System.EventHandler* delegate and pass our method name as a parameter:

```
new System.EventHandler(cmdClickMe_Click);
```

Since *cmdClickMe_Click* matches the *System.EventHandler* delegate's signature, we can assign it to handle any standard system event. The *System.EventHandler* delegate is a predefined delegate especially declared to be used for handling standard system events. We can use it to instantiate an instance of a delegate through which our event handler will be called.

To assign our event handler to the **cmdClickMe** button click event, we can take advantage of the overloaded + operator. Specifically, we can use the += operator to add our delegate to the button's click event handler list, like this:

```
cmdClickMe.Click += new
    System.EventHandler(cmdClickMe_Click);
```

It's as simple as that! If we click the **cmdClickMe** button, we will see a message box that says, "cmdClickMe was clicked!" We used the += operator to add an event handler for the *click* event, which we constructed using the global *EventHandler* delegate. This same convention is used for consuming any standard system event in C#. Creating GUI applications will be discussed again in Chapter 12.

## Using System.EventArgs

For simple events, like button clicks, the *System.EventArgs* argument has very little data in it, since there is not really any information to pass. For more complex events, however, our handler generally will use a subclass of *System.EventArgs* that has some real data in it. For instance, if we are consuming mouse events, our handler will take an argument of type *System.Windows.Forms.MouseEventArgs*.

*MouseEventArgs* contains information specific to mouse clicks, such as which button was clicked, how many times it was clicked, what the x and y screen coordinates of the mouse were at the time, and so on. To illustrate this further, the following section will show how you can extend *System.EventArgs* and create your own events.

# Creating and Handling Events

In many applications, especially multithreaded ones, creating, firing, and handling your own events can be extremely useful. Take, for example, a socket-based application. You could use a single thread to do all of your processing, including checking the socket for incoming data. It would be much tidier, however, to spawn a separate thread that listens on the socket for incoming data while another thread performs the processing. When new data is received, it could fire an event, and we could create an event handler to get called when new data arrives on the socket.

Events are also useful when an application needs to receive data from external sources. Often, this communication is accomplished using messages. Such messages generally are transferred using message queues, or are sent directly to an application. To get the full effect of events, let's create an application where we create, fire, and handle our own events when a message is received. Our application will allow messages to be sent to it, and when it receives messages, it will fire an event to the clients subscribing to the messages. It will have these parts:

- A *MessageData* class, derived from *System.EventArgs*, that will contain our message data when events are fired

- A *MessageManager* class that receives messages and then fires events

- A *MessageClient* class that handles events fired by the *MessageManager*

- A *MainApplication* class that creates our other class instances and sends messages to the *MessageManager*

## *The* MessageData *Class*

The *MessageData* class encapsulates the data that will be sent as the second argument to the event handler. As discussed previously, this object must derive from *System.EventArgs*. Our class will have only one property, namely a string that will contain the text of the message that was sent. We will also provide a constructor to initialize our string. Our class will look like this:

```
class MessageData : System.EventArgs
{
  //This is the string that will contain the message text.
  public string sMessageText;

  //A constructor to initialized sMessageText
  public MessageData(string sText)
  {
    sMessageText = sText;
  }
}
```

## *The* MessageManager *Class*

The *MessageManager* class actually will receive the messages. It will be called by other components, which will pass the message to it. It is then responsible for firing the event that will notify subscribed clients that a message has been received.

To define the type of event handler that it is able to call, the *MessageManager* declares a delegate named *MessageEventHandler*, which returns *void* and takes two parameters, an object and a *MessageData* parameter. Since *MessageData* is derived from *System.EventArgs*, our *MessageEventHandler* delegate fits the mold for a standard event handler. The declaration looks like this:

```
public delegate void MessageEventHandler(object sender,
 MessageData e);
```

> **NOTE**
>
> We named our *MessageData* parameter e. This is not really descriptive, and you can call your *EventArgs* object something more useful. In this example, e is used simply to follow the precedence set by the rest of the .NET Framework, where this object is always named e.

*MessageManager* also defines the event that we will fire when we receive a new message. This event is defined using the *event* keyword. When we use the *event* keyword, the compiler will look for two things after it: the delegate type that will be allowed to handle this event, and the name of the event. In our example, the event declaration looks like this:

```
public event MessageEventHandler OnMessageReceived;
```

This basically says that we have declared a new event that can be handled by delegates of type *MessageEventHandler*. The name of the event will be *OnMessageReceived*.

Since the *MessageManager* class is responsible for receiving messages, we need to implement a method through which clients can send messages. We'll call the method *SendMessage*. This method will also be responsible for creating a *MessageData* class with the message text in it, and then sending the *MessageData* out as part of an *OnMessageReceived* event that it will fire. The *MessageData* object is created by using its constructor. The *OnMessageReceived* event can then be fired by calling the *OnMessageReceived* event as if it were a method. We'll supply a reference to ourselves using the *this* keyword along with the *MessageData* object when we fire the event. The entire *SendMessage()* method will look like this:

```
public void SendMessage(string sMessage)
{
    MessageData msgData=new MessageData(sMessage);
    OnMessageReceived(this, msgData);
}
```

To put all of those segments together, the entire *MessageManager* class will look like this:

```
class MessageManager
{
    public delegate void MessageEventHandler(object sender,
    MessageData e);

    public event MessageEventHandler OnMessageReceived;

    public void SendMessage(string sMessage)
    {
        Console.WriteLine("MessageManager - Received message: " + sMessage);

        MessageData msgData=new MessageData(sMessage);
        OnMessageReceived(this, msgData);
```

```
    }
}
```

## *The* MessageClient *Class*

The primary purpose of the *MessageClient* is to consume the events that the *MessageManager* publishes. For it to subscribe to *MessageManager's* events, it needs a reference to the *MessageManager* itself. We therefore provide one through *MessageClient's* constructor. Inside of the constructor, we associate *MessageManager's* *OnMessageReceived* event with our message handler using the overloaded += operator:

```
public MessageClient(MessageManager mgr)
{
 mgr.OnMessageReceived += new
 MessageManager.MessageEventHandler(HandleMessageReceived);
}
```

The message handler *HandleMessageReceived* that we assigned to the event has not been implemented yet—that is the next step. We will make it write a message to the console to alert us that a message has been received:

```
public void HandleMessageReceived(object sender,
 MessageData e)
{
     Console.WriteLine("MessageClient - The message text is: " +
         e.sMessageText);
}
```

## *The* MainApplication *Class*

We're all done implementing our messaging system. Now we just need an entry point where we can create our class instances and send a message. First we'll create an instance of the *MessageManager*. Then we'll create an instance of the *MessageClient*, and pass our reference to *MessageManager* into its constructor. Finally, we'll send a message.

```
class MainApplication
{
  static void Main(string[] args)
  {
```

```
      MessageManager mgr=new MessageManager();
      MessageClient client=new MessageClient(mgr);


      mgr.SendMessage("Here is a new message");
    }
  }
```

## Our Complete Messaging Example

Our event publisher/subscriber system is now complete. Here is the complete
code listing for our messaging system:

```
using System;
namespace EventSample
{
//This is the data that will be sent with the event when
// it fires. Note that is derived from System.EventArgs.
class MessageData : System.EventArgs
{
  public string sMessageText;

  public MessageData(string sText)
  {
     //This will hold the actual text of the message.
     sMessageText=sText;
  }
}


//The message manager receives messages, and fires an
// event when it receives a message.
class MessageManager
{
  //This delegate defines what our event handlers have
  // to look like.
  public delegate void MessageEventHandler(object sender, MessageData e);

  //This is the actual event that we will fire.
  // 'MessageEventHandler' is the delegate type that
```

```
   // can handle this event.
   public event MessageEventHandler OnMessageReceived;


   //This is the method through which applications can
   // send messages.
   public void SendMessage(string sMessage)
   {
     Console.WriteLine("MessageManager - Received message: " + sMessage);


     //We have received a message. First create our
     //message data class, supplying the message text to
     //the constructor.
     MessageData msgData=new MessageData(sMessage);


     //Now fire the event.
     OnMessageReceived(this, msgData);
   }
 }


//The MessageClient registers for and handles the
// OnMessageReceived event from MessageManager.
class MessageClient
{
  //Our constructor takes a reference to a
  //MessageManager object so we can register to receive
  //its events.
  public MessageClient(MessageManager mgr)
  {
    //Use the overloaded += operator to register for
    //the OnMessageReceived event.
    mgr.OnMessageReceived += new
    MessageManager.MessageEventHandler(
      HandleMessageReceived);
  }

    //This is our actual event handler.
    public void HandleMessageReceived(object sender,
```

```
      MessageData e)
    {
      //Our MessageData object contains the message
      //text.  Write the message to the console.
      Console.WriteLine("MessageClient - The message text is: " +
          e.sMessageText);
    }
}


//This is the main entry point.
class MainApplication
{
    static void Main(string[] args)
    {
      //Create a new MessageManager.
      MessageManager mgr=new MessageManager();

      //Create a new MessageClient and supply it with a
      // reference to the MessageManager so it can register
      // for MessageManager's events.
      MessageClient client = new MessageClient(mgr);

      //Send a message to the MessageManager. This will then
      // in turn cause an event to be fired to the
      // MessageClient.
      Console.WriteLine("Sending a message to MessageManager");
      mgr.SendMessage("Delegates are cool!");
    }
  }
}
```

## Output

```
Sending a message to MessageManager
MessageManager - Received message: Delegates are cool!
MessageClient - The message text is: Delegates are cool!
```

We send the message, the message is received, and the event fires. Our handler then fires and prints out the final line in the output. Note that, in fact, we could add as many handlers as we want to the *OnMessageReceived* event. Each of these handlers then would get called when the event fires. This ability is called *multicasting*, and will be discussed in the next section.

# Multicasting

Multicasting involves sending one event notification to many different event subscribers. For example, consider using an e-mail client to send an e-mail. When you click the **Send** button, there are several different components that need to know about it. The windowing component needs to know you clicked the **Send** button so it can animate the button pushing in. It might also automatically close the window in which you were composing the e-mail. The network spooling component needs to know so that it can queue the e-mail and then send it. Depending on the architecture of the e-mail client, there may even be a thread that needs to be notified so that it can place the e-mail in a folder of items that have been sent. In such a scenario, multicasting can be useful. By allowing different components to subscribe to the same event, we can allow many different actions to take place in response to the event.

C#'s delegates, of course, support multicasting. We can use the overloaded += operator to assign as many delegates as we want to an event. For an example, let's revisit the messaging application we created earlier. We'll add another class to it, called *MessageLogger*. The purpose of the *MessageLogger* will be to write any messages that are received to a file. We will subscribe it to the *MessageManager.OnMessageReceived* event, just as we did with *MessageClient*. In other words, both *MessageLogger* and *MessageClient* will be subscribing to the same event at the same time. Thus, the event will be multicast to both.

The *MessageLogger* will have much the same structure as the *MessageClient* class. The constructor, for instance, will be almost identical. It will take a reference to the *MessageManager* class and then subscribe to the *MessageManager's OnMessageReceived* event:

```
public MessageLogger(MessageManager mgr)
{
  mgr.OnMessageReceived += new
  MessageManager.MessageEventHandler(WriteMessageToFile);
}
```

Our handler in this case will be called *WriteMessageToFile*. It will follow the same format that *MessageClient's* handler follows, in that it will take argument types of *object* and *MessageData*. It will then use a *StreamWriter* to write the message to a file:

```
public void WriteMessageToFile(object sender,
 MessageData e)
{
  System.IO.StreamWriter writer = new
  System.IO.StreamWriter("c:\\log.txt", true);
  writer.WriteLine(e.sMessageText);
  writer.Close();
}
```

The *StreamWriter* object takes two arguments. The first is the path to our log file, and the second is a *boolean* that signifies that we wish to open the file in append mode. Chapter 11 discusses the *System.IO* namespace in full detail. For the time being, all you need to know is that our example will create a file called *log.txt* located in the root of the C drive (c:\ directory). All of our messages will be written to that file.

The final step is to instantiate an instance of *MessageLogger* in our *Main* method. The rest of the code will be similar to the preceding one except for the following additions:

```
using System:
namespace EventSample
{
...
//Rest of the code removed for simplicity
...


//The MessageLogger class responds to the
// MessageManager.OnMessageReceived event and writes the
// message that was received to a file.
class MessageLogger
{
    public MessageLogger(MessageManager mgr)
    {
      mgr.OnMessageReceived += new
```

```
        MessageManager.MessageEventHandler(WriteMessageToFile);
    }


    public void WriteMessageToFile(object sender,
    MessageData e)
    {
        Console.WriteLine("MessageLogger - Writing message to file: " +
            e.sMessageText);
        //Create a stream writer object to write the file to.
        System.IO.StreamWriter writer = new
      System.IO.StreamWriter("c:\\log.txt", true);


        //Write the message text to file.
        writer.WriteLine(e.sMessageText);
        writer.Close();
    }
}


class MainApplication
{
    static void Main(string[] args)
    {
        //Create a new MessageManager.
        MessageManager mgr=new MessageManager();

        //Create a new MessageClient and supply it with a
        // reference to the MessageManager so it can register
        // for MessageManager's events.
        MessageClient client = new MessageClient(mgr);

        //Create a new MessageLogger and supply it with a
        // reference to the MessageManager.
        MessageLogger logger = new MessageLogger(mgr);

        //Send a message to the MessageManager. This will then
        // in turn cause an event to be fired to the
        // MessageClient.
```

```
        Console.WriteLine("Sending a message to MessageManager");
        mgr.SendMessage("Here is a new message");
    }
}
}
```

The net effect here is that we will now perform two actions when a message is sent to the *MessageManager*: the *MessageClient* will write a message to the console and the *MessageLogger* will write the message to a file. The output is as follows:

```
Sending a message to MessageManager
MessageManager - Received message: Delegates are cool!
MessageClient - The message text is: Delegates are cool!
MessageLogger - Writing message to file: Delegates are cool!
```

In addition to the console output, a new file has been created, namely C:\log.txt. Opening the file reveals that it contains the following text:

```
Delegates are cool!
```

## Order of Operations in Multicasting

Multicast events are published to subscribers in the order in which they are assigned. In the example in the previous section, for instance, the message will first be written to the console, then the message will be written to a file.

Note that multicasting is also single threaded. In other words, when an event is fired, control does not return to the firing thread until the consuming event handler returns. This becomes significant if you have a multithreaded application and are multicasting an event to different threads. The event will be published on a single thread, so it is up to the subscribing threads to consume it responsibly and return properly so that the other subscribers can also receive the event.

In a worst-case scenario, a subscriber could receive an event and put up, say, a modal dialog box waiting for user input. If the computer happens to be unattended, the multicasting thread will block and no other subscribers will receive the event until the dialog box is dismissed.

# Advanced Delegate Usage

You have already learned most of the important concepts behind delegates. As a matter of fact, you now know enough to use delegates very successfully! This section covers some more advanced concepts with delegates to augment your knowledge and maybe make your life a little easier.

# Declaring Delegates as Static Members

As we discussed earlier, an instance of a delegate must be created before it can be used. In our database engine example, we first had to instantiate an instance of our class that contained the callback function so that we could use the instance of the callback function to create the delegate. We also explicitly had to instantiate our delegate before it could be used. Specifically, I'm referring to the following code segment:

```
class DBEngine
{
  static void Main(string[] args)
  {
    DBEngine dbEngine = new DBEngine();

    DBIndexer.DoneIndexingCallback callback = new
  DBIndexer.DoneIndexingCallback(dbEngine.DoneIndexing);




  }
}
```

We could simplify this code segment somewhat by taking advantage of the fact that a delegate can be a reference to a static member method, and we can also declare the delegate itself as a static member. The new *DBEngine* would look like this:

```
class DBEngine
{
  //We will declare and instantiate the delegate here as a
  // static member.
  public static DBIndexer.DoneIndexingCallback callback = new
DBIndexer.DoneIndexingCallback(DBEngine.DoneIndexing);

  static void Main(string[] args)
  {
```

```
DBIndexer indexer = new DBIndexer();
Console.WriteLine("Calling the DBIndexer…");
//Index the DB!
indexer.Index(callback);

//Continue doing some work while waiting for the
//callback.  But since it's not asyncronous it will
//actually block before continuing.
for(int i=0; i<100; i++)
{
  Console.WriteLine(i);
}
}


//Note we have made this callback method static.
public static void DoneIndexing(int nNumberOfIndexes)
{
  Console.WriteLine("Done indexing, there are " +
nNumberOfIndexes + " indexes in the database");
}
}
```

The method is now a bit simpler. Additionally, our delegate is created statically. This would be especially beneficial if we needed to access the delegate many different times and from different parts of our class. Creating it statically saves us the need for recurring instantiation.

# Delegates and Thread Creation

In Java, thread creation generally is accomplished by making a class implement the *Runnable* Interface. Since C# already has the flexibility of delegates, however, they make for an easy solution to creating threads. We use a delegate to get a reference to a thread's entry point, and use it when creating the thread. When we tell the thread to run, that delegate will then be used to start the thread's main method.

Threads are constructed via a predefined delegate called *System.Threading.ThreadStart*, which returns *void* and takes no parameters. You can assign any method with this signature to this delegate and have it run as a separate thread. Here's an example:

```
using System;
using System.Threading;

namespace ThreadingSample
{
  class ThreadSample
  {
    static void Main(string[] args)
    {
      Thread thread;

      //Create a thread using the predefined ThreadStart
      // delegate declaration.
      thread = new Thread(new ThreadStart(MyThread));

      //Tell the new thread to start execution.
      thread.Start();
      Console.WriteLine("In main thread");
    }

    static void MyThread()
    {
      Console.WriteLine("In new thread");
    }
  }
}
```

Don't worry too much about understanding the ins and outs of this example now, as threads and multithreading programming are covered in more detail in Chapter 10. Just be aware of the existence of the *System.Threading.ThreadStart* delegate and how you can assign a method to this delegate, which can then be executed as separate thread.

# Summary

In this chapter, we talked about delegates, and how they are type-safe and object-oriented. We also discussed how they are references to a method. They can reference any method, as long as that method conforms to the signature with which the delegate was declared.

After learning about what delegates are, we learned how they could be used as callback functions, or for asynchronous processing. We looked at how they are declared, instantiated, and invoked. We then created the *DBIndexer* sample application, where we used a delegate to alert us through a callback when the *DBIndexer* was finished processing.

Next, we discussed how delegates are used in event handling. We learned that there are many delegates already defined in the .NET Framework, and they all have the same signature as *System.EventHandler*. They return *void* and take two arguments: an object and a class derived from *System.EventArgs*. We then built our own event publisher/subscriber system, where we sent messages to an object, and that object then fired the events to subscribed handlers.

Next, we learned about how delegates are used to handle events in GUI applications, like button clicks or other windowing events. We created a form that had a single button, implemented a handler, and then assigned the handler to the button's click event.

After our discussion on GUI events, we took a look at multicasting, which is firing the same event to multiple subscribers. We revisited the messaging example and added another subscriber to receive the *OnMessageReceived* event. The event was then multicast to both subscribers.

As a final note, we talked about how delegates can be declared statically to simplify coding. We also took a look at how delegates are used as part of the .NET Framework's threading model.

# Solutions Fast Track

## Delegates

- ☑ Delegates are similar to C/C++ function pointers.
- ☑ Delegates reference a method.
- ☑ Delegates are object-oriented, type-safe, and secure.

# Using Delegates as Callbacks

☑ Using delegates as callbacks is useful for receiving notifications.

☑ Using delegates as callbacks is helpful in asynchronous processing.

# Using Delegates for Event Handling

☑ Using delegates for event handling is the standard publisher/subscriber model.

☑ Handlers take two arguments: a reference to the event source and an object derived from *System.EventArgs*.

☑ Event delegates are constructed using the predefined delegate declaration *System.EventHandler*.

# Multicasting

☑ Multicasting publishes one event to multiple subscribers.

☑ Multicasting is single threaded.

# Advanced Delegate Usage

☑ The delegate and the handler are both declared static.

☑ Declaring delegates as static members yields more concise and easier-to-read code.

☑ The predefined delegate *System.Threading.ThreadStart* is used to create a delegate.

☑ The new delegate holds a reference to the thread's entry point.

# Frequently Asked Questions

The following Frequently Asked Questions, answered by the authors of this book, are designed to both measure your understanding of the concepts presented in this chapter and to assist you with real-life implementation of these concepts. To have your questions about this chapter answered by the author, browse to **www.syngress.com/solutions** and click on the **"Ask the Author"** form.

**Q:** What is the Java equivalent of a delegate?

**A:** There really is no Java equivalent to delegates. Java does provide elements that give similar functionality (like the *ActionListener* interface for event handling), but the concept of using a variable to reference to a method does not really exist in Java.

**Q:** Are delegates really function pointers?

**A:** No. Though they are similar, delegates are much more than function pointers. Most importantly, they can hold references to multiple methods, and they are type-safe.

**Q:** How many event handlers can be assigned to a multicast delegate?

**A:** A multicast delegate stores its invocation list in a linked list. That being the case, the number of references it can hold theoretically is limited only by system resources (and practicality!).

**Q:** Why did Microsoft choose to use delegates instead of a more Java-like architecture?

**A:** This is perhaps best answered by Microsoft. Recently, Microsoft published an article at http://msdn.microsoft.com/visualj/technical/articles/delegates/truth.asp, which explains the issue very well. The article was posted in response to a white paper published by Sun at http://java.sun.com/docs/white/delegates.html, criticizing Microsoft's use of delegates in J++ and C#.

# Chapter 9

# Attributes and Assemblies

## Solutions in this chapter:

- **Working with Attributes**
- **Using Reflection**
- **Creating Assemblies**
- **Versioning**

☑ **Summary**

☑ **Solutions Fast Track**

☑ **Frequently Asked Questions**

# Introduction

One of the features of the Common Language Runtime (CLR) is that any types built for the CLR with any .NET languages can be shared among other applications in the Microsoft .NET Framework. In this section we will look at building, packaging, and deploying applications for the .NET Framework. More specifically, we will learn about attributes and assemblies.

The first part of this chapter will look at attributes. Attributes are used to give extra information to the .NET compiler. Java uses a combination of /** and @ tag comments for including additional documentation information about classes, methods, fields, and even individual parameters. However, this information is not included as parts of the bytecode after you compile your class. With attributes you have the ability to provide custom information about any element of your code that gets compiled as part of your program. This information or metadata can then easily be retrieved at runtime through a process known as *reflection*.

The second part of the chapter will look at assemblies, which are C#'s version of packaging. Assemblies are *.exe*'s or *.dll*'s generated from compiling a project of files. The .NET runtime uses the configurable attributes and versioning rules built into assemblies to greatly simplify application deployment. Finally, you will learn about versioning, which will prevent a common Windows application development problem referred to as "DLL Hell."

# Working with Attributes

The most useful thing to know about attributes is that the information supplied in the attribute is compiled as part of the Intermediate Language (IL) file for your class. Therefore, any information stored as C# attributes is available at runtime. This can be very handy, as you'll learn in the following sections.

Attributes store their information in the application metadata. This is a binary form of information storage that is included with every compiled application or dynamic link library (DLL) in the .NET framework. Program information such as assembly information, types and resources in an assembly, and various other pieces of data about the application or DLL is stored here. As a matter of fact, every type and member defined or referenced in your code is described in the application metadata.

As the programmer, you also have the ability to include information in the metadata of your program or DLL. This information can then be read at runtime, or can be accessed via a third-party application. Information can be placed into the metadata using either default or custom attributes.

Why would you want to add attributes? A couple of very useful implementations of attributes would be to use them for bug tracking or for code-check verification. If you need a way to verify that the code in particular sections has been checked or reviewed, attributes can provide an easy way to implement this. Project tracking and bug tracking are just two of the useful applications for this new feature.

### Developing & Deploying…

## Application Security

Keep in mind that attribute information will be stored in the application metadata and included with your runtime executable. This means that anybody can read this information by using a third-party application capable of reading application metadata. This can be useful if you're including information on how to use your distributed DLL files successfully, but not as useful if you include proprietary information. Just keep this in mind when deciding what to include in your attributes.

# Using Attributes

Attributes can be applied to many locations and scopes within your code. These elements are called *Attribute Targets*. The following elements are able to have attributes applied to them:

- *Assemblies*
- *Classes*
- *Constructors*
- *Delegates*
- *Enums*
- *Events*
- *Fields*
- *Interfaces*

- *Methods*
- *Modules*
- *Parameters*
- *Properties*
- *Return Values*
- *Structs*

As mentioned previously, you can use either default attributes or define custom attributes in your code. All attributes have specific targets that they are assigned to support. This is defined by the *AttributeTargets* parameter of the attribute. We'll examine this parameter in more detail in the section, "Creating Custom Attributes."

Table 9.1 lists some of the default attributes that are included with C# (which are all members of the *System.Attribute* namespace). This list shows only some of the more common, practical attributes that you'll encounter. There are hundreds of default attributes available in C#, plus the ability to create your own custom attributes.

**Table 9.1** Common Default Attributes

| Attribute | Description |
| --- | --- |
| System.SerializableAttribute [Serializable] | Allows your class to be serializable to disk or over a network. |
| System.NonSerializedAttribute [NonSerialized] | Allows certain members to be nonserialized so that data won't be saved to disk or over a network. Similar to the *transient* keyword in Java. |
| System.Web.Services.WebServiceAttribute [WebService] | Allows you to specify a name and description for a Web service. |
| System.Web.Services.WebMethodAttribute [WebMethod] | Marks a method to be exposed as part of a Web service. |
| System.AttributeUsageAttribute [AttributeUsage] | Defines the usage parameters for custom attributes. |

**Continued**

**Table 9.1** Continued

| Attribute | Description |
| --- | --- |
| System.Diagnostics.ConditionalAttribute [Conditional] | Makes the execute of a method optional depending on specific preprocessor directives. |
| System.ObsoleteAttribute [Obsolete] | Marks a specific section of code as obsolete. |
| System.Reflection.AssemblyCultureAttribute [AssemblyCulture] | Specifies a specific culture supported by the assembly. |
| System.Reflection.AssemblyVersionAttribute [AssemblyVersion] | Specifies the version number of the assembly. |
| System.Reflection.AssemblyKeyFileAttribute [AssemblyKeyFile] | Specifies a key file to use when assigning a "strong name" to an assembly. |

To use an attribute, simply specify the attribute you wish to use and encapsulate it within a pair of brackets. You will notice that all of the attributes in Table 9.1 end with the text *Attribute*. In C#, when you specify an attribute, you can leave off this portion of the attribute name. In addition, if you have specified the *using System* statement in your code, you can leave off the *System* namespace identifier. As a result of this, the *System.NonSerializedAttribute* attribute would simply be referenced as *[NonSerialized]*.

You can apply your attribute to your target by placing it immediately before the target element. For example, to apply the *[Serializable]* attribute to a class, you would do the following:

```
using System;
[Serializable]
class SerialaizableClass
{
  //Class definition here
}
```

To apply more than one attribute to a target, you can simply stack them one on top of the other, or you can separate them using commas. For example, these two declarations are the same:

```
[Serializable]
[WebService]
```

```
or
```

```
[Serializable, WebService]
```

As I've mentioned, attributes can be applied on most elements within your application, depending on which attribute targets the attribute has defined. Attributes are applied to all of these in the same way, with one exception. When applying attributes to the assembly level, they must be specified as *[assembly: Attribute]*. This designates that the attribute refers to the assembly level and it will be applied to the assembly element. In all other cases, the compiler will determine the attribute target based on the attribute's location.

Some attributes accept a string parameter and use it as part of their function. A good example of this would be to use the *System.ObsoleteAttribute* attribute. This attribute is used to mark a program element as obsolete and destined to be removed in a future version. The following code sample shows how this attribute would be used:

```
using System;

class AttributesSample
{
  static void Main()
  {
    string FullString = ConcatStrings("This is our ",
            "attributes example.");

    Console.WriteLine(FullString);

    FullString = ConcatTwoStrings("Compiler generates ",
            "a warning when this line is compiled.");

    Console.WriteLine(FullString);

    FullString = ConcatStrings("This example ",
            "is ", "complete.");

    Console.WriteLine(FullString);
  }
```

```
[Obsolete("Use ConcatStrings instead.")]
public static string ConcatTwoStrings(string StringOne,
                                             string StringTwo)
{
     return (StringOne + StringTwo);
}

public static string ConcatStrings()
{
     return ("No strings submitted");
}

public static string ConcatStrings(string StringOne,
                                        string StringTwo)
{
     return (StringOne + StringTwo);
}

public static string ConcatStrings(string StringOne,
                                        string StringTwo,
                                        string StringThree)
{
     return (StringOne + StringTwo + StringThree);
}
}
```

When the preceding code is compiled, a warning is generated that notifies you that you are using a method that is obsolete. It includes the text specified with the *[Obsolete]* attribute, which can include redirecting someone to use a different method. The actual warning is as follows:

```
Microsoft (R) Visual C# Compiler Version 7.00.9254 [CLR version v1.0.2914]
Copyright (C) Microsoft Corp 2000-2001. All rights reserved.

AttributesSample.cs(12,15): warning CS0618:
     'AttributesSample.ConcatTwoStrings(string, string)' is obsolete:
'Use
     ConcatStrings instead.'
```

As you can see, this attribute alone can help a great deal when working with an application that will end up with multiple version releases as it is developed. This and all the other built-in attributes can be very useful as a project continues through the development phases.

# Creating Custom Attributes

Generally, the built-in attributes will cover most situations that would require the use of attributes. Situations do tend to arise, however, where the default attributes just don't provide the necessary information or functions that you require. This eventuality is provided for in the .NET architecture by allowing you to define your own custom attributes.

There are several situations when this may be useful. In a case where code development is done by several distinct groups, a custom attribute could be defined to pass information about certain sections of code between groups. Another good example of this would be when using a third-party change management system to track code development. Custom attributes that relate to the data needed for the change management system could be defined and then later extracted into a database. Finally, when developing a program that has the ability to run in both a demo or licensed mode, you could define a custom attribute to designate which sections of code are designed to work in each mode.

A custom attribute is really just an attribute class. These classes are derived from *System.Attribute* either directly or indirectly. There are several steps involved in creating an attribute class. First, the allowed targets for your custom attribute must be defined. This is done by adding the *AttributeUsageAttribute* to your class.

Second, you must declare the class itself as either a direct derivative or an indirect derivative of *System.Attribute*. In addition to this requirement, the class must also be defined as a *public* class. It is highly recommended, though not required, that you end the class name with *Attribute*. Next, the constructors for your class must be declared. This can be done in the same way as any other class and does support overloading the constructor. This leads us to our final step of defining properties. Defining properties allows optional parameters to be passed to the constructor.

Due to the number of steps involved in creating custom attributes, we will go through each step individually and examine the options available to us each step of the way. As we work through each step, we'll watch as our code evolves until finally we have a new custom attribute defined and implemented.

Debugging…

## Conflicting Attributes

When writing your own custom attributes, it is always best to make sure that there isn't a built-in attribute with the same name. If there is, this can lead to conflicts and compile errors. It's also a good idea to see if there is an existing built-in attribute that will fulfill your needs rather than creating a custom attribute. There's no point in reinventing the wheel!

## Defining the *AttributeUsage* Attribute

The first step of designing our custom attribute is to define the target of the new custom attribute. This defines the elements to which the attribute can be applied. So, we first need to determine whether the attribute should be applied to specific elements or available to all elements. The available target values are shown in Table 9.2 along with a description of the elements to which an attribute can be applied when using each target:

**Table 9.2** Attribute Targets

| Target | Description |
| --- | --- |
| All | Any element |
| Assembly | An assembly |
| ClassMembers | Any class member |
| Class | A class |
| Constructor | A constructor |
| Delegate | A delegate |
| Enum | An enumeration |
| Event | An event |
| Field | A field |
| Interface | An interface |
| Method | A method |
| Module | A module |
| Parameter | A parameter |

Continued

**Table 9.2** Continued

| Target | Description |
| --- | --- |
| Property | A property |
| ReturnValue | A return value |
| Struct | A structure |

In addition to the target, there are two additional properties that need to be set for the *AttributeUsage* attribute. The *Inherited* property is a *boolean* property that specifies whether your attribute can be inherited by any classes derived from a class to which your attribute has been applied. The default value for this property is *true*, but you can specify it as *false* to prevent this behavior.

The second property is the *AllowMultiple* property. This property is a *boolean* as well, and specifies whether multiple instances of your attribute can exist on any given element to which it is applied. The default value for this property is *false*, but you can specify it as *true* to allow your attribute to be specified multiple times on a given element.

So, for our example, let's define an *AttributeUsage* attribute and give it targets of *Assembly*, *Class*, and *Method*. We'll also leave the *Inherited* property with its default of *true*, but set the *AllowMultiple* property to true. In our code, this would look like the following:

```
[AttributeUsage(AttributeTargets.Assembly
      | AttributeTargets.Class
      | AttributeTargets.Method, AllowMultiple=true)]
```

(Note that you separate multiple attribute targets by using the pipe | character.)

# Declaring an Attribute Class

Before declaring our attribute class, we must keep the rules for doing this properly in mind to make sure we get it right the first time.

- An attribute class must directly or indirectly derive from *System.Attribute*.

- An attribute class must be declared as *public*.

- An attribute class should follow the attribute naming convention.

So, with that in mind, let's declare our attribute class. For this example, we'll name our attribute class *CodeTrackerAttribute*. We'll be using this attribute to track the development of code within our project. A perfect scenario for the usage of this would be in a situation when a very large code project has been divided between several companies, with each wanting to keep their source code restricted from the other. This custom attribute could be included in a compiled assembly and distributed for the other companies to use. XML documentation comments could also be used to accomplish the same goal, but this is simply another alternative. The following code sample shows how we would define this while complying with our rules:

```
[AttributeUsage(AttributeTargets.Assembly
        | AttributeTargets.Class
        | AttributeTargets.Method, AllowMultiple=true)]
public class CodeTrackerAttribute : System.Attribute
{
}
```

## Declaring Attribute Class Constructors and Properties

Attribute class constructors function in the same way as normal constructors, and can be overloaded in the same manner as you would in a normal class. You can also specify required and optional parameters for your attribute class constructor. Generally, this is done by using properties with your constructor.

For our example, we'll want our attribute to take the programmer's name, a coding phase designator, and an optional notes field as parameters. In order to do this, we'll create our constructor and require the *name* and *phase* fields while leaving the *notes* field as optional. In order to define the *notes* field as optional, all we have to do is leave it out of the constructor and it automatically becomes an optional field. The following code demonstrates how we could do this by using properties:

```
using System;

[AttributeUsage(AttributeTargets.Assembly
        | AttributeTargets.Class
        | AttributeTargets.Method, AllowMultiple=true)]
public class CodeTrackerAttribute : System.Attribute
{
  private string name;
  private string phase;
  private string notes;
```

```
//We'll require the name and phase parameters.
public CodeTrackerAttribute(string name, string phase)
{
   this.name=name;
   this.phase=phase;
   this.notes=notes;
}

//Define the name property.
public virtual string Name
{
   get {return name;}
}

//Define the phase property.
public virtual string Phase
{
   get {return phase;}
}

//Define the notes optional property.
public virtual string Notes
{
   get {return notes;}
   set {notes=value;}
}
}
```

Just to review, we first use the *AttributeUsage* attribute to define the targets for our new attribute class. Then we define the attribute class as a derivative of the *System.Attribute* class. We then define our three string variables as private and define our constructor. In the constructor, we specify the *name* and *phase* parameters so that they are required fields. We then define these two properties as well as the *notes* property, which is optional.

# Using Custom Attributes

Now that we've created our custom attribute class, all that remains is to actually make use of our new attribute. Custom attributes are used in the same way as the built-in attributes. Since our new custom attribute is defined with targets of *Assembly*, *Class*, and *Method*, the attribute can be applied to any of these three elements. The following code gives us an example of using this new attribute:

```
[CodeTracker("Jeremy Faircloth", "R1",
        Notes = "This is only for testing.")]
class AttribTest
{
  public AttribTest()
  {
    Console.WriteLine ("AttribTest initialized");
  }


  [CodeTracker("Jeremy Faircloth", "R2")]
  public void AttribMessage(string Message)
  {
    Console.WriteLine(Message);
  }
}
```

In the preceding code, we have declared the *CodeTracker* attribute on the *AttribTest* class. In this case, we have also included the optional *notes* field. You will notice that in order to specify that the additional parameter is to be used for the *notes* property, we have specified *Notes* = prior to the string. The required fields do not have this requirement as they are included as part of the constructor of our attribute class. Since the notes field is not a part of the constructor, the constructor needs to know that the additional incoming parameter is to be used for this property.

We have also declared the *CodeTracker* attribute on the *AttribMessage* method. In this case, we are simply including the two required fields and not making use of our optional notes property. Therefore, each parameter is sent simply as a string and does not require any additional parameter to specify for what they are to be used.

# Using Reflection

Now that we have learned how to use the built-in attributes and how to create and use our own custom attributes, it's time to move on to how we can retrieve information from our attributes. To do this, we have to retrieve the attribute information out of the metadata. This process is called *reflection*.

By using reflection, you can pull information from the metadata at runtime or during the compile. Reflection actually offers us much more than just the ability to gather information about properties, however. By using reflection, you also have the ability to:

- Define and load assemblies
- Load modules listed in the assembly manifest
- Create new instances of a type from an assembly
- Discover information about modules
- Discover information about classes
- Discover information about constructors
- Invoke a constructor
- Discover information about methods
- Invoke a method
- Discover information about fields
- Set or get field values
- Discover information about events
- Add or remove event handlers
- Discover information about properties
- Set or get property values
- Discover information about parameters

As you can see, reflection is a very powerful tool. As it relates to attributes, we can obtain the information that has been stored in the metadata by our attribute classes and display or work with that data. This is done by using the *GetCustomAttributes()* method, which is part of the *System.Reflection* namespace.

We can use this method in one of two ways: as a discovery tool to determine which members of our application have attributes and what those attributes are; or to determine the values of the attributes within our application.

To use the *GetCustomAttributes()* method to discover attributes, we need to obtain an array of members within our application. After we have this array, we apply the *GetCustomAttributes()* method to each member in the array and determine whether it returns a value. If data is returned, it will be returned as an array containing the names of the attributes applied to the member. We'll then need to parse through that array and display the contents. An example of how to perform this is as follows:

```
Type ClassType = typeof(AttribTest);
MemberInfo[] AttribMembers = ClassType.GetMembers();
for(int i = 0; i < AttribMembers.Length; i++)
{
  Object[] OurAttributes =
     AttribMembers[i].GetCustomAttributes(false);
  if(OurAttributes.Length > 0)
  {
    Console.WriteLine("The attributes for the member {0}
                      are: ", AttribMembers[i]);
    for(int j = 0; j < OurAttributes.Length; j++)
      Console.WriteLine("{0}", OurAttributes[j]);
  }
}
```

In this code, we go through several operations, which end with the result of each member with attributes being displayed as well as the attributes assigned to the member. Let's go through this example and see exactly how it all works. First, we determine the object type of *AttribTest* by using the *typeof* operator. This operator, when used in this context, returns the *System.Type* object for the member that has been passed to it. In this case, it returns *AttribExample.AttribTest*.

```
Type ClassType = typeof(AttribTest);
```

We then create a new instance of the *System.Type* class called *ClassType*, and set it to contain the value *AttribExample.AttribTest* as previously determined by the use of the *typeof* operator. The *System.Type* class is the fundamental class that allows you to perform reflection on the members of your assembly. Once a *System.Type* object is created, you can use the object's methods, fields, properties, and classes to gather any information about the type. In this case, we are creating a new *System.Type* object, which allows us to access information on the *AttribExample.AttribTest* member.

There are several methods available for the *System.Type* object. In this case, we're going to use the *GetMembers()* method to return a list of all of this object's members, which we will store in a *System.Reflection.MemberInfo* array called *AttribMembers*. The *MemberInfo* class is used to obtain information about members of a class such as constructors, events, fields, methods, or properties. This declaration is as follows:

```
MemberInfo[] AttribMembers = ClassType.GetMembers();
```

Stepping through this array with a *for* loop, we now use the *GetCustomAttributes()* method on each member listed in the array. Basically, the *GetCustomAttributes()* method causes objects to be constructed for each custom attribute defined on the member and stores these constructed objects in an array. In this example we are storing them in an *Object* array named *OurAttributes*.

```
Object[] OurAttributes =
    AttribMembers[i].GetCustomAttributes(false);
```

Before continuing to the next step, we need to determine whether the array of attribute objects actually contains anything. This is done by using an *if* statement. If there are attribute objects defined on the member we're working on, we output the name of the member and a list of the attributes defined on the member to the console.

Through this series of operations, we've determined which members of the *AttribTest* class have attributes and have also determined what those attributes are. Now, let's move on to determining the value of an attribute.

To use the *GetCustomAttributes()* method to discover the values of an attribute, we need to know the name of the attribute from which we wish to gather information and the values available in the attribute. With this knowledge in hand, we obtain a list of attributes by using the *GetCustomAttributes()* method with the class from which we wish to obtain the attribute information. By using the resulting object as a new attribute object based on the attribute about which we wish to obtain the information, we can pull the individual attribute parameters from the attribute. The following code illustrates this process:

```
Type type = typeof(AttribTest);
foreach (object MyObj in type.GetCustomAttributes(true))
{
```

```
  CodeTrackerAttribute att = MyObj as CodeTrackerAttribute;
  if (att != null)
  {
    Console.WriteLine("Name: {0}", att.Name);
    Console.WriteLine("Phase: {0}", att.Phase);
    Console.WriteLine("Notes: {0}", att.Notes);
  }
}
```

Stepping through this code, we first create a new *System.Type* object of the same type as *AttribTest*, just as we did in the last code sample. We then use the *GetCustomAttributes* method on each object of that type.

Next, we create a new *CodeTrackerAttribute* object named *att* using the previously created object as a *CodeTrackerAttribute* object. If this object is null after this procedure, it would mean that there were no *CodeTrackerAttribute* attributes defined on the object. Therefore, we check to see if this is the case and if not, we proceed.

Since we have now identified that there is a *CodeTrackerAttribute* attribute defined on the member we're working with, we can now iterate through the information that we know is stored in that attribute and display it to the console.

Now that we know how to use the *GetCustomAttributes()* method, let's take a look at how to put it all together. The following code sample takes our previous custom attribute sample and expands on it. Included in this code is the definition of a new custom attribute, then an example of how to obtain the information contained within the attribute.

```
using System;
using System.Reflection;


[AttributeUsage(AttributeTargets.All, AllowMultiple-true)]
public class CodeTrackerAttribute : System.Attribute
{
  private string name;
  private string phase;
  private string notes;

  //We'll make the name and phase parameters required
  //and the notes property optional.
  public CodeTrackerAttribute(string name, string phase)
```

```
  {
    this.name=name;
    this.phase=phase;
    this.notes=notes;

  }


  //Define the name property.
  public virtual string Name
  {
    get {return name;}
  }


  //Define the phase property.
  public virtual string Phase
  {
      get {return phase;}
  }


  //Define the notes optional property.
  public virtual string Notes
  {
      get {return notes;}
      set {notes=value;}
  }
}


[CodeTracker("Jeremy Faircloth", "R1",
                Notes = "This is only for testing.")]
public class AttribTest
{
  [CodeTracker("Jeremy Faircloth", "R1")]
  public AttribTest()
  {
    //Insert useful constructor code here.
  }


  [CodeTracker("Jeremy Faircloth", "R2",
```

```
                    Notes="Revision 2 for this method")]
    public void AttribMessage(string Message)
    {
      Console.WriteLine("*****" + Message + "*****");
    }
}


public class AttribInfo
{
  public AttribInfo()
  {
    Type type = typeof(AttribTest);
    MemberInfo[] AttribMembers = type.GetMembers();
    for(int i = 0; i < AttribMembers.Length; i++)
    {
      Object[] OurAttributes =
              AttribMembers[i].GetCustomAttributes(false);
      if(OurAttributes.Length > 0)
      {
        Console.WriteLine("The attributes for the " +
              "member {0} are: ", AttribMembers[i]);

        for(int j = 0; j < OurAttributes.Length; j++)
          Console.WriteLine("{0}", OurAttributes[j]);
        Console.WriteLine("*****");
        foreach (object MyObj in OurAttributes)
        {
          CodeTrackerAttribute att = MyObj as
                    CodeTrackerAttribute;
          if (att != null)
          {
            Console.WriteLine("The CodeTracker attribute"
                    + " values for this member are:");
            Console.WriteLine("Name: {0}", att.Name);
            Console.WriteLine("Phase: {0}", att.Phase);
            Console.WriteLine("Notes: {0}", att.Notes);
            Console.WriteLine("*****");
```

```
                    }
                 }
              }
           }
        }
}


class AttribWork
{
   static void Main()
   {
      AttribTest attrib = new AttribTest();
      attrib.AttribMessage ("Attribute Example");

      AttribInfo attinfo1 = new AttribInfo();
   }
}
```

This code example is a little more complex, so let's examine it and see exactly what is happening. In the first part of the code, we're creating a new custom attribute called *CodeTracker*. This is very similar to our original *CodeTracker* custom attribute, with the notable difference that this attribute has the attribute target *All*. Since we've already gone over how this custom attribute works, we'll move on to the *AttribTest* class.

First of all, we've declared our *CodeTracker* attribute on the *AttribTest* class. This class contains a constructor and one method. The constructor really doesn't do anything, but we have declared our attribute on it as well. The *AttribMessage* method simply outputs an incoming string to the console after encapsulating it within ten asterisks.

The real functionality of this application is in the *AttribInfo* class, which performs the reflection and examines the attributes contained in the *AttribTest* class. This class first creates a *System.Type* object based on the *AttribTest* class. We then gather a list of the members in the class into a *System.Reflection.MemberInfo* array called *AttribMembers*. Now that we have the array of members in the class, we iterate through them all.

For each member, we create an object called *OurAttributes*, containing the custom attributes declared on the object based on the objects returned by the

*GetCustomAttributes* method. If there are custom attributes defined on the member, we output the member name and the attributes defined on it.

At this point, we change things a little from our previous example code. We now iterate through each object in the *OurAttributes* array using a *foreach* statement. With each iteration, we create a new *CodeTrackerAttribute* object using the current object in the array. If the object is a valid *CodeTrackerAttribute* object, we write the values of the attribute to the console.

The *AttribWork* class serves as a container for our *Main()* method. In the *Main()* method, we simply create a new *AttribTest* object and use its *AttribMessage* method to send a message to the console. Then we create a new *AttribInfo* object causing the attribute information to be written to the console as well.

When we run this code, we are presented with the following output:

```
*****Attribute Example*****
The attributes for the member Void AttribMessage(System.String) are:
CodeTrackerAttribute
*****
The CodeTracker attribute values for this member are:
Name: Jeremy Faircloth
Phase: R2
Notes: Revision 2 for this method
*****
The attributes for the member Void .ctor() are:
CodeTrackerAttribute
*****
The CodeTracker attribute values for this member are:
Name: Jeremy Faircloth
Phase: R1
Notes:
*****
```

**NOTE**

The *.ctor()* method is the constructor name for the class.

As you can see with the use of reflection we were able to examine the metadata information contained in the *AttribTest* class. Viewing metadata is just one of the major uses of reflection. Using the classes in the *Reflection* namespace along with the *System.Type* class, you can examine and interact with the metadata of a class to perform type discovery, dynamically invoke properties and methods, or create new types at runtime.

# Creating Assemblies

If you're familiar with Java's *packages* then you'll easily understand the basic concepts of C#'s *assemblies*. When working with large applications, the code quickly becomes unwieldy due to the number of classes that eventually are defined. In addition, naming conflicts for classes quickly arise in the application. By managing the namespace, these conflicts can be avoided. In addition, your code is more portable, with programmers needing to check out only the particular portion of the namespace on which they are currently working.

Whereas Java packages are stored in .JAR files, C# assemblies are stored in either a .CAB or a .MSI file. However, a compiled .EXE or .DLL file is also considered an assembly. These files contain all of your interfaces and classes as well as any additional resources necessary for your assembly, such as graphic files or configuration files. They also include the metadata for your application.

Although similar to Java packages, assemblies do differ in many ways. First is the ability to perform versioning. This allows you to create and track multiple versions of an assembly. Second, assemblies can actually be written in any of the .NET languages, and then referenced by any other .NET language. This allows a program to actually be composed of code written in different languages, all working together.

The data contained in your assembly contains an intermediate form of your compiled code. As we mentioned before, this is known as IL, and is the bytecode form of your code. This bytecode can be disassembled by a utility included with the .NET Framework SDK called *ILDasm*. This utility allows you to view the manifest of your assembly, or to disassemble and view the bytecode contained within it. The *ILDasm* utility works in both a graphical or command-line form and can show you any information about an assembly simply by opening the assembly within the utility. Command-line options for the utility can be found by using the /? parameter.

# Manifest Data

Assemblies are similar to Java's packages in some other ways as well. Assemblies contain a manifest, which is similar to a manifest within a Java package. This manifest is basically metadata, containing information about the assembly. This metadata contains information describing the relationship between all of the parts of your assembly. Information such as what classes are included in the assembly, what methods are included, which outside assemblies are referenced, what graphic files are included, and various other bits of information are stored here.

The manifest is also where versioning information for the assembly is stored. This allows you to determine and control which versions of an assembly are in use. Also, the manifest is digitally signed, which allows you to determine authenticity of an assembly.

# Building Assemblies

Assemblies can be created in two primary forms, a single-file assembly or a multi-file assembly. When working with a single-file assembly, you can create either an executable assembly or a library assembly.

Creating a single-file executable assembly is done in the same way as we've been compiling our sample applications. Using the command-line compiler with the following syntax creates an executable assembly named after the source file:

```
csc MyAssembly.cs
```

You can also specify a different filename for your executable assembly, by using the */out:* command-line parameter. By using the following syntax, our code will be compiled into an executable assembly with a name that differs from the name of the source file:

```
csc /out:MyNewAssembly.exe MyAssembly.cs
```

Keep in mind that any code used for a single-file executable assembly must contain an entry point. More than one entry point can be defined in the code, but only one can be used by the compiled executable. The entry point to use can be specified at the command line with the following syntax specifying the class containing the entry point that you wish to use:

```
csc /main:MyClass MyAssembly.cs
```

A library assembly is defined as an assembly containing multiple classes, but no entry point. The classes within these assemblies can be called and used by other assemblies. To compile a library assembly, simply add the command-line parameter *t:library* to your compiler command line. This is shown in the following example:

```
csc /out:MyNewAssembly.dll /t:library MyAssembly.cs
```

# Multiple Module Assembly

Creating a multiple module assembly easily lets you segment your namespace into multiple files. An example for this would be where a code module references a namespace from another code module. This is very useful when segmenting programming work between multiple programmers. In addition, by using multiple files in your assemblies, each file could be written in a different language under the .NET architecture and still interact.

As with a single-file assembly, a multiple module assembly must have an entry point defined if it is to be compiled into an executable assembly. Also, the manifest for your assembly must be stored in one file that you specify within the assembly. For example, if you have a code file that references a namespace within another code file and contains the *Main* method, your assembly would contain the two code files and one additional file that contains the manifest, references both code modules, and launches the application.

There is a specific order that should be followed when creating a multi-module assembly. By following these steps, you will be able to generate a multi-module assembly successfully:

1. All code files containing namespaces referenced in other code files should be compiled into code modules first.

2. All other code files should be compiled into modules.

3. Use the *Assembly Generation Tool* to create an output file containing the assembly manifest. This file can also act as the executable for the application.

We'll take a look at each of these steps in detail. First, let's create two code files with one code file referencing a namespace within the other. The following two sample files will work for this example.

## *Messaging.cs*

```
using System;
```

```
namespace Messaging
{
  class MyMessage
  {
    public MyMessage(string InMsg)
    {
      Console.WriteLine("The author says: " + InMsg);
    }
  }
}
```

## MainApp.cs

```
using System;
using Messaging;

class SendMsg
{
  public static void Main()
  {
    MyMessage MyMsg = new MyMessage("Greetings!");
  }
}
```

So we now have our two code samples and are ready to compile our assembly. The first step in the process is to compile the code file with the namespace that is being referenced into a module. In our example, this is the *Messaging.cs* file. To compile a code file into a module, we must pass the */t:module* command-line parameter to the compiler. For this example, our command-line syntax would be:

```
csc /t:module Messaging.cs
```

Now that our referenced namespace has been compiled into a module, we can proceed to step two. Note that the filename of the module we compiled is, by default, *Messaging.netmodule*. Now we need to compile our referencing code file into a module. For this, we need to use the same command-line parameter specifying that the file should be compiled into a module. We also need to add a command-line parameter specifying that the *Messaging.netmodule* module is referenced by this module. Our syntax for this would be:

```
csc /addmodule:Messaging.netmodule /t:module MainApp.cs
```

Now for our final step, we need to use the Assembly Generation Tool to compile our final multifile assembly. This will create the manifest and add it to our final executable assembly. To do this, we will run the *al.exe (assembly linker)* utility with the following syntax (note that it should be written on a single line):

```
al Messaging.netmodule MainApp.netmodule /main:SendMsg.Main
   /out:MainProg.exe /target:exe
```

Let's go over the options that we're specifying in that command line. The first parameters following your call to the *al.exe* executable are the modules that are to be included in the assembly. The */main:* parameter specifies where your application starting point is. In our case, this is the *Main()* method in the *SendMsg* class. The */out:* parameter specifies the filename for our final assembly, which will also contain the assembly manifest. And finally, the */target:* parameter specifies the type of assembly to compile. The options for this are *exe* for a console application, *win* for a Windows executable, or *lib* for a library.

Now that we have a compiled executable assembly, we can run our *MainProg.exe* application. This generates the following output:

```
The author says: Greetings!
```

There is one very important thing to remember when working with a multimodule assembly: When you distribute your application, you must be sure to include the final executable assembly as well as all compiled modules referenced by the final assembly. Without these compiled modules, the executable assembly will generate a file not found exception.

# Versioning

One of the most common problems encountered with software development is the issue of supporting files and multiple versions of an application. Questions arise with each new software release regarding which support files are to be used with which version. Is the new version of the software compatible with the old components? Are the new components backward-compatible with the old version of the software? Will these new components break another installed application? And then on the developer side, which component should be included in a new application assembly?

This problem is fondly referred to as "DLL Hell," and is a plague on application users and developers alike. The .NET architecture solves this with the inclusion of versioning capability into its assemblies. With versioning, you have the capability to specify which versions of a component are compatible with your final application. You also have the ability for multiple versions of a component to run side-by-side.

The idea is to end the problems associated with multiple versions of components. This gives the end user a better experience, eliminates many software support headaches, and makes development of new software versions easier for developers to create and distribute.

In order to do versioning of assemblies, the .NET architecture stores the version number of each assembly in the assembly manifest. In addition, a culture identifier and digital key can be stored in the assembly manifest to provide for further versioning based on region, and in order to verify that the correct assembly is being used. When the runtime is attempting to bind to an assembly, all of these values are checked and you have the ability to stop the application from executing if the wrong version of any assembly is found.

On top of all this, you also have the ability to use private or shared assemblies. Basically, you can set up an assembly to be installed with your application and have it installed in your application's directories. This would be considered a private assembly and would be used only by your application. The alternative would be to set up a shared assembly, which could be located in the *global assembly cache*. This global assembly cache is a machinewide code cache that is set up wherever the Common Language Runtime is installed. It allows you to place your assemblies into a central location for sharing between multiple applications. These assemblies are considered shared assemblies, and this is where versioning can really show its usefulness. For example, if your company has developed multiple applications that share components, and then a new application is released with updated components, you could specify that the components are a newer version and should not be used by the applications released previously. This eliminates the need to include backward-compatibility in the new components.

# Creating Versioned Assemblies

To create a versioned assembly you must first create an assembly with a *strong name*. A strong name is basically the assembly's identity, a public key, and a digital signature. This strong name is stored in the assembly file containing the assembly manifest and is generated using a private key.

This public-private key pair is used to validate the authenticity of the assembly. A bytecode hash is generated for the assembly, and then digitally signed using the private key. When an assembly with a strong name is used, the validity of the assembly is verified by first checking the signature using the public key. If this test passes, the hash code is checked against a current hash code of the assembly to verify that they are identical. If this test passes, the assembly is considered authentic and untampered.

So, before we can create our versioned assembly, we must first give it a strong name. This can be done at the command line using tools included with the .NET Framework SDK. This requires two tools: the assembly generation tool, with which you're already familiar, and a new tool called the *strong name tool*. The strong name tool is used to create the cryptographic key pair, and then the assembly generation tool is used to assign the key pair to the assembly.

To create the key pair, simply run the following command at a command prompt:

```
sn -k MyKey.snk
```

This will generate your private key and store it in a file called *MyKey.snk* (*snk* is the standard extension for private keys in the .NET Framework). After this file is generated, your next step is to extract the public key from your private key. This is done by using the following syntax:

```
sn -p MyKey.snk MyPublicKey.snk
```

Running this command will extract the public key from the file containing your key pair and store it in the *MyPublicKey.snk* file. Now we have two key files with one containing our key pair and one containing only the public key. At this point we need to assign the key to an assembly and assign a version number to our assembly. For this example, let's use the *Messaging.cs* file from the previous source example.

In order to do this, we must add an attribute to the code specifying the name of the key file to use. This is an assembly level attribute called *AssemblyKeyFileAttribute*. It is also important to note that this attribute is in the *System.Reflection* namespace, so we'll have to be sure and insert a *using* statement for *System.Reflection*. This attribute accepts a string parameter, which specifies the filename (assumed to be in the current directory) for the key file containing the private key. In our case, this file is the *MyKey.snk* file. So we'll add the following statements to the top of our code file:

```
using System.Reflection;
[assembly:AssemblyKeyFileAttribute("MyKey.snk")]
```

Now, we need to add a version number to our assembly, using the *AssemblyVersionAttribute*. This attribute is also an assembly level attribute, and is located in the *System.Reflection* namespace. This attribute accepts a string value specifying the version number of the assembly in the format of *major.minor.build .revision*. For our file, let's go ahead and set this to *1.1.0.0*, as follows:

```
[assembly:AssemblyVersionAttribute("1.1.0.0")]
```

If we choose, we can also add a culture attribute to the assembly, which specifies that this is intended for a specific culture. This is done using the *AssemblyCultureAttribute*, which is also an assembly level attribute from the *System.Reflection* namespace. It accepts a string parameter specifying the culture code. This does not work for executable assemblies that include modules. This is intended primarily for executable assemblies referencing libraries instead. So as a consequence, this will not work in our sample application. For this example, we'll use *en* as our culture:

```
[assembly:AssemblyCultureAttribute("en")]
```

If you'll think back to the information on how attributes work from earlier in this chapter, you might recall that attributes are named with the *Attribute* suffix—this is not required when referring to them. Based on this, the following statements also work:

```
using System;
using System.Reflection;
[assembly:AssemblyKeyFile("MyKey.snk")]
[assembly:AssemblyVersion("1.1.0.0")]
```

Now we'll need to compile our code into a module. To do this, we need to make sure that the *MyKey.snk* file is located in the same directory as our source file and run the compiler with the */t:module* command-line parameter. This would result in the following command line:

```
csc /t:module Messaging.cs
```

At this point, we now have a compiled module with has a strong name. In order to make use of this module, we now need to compile the source file referencing the *Messaging* namespace with a reference to the new *Messaging.netmodule* file. This is done the same way as our compile of the *MainApp.cs* file, referenced earlier in the chapter. This syntax would look like the following:

```
csc /t:module MainApp.cs /addmodule:Messaging.netmodule
```

Now that our modules are compiled, we can compile our executable assembly and complete our application using the assembly generation tool. The syntax for this is:

```
al MainApp.netmodule Messaging.netmodule /main:SendMsg.Main
   /out: MyVersionedApp.exe /t:exe
```

If we run our new executable assembly, we'll receive the following result:

```
C:\chapt9-code>myversionedapp
The author says: Greetings!
```

Of course, this is the same result that we previously obtained when we went through the same procedure without versioning. How is this any different than the previous compile? Well, this can easily be shown by making a small modification to our *Messaging.cs* file and recompiling it. If we change the version number to *2.1.0.0*, then recompile the file into a module, we end up with a module containing a different version number. If you attempt to run your previously compiled version of *MyVersionedApp.exe* without recompiling it with the new version of the module, you receive the following message:

```
C:\chapt9-code>myversionedapp

Unhandled Exception: System.IO.FileLoadException: The check of the
   module's hash failed for file 'Messaging.netmodule'.
File name: "Messaging.netmodule"
   at SendMsg.Main()
```

Based on this, you can see how a versioned application reacts when presented with a module of the wrong version. This allows us to have a great deal of flexibility when dealing with versioning problems and gives us a new weapon to combat the nemesis of DLL Hell.

# Summary

This chapter has covered a lot of ground in two distinct sections. In the first part of the chapter, we learned about attributes. C# has a plethora of default (or built-in) attributes available for you to use in your applications. These attributes cover everything from setting up Web services to code obsolescence. C# also provides you with the ability to design your own custom attributes as needed for your applications. These custom attributes are attribute classes and can contain both required and optional parameters. The entities upon which they can be defined are also customizable with the use of attribute targets. These attributes, both default and custom, provide you with a powerful method of providing information or performing operations upon your application.

We also created our own custom attribute called *CodeTracker*, and learned how to gather information about our custom attribute through a process called reflection. Reflection is a powerful tool that allows us to gather information out of the assembly manifest at runtime as well as perform many other functions. In our examples, we used reflection to determine the members of a class, which attributes are defined on these members, and what the properties of any *CodeTracker* attributes on the members are.

In the second part of the chapter, we learned about assemblies. Assemblies are the basic containers of compiled code for C# and are similar in function to Java's .JAR files. Assemblies can be in the form of .DLL files and can be used to provide additional functionality to an application, or they can be compiled as executable assemblies with an .EXE extension. We also learned the difference between single-file and multimodule assemblies, and how to properly compile each.

In this section we also learned about assembly manifests and how they are used. All data in the assembly manifest can be read either from within the assembly itself, or from external utilities. The assembly manifest does have to be generated slightly different for multimodule assemblies and we learned how to do this as well.

Finally, we covered the new versioning features available to us in C#. We learned how to assign versions to assemblies and how to *sign* or assign a strong name to an assembly. We also created a versioned assembly and learned what happens if an incorrect version of an assembly is used when a specific version is expected.

# Solutions Fast Track

## Working with Attributes

☑ Attributes are additional pieces of information that the developer can choose to store in the application metadata.

☑ There are many built-in attributes, but custom attributes can also easily be created and used.

☑ Attributes are defined on specific targets, and can be limited as to which targets are available.

## Using Reflection

☑ Reflection is a process that allows us to retrieve and work with data stored in the application metadata.

☑ Data in the application metadata can be retrieved either at compile time or runtime by using this process.

☑ Reflection allows us to list attributes defined on a target as well as list the values of defined attributes.

## Creating Assemblies

☑ Assemblies are the C# equivalent to Java's packages and are used to segment namespaces.

☑ Assemblies in the .NET architecture can be written and compiled in different languages, and still work together.

☑ All information about an assembly is stored in the assembly manifest.

## Versioning

☑ Versioning allows developers to prevent DLL conflicts and make sure that their application is using the correct version of a component.

☑ In order to implement versioning, an assembly must have a *strong name* and be compiled with a public-private key pair.

☑ If a component is used that is not the correct version, exceptions can be generated and handled.

# Frequently Asked Questions

The following Frequently Asked Questions, answered by the authors of this book, are designed to both measure your understanding of the concepts presented in this chapter and to assist you with real-life implementation of these concepts. To have your questions about this chapter answered by the author, browse to **www.syngress.com/solutions** and click on the **"Ask the Author"** form.

**Q:** Are attributes required in an application?

**A:** Yes, but you don't have to define them. There are attributes that the compiler adds into the application metadata, and these are required. However, you also have the option of adding your own.

**Q:** Why would I want to limit the targets available for my custom attribute?

**A:** A good example of this would be the built-in *AssemblyVersionAttribute*. This attribute specifies the version number for your assembly. If this could be defined at more levels than the assembly target, it could cause confusion as to what the version number of the assembly really is.

**Q:** Is reflection the only way to view information stored in an application's metadata?

**A:** No. Since the metadata is included with the compiled assembly, any utility capable of viewing an assembly could see this as well. An example of this is the *ILDasm.exe* utility included with the .NET Framework.

**Q:** Why should I use assemblies?

**A:** Assemblies can really be useful when developing a very large program or even when developing code that you think you might use again. In large programs, assemblies help make the namespace more manageable as well as making it easy for programmers to work on specific sections of the application. When you develop useful code that you think you might be able to use sometime in the future, you could simply compile it as an assembly and reuse it later.

**Q:** So with assemblies, I can write anything in any of the languages supporting the common language runtime and the assemblies will always work together?

**A:** No, this is not always the case. There are some functions that will work in some languages that just aren't supported in others. Therefore, there are specific rules that define what code is or is not compatible for this purpose.

# Chapter 10

# Multithreading

## Solutions in this chapter:

- Threads
- Creating Threads
- Managing Threads
- Scheduling Threads
- Synchronizing Threads
- Avoiding Deadlocks and Starvation

☑ Summary

☑ Solutions Fast Track

☑ Frequently Asked Questions

# Introduction

In this chapter you will learn about the *System.Threading* namespace, which is one of the main class libraries provided by the .NET Framework for creating multi-threaded programs. Multithreaded programs are similar to multitasking—the ability to have more than one program working at the same time—except that it's one step lower. Multithreaded applications give individual programs the ability to do multiple tasks at the same time.

The first part of the chapter will discuss threads and synchronization. Threads are lightweight processes used for multitasking within a single application. Just like Java, C# provides us with a simple way to build multithreaded programs and synchronizing resources accessed by multiple threads.

To end the chapter we will look at some of the trouble you can get into when you're writing multithreaded programs. We will look at conditions that can cause deadlocks and starvation to your running application, as well as how best to avoid these conditions.

# Threads

Threads are an excellent way for programmers to parallelize multiple operations efficiently. Very much like multiple processes in multitasking operating systems, multiple threads within a single process can time-share critical resources such as the CPU and memory. Often threads are used to speed up response time to a program. For example, one thread can perform computations while another performs memory updates. The two threads would make the compute and update operations seem simultaneous.

Although threads generally tend to improve the performance of a program, they can negatively impact a program if there are not enough shared resources. Because a substantial amount of overhead is involved in switching from one thread to another, having threads in an environment where resources are relatively limited (such as a single CPU, for example) can cause an adverse slowing effect as a result of frequent context switching. Therefore the use of threads must be considered carefully in light of available resources in a particular operating environment and whether the availability of these resources can balance out the thread switching overheads. Improvement in performance must also be adequate to justify the extra time required to verify and debug multiple threads.

Very much like threads in Java, threads in C# within the .NET Framework are concurrent, lightweight control flows of individual sequential operations.

However, although very similar to its counterpart in Java, threads in C# have a slightly simplified and different model.

The .NET Framework provides us with the *System.Threading* namespace for creating and managing threads. This namespace contains a wealth of classes and interfaces to facilitate multithreaded programming and to simplify most threading tasks. The *System.Threading* namespace provides the *Thread* object as well as several classes for managing threads. Here's a list of other useful classes in the namespace:

- **Timer** Enables the programmer to execute methods at certain time intervals.

- **Interlocked** Enables the programmer to perform atomic operations for variables shared by multiple threads.

- **Monitor** Enables the programmer to synchronize access to thread objects.

- **WaitHandle** Enables the programmer to perform wait notification by encapsulating operating system-specific objects that wait for exclusive access to shared resources.

- **Mutex** With the *WaitHandle* class, enables the programmer to manage interprocess thread synchronization.

- **ThreadPool** With the *WaitHandle* class, enables the programmer to manage thread groups by providing a pool of threads that can post work items, process asynchronous I/O, wait on behalf of other threads, and process timers.

Several classes of methods for managing thread objects are derived from these classes. Examples for using some of these classes will be presented in the following sections.

# Creating Threads

In Java, threads are created either by extending the *java.lang.Thread* class and overriding its *run()* method or by implementing the *java.lang.Runnable* interface and its corresponding *run()* method. In C# the simplest way to create a thread is to create an instance of the *Thread* class found in the *System.Threading* namespace. The *Thread* constructor takes a single argument, which is a delegate type.

As mentioned, there are several ways you can create a thread in Java, but for the following example we will use anonymous inner classes to resemble the C# model closely (inner classes are comparable to delegates; refer to Chapter 8). Let's write a program that will create two threads; each thread will count from 0 to 9. Here's how you would write it in Java:

## Java

```
class ThreadExample
{
  public static void main (String[] args)
  {
    Thread threadA = new Thread(new Runnable() {
      public void run() { count("threadA"); } } );

    Thread threadB = new Thread(new Runnable() {
      public void run() { count("threadB"); } } );

    threadA.start();
    threadB.start();
  }

  public static void count(String name)
  {
    for(int i = 0; i < 10; i++)
    {
      System.out.println(name + " " + i);
    }
  }
}
```

In this example, a thread is created by passing it an anonymous inner class that implements *java.lang.Runnable* and contains the *count* method.

Let's now look at an example of how you would create threads in C#. Let's look at the C# equivalent of the previous Java program example:

## C#

```
using System;
using System.Threading;

class ThreadExample
```

```
{
  public static void Main()
  {
    Thread threadA = new Thread(new ThreadStart(count));
    Thread threadB = new Thread(new ThreadStart(count));

    threadA.Start();
    threadB.Start();
  }

  public static void count()
  {
    for(int i = 0; i < 10; i++)
    {
      Console.WriteLine(i);
    }
  }
}
```

As you can see, creating threads in C# is pretty straightforward, and the code is fairly similar to Java. Just like in Java, you implement a thread by creating a thread object and calling its *Start()* method. In C# thread objects are created by passing the intended instance object method (*count* in this case) to a *ThreadStart()* delegate. The *ThreadStart()* delegate thus points to a method you supply, which the CLR will execute as soon as the thread is started. The delegate declaration looks like this:

```
public delegate void ThreadStart();
```

The method that you pass to this delegate must match its signature. This means that it must return *void* and takes *no* parameters. Therefore, if you wish to create a thread, your declaration will look something like this:

```
Thread myThread = new Thread(new ThreadStart(myMethod));
```

If you are paying close attention, you may notice that the codes aren't completely identical. In the Java version, we were able to pass a variable to the count method, but since the method that you pass to the *ThreadStart()* delegate must take no parameters, we cannot do the same thing in C#. The reason for this is that unlike Java where we can extend the *java.lang.Thread* class or implement *java.lang.Runnable* interface, C#'s thread class is *sealed* and cannot be extended;

thus, whatever is passed to the delegate must match its signature exactly, as previously mentioned. One way around this is to create a new object that can hold variables that you want to keep track of and can pass a method from the object that you wish to be threaded. Here's an example to illustrate how this can be done:

```
using System;
using System.Threading;

class ThreadExample
{
  public static void Main()
  {
    Counter counterA = new Counter("threadA");
    Counter counterB = new Counter("threadB");

    Thread threadA =
        new Thread(new ThreadStart(counterA.count));
    Thread threadB =
        new Thread(new ThreadStart(counterB.count));

    threadA.Start();
    threadB.Start();
  }
}

class Counter
{
  private String name;

  public Counter(String name)
  {
    this.name = name;
  }

  public void count()
  {
    for(int i = 0; i < 10; i++)
    {
```

```
        Console.WriteLine(name + " " + i);
    }
  }
}
```

Note that in this case since the *count()* method is not static, an object instance of the *Counter* class must be created in the *Main()* method and then passed to the *ThreadStart* delegate.

When threads are executed in the .NET environment, they alternate and time-share the computing resources. To observe this, first we will slow down each thread by using the *Sleep()* method:

```
public void count()
{
  for(int i = 0; i < 10; i++)
  {
    Console.WriteLine(name + " " + i);
    Thread.Sleep(2);
  }
}
```

The *Sleep()* method takes in a parameter of type *long*, which tells the thread to block for a specified number of time in milliseconds. Therefore, *Sleep(2)* gives the thread a slight two millisecond pause. Now if we execute the program we can see how the operating system switches between the two threads in order to share the CPU processing. Here's the output of the program.

## *Output*

```
threadA 0
threadB 0
threadA 1
threadB 1
threadA 2
threadB 2
threadA 3
threadB 3
threadA 4
threadB 4
threadA 5
```

```
threadB 5
threadA 6
threadB 6
threadA 7
threadB 7
threadA 8
threadB 8
threadA 9
threadB 9
```

The output might vary from computer to computer because the thread scheduler is dependent on many factors, such as processor speed, other programs running, and so forth. Scheduling threads will be discussed in greater detail later in this section.

As a last note on creating threads, threads in C# can be given names by setting the *Name* property of the thread object:

```
threadA.Name = "thread A";
threadB.Name = "thread B";
```

Other properties of the *Thread* object will be discussed in the following section when we discuss how to manage threads.

# Managing Threads

Once threads are started, they can be managed with methods and properties provided by the *Thread* and *ThreadPool* classes. For example, the threads *IsAlive* and *ThreadState* properties can be used to check on the execution status and states of a thread. Furthermore, the thread's *Join()* method can be used to join two threads together. Similar to its counterpart in Java, C#'s *Join()* method is a wait for the child thread's termination or timeout mechanism. However, unlike its counterpart in Java, *Join()* in C# can return a *boolean* to signify whether a thread died (true) or timed out (false). C#'s *Join()* method is overloaded with three types of parameters:

- **Null** The calling thread is blocked until a particular thread terminates:

```
public void Join();
```

- **Integer** The calling thread is blocked until a particular thread either terminates or the specified number of milliseconds (*integer*) has elapsed, whichever comes first:

```
public bool Join(int);
```

■ **TimeSpan** The calling thread is blocked until the thread either terminates or the specified amount of time (timespan) has elapsed, whichever comes first:

```
public bool Join(TimeSpan);
```

The following example illustrates the use of the *Join()* method. Suppose there are three threads: the parent thread opens and prepares a file for writing and then starts a couple of child threads to read and collect data from network sockets. The parent thread needs to wait until both child threads complete before it can actually write the collected data into the file. The *Join()* method can be used to make sure the child threads complete before writing to the file:

```
using System;
using System.IO;
using System.Net;
using System.Threading;

public class JoinExample
{
  public static void Main()
  {
    Thread myParent =
       new Thread(new ThreadStart(Parent));

    myParent.Start();
  }

  public static void Parent()
  {
    //Prepares file for writing

    //Creates and dispatches the reader threads
    Thread mySocketReader1 =
       new Thread(new ThreadStart(SocketReader));
    Thread mySocketReader2 =
       new Thread(new ThreadStart(SocketReader));
```

```
        mySocketReader1.Start();
        mySocketReader2.Start();

        //Waits for reader threads to complete
        mySocketReader1.Join();
        mySocketReader2.Join();

        //Writes to file
        FileWriter();
    }

    public static void SocketReader()
    {
        //Reads from socket here
    }

    public static void FileWriter()
    {
        //Writes to file here
    }
}
```

*Join()* makes sure all the reader threads are completed before starting the writer that writes the contents to files.

## Using *Suspend()/Resume()* and *Abort()*

Oftentimes the programmer wants to stop the execution of a thread temporarily, until another event takes place. For example, after a certain computation, it might be desirable to wait for an update to be successfully displayed before another computation is performed. In this case the thread can be paused, and once the update completion event is detected, restarted at the point where it was paused. In C# a thread can be suspended and resumed using the *Suspend()* and *Resume()* methods of the *Thread* object as follows:

## *Suspending*

```
if (threadA.ThreadState = ThreadState.Running)
{
    threadA.Suspend();
}
```

## *Resuming*

```
if (threadA.ThreadState = ThreadState.Suspended)
{
    threadA.Resume();
}
```

First the state of the thread is checked (this usually is a good idea since we want to make sure the thread is in a state where *Suspend()* and *Resume()* can be performed), and then the thread itself is suspended or resumed accordingly.

### Developing & Deploying…

### Suspend/Resume May Be Deadlock Prone

Note that *Suspend()* does not release locks. Thus care must be taken to make sure any locked objects do not inadvertently block other threads and cause the program to deadlock (deadlock will be discussed in more detail in the section "Avoiding Deadlock and Starvation").

There might also be times when a thread must be terminated upon a certain event. For example, if in the middle of a heavy computation the user changes his or her mind and decides to stop the computation, he or she might press a certain key that would in turn trigger an event that can be used to signal a thread that it should be killed. A thread can be killed using the *Abort()* method of the *Thread* object as follows:

```
if (threadA.IsAlive)
{
    try
    {
```

```
      threadA.Abort();
   }
   catch (ThreadAbortException ta)
   {
      Console.WriteLine(ta.ToString());
   }
}
```

Again the state of the thread is checked to see whether it is a live thread, then the abort operation is attempted and exceptions are caught (if any, should the *Abort()* operation fail).

# Scheduling Threads

When there are limited resources, such as in a single CPU environment, only one task or thread can be serviced at a time. Multitasking is done by switching back and forth between the different threads. In such cases, it might be a good idea to give certain threads higher priorities than others. For example, in GUI applications, the thread that is refreshing and updating the user interface window might be given a higher priority in order to improve the apparent responsiveness of the program to the user.

Similar to Java, threads in the .NET environment are scheduled for execution according to their priorities. The *Priority* property of the *Thread* object provides the means for setting the priority level. There are five possible priority levels, listed in Table 10.1.

**Table 10.1** Different Thread Priorities

| Priority | Description |
| --- | --- |
| AboveNormal | Scheduled after threads with **Highest** priority and before those with **Normal** priority |
| BelowNormal | Scheduled after threads with **Normal** priority and before those with **Lowest** priority |
| Highest | Scheduled before threads with any other priority |
| Lowest | Scheduled after threads with any other priority |
| Normal | Default |

Suppose there is a thread called *guiUpdater* that refreshes the graphical user interface, and another thread called *calculator*. You would want the *guiUpdater* thread to have a higher priority than *calculator* because you want the user interface to be responsive. You wouldn't want the *calculator* thread to tie up the processor and make it seem to the user that the application has "frozen." The following assignment statement can be used to set the priority of *guiUpdater* to highest before starting thread execution:

```
guiUpdater.Priority = ThreadPriority.Highest;
```

This will give *guiUpdater* the highest possible priority during execution when a critical computing resource is limited. This way if the *calculator* thread, for example, is doing some heavy calculations, the thread scheduler will give more priority to the *guiUpdater* so that the GUI can be updated first before proceeding with the calculation.

Threads can also be scheduled to execute at certain time intervals. This is supported by the *Timer* class in the .NET environment. After a start time and a period (time between execution) are specified, a *TimerCallback* delegate is used to designate which methods to execute. The timer can be changed and disposed on the fly. This is best illustrated by an example—the following program creates a timer that has an initial interval of two seconds, then it switches to two tenths of a second.

First, create an empty *Timer* placeholder class. In this class, an integer counter is declared and a dummy *Timer* handle (for the purpose of being able to dispose this object later) is created—it will be assigned to point to the actually timer later:

```
class TimerExampleState
{
    public int counter = 0;
    public Timer tmr;
}
```

Next, create a timer and a delegate that will invoke the timer itself. The delegate creation part is done by declaring a *TimerCallback* delegate and providing the method to call (*CheckStatus()* in this case). The delegate is then tied to the object we created and the time intervals are specified. The *Timer* constructor can take the time specification in either milliseconds or *TimeSpan*:

```
public Timer(callback, object, int/long, int/long);
```

```
public Timer(callback, object, TimeSpan, TimeSpan);
```

Here's the code listing for our *TimerExample* class. The *Main()* method first creates the *timerDelegate* and assign the *CheckStatus()* method to it. It then creates a *stateHandler* to keep track of the timer, so that we can dispose it later. Then, a new instance of the *Timer* class is created by passing our *timerDelegate* and *stateHandler* to its constructor. Afterward, we put the main thread to sleep while we execute the timer.

Next, we declare our delegated method *CheckStatus()*. This method increments the counter every time it is called. It also shortens the timer period to two-tenths of a second when the counter reaches 10 and kills the timer when the counter reaches 20. *WriteLine()* is called to print out the time and the counter for illustration. Following is the full code listing for our example.

```
using System;
using System.Threading;

class TimerExampleState
{
    public int counter = 0;
    public Timer tmr;
}

class TimerExample
{
    public static void Main()
    {
        TimerCallback timerDelegate =
            new TimerCallback(CheckStatus);

        TimerExampleState stateHandler = new
            TimerExampleState();
        Timer timer = new Timer(timerDelegate,
            stateHandler, 1000, 2000);

        //Now we can assign the handle we created earlier to
        //point back to the timer itself:
        stateHandler.tmr = timer;

        //We can now put the main thread to sleep while we
```

```
    //execute the timer:
    while(stateHandler.tmr != null)
      Thread.Sleep(0);


    Console.WriteLine("Timer example done.");
  }


  static void CheckStatus(Object state)
  {
    TimerExampleState s =(TimerExampleState) state;
    s.counter++;


    Console.WriteLine( "{0}:{1} Checking Status {2}.",
      DateTime.Now.Minute, DateTime.Now.Second,
      s.counter);


     if(s.counter == 10)
     {
       // Restarts after ten seconds and shortens the
       // period to 2/10th of a second
       (s.tmr).Change(10000, 200);
       Console.WriteLine("changed...");
     }


     if(s.counter == 20)
     {
       Console.WriteLine("disposing of timer...");
       s.tmr.Dispose();
       s.tmr = null;
     }
   }
 }
```

The output of this timer example follows. As we can see, the timer switches to a smaller interval when the count reaches 10:

# Output

```
29:56 Checking Status 1.
29:58 Checking Status 2.
30:0 Checking Status 3.
30:2 Checking Status 4.
30:4 Checking Status 5.
30:6 Checking Status 6.
30:8 Checking Status 7.
30:10 Checking Status 8.
30:12 Checking Status 9.
30:14 Checking Status 10.
changed...
30:24 Checking Status 11.
30:24 Checking Status 12.
30:24 Checking Status 13.
30:25 Checking Status 14.
30:25 Checking Status 15.
30:25 Checking Status 16.
30:25 Checking Status 17.
30:25 Checking Status 18.
30:26 Checking Status 19.
30:26 Checking Status 20.
disposing of timer...
Timer example done.
```

As a closing remark for this section, Table 10.2 summarizes some of the major methods available to the *Thread* object, and their equivalents in Java. Note that the C# methods appear to be either the same as or only a little more flexible than their corresponding Java equivalents.

**Table 10.2** Common C# and Java Equivalent Thread Methods and Properties

| C# | Java | Function | Notes |
| --- | --- | --- | --- |
| IsBackground set property | setDaemon() | Sets the thread to run as a daemon | In C#, a property needs to be set. |
| IsBackground get property | isDaemon () | Determines whether a thread is a daemon | In C#, this property will return true if it is a daemon. |

**Continued**

**Table 10.2** Continued

| C# | Java | Function | Notes |
|---|---|---|---|
| IsAlive get property | isAlive () | Determines whether a thread is alive | In C#, this property will return true is it is alive. |
| Sleep() | sleep() | Pauses thread execution for specified time | In C#, this method can take the TimeSpan structure. |
| Join() | join() | Serializes thread execution by waiting for completion | In C#, a Boolean value is returned to indicate whether the thread died (true) or timer expired (false). |
| Suspend() | suspend() | Suspends a thread | This is deprecated in Java. |
| Resume() | resume() | Resumes a thread | This is deprecated in Java. |
| Abort () | stop() | Kills a thread | This is deprecated in Java. |

# Synchronizing Threads

Since different threads can operate on the same data structure set, problems of ordering and consistency can arise if there is a lack of synchronization. Like Java, the .NET environment provides synchronization as a mean of ensuring serialized execution of critical sections (codes that operate on the same data structure) and atomic operations in consistent order. Two methods of synchronization are provided for this purpose: using the *lock* statement (similar to Java's *synchronized* statement), which in turn calls the underlying *Monitor* class of *System.Threading* namespace in the .NET environment, or using the *Monitor* class' *Enter()* and *Exit()* methods directly. However, just as in Java, if synchronization is done incorrectly critical sections can pose a danger for one thread either to block another (*deadlock*) or to hog available resource (*starvation*) indefinitely. Therefore extreme care must be taken to synchronize multiple threads correctly.

## Using the *lock* Statement

If a critical section operates on the same data structure in a multithreaded environment, unpredictable ordering can occur unless care is taken to serialize the different threads (i.e., make sure when one thread is accessing the common data structure, the data structure is locked from being accessed by another thread). In Java, this synchronization can be done using the *synchronized* keyword. For example, suppose there are two threads both sharing the same *Counter* object. Since both can call the *Increment()* method at the same time, we would want to synchronize access to the shared *count* variable. We can use the *synchronized* keyword to accomplish serializing the critical section as follows.

## *Java*

```
public class Counter
{
  private int count = 0;

  public void Increment()
  {
     synchronized(this)
     {
        for( int i = 0; i < 10; i++ )
           count++;
     }
  }
}
```

The same thing can be accomplished in C# using the corresponding *lock* keyword. The *lock* keyword locks the shared resource before performing the increment. If the *Increment()* method is called from two simultaneous threads one will lock the object before the other. Therefore, only one thread can increment the *count* variable at a time. The lock is released upon completion of the code block, which is enclosed by the curly braces {}:

## *C#*

```
public class Counter
{
  private int count = 0;

  public void Increment()
  {
    lock(this)
    {
       for( int i = 0; i < 10; i++ )
```

```
        count++;
    }
  }
}
```

The locked item can be any object. In the preceding example the lock is placed on the object *this*. This aspect will be discussed in more detail in the following sections, where the underlying mechanisms that make synchronization with the *lock* statement possible are discussed.

## Developing & Deploying...

### Interlocked Class

Since incrementing and decrementing a variable in a synchronized fashion is such a common programming concept, C# offers the *Interlocked* class for just this purpose. This class has two methods, *Increment()* and *Decrement()*, which will increment and decrement a variable under a synchronized control. The variable *count* in the previous example can actually be locked as follows:

```
public int count = 0;


public void Increment()
{
    for( int i = 0; i < 0; i++)
        Interlocked.Increment(ref count);
}
```

## Using the Monitor Class

When the *lock* statement is used, it actually calls the underlying *Monitor* class provided by the .NET environment to perform its locking task. The *Monitor* class contains various methods to control synchronization of threads. If desired, the programmer can access these methods directly rather than using the *lock* statement to achieve the same purpose. The following code shows how the synchronization example in the previous section can be done the same way using the *Monitor* class methods directly:

```
public static void Increment()
{
  try
  {
    Monitor.Enter(this);
    for( int i = 0; i < 10; i++ )
      count++;
  }
  finally
  {
    Monitor.Exit(this);
  }
}
```

**NOTE**

When using *Monitor's Enter()* and *Exit()* it is a good idea to use a *try/finally* construct to prevent possible exceptions from blocking out the *Exit()*. For example, suppose *count++* is some other operation that throws an exception; the *Exit()* would have been lost if we did not enclosed it within a try/finally block.

The *Monitor.Enter()* and *Exit()* pair performs the same task, and they can coexist with *lock* statements. However, using the *Monitor* methods directly gives the programmer a lot more flexibility in controlling the synchronization. The *Monitor* class also provides the *Pulse()* and *Wait()* methods. The *Wait()* method tells the thread to wait until the object protected by the monitor becomes available. The *Pulse()* method signals that there has been a change in state, and other waiting threads can have control of the monitor object. Let's look at an example. Suppose we have a *MessageBoard* class where individual threads can post and read messages. We will synchronize access to this class so that only one thread can perform a read or write at a time. Our *MessageBoard* class will have a *Reader()* method and a *Writer()* method.

The *Reader()* method checks the string *messages* to see if messages are available, and the *Writer()* method writes to same string. If there are *no messages* during reading, the *Reader()* method waits via *Wait()* until the *Writer()* method has written the messages and sent out a signal via *Pulse()* to tell the *Reader()* method to stop waiting and go on. The following is a code listing for the *MessageBoard* class:

```
using System;
using System.Threading;

class MessageBoard
{
  private String messages = "no messages" ;

  public void Reader()
  {
    try
    {
      Monitor.Enter(this);

      //If there are no messages then wait.
      if (messages == "no messages")
      {
        Console.WriteLine("{0} {1}",
          Thread.CurrentThread.Name, messages);

        Console.WriteLine("{0} waiting...",
          Thread.CurrentThread.Name);

        Monitor.Wait(this);
      }

      //Means that messages state has changed
      Console.WriteLine("{0} {1}",
        Thread.CurrentThread.Name, messages);
    }
    finally
    {
      Monitor.Exit(this);
    }
  }
```

```
public void Writer()
{
  try
  {
    Monitor.Enter(this);
    messages = "Greetings Caroline and Marianne!";

    Console.WriteLine("{0} Done writing message...",
        Thread.CurrentThread.Name);

    //Signal waiting threads that there's data to be read
    Monitor.Pulse(this);
  }
  finally
  {
    Monitor.Exit(this);
  }
}


public static void Main()
{
  MessageBoard myMessageBoard = new MessageBoard();

  Thread reader = new Thread(new
    ThreadStart(myMessageBoard.Reader));

  //Assign the thread a name.
  reader.Name = "ReaderThread:";

  Thread writer = new Thread( new
    ThreadStart(myMessageBoard.Writer));

  //Assign the thread a name.
  writer.Name = "WriterThread:";

  reader.Start();
```

```
        writer.Start();
    }
}
```

## Output

```
ReaderThread: no messages
ReaderThread: waiting...
WriterThread: Done writing message...
ReaderThread: Greetings Caroline and Marianne!
```

As you can see from the output, since we started the *reader* thread first, it locks the *MessageBoard* class first, which means that it has exclusive access to the *messages* string variable. But since the *messages* still contains *no message*, the *reader* releases the lock by calling the *Wait()* method. The *writer* thread then gets a chance to lock the object and write its message. Then it calls the *Pulse()* method to signal the waiting *reader* thread that it can proceed.

### Developing & Deploying…

#### Monitor.Wait() Parameters

The *Wait()* method can take on a variety of parameters, including an integer specifying the number of milliseconds to wait as well as a *TimeSpan* structure. In the event that the specified time expires before it is notified by a corresponding *Pulse()*, *Wait()* returns a *boolean* value of *false*.

# Avoiding Deadlock and Starvation

Like in Java, deadlock and starvation can occur if synchronization is not done correctly. *Deadlock* occurs when multiple threads interfere with one another, causing one or more of them to wait forever on one another's resource. *Starvation* is a similar problem in which one thread grabs all the available resources forever, thus depriving the other threads from utilizing their shared resource.

Consider the classic dining philosophers' example whereby five philosophers are sitting around a round table. Between each pair of philosophers is one chopstick. Each philosopher must get two chopsticks before he can eat. They must find a way to share chopsticks such that they all get to eat. Suppose they come up with a *GetChopSticks()* function where each philosopher first reaches for a chopstick on his right, and then his left. If he gets both chopsticks, he eats and then puts them down and signals to the other philosophers. If he gets only one chopstick, then he waits. However, suppose every philosopher reaches for the chopstick on his right at the same time—then *deadlock* occurs because after each philosopher picks up one chopstick from his right, the chopstick on his left is no longer available and then everybody waits for the second chopstick indefinitely. This is an example of *deadlock*.

Now consider an alternate case where one of philosophers does get two chopsticks, but he keeps on eating and never releases either one of his chopsticks. In this case the other philosophers will also wait indefinitely. This is an example of *starvation*.

The best way to prevent deadlock and starvation is to avoid it, either by making sure that each thread accesses the shared resources in an orderly sequential fashion or releases the resources when it is not using them. The first method can be done via the *Join()* method of the *Thread* object, and the latter can be accomplished via the use of *Wait()* and *Pulse()* methods of the *Monitor* class. Let's go through an example.

The best way to avoid deadlock and starvation is to make sure that either the threads access the shared resource in a fixed order or the shared resource is released before the next thread can acquire the same resource. In our example, the philosophers' *GetChopSticks()* attempts must be ordered. As illustrated previously, the *Join()* method enables one thread to wait for another. The same mechanism can be used to ensure orderly resource acquisition and release.

Let's simplify the philosopher's dilemma problem to two philosophers and two chopsticks. Now suppose there are two variables indicating the availability of the chopsticks and two *GetChopSticks()* methods used by the philosophers. Each of the methods picks up one chopstick at a time and sets the corresponding variable to false. Once both chopsticks are picked up the philosopher uses the chopsticks and makes both chopsticks available again for use:

```
using System;
using System.Threading;

class PhilosopherExample
{
    public static bool chopStick1Available = true;
```

```
public static bool chopStick2Available = true;

public static void Main()
{
   Thread philosopher1 =
      new Thread(new ThreadStart(GetChopSticks1));
   Thread philosopher2 =
      new Thread(new ThreadStart(GetChopSticks2));

   philosopher1.Start();
   philosopher2.Start();
}


public static void GetChopSticks1()
{
   while (!chopStick1Available)
   {
      Console.WriteLine("#1 waiting for 1st chopstick.");
      Thread.Sleep(0); // Wait until available
   }
   Console.WriteLine("#1 got 1st chopstick.");
   chopStick1Available = false;

   while (!chopStick2Available)
   {
      Console.WriteLine("#1 waiting for 2nd chopstick.");
      Thread.Sleep(0); // Wait until available
   }
   Console.WriteLine("#1 got 2nd chopstick.");
   chopStick2Available = false;

   // Uses chopsticks then makes them available again
   Console.WriteLine("#1 uses and releases chopsticks.");

   chopStick1Available = true;
   chopStick2Available = true;
}
```

```
public static void GetChopSticks2()
{
    while (!chopStick2Available)
    {
        Console.WriteLine("#2 waiting for 1st chopstick.");
        Thread.Sleep(0); // Wait until available
    }
    Console.WriteLine("#2 got 1st chopstick.");
    chopStick2Available = false;

    while (!chopStick1Available)
    {
        Console.WriteLine("#2 waiting for 2nd chopstick.");
        Thread.Sleep(0); // Wait until available
    }
    Console.WriteLine("#2 got 2nd chopstick.");
    chopStick1Available = false;

    // Uses chopsticks then makes them available again
    Console.WriteLine("#2 uses and releases chopsticks.");

    chopStick1Available = true;
    chopStick2Available = true;
}
}
```

Now here's the problem. What if philosopher1 picks up chopstick #1 while philosopher #2 picks up chopstick #2? Deadlock then occurs because everybody is waiting for the second chopstick:

```
#1 waiting for 2nd chopstick.
#2 waiting for 2nd chopstick.
```

To solve this problem, the *Join()* method can be used to serialize the operations. As illustrated previously, the *Join()* method waits for one thread to finish before going on. The previous deadlock condition can be prevented if the following codes were used:

```
philosopher1.Start();
```

```
philosopher1.Join();
philosopher2.Start();
```

This way, philosopher2 will wait for philosopher1 to finish before attempting to pick up any chopsticks, thus avoiding deadlock.

In our simple program it was very easy to see where a deadlock can occur and where we can correct it. However, in a program running many threads, it might not be so intuitive to see where a deadlock can occur. One good rule to follow is to try to get all the locks you need, and if you can't, release all the locks you have and try again. Another good rule is to try to hold your locks as briefly as possible.

## Developing & Deploying...

### Semaphores

Semaphores are classical examples of synchronizing two or more threads where one set of threads is producing results and another set of threads is consuming the results. A semaphore is basically a count that maintains the number of users for a particular lock. A semaphore class is typically created to make available one counter and two methods: one to acquire the semaphore and other to release a semaphore. As it turns out, the *Monitor* class's *Pulse()* and *Wait()* methods make it very simple to implement such a semaphore class. The following code is an example of such a class—*acquire()* tries to acquire the semaphore and decrements the count, and *release()* releases the semaphore and increments the count. If the semaphore is not available when it is being acquired, *acquire()* will *Wait()* until someone else releases the semaphore and signals a *Pulse()*:

```
class Semaphore
{
    int s_count;


    public Semaphore(int count)
    {
        s_count = count;
```

**Continued**

```
        }

    public void acquire()
    {
        lock(this)
        {
   // Keep waiting until a semaphore is
   // available.
            while(s_count <= 0)
            {
                Monitor.Wait(this);
            }
            s_count--;
        }
    }


    public void release()
    {
        lock(this)
        {
            s_count++;
            Monitor.Pulse(this);

        }
    }
}
```

A typical use of the semaphore would be to initialize the semaphore in the parent:

```
Semaphore s = new Semaphore(1);
```

You would then do the following in each of the threads:

```
s.acquire();


// Perform critical operation


s.release();
```

# Summary

Multithreading is essential to providing superior performance and effective resource utilization. Like Java, the .NET environment provides the means needed for creating and managing as well as scheduling threads. The *Threading* namespace and the *Thread* object, along with classes such as *Timer*, *Monitor*, *WaitHandle*, *Mutex*, and *ThreadPool*, provide the means for seamless handling of threads. Although similar to their counterparts in Java, threads in C# are simpler in model and more flexible in terms of usage. The methods available for thread management in C# are designed to fit both the novice and expert programmers' intents.

Threads in C# are created using the *Threading* namespace and the *ThreadStart()* delegate. The *ThreadStart()* delegate takes an instance object method that take *no* parameters and returns *void*. Furthermore, if the threaded method is nonstatic it must be created first in the calling method.

The *Join()* method can be used to serialize thread execution. Similarly, *Suspend()* and *Resume()* can be used to pause and restart threads. Lastly, the *Abort()* method can be used to terminate a thread.

Threads can be given priorities in execution by setting their priorities to one of five levels. Setting of priorities must be weighed carefully against the resource utilization associated with each of the prioritized threads.

Synchronization of threads can be done with either the *lock* statement (which in turns call the underlying *Monitor* class in the .NET environment) or the *Monitor* class methods themselves. The choice of which one to use would have to depend on whether the programmer prefers convenience (in the case of the *lock* statement) or control flexibility (in the case of *Monitor* class methods).

Last but not least, the .NET environment also provides support for preventing deadlock and starvation. Deadlock and starvation are best prevented during planning in the design stage by using proper lock and release mechanisms provided by either the *Join()* method or the *Monitor()*/*Wait()* pair of the *Monitor* class. Proper serialization guarantees that critical sections will not consume all available resources inadvertently without releasing them.

# Solutions Fast Track

## Threads

☑ Threads are an excellent way for programmers to efficiently parallelize multiple operations.

☑ Threads can negatively impact a program if there are not enough shared resources.

☑ The .NET framework provides us with the *System.Threading* namespace for creating and managing threads.

## Creating Threads

☑ Use the *Threading* namespace and the *ThreadStart()* delegate to create a thread.

☑ Threaded methods take *no* parameters and return *void*.

☑ If the threaded method is nonstatic it must be created first in the caller.

## Managing Threads

☑ Threads can be serialized using *Join()*.

☑ Threads can be paused/restarted using *Suspend()/Resume()*.

☑ Threads can be killed using *Abort()*.

## Scheduling Threads

☑ Threads are scheduled for execution based on their priorities.

☑ There are five priority levels.

☑ Balance thread priority with resource demands according.

## Synchronizing Threads

☑ Threads can be synchronized using the *lock* statement.

☑ Threads can also be synchronized using the intrinsic *Monitor* class.

☑ Choice of the *lock* statement versus the *Monitor* class depends on flexibility versus convenience.

## Avoiding Deadlocks and Starvation

☑ Deadlocks and starvation are best avoided with proper planning in the design stage.

☑ To avoid deadlock and starvation, use the proper *lock* and *release* mechanism via the *Join()* method.

☑ The *Monitor.Wait()* and *Monitor.Pulse()* methods can also be used to synchronize resource utilization properly.

# Frequently Asked Questions

The following Frequently Asked Questions, answered by the authors of this book, are designed to both measure your understanding of the concepts presented in this chapter and to assist you with real-life implementation of these concepts. To have your questions about this chapter answered by the author, browse to **www.syngress.com/solutions** and click on the **"Ask the Author"** form.

**Q:** The *lock* statement and *Monitor.Enter/Exit* methods allow me to synchronize threads within the same process. Are there mechanisms that will allow me to synchronize threads across *different* processes?

**A:** The .NET environment provides a *Mutex* class that is derived from *WaitHandle* for this purpose. A *Mutex* object is a named synchronization object that can be obtained from any thread within any process. The *Mutex* class takes as its argument a *bool* indicating whether the current thread initially owns the *Mutex* object or not. Once created, a *Mutex* object is referenced by its handle (similar to a file handle). *Mutex* provides several synchronization support methods such as *WaitOne* to request for a *Mutex* and *ReleaseMutex* to release a *Mutex*. An example code of how this is used follows:

```
public static void Increment()
{
    Mutex myMutex = new Mutex(false);
    myMutex.WaitOne ();
    count++;
    myMutex.Close ();
}
```

Please refer to the MSDN documentation for more details on the Mutex class.

**Q:** If a have a COM callable wrapper that invokes an unmanaged thread during runtime, can they coexist with my managed threads (ones created with the *Thread* class)?

**A:** Yes. The .NET environment's runtime support monitors all threads, managed and unmanaged.

**Q:** Is it possible to store data that is unique to a particular thread or application?

**A:** Thread local storage (TLS) and thread relative static fields support in the .NET environment enable programmers to store data associated with a particular managed thread. Please consult the MSDN documentation for more details.

**Q:** Where on the Web can I find resources and sample codes for multithreaded programming?

**A:** Besides MSDN (msdn.microsoft.com), additional resources can be found on third-party sites such as www.codeproject.com and www.c-sharpcorner.com.

# Chapter 11

# Working with I/O Streams

## Solutions in this chapter:

- **File System**
- **Streams**
- **Encoding Data Types**
- **Text**
- **Network I/O**
- **Synchronous vs. Asynchronous**
- **Web Streams**
- **Serialization**

☑ **Summary**

☑ **Solutions Fast Track**

☑ **Frequently Asked Questions**

# Introduction

One of Java's great features is providing a layer of abstraction for performing input/output and networking operations. The Java model for IO uses streams, something familiar to most Java programmers. C# also uses streams and provides a rich set of libraries for hiding the complications of data transfer. The counterpart of the *java.io* package is the *System.IO* namespace. Classes in the *System.IO* namespace allow you to read and write information to a file, or to the console. Other packages, such as *System.Net.Socket,* support streams for network connections.

# File System

In Java, files and directories are handled using a single class called *File*. This ambiguous design sometimes leads to confusion since it can be difficult to determine if a file or directory is being used. C# distinguishes between files and directories by giving us two classes to handle disk operations: *File* and *Directory*. These two classes use only static methods to perform disk operations, but there are also two corresponding classes that perform disk operations on instances: *FileInfo* and *DirectoryInfo*. For Java programmers, the latter seems more familiar.

   C# uses a base class for *FileInfo* and *DirectoryInfo* called *FileSystemInfo*. This base class contains only methods that are common to both directories and files. Many of the methods in *FileSystemInfo* have counterparts in *java.io.File*. C# also has methods that have no counterpart in Java, since the Java strategy is to create only methods that are universal across different platforms. For example, methods for accessing the last time a file was accessed or when a file was created are unique to C#.

## Directories

The two classes for handling directories are *Directory* and *DirectoryInfo*. Both of these classes have almost identical methods, except that *Directory* contains static methods (as shown in Table 11.1), which are called from the class meta-object. Because an instance is not used, it is necessary to specify the directory path (as a *String* argument) for most of these method calls. A typical Directory call is as follows:

```
bool exists = Directory.Exists("c:\\Program Files");
```

**Table 11.1** The Directory API

| C# | Java Equivalent | Description |
|---|---|---|
| CreateDirectory() | File.mkDir() | Creates all directories and sub-directories as specified by path. |
| Delete() | File.delete() | Deletes a directory and its contents. |
| Exists() | File.exists() | Determines whether the given path refers to an existing directory on disk. |
| GetCreationTime() | Not Available | Gets the creation date and time of a directory. |
| GetCurrentDirectory() | Not Available | Gets the current working directory of the application. |
| GetDirectories() | File.list() or File.listFiles() | Gets the names of subdirectories in the specified directory. |
| GetDirectoryRoot() | File.getAbsolutePath() | Returns the volume information, root information, or both for the specified path. |
| GetFiles() | File.list() or File.listFiles() | Returns the names of files in the specified directory. |
| GetFileSystemEntries() | File.list() | Returns the names of all files and subdirectories in the specified directory. |
| GetLastAccessTime() | Not Available | Returns the date and time the specified file or directory was last accessed. |
| GetLastWriteTime() | File.lastModified() | Returns the date and time the specified file or directory was last written to. |
| GetLogicalDrives() | File.listRoots() | Retrieves the names of the logical drives on this computer in the form "<drive letter>:\". |
| GetParent() | File.getParent() | Retrieves the parent directory of the specified path, including both absolute and relative paths. |
| Move() | File.renameTo() | Moves a file or a directory and its contents to a new location. |

**Continued**

**Table 11.1** Continued

| C# | Java Equivalent | Description |
|---|---|---|
| SetCreationTime() | Not Available | Sets the creation date and time for the specified file or directory. |
| SetCurrentDirectory() | Not Available | Sets the application's current working directory to the specified directory. |
| SetLastAccessTime() | Not Available | Sets the date and time the specified file or directory was last accessed. |
| SetLastWriteTime() | File.setLastModified() | Sets the date and time a directory was last written to. |

## Debugging...

### The Directory Separator

One of the most frequent bugs when programming with the file system is the backslash used to identify directory structures. Notice the need to use two backslashes in the preceding example. This is because the backslash is an escape character, so it is necessary to nullify the first by using two backslashes. An even better solution is to indicate a verbatim string literal by placing the @ symbol in front of the string, as follows:

```
String filename = @"c:\Program Files";
```

Unlike *Directory*, in order to use *DirectoryInfo* it must be instantiated. *DirectoryInfo* contains several properties (as shown in Table 11.2), whereas *Directory* contains none since all the methods are static. A single *DirectoryInfo* instance represents a single directory, much like the Java counterpart *File*. Let's examine the use of *DirectoryInfo* in a simple example. Directories are a perfect opportunity to use recursion, so we'll create a simple recursive method called *CountDirectories()* that will drill down through the hierarchy, counting the directories it encounters.

```
using System;
using System.IO;
```

```
namespace IOTest
{
    public class DirectoryCounter
    {
        public static void Main()
        {
            DirectoryInfo myDir = new
                DirectoryInfo(@"c:\Program Files");
            int total = CountDirectories(myDir);
            Console.WriteLine("Total for " + myDir.FullName);
            Console.WriteLine(total);
        }


        public static int CountDirectories(DirectoryInfo dir)
        {
            DirectoryInfo [] dirs = dir.GetDirectories();
            int count = dirs.Length;
            foreach(DirectoryInfo subDir in dirs)
            {
                count += CountDirectories(subDir);
            }
            return count;
        }
    }
}
```

This program begins by creating a new *DirectoryInfo* object representing the directory "Program Files." It then calls a custom method called *CountDirectories()*, which counts the number of subdirectories in the directory. For every directory it encounters it recursively calls *CountDirectories()*. This program may take a while as it seeps through the directory structure, so be patient as it explores.

**Table 11.2** *DirectoryInfo* Methods and Properties

| C# | Java Equivalent | Description |
| --- | --- | --- |
| Create() | File.mkDir() | Creates a directory. |

**Continued**

**Table 11.2** Continued

| C# | Java Equivalent | Description |
|---|---|---|
| CreateSubdirectory() | Not Available | Creates a subdirectory or subdirectories on the specified path. The specified path can be relative to this instance of the *DirectoryInfo* class. |
| Delete() | File.delete() | Deletes a *DirectoryInfo* and its contents from a path. |
| GetDirectories() | File.list() or File.listFiles() | Returns the subdirectories of the current directory. |
| GetFiles() | File.list() or File.listFiles() | Returns a file list from the current directory. |
| GetFileSystemInfo() | Not Available | Retrieves an array of strongly typed *FileSystemInfo* objects. |
| MoveTo() | File.renameTo() | Moves a *DirectoryInfo* instance and its contents to a new path. |
| Attributes | Not Available | Gets or sets the *FileAttributes* of the current *FileSystemInfo*. |
| CreationTime | Not Available | Gets or sets the creation time of the current *FileSystemInfo* object. |
| Exists | File.exists() | Gets a value indicating whether the directory exists. |
| Extension | Not Available | Gets the string representing the extension part of the file. |
| FullName | File.getAbsolutePath() | Gets the full path of the directory or file. |
| LastAccessTime | Not Available | Gets or sets the time the current file or directory was last accessed. |
| LastWriteTime | File.lastModified() | Gets or sets the time when the current file or directory was last written to. |
| Name | File.getName() | Gets the name of this *DirectoryInfo* instance. |
| Parent | File.getParent() | Gets the parent directory of a specified subdirectory. |
| Root | Not Available | Gets the root portion of a path. |

# Files

File handling in C# is structured in almost the same way as directories. There are two classes: *File* and *FileInfo*, which work much the same as their directory counterparts. *File* contains all static methods and cannot be instantiated, so most of the methods require the file name to be specified. Table 11.3 lists the relevant methods of the *File* class and their Java counterparts. Notice there are no properties in the class, since this class is not instantiated.

**Table 11.3** The File API

| C# | Java Equivalent | Description |
| --- | --- | --- |
| AppendText() | Not Available | Creates a *StreamWriter* that appends UTF-8 encoded text to an existing file. |
| Copy() | Not Available | Copies an existing file to a new file. |
| Create() | File.createNewFile() | Creates a file in the specified fully qualified path. |
| CreateText() | Not Available | Creates or opens a new file for writing UTF-8 encoded text. |
| Delete() | File.delete() | Deletes the file specified by the fully qualified path. An exception is not thrown if the specified file does not exist. |
| Exists() | File.exists() | Determines whether the specified file exists. |
| GetAttributes() | Not Available | Gets the *FileAttributes* of the file on the fully qualified path. |
| GetCreationTime() | Not Available | Returns the creation date and time of the specified file or directory. |
| GetLastAccessTime() | Not Available | Returns the date and time the specified file or directory was last accessed. |
| GetLastWriteTime() | File.lastModified() | Returns the date and time the specified file or directory was last written to. |
| Move() | File.renameTo() | Moves a specified file to a new location, providing the option to specify a new filename. |

**Continued**

**Table 11.3** Continued

| C# | Java Equivalent | Description |
|---|---|---|
| Open() | Not Available | Opens a *FileStream* on the specified path. |
| OpenRead() | File.setReadOnly() | Opens an existing file for reading. |
| OpenText() | Not Available | Opens an existing UTF-8 encoded text file for reading. |
| OpenWrite() | Not Available | Opens an existing file for writing. |
| SetAttributes() | Not Available | Sets the specified *FileAttributes* of the file on the specified path. |
| SetCreationTime() | Not Available | Sets the date and time the file was created. |
| SetLastAccessTime() | Not Available | Sets the date and time the specified file was last accessed. |
| SetLastWriteTime() | File.setLastModified() | Sets the date and time that the specified file was last written to. |

*FileInfo* is almost identical to the Java class *File*, except *FileInfo* cannot represent a directory. A complete list of methods and properties can be found in Table 11.4.

**Table 11.4** *FileInfo* Methods and Properties

| C# | Java Equivalent | Description |
|---|---|---|
| AppendText() | Not Available | Creates a *StreamWriter* that appends text to the file represented by this instance of the *FileInfo*. |
| CopyTo() | Not Available | Copies an existing file to a new file. |
| Create() | File.createNewFile() | Creates a file. |
| CreateText() | Not Available | Creates a *StreamWriter* that writes a new text file. |
| Delete() | File.delete() | Permanently deletes a file. |
| MoveTo() | File.renameTo() | Moves a specified file to a new location, providing the option to specify a new filename. |
| Open() | Not Available | Opens a file with various read/write and sharing privileges. |
| OpenRead() | File.setReadOnly() | Creates a read-only *FileStream*. |

**Continued**

**Table 11.4** Continued

| C# | Java Equivalent | Description |
|---|---|---|
| OpenText() | Not Available | Creates a *StreamReader* with UTF8 encoding that reads from an existing text file. |
| OpenWrite() | Not Available | Creates a write-only *FileStream*. |
| Refresh() | Not Available | Refreshes the state of the object. |
| Attributes | Not Available | Gets or sets the *FileAttributes* of the current *FileSystemInfo*. |
| CreationTime | Not Available | Gets or sets the creation time of the current *FileSystemInfo* object. |
| Directory | Not Available | Gets an instance of the parent directory. |
| DirectoryName | Not Available | Gets a string representing the directory's full path. |
| Exists | File.exists() | Gets a value indicating whether a file exists. |
| Extension | Not Available | Gets the string representing the extension part of the file. |
| FullName | Not Available | Gets the full path of the directory or file. |
| LastAccessTime | Not Available | Gets or sets the time the current file or directory was last accessed. |
| LastWriteTime | File.lastModified() | Gets or sets the time when the current file or directory was last written to. |

An instance of *FileInfo* can be obtained from *DirectoryInfo* using a method called *GetFiles()*, which returns an array of *FileInfo* objects. This can be useful when searching through directories, as the following example demonstrates.

```
using System;
using System.IO;
namespace IOTest
{
    public class FileSearch
    {
        public static void Main()
        {
            String searchName = "win";
```

```
        DirectoryInfo myDir = new
            DirectoryInfo( @"c:\Program Files");
        SearchDirectories(myDir, searchName);

    }


    public static void SearchDirectories(
        DirectoryInfo dir, String target)
    {

        FileInfo[] files = dir.GetFiles();
        foreach(FileInfo file in files)
        {
            // Check if name is in any files
            if(file.Name.IndexOf(target) > -1)
            {
                Console.WriteLine(file.Name);
            }
        }


        DirectoryInfo [] dirs = dir.GetDirectories();
        foreach(DirectoryInfo subDir in dirs)
        {
            SearchDirectories(subDir, target);
        }
    }
  }
}
```

This program starts by creating a *DirectoryInfo* object pointing to the "Program Files" directory. It calls the *SearchDirectories()* method, which retrieves an array of *FileInfo* objects, representing all files in the directory. It then goes through the array checking if the filename matches the search string *win*. This is done using the *String* method *IndexOf()*, which will return −1 if no substring is found; otherwise it returns the index number representing the start of the sub-string. Any matching substrings cause the program to output the filename to the console. In other words, this program will output any file that has *win* in its file-name. The *SearchDirectories* then performs the same search on the other subdirec-tories using recursion.

# Streams

Most Java programmers are familiar with the concept of *streams*. Briefly, streams allow a programmer to layer different stream classes to provide functionality. For example, imagine a program that will be used to send double values across a network, while buffering the data. In Java the first step is to obtain an *OutputStream* from a *Socket* object, using the *getOutputStream()* method. The next step is to create a *BufferedOutputStream* object with the original *OutputStream* object in the constructor. Finally, a *DataOutputStream* object is created with the *BufferedOutputStream* object in the constructor. In this example we've added three layers of functionality to the stream of data.

C# uses the streams concept as well, with some changes. Probably the most surprising change in the way C# handles streams is combining *Input* and *Output* streams into one class. For example, C# combines *BufferedInputStream* and *BufferedOutputStream* into a single *BufferedStream* class. Let's explore the available stream classes in C# and their functionality. Table 11.5 shows the C# stream classes and their Java equivalents (all of these classes will be covered later in this chapter).

**Table 11.5** The *System*.IO Namespace and Corresponding Java Classes

| C# | Java | Description |
|---|---|---|
| Stream | InputStream OutputStream | Provides a generic view of a sequence of bytes. |
| BinaryReader | DataInputStream | Reads primitive data types as binary values in a specific encoding. |
| BinaryWriter | DataOuptutStream | Writes primitive types in binary to a stream and supports writing strings in a specific encoding. |
| BufferedStream | BufferedInputStream BufferedOutputStream | Reads and writes to another stream. This class cannot be inherited. |
| FileStream | FileInputStream FileOutputStream | Exposes a stream around a file, supporting both synchronous and asynchronous read and write operations. |
| MemoryStream | Not Available | Creates a stream whose backing store is memory. |
| NetworkStream | (hidden; returned by java.net.Socket) | Creates a network stream using TCP/IP. |

**Continued**

**Table 11.5** Continued

| C# | Java | Description |
| --- | --- | --- |
| StreamReader | InputStreamReader | Implements a *TextReader* that reads characters from a byte stream in a particular encoding. |
| StreamWriter | PrintWriter, OutputStreamWriter | Implements a *TextWriter* for writing characters to a stream in a particular encoding. |
| StringReader | StringReader | Implements a *TextReader* that reads from a string. |
| StringWriter | StringWriter | Writes information to a string. The information is stored in an underlying *StringBuilder*. |
| TextReader | Reader | Represents a reader that can read a sequential series of characters. |
| TextWriter | Writer | Represents a writer that can write a sequential series of characters. This class is abstract. |

# Stream

*Stream* is an abstract class from which all other stream classes are derived. Most methods in this class are very similar to those found in Java streams: *WriteByte(), ReadByte(), Flush(),* and *Close().*

Additionally, there are four methods used for asynchronous data transfer: *BeginRead(), BeginWrite(), EndRead(),* and *EndWrite().* In Java, data is handled in a *synchronous* fashion, where method calls to the various read and write methods cause the program to halt while it finishes IO (unless you specifically call the IO method from a separate thread). *Asynchronous* IO allows the program to start reading data (from a file, network, or other source) and then continue with other tasks. Once the data operation is completed, a callback method will notify the program it has finished, and the program can then process the data. Asynchronous data transfer will be discussed in depth later in this chapter.

Table 11.6 shows the methods of the *Stream* class. These methods are present in *FileStream, MemoryStream, BufferedStream,* and *NetworkStream* (mentioned later), since *Stream* is the base class for all other streams. For this reason there is no need to go over the API for all four of these classes.

**Table 11.6** Stream Methods and Properties

| C# | Java | Description |
|---|---|---|
| BeginRead() | Not Available | Begins an asynchronous read operation. |
| BeginWrite() | Not Available | Begins an asynchronous write operation. |
| Close() | InputStream.close() and OutputStream.close() | Closes the current stream and releases any resources (such as sockets and file handles) associated with the current stream. |
| EndRead() | Not Available | Waits for the pending asynchronous read to complete. |
| EndWrite() | Not Available | Ends an asynchronous write operation. |
| Flush() | OutputStream.flush() | When overridden in a derived class, clears all buffers for this stream and causes any buffered data to be written to the underlying device. |
| Read() | InputStream.read(byte [] b) | When overridden in a derived class, reads a sequence of bytes from the current stream and advances the position within the stream by the number of bytes read. |
| ReadByte() | InputStream.read() | Reads a byte from the stream and advances the position within the stream by one byte, or returns −1 if at the end of the stream. |
| Seek() | InputStream.skip() | When overridden in a derived class, sets the position within the current stream. |
| SetLength() | Not Available | When overridden in a derived class, sets the length of the current stream. |
| Write() | OutputStream.write(byte [] b) | When overridden in a derived class, writes a sequence of bytes to the current stream and advances the current position within this stream by the number of bytes written. |

**Continued**

**Table 11.6** Continued

| C# | Java | Description |
| --- | --- | --- |
| WriteByte() | OutputStream.write(byte b) | Writes a byte to the current position in the stream and advances the position within the stream by one byte. |
| CanRead | Not Available | When overridden in a derived class, gets a value indicating whether the current stream supports reading. |
| CanWrite | Not Available | When overridden in a derived class, gets a value indicating whether the current stream supports writing. |
| CanSeek | InputStream.markSupported() | When overridden in a derived class, gets a value indicating whether the current stream supports seeking. |
| Length | InputStream.available() | When overridden in a derived class, gets the length in bytes of the stream. |
| Position | InputStream.mark() | When overridden in a derived class, gets or sets the position within the current stream. |

# FileStream

There are several ways to obtain a *FileStream*. The first way to obtain an instance is to use one of the nine overloaded constructors of *FileStream*. A *FileMode* enumeration is used to specify how to obtain the *FileStream* (*Append, Create, CreateNew, Open, OpenOrCreate,* or *Truncate*). The following example creates a new file on disk or overwrites an existing file if it has the same name.

```
FileStream ioStream = new FileStream(@"c:\data\test.dat",
    FileMode.Create);
```

An instance of *FileStream* can also be obtained from the *File* class. The following example opens an existing file for write access only:

```
FileStream outputStream = File.OpenWrite(@"c:\test.dat");
```

Finally, *FileStream* can be obtained from a *FileInfo* instance:

```
FileInfo file = new FileInfo(@"c:\data\test.dat");
FileStream outStream = file.OpenRead();
```

# MemoryStream

*MemoryStream* is a new addition to the streams family, and is probably unfamiliar to Java programmers. A *MemoryStream* is simply a stream with a backing store that originates in memory, in the form of an array of bytes. There are seven constructors for *MemoryStream*, but essentially two different kinds, depending on the parameters used in the constructor. The first type of *MemoryStream* accepts an array of bytes in the constructor.

```
byte [] b = {1,2,3,4,5,6};
MemoryStream memOut = new MemoryStream(b);
```

A *MemoryStream* with an array of bytes in the constructor is not resizable. Byte values within the stream may be changed (as long as it is not specifically created as read only), but the size of the internal array will remain constant. The other kind of *MemoryStream* is resizable.

```
MemoryStream memOut = new MemoryStream();
```

This kind of *MemoryStream* does not use a byte array in the constructor. Some of the constructors also allow an *int* parameter that determines the initial array size. Data is stored in the *MemoryStream* using the *Write()* method, as shown in this example.

```
using System;
using System.IO;

namespace IOTest
{
    public class MemTest
    {
        public static void Main()
        {
            MemoryStream memOut = new MemoryStream();

            byte [] bs = {1,2,3,4,5,6};
            memOut.Write(bs,0,bs.Length);
```

```
        memOut.Seek(+3, SeekOrigin.Begin);
        byte b = (byte)memOut.ReadByte();
        Console.WriteLine("Value: " + b);
    }
  }
}
```

## *Output*

4

This program creates an empty *MemoryStream* and writes an array of bytes to it in regular stream fashion. It then uses the *Seek()* method to move the pointer to the beginning (+3) and reads in a value. The capacity of this *MemoryStream* will grow automatically as it is written to by increments of 256. You can also manually change the capacity using the *SetLength()* method.

So what are *MemoryStream* objects used for? Generally for buffering purposes, where it is better to have the image in memory than residing on the network or on disk. The following example shows how to obtain a stream of a binary file (for example, an image) and store it in memory so it can be analyzed.

Image analysis programs typically process large amounts of data. Bitmap color images are made up of thousands of byte values. Each byte represents the intensity of one of three colors: red, green, or blue. A value of 0 represents no color, whereas a value of 255 has an intense color. So for a single pixel in a bitmap image, the value 255,127, 0 has intense blue, medium green and no red in it. Using these assumptions, let's create a program to analyze the overall intensity of each color in a picture.

The following example will read in all the bytes from a jpeg image and converts the data into a basic bitmap image (raw bytes). It then sums all the various bytes in the image in threes and stores them to an array—for example, all blue values belong to array 0, green to array 1, and red to array 2. From the stats, you can then tell what the mood of the picture is by looking at the occurrence of the different colors.

**N**OTE

For this example you can use any jpeg images you want. Windows XP users have four sample pictures located in the shared folder C:\Documents and Settings\[username] \Documents\My Pictures\Sample Pictures\. These pictures all have only one dominant color, which will allow us to easily verify the results. The images are Blue Hills.jpg (very blue), Winter.jpg (blue), Sunset.jpg (red), and Water lilies.jpg (green).

```csharp
using System;

using System.IO;

using System.Drawing;

using System.Drawing.Imaging;


namespace ImageAnalyzer
{
    public class Analyzer
    {
        public byte [] currentImage;

        public Analyzer(String file)
        {
            Image sample = new Bitmap(file);
            MemoryStream buf = new MemoryStream();
            sample.Save(buf, ImageFormat.Bmp);
            currentImage = buf.GetBuffer();
        }

        public int [] GetStats()
        {
            int [] stats = new int[3];
            for(int i=0;i<currentImage.Length;)
                for(int j=0;j<3;j++){
                    stats[j] += currentImage[i];
                    ++i;
                }
```

```
        return stats;
    }


    public static void Main()
    {
        String f = @"C:\Documents and Settings\All Users\
            Documents\My Pictures\Sample Pictures\
            Blue Hills.jpg";
        Analyzer a = new Analyzer(f);
        int [] stats = a.GetStats();
        Console.WriteLine("Blue: " + stats[0]);
        Console.WriteLine("Green: " + stats[1]);
        Console.WriteLine("Red: " + stats[2]);
        if((stats[0] > stats[1]) && (stats[0] > stats[2]))
            Console.WriteLine("This is a cold picture.");
        if((stats[1] > stats[0]) && (stats[1] > stats[2]))
            Console.WriteLine("This is a summer picture.");
        if((stats[2] > stats[0]) && (stats[2] > stats[1]))
            Console.WriteLine("This is a fiery picture.");
    }
}
}
```

In the preceding code, the *Analyzer* constructor creates a new *Image* object from the jpeg image on disk. The next line creates an empty *MemoryStream* object, then sends the entire Image into the stream in bitmap format, using the *Image.Save()* method. The entire byte array is then retrieved from the *MemoryStream* object and sent to the *GetStats()* method. This method contains an array of three values. The method loops through the entire image byte array, and each byte it encounters increments the appropriate value in the stats array. In this manner it counts each byte in the image array. The output of the program follows. From the output we can see that the most intense color in this image is blue.

## Output

```
Blue: 100706587
Green: 63844498
```

```
Red: 28778940
This is a cold picture.
```

# BufferedStream

The previous section showed how to manually buffer an individual binary file. Most Java programmers are aware of *BufferedInputStream* and *BufferedOutputStream* from Java. C# contains this functional layer in one class, *BufferedStream*. The use of *BufferedStream* should be very familiar to Java programmers since it is so similar. Buffering is added to a stream by accepting a *Stream* object in the *BufferedStream* constructor. The new *BufferedStream* object will provide buffering automatically, on the fly. Let's examine this in code.

```
FileStream fs = new
    FileStream(@"c:\test.txt", FileMode.Open);
BufferedStream bs = new BufferedStream(fs);
```

> **WARNING**
>
> Remember to call *Flush()* after all write operations, otherwise the stream could have unsent bytes that will not arrive at the destination.

# Encoding Data Types

All data is sent as byte values (0 to 255). This is useful as a building block for other data types, but other classes are required if we want to send larger types such as integers, floating point numbers, or even *Strings*. In order to send these data types the class must be able to encode byte values into the respective data types using some sort of algorithm. And of course, at the other end of the stream a class must be able to decode these bytes and convert them back into the respective data types.

Java programmers are used to the *DataInputStream* and *DataOutputStream* classes to perform this task. C# provides an equivalent pair of classes, but they are not *Stream* classes (they do not inherit *Stream*). Instead, C# uses *BinaryWriter* and *BinaryReader* to perform data encoding and decoding. Both of these classes accept a *Stream* parameter in their constructors, however.

So why not follow the pattern set by Java and use *DataStream* instead? Probably because this class is meant to be the last class added to a chain of streams. *BufferedStream* works fine sandwiched in the middle of a stream, because none of the methods in *BufferedStream* need to be accessed directly by a programmer. With *BinaryReader* and *BinaryWriter*, however, the methods must be accessible to the programmer (methods such as *ReadInt()*, for example). In other words, it does no good to sandwich *BinaryReader* in the middle layer of many streams since that would hide the useful encoding/decoding methods from being accessed. Let's take a look at a problem that can occur in Java.

## Java

```
FileInputStream file = new FileInputStream("c:\\data.dat");
DataInputStream dIn = new DataInputStream(file);
BufferedInputStream bIn = new BufferedInputStream(dIn);
```

This example shows a continuous chain of streams consisting of a *FileInputStream*, a *DataInputStream*, and a *BufferedInputStream*. But once we have created the last object, the *DataInputStream* is no longer useful for anything. *BufferedInputStream* will use only the *read()* methods of *DataInputStream*, but the other methods for reading data types will be hidden from the final *BufferedInputStream* instance.

By using a different class type (*BinaryReader* and *BinaryWriter*), C# ensures this cannot happen. It is a one-way street, where streams can be added to the *BinaryReader/Writer*, but the *Writer* cannot be added to another stream. The following code demonstrates this.

## C#

```
FileStream file = new
                FileStream("c:\\data.dat",FileMode.Open);
BufferedStream bIn = new BufferedStream(file);
BinaryReader dIn = new BinaryReader(bIn);
```

It would be impossible to sandwich *BinaryReader* in the middle layer of these streams. In this respect, the C# API has just a little more enforcement than the Java API.

Table 11.7 shows the methods in *BinaryReader* and the corresponding methods in Java. Notice the method names for integers and floating point numbers seem quite general. For example, C# uses *ReadInt16()* rather than *ReadShort()*. This is because these classes are shared by Visual Basic and C++, and those languages don't use the same names for their primitive types; hence the generalization of method names.

**Table 11.7** *BinaryReader* Methods vs. *DataInputStream* Methods

| C# | Java | Description |
| --- | --- | --- |
| PeekChar() | Not Available | Returns the next available character and does not advance the byte or character position. |
| Read() | Not Available | Reads characters from the underlying stream and advances the current position of the stream. |
| ReadBoolean() | ReadBoolean() | Reads a Boolean from the current stream and advances the current position of the stream by one byte. |
| ReadByte() | readByte() | Reads the next byte from the current stream and advances the current position of the stream by one byte. |
| ReadBytes() | read() | Reads a specific number of bytes from the current stream into a byte array and advances the current position by count bytes. |
| ReadChar() | readChar() | Reads the next character from the current stream and advances the current position of the stream in accordance with the encoding used and the specific character being read from the stream. |
| ReadChars() | Not Available | Reads a specific number of characters from the current stream, returns the data in a character array, and advances the current position in accordance with the encoding used and the specific character being read from the stream. |
| ReadDecimal() | Not Available | Reads a decimal value from the current stream and advances the current position of the stream by 16 bytes. |
| ReadDouble() | readDouble() | Reads an 8-byte floating point value from the current stream and advances the current position of the stream by eight bytes. |

**Continued**

**Table 11.7** Continued

| C# | Java | Description |
|---|---|---|
| ReadInt16() | readShort() | Reads a 2-byte signed integer from the current stream and advances the current position of the stream by two bytes. |
| ReadInt32() | readInt() | Reads a 4-byte signed integer from the current stream and advances the current position of the stream by four bytes. |
| ReadInt64() | readLong() | Reads an 8-byte signed integer from the current stream and advances the current position of the stream by four bytes. |
| ReadSByte() | readByte() | Reads a signed byte from this stream and advances the current position of the stream by one byte. |
| ReadSingle() | readFloat() | Reads a 4-byte floating point value from the current stream and advances the current position of the stream by four bytes. |
| ReadString() | readUTF() | Reads a string from the current stream. The string is prefixed with the length, encoded as an integer 7 bits at a time. |
| ReadUInt16() | readUnsignedShort() | Reads a 2-byte unsigned integer from the current stream using little endian encoding and advances the position of the stream by two bytes. |
| ReadUInt32() | Not Available | Reads a 4-byte unsigned integer from the current stream and advances the position of the stream by four bytes. |
| ReadUInt64() | Not Available | Reads an 8-byte unsigned integer from the current stream and advances the position of the stream by eight bytes. |

*BinaryWriter* is a little different from *BinaryReader*. All of the methods in *BinaryReader* read a specific type, but *BinaryWriter* has one overloaded method to handle all of this: *Write()*. So depending on the type of parameter used in the *Write()* method, C# will choose the proper encoding for that data type. There are 18 overloaded *Write()* methods that can encode all primitive types (see Table 11.8), including *byte*, *short*, *int*, *long*, *double*, *bool*, *char*, *float*, *double*, *string*, and the unsigned integer types.

**Table 11.8** *BinaryWriter* Methods

| C# | Description |
| --- | --- |
| Write(bool) | Writes a one-byte Boolean value to the current stream, with zero representing false and one representing true. |
| Write(byte) | Writes an unsigned byte to the current stream and advances the stream position by one byte. |
| Write(byte[]) | Writes a byte array to the underlying stream. |
| Write(char) | Writes a Unicode character to the current stream and advances the current position of the stream in accordance with the encoding used and the specific characters being written to the stream. |
| Write(char[]) | Writes a character array to the current stream and advances the current position of the stream in accordance with the encoding used and the specific characters being written to the stream. |
| Write(decimal) | Writes a decimal value to the current stream and advances the stream position by eight bytes. |
| Write(double) | Writes an 8-byte floating point value to the current stream and advances the stream position by eight bytes. |
| Write(short) | Writes a 2-byte signed integer to the current stream and advances the stream position by two bytes. |
| Write(int) | Writes a 4-byte signed integer to the current stream and advances the stream position by four bytes. |
| Write(long) | Writes an 8-byte signed integer to the current stream and advances the stream position by eight bytes. |
| Write(sbyte) | Writes a signed byte to the current stream and advances the stream position by one byte. This method is not CLS-compliant. |
| Write(float) | Writes a 4-byte floating-point value to the current stream and advances the stream position by four bytes. |
| Write(string) | Writes a length-prefixed string to this stream in the current encoding of the *BinaryWriter*, and advances the current position of the stream in accordance with the encoding used and the specific characters being written to the stream. |

**Continued**

**Table 11.8** Continued

| C# | Description |
|---|---|
| Write(ushort) | Writes a 2-byte unsigned integer to the current stream and advances the stream position by two bytes. This method is not CLS-compliant. |
| Write(uint) | Writes a 4-byte unsigned integer to the current stream and advances the stream position by two bytes. This method is not CLS-compliant. |
| Write(ulong) | Writes an 8-byte unsigned integer to the current stream and advances the stream position by two bytes. This method is not CLS-compliant. |
| Write(byte[],int,int) | Writes a region of a byte array to the current stream. |
| Write(char[],int,int) | Writes a section of a character array to the current stream, and advances the current position of the stream in accordance with the encoding used and perhaps the specific characters being written to the stream. |

# Text

Most languages contain support for reading and writing text. C# happens to contain text classes that are very similar to Java's. Java contains two abstract classes called *Reader* and *Writer* that are used specifically for character streams. From the *Reader* class we get a whole slew of subclasses: *BufferedReader, CharArrayReader, FilterReader, InputStreamReader, PipedReader, StringReader,* and *FileReader.* Likewise, *Writer* also produces many subclasses: *BufferedWriter, CharArrayWriter, FilterWriter, OutputStreamWriter, PipedWriter, PrintWriter, StringWriter,* and *FileWriter.*

In C#, the base classes used for handling text are *TextReader* and *TextWriter,* both abstract classes. C# offers a much more simplified collection of *TextReaders* and *TextWriters. TextReader* has only two subclasses:

- *StreamReader*
- *StringReader*

*TextWriter,* on the other hand, has five subclasses:

- *StreamWriter*
- *StringWriter*
- *System.Web.HttpWriter*

- *System. Web. UI. HtmlTextWriter*
- *System. CodeDom. Compiler. IndentedTextWriter*

**NOTE**

*BinaryReader* and *BinaryWriter* do not inherit from *TextReader* or *TextWriter*.

# *StreamReader* and *StreamWriter*

The Java strategy for *Readers* and *Writers* is to have a lot of different classes that specialize. C# uses fewer classes that allow specialized behavior to be chosen through the constructors. *StreamReader* has 10 constructors that determine the source (file or stream), buffer size, character encoding, and whether it allows mark detection. Let's try obtaining a *StreamReader* using one of these constructors:

```
StreamReader txtFile = new StreamReader(@"c:\data\readme");
```

It is also possible to obtain a *StreamReader* from other objects, such as a *FileInfo* object:

```
FileInfo readme = new FileInfo(@"c:\data\readme");
StreamReader txtFile = readme.OpenText();
```

*TextReaders* have the ability to read one line at a time using the *ReadLine()* method. The following code opens a file and outputs the text to the console.

```
using System;
using System.IO;

namespace IO
{
    public class LicenseViewer
    {
        public static void Main()
        {
            FileInfo license = new
                FileInfo(@"c:\jdk1.3.1_02\LICENSE");
```

```
        StreamReader txtIn = license.OpenText();
        String line;
        do
        {
            line = txtIn.ReadLine();
            Console.WriteLine(line);
        } while(line != null);
    }
  }
}
```

This class is quite simple. It creates a *FileInfo* object referencing the JDK license. It then calls the *OpenText()* method to retrieve a *StreamReader* object. Once it has this it is simple to read in text line by line.

The *Read()* method is overloaded with two methods. If we used *Read()* it would read in a single character at a time. It is also possible to read in sections of the data at a time by using *Read()* with parameters including a *char* array and an index value.

## *StringReader* and *StringWriter*

*StringWriter* and *StringReader* both inherit from *TextWriter* and *TextReader*, respectively; therefore they function the same way as other *Readers* and *Writers*. The crucial difference is that rather than using a *Stream* as the source it uses a *String*. A constructor for a typical *StringReader* is as follows:

```
MyString = "a1b2c3d4e5";
StringReader sr = new StringReader(myString);
```

*StringReader's* and *StringWriter's* each have their own uses. These classes are useful because strings are perhaps the most popular currency for handling text in C#. So it makes sense to be able to write directly to a string from a stream source. Let's look at an example.

```
using System;
using System.IO;
using System.Xml;
namespace IO
{
    public class BookListing
    {
```

```
public static void Main()
{
    XmlDocument doc = new XmlDocument();
    String entry = "<book genre='biography'" +
        " ISBN='0553256742'><title>Yeager</title>" +
        "</book>";
    doc.LoadXml(entry); // to XmlDocument

    StringWriter writer = new StringWriter();
    doc.Save(writer); // to StringWriter
    String strXML = writer.ToString(); // to String
    Console.WriteLine(strXML);
}
}
}
```

## Output

```
<?xml version="1.0" encoding="utf-16"?>
<book genre="biography" ISBN="0553256742">
  <title>Yeager</title>
</book>
```

This example demonstrates how smoothly C# can convert data between various data types. This code creates an XML document, then saves the data to a *StringWriter*, then uses *ToString()* to convert to a string and output the data to the console. The *StringReader* and *StringWriter* allow conversions to be that much simpler, since streams, writers, and strings are the most popular objects for exchanging text data.

# Network I/O

Network IO is one of the strong points of Java. The *java.net* package provides intuitive classes for obtaining a socket connection to another computer. C# essentially uses the same model, but there are some differences in the way they choose to implement the methods for retrieving a stream. Let's dive right in and see how this is done.

# Server Side

In Java, a server is created using a *ServerSocket* object, which defines a port number. The *ServerSocket* accepts connection and returns a *Socket* with which the program can communicate with the client.

## *Java*

```
ServerSocket server = new ServerSocket(55555);
Socket client = Server.accept();
OutputStream out = client.getOutputStream();
```

In C# the equivalent to *ServerSocket* is *TcpListener*, found in the *System.Net .Sockets* namespace. This class accepts a connection using the *AcceptSocket()* method, which returns a *Socket* object. The names might be different but the functionality is about the same, except for one minor difference. The *TcpListener* does not start listening for connections until *Start()* is called.

## *C#*

```
TcpListener server = new TcpListener(55555);
server.Start();
Socket client = server.AcceptSocket();
```

The *AcceptSocket()* method waits for connection, just like Java. The program essentially halts at this point until the method call returns with a *Socket* object.

Now things start to diverge slightly from what Java programmers are used to. In Java, once a *Socket* has been obtained we can simply call *getInputStream()* or *getOutputStream()*. This contrasts with C#, which requires the program to create a new instance of *NetworkStream*. The *NetworkStream* class accepts a *Socket* in the constructor. Since *NetworkStream* inherits from *Stream*, it can be used in any classes using *Stream*, such as *BinaryWriter*.

```
NetworkStream netStream = new NetworkStream(client);
BinaryWriter dataOut = new BinaryWriter(netStream);
```

Let's create a complete *Server* to demonstrate these concepts. This server will send the time using *BinaryWriter* to any client that connects to it. And any good server should be able to handle multiple connections, so this server will spawn a new thread to handle each client.

```
using System.Net.Sockets;
using System.IO;
```

```
using System;
using System.Threading;

namespace IO
{
public class TimeServer
{
  public static void Main()
  {
    TcpListener server = new TcpListener(55555);
    server.Start();
    Console.WriteLine("Waiting for connections...");
    while(true)
    {
      Socket client = server.AcceptSocket();
      Console.WriteLine("New connection detected on "
                          + client.Handle);
      ClientHandler ch = new ClientHandler(client);
    }
  }

  class ClientHandler
  {
    private Socket client;

    public ClientHandler(Socket client)
    {
      this.client = client;
      Thread clientThread = new Thread(new
              ThreadStart(ClientSession));
      clientThread.Start();
    }

    public void ClientSession()
    {
      NetworkStream netStream = new
              NetworkStream(client);
```

```
         BinaryWriter timeOut = new
                   BinaryWriter(netStream);
      String time = DateTime.Now.ToString();
      timeOut.Write(time);
      timeOut.Close();
      netStream.Close();
      client.Close();
    }
  }
}
}
```

The main loop for this program occurs in the *Main()* method. This method creates a *TcpListener* with a port number of 55555. It then waits for a client to connect. Upon connection it spawns a new thread to handle all client interactions—in this case, sending the current time. As you can see there's really not that much to handling network connections using C#.

## Developing & Deploying…

### Avoiding Conflicting Ports

Each network application you create needs a unique port number with which to communicate. Since users may run more than one networked application on their computer it is important that no two applications use the same port. The Internet Assigned Numbers Authority (IANA) assigns port numbers to programs. Port numbers 0 through 49151 are registered to programs as connection ports. Ports 49152 through 65535 are assigned dynamically by the server, therefore they may not be registered. Once a computer connects to a server through the connect port, the connection is shuffled over to a dynamic port so the connection port is not tied up. To see an up-to-date listing of all registered port numbers, visit the IANA at www.iana.org/assignments/port-numbers.

# Client Side

There are a few differences with creating network clients as well. In Java we simply use the *Socket* class to create a client socket.

## *Java*

```
Socket client = new Socket("127.0.0.1",55555);
```

C# has a few ways of obtaining a socket connection with another client. The most familiar way for Java programmers is to create a *Socket* object (see the sidebar, "Using a Socket"), but in C# the equivalent class in terms of functionality is *TCPClient*.

C# can also create a socket by using objects that are tailor-made for a specific transport protocol. Currently the *System.Net.Sockets* namespace includes two such classes: *TcpClient* and *UdpClient*. The *TcpClient* constructor requires the IP address and port number to connect to, much like *Socket* in Java:

```
TcpClient client = new TcpClient("127.0.0.1",55555);
```

When the *TcpClient* is initialized it connects automatically to the server described in the parameters. *TcpClient* (and *UdpClient*) are like convenience classes, making it easier to create a socket using a TCP connection. *TcpClient* contains the *GetStream()* method for retrieving a stream. Let's examine this code in a complete client program.

```
using System.Net.Sockets;
using System.IO;
using System;


namespace IOClient
{
    public class TimeClient
    {
        TcpClient client;

        public TimeClient()
        {
            client = new TcpClient("127.0.0.1",55555);
        }
```

```
public static void Main()
{
    TimeClient tc = new TimeClient();
    String time = tc.RetrieveTime();
    Console.Write("The time is: ");
    Console.WriteLine(time);
}

public String RetrieveTime()
{
    NetworkStream netStream = client.GetStream();
    BinaryReader timeIn = new BinaryReader(netStream);
    return timeIn.ReadString();
}
}
}
```

This program will connect to the server we made previously. If you are using Visual Studio you will need to open two instances of the IDE. Start the *TimeServer* program first, and then switch over to the second Visual Studio instance and run *TimeClient*. The output window will display the current time, retrieved from the server program.

The constructor for this program creates an instance of *TcpClient*, connecting to the local IP address and port 55555. It then calls the *RetrieveTime()* method. This method obtains a network stream by using *GetStream()*, then reads in a single string representing the time. As you can see, it is much more convenient to use a *TcpClient* object as opposed to a *Socket* object (see the sidebar, "Using a Socket"). However, if you need to use a different transport protocol, C# gives you the flexibility with the *Socket* class.

## Developing & Deploying…

### Using a Socket

The C# *Socket* class is much more complicated to use than the Java *Socket* class. The reason for the complexity is because C# allows a lot more flexibility in deciding the type of connection to establish. Let's try this out in a quick example to demonstrate these complexities.

The first step is to obtain a resolved IP address, in the form of an *IPAddress* object. This can be obtained from the *Dns* class using the *Resolve()* method, which returns an *IPHostEntry* object, from which an *IPAddress* may be obtained. Simple, isn't it? There's more. Once an *IPAddress* is obtained, an *IPEndpoint* must be obtained, which specifies a port number to connect to. In code it takes up only three lines, but there's more to come.

```
// Use Dns to get the first IPAddress in the list.
IPHostEntry host = Dns.Resolve("localhost");
IPAddress serverIP = host.AddressList[0];
IPEndPoint serverEP = new IPEndPoint(serverIP, 80);
```

OK, we've got an *IPEndPoint*, but so far there is no Socket object, so now what do we do? The next step is to create a *Socket* object. There are three enumerations used to define the socket: *AddressFamily*, *SocketType*, and *ProtocolType*. *AddressFamily* specifies the addressing scheme that this instance of *Socket* will use. For example, it could use AppleTalk, Banyan, IPX, or UNIX, among many. We're going to use an IP address (four bytes separated by decimals), which is indicated by the *InterNetwork* enumerator. *SocketType* determines the type of socket to create. In our case, we're going to use *Stream*. For the final parameter, we will select the TCP protocol.

```
//Create TCP Socket
Socket server = new Socket(
    AddressFamily.InterNetwork, SocketType.Stream,
    ProtocolType.Tcp );
server.Connect(serverEP);
NetworkStream inout = new NetworkStream(server);
```

*Continued*

It should be noted in the preceding example that *SocketType* and *ProtocolType* are directly related within an *AddressFamily*. For example, when the *SocketType* is *Dgram* the *ProtocolType* must always be UDP. When the *SocketType* is *Stream* the *ProtocolType* must always be TCP.

Once the socket has connected to the server it's possible to create a new *NetworkStream* using the *Socket* object in the constructor. As you can see from this example, it's not the most intuitive process in the world for most programmers, which is why Java programmers might feel more at home with the *TcpClient* class. However, it does provide you with great flexibility when you need to create different types of network connection.

# Synchronous vs. Asynchronous

The examples presented so far have used *synchronous* data access, meaning when a method is called to read or write, the method does not return until the process is done. The *Stream* class in C# also allows *asynchronous* access, meaning read and write methods will immediately return, accessing the data in the background. All streams allow asynchronous data transfer. There are two methods to use for asynchronous data access (see Table 11-6), *BeginRead()* and *BeginWrite()*.

Let's look at *BeginRead()* first. This method accepts five parameters:

```
public override IAsyncResult BeginRead(
    byte[] array,
    int offset,
    int numBytes,
    AsyncCallback userCallback,
    object stateObject
)
```

In this method definition the byte array acts as the buffer to read the data into. The second and third parameters, *offset* and *numBytes*, determine the byte at which to start reading, and the maximum number of bytes to read.

The fourth parameter is an *AsyncCallback* object, which is a delegate (see Chapter 8). This object references an event handler to notify the program when the operation is finished. You may optionally choose not to use a delegate by passing *null* as the parameter, in which case the program will not be notified when the read has completed. In this case you must program the class to manually check if the file read has completed.

The final parameter can be any object, such as the caller itself, which is used to distinguish this asynchronous request from other requests. This parameter, and the delegate object, are optional. The user may ignore these parameters by passing *null* values instead. Let's look at an example of asynchronous data transfer. We'll modify our previous *LicenseViewer* example to read the text asynchronously.

```csharp
using System;
using System.IO;
using System.Text;

namespace IO
{
    public class LicenseViewer
    {
        FileStream license;
        private AsyncCallback doneDelegate;
        private byte [] buff = new byte[100];
        public LicenseViewer(String file)
        {
            license = new FileStream(file, FileMode.Open);
            doneDelegate = new AsyncCallback(UpdateConsole);
        }

        /** Read in the license in blocks at a time */
        public void ReadLicense()
        {
            if (buff[0] > 0)
                {
                    license.BeginRead(buff, 0,
                    buff.Length, doneDelegate, this);
                }
        }

        public void UpdateConsole(IAsyncResult result)
        {
            // Suspend reading, then output contents:
            int totalBytes = license.EndRead(result);
            if(totalBytes > 0)
            {
```

```
                                   String s = Encoding.ASCII.GetString(buff, 0,
                                         totalBytes);
                                   Console.WriteLine(s);
                                   // Continue reading:
                          }
                          ReadLicense();
                          }


          }


     public class Test
     {
          public static void Main()
          {
                     String file = @"C:\jdk1.3.1\LICENSE";
                     LicenseViewer lv = new LicenseViewer(file);
                     //Read in licence asynchronously
                     lv.ReadLicense();
                     //Continue processing, this loop will be performed
                     //concurrently with the read.
                     long tally = 0;
                     for(int i=0;i<50000;++i)
                     {
                            tally += i;
                            Console.WriteLine(tally);
                     }
               }
        }
}
```

This program starts an asynchronous read on the JDK license. Notice in the constructor for *LicenseViewer,* that the method *UpdateConsole* is specified as the delegate. This is done by creating an *AsyncCallback* object and using the method name as a parameter. Once an *AsyncCallback* object is obtained (*doneDelegate*) it is used as a parameter in the *BeginRead()* method in the *ReadLicense()* method.

The *ReadLicense()* method initiates the read, and reads in 100 bytes at a time. Once the asynchronous read has begun it goes into a loop where it counts off numbers and outputs them to the console, providing a visible demonstration that the program has continued to execute. After each 100 byte block is read, the delegate will be notified via the callback method *UpdateConsole()* we created. This method suspends disk access to the file, outputs the contents of the *buff* variable, and then continues reading.

> **NOTE**
>
> Java has no built-in support for asynchronous file reads, but it can easily perform them by reading all data from a separate thread.

# Web Streams

The C# language wisely contains classes made specifically for interacting with the Internet. At the code level, it can be useful to retrieve information from a Web site that is used within an application. C# provides some useful classes for reading data directly from Web pages using any valid Web address.

Retrieving information from a Web server is essentially a two-step process. The first step is to send a request to the server. If all goes well, your computer will connect to a server somewhere across the Internet. Step two is receiving a response from the server, in the form of a data file. C# breaks up the request and response into two separate classes: *HttpWebRequest* and *HttpWebResponse*. The ultimate goal is to receive a stream with a Web page as the backing-store.

An *HttpWebRequest* object can be obtained from a static method contained in the *WebRequest* class (which is also the base class of HttpWebRequest). This method is called *Create()* and it accepts either a URI object (Uniform Resource Identifier) or simply a string of the Web address.

```
String page = "http://www.mts.net/~bbagnall/index.html";
HttpWebRequest site =
    (HttpWebRequest)WebRequest.Create(page);
```

Once we have an *HttpWebRequest* object we can use it to receive an *HttpWebResponse*. This is accomplished using the *HttpWebRequest.GetResponse()* method.

```
HttpWebResponse response =
    (HttpWebResponse)site.GetResponse();
```

And finally, we can achieve our ultimate goal, obtaining a stream using the *GetResponseStream()* method.

```
Stream dataStream = response.GetResponseStream();
```

The completed code for an application to retrieve the contents of a Web page is as follows:

```
using System;
using System.Net;
using System.IO;

namespace IO
{
    public class WebApp
    {
        public static void Main()
        {
            String page =
                "http://www.mts.net/~bbagnall/index.html";
            HttpWebRequest site =
                (HttpWebRequest)WebRequest.Create(page);
            HttpWebResponse response =
                (HttpWebResponse)site.GetResponse();
            Stream dataStream = response.GetResponseStream();
            StreamReader read = new StreamReader(dataStream);
            String data = read.ReadToEnd();
            Console.WriteLine(data);
        }
    }
}
```

## Output

```
<TITLE>Homepage of Brian Bagnall</TITLE>
<H1>
Welcome to my web page...
</H1>
(abbreviated)
```

The flow of this program is quite basic. It creates an *HttpWebRequest* object pointing to a Web page. It then retrieves an *HttpWebResponse* using the *GetResponse()* method. From this it harvests a *Stream* object and uses it to create a

*StreamReader* for handling text. It reads to the end of the stream using *ReadToEnd()*, which returns a *String*. It then outputs the entire *String* to the console. As you can see from the output, the HTML code for the Web page is displayed.

# Serialization

One of the best features of Java I/O is the ability to send objects through a stream, a process known as *serialization*. Java has two classes for object transfer: *ObjectOutputStream* and *ObjectInputStream*. These classes can send any object through any stream, provided the object implements the *Serializable* interface.

C# takes a different approach to serialization. Instead of creating a stream capable of sending objects, C# uses two methods in the *BinaryFormatter* class: *Serialize()* and *Deserialize()*. The *Serialize()* method requires two parameters: a stream to write to, and the object that will be sent. The *Deserialize()* method requires only a stream to read from, and it returns an object (which can be cast to the appropriate type).

## Creating a Serializable Object

Before we get into serialization and deserialization, let's try creating a serializable object. Rather than implement a *Serializable* interface as Java does, C# requires an object to be marked with the *[Serializable]* attribute. This attribute is actually defined in the *System.SerializableAttribute* class.

For our example, we will create a simple class that stores a *String* and an *int*. This class could just as easily be a *struct*—it makes no difference for serialization purposes.

```
using System;

namespace IO
{
    [Serializable]
    public class BookRecord
    {
        public String title;
        public int asin;

        public BookRecord(String title, int asin)
        {
```

```
                this.title = title;
                this.asin = asin;
        }
    }
}
```

This class represents a book record. It stores a string representing the title of a book and an integer representing an ASIN number. The most obvious difference is the use of the *[Serializable]* attribute located just above the class definition. This indicates that this object is eligible for serialization. Without this attribute, it will not be accepted by the methods in the *BinaryFormatter* class.

# Serializing an Object

Now that we have a serializable object we can try sending it through a stream. We'll create a *FileStream* to create a new file to disk.

```
using System;
using System.Runtime.Serialization.Formatters.Binary;
using System.IO;

namespace IO
{
    public class SerializeObject
    {
        public static void Main()
        {
            BookRecord book = new BookRecord(
                "Building Robots with Lego Mindstorms",
                1928994679);
            FileStream stream = new FileStream(@"book.obj",
                FileMode.Create);

            BinaryFormatter bf = new BinaryFormatter();
            bf.Serialize(stream, book);
            stream.Close();
        }
    }
}
```

This program creates a new *BookRecord* object that will act as our test subject. It then creates a new *FileStream* object pointing to the file *book.obj*. Note that any stream can be used, including a *NetworkStream*. In order to use the methods of *BinaryFormatter* we need an instance, so the code creates a new one. It then calls the method *Serialize()* and writes the given object to the stream. Once this program has finished, a new file called *book.obj*, will appear in the current project directory.

## Deserializing an Object

It is just as easy to retrieve an object through a stream. This example opens a stream with the *book.obj* file as a backing-store. The hardest part of reading an object is to remember to cast it to the appropriate type.

```
using System;
using System.Runtime.Serialization.Formatters.Binary;
using System.IO;


namespace IO
{
    public class DeserializeObject
    {
        public static void Main()
        {
            FileStream streamIn = new FileStream(
                @"book.obj", FileMode.Open);
            BinaryFormatter bf = new BinaryFormatter();
            BookRecord book =
                (BookRecord)bf.Deserialize(streamIn);
            streamIn.Close();
            Console.Write(book.title + " " + book.asin);
        }
    }
}
```

*Output*

```
Building Robots with Lego Mindstorms 1928994679
```

As you can see from the output, all the data within the class was successfully stored and retrieved. The *Main()* method starts by creating a *FileStream* to the *book.obj* file. It then creates a *BinaryFormatter* and calls the *Deserialize()* method to read in the object. The object is cast into a *BookRecord* and then the two public fields are output to the console.

# Transient Data

Transient data is data that you do not want to travel with the object when it is serialized. In Java it is easy to mark data as transient—just declare the variable with the *transient* keyword.

## *Java*

```
transient int total_sales;
```

The only difference with the C# language is that it uses the *[NonSerialized]* attribute instead.

## *C#*

```
[NonSerialized] int total_sales;
```

Now when an object is sent through the stream, the *total_sales* variable will not be sent. On the other end of the stream, when the object is *Deserialized* it will equal 0. This leads us to the next topic.

# Deserialization Operations

Sometimes it is necessary to perform some data processing just after an object is deserialized. For example, a transient field might need to be recalculated upon deserialization. The data for a field in an object might be large but repetitive; hence memory can be saved by recalculating the data once it is deserialized rather than transferring it through the stream. Or the data may come from another source, such as the Internet, and should be updated when the object is deserialized.

C# has the *IDeserializationCallback* interface with one method for performing this kind of operations. The method *OnDeserialization()* must be implemented when this interface is used. This method is called automatically by the CLR once the object has been deserialized.

The following example is the *BookRecord* class, only it has been modified to include a field of the sales rank. This field is transient so it will not be sent through a stream. When the object is reassembled on the other side it will have the default value (a value of 0), therefore it is up to the *OnDeserialization()* method to update the field with the appropriate data.

```csharp
using System;
using System.Runtime.Serialization;

namespace IO
{
    [Serializable]
    public class BookRecord: IDeserializationCallback
    {
        public String title;
        public int asin;
        [NonSerialized] public int sales_rank;

        public BookRecord(String title, int asin)
        {
            this.title = title;
            this.asin = asin;
            sales_rank = GetSalesRank();
        }

        public int GetSalesRank()
        {
            Random r = new Random();
            return r.Next(5000);
        }

        public void OnDeserialization(Object o)
        {
            sales_rank = GetSalesRank();
        }
    }
}
```

The major changes to the original *BookRecord* code have been highlighted. A new field has been added that keeps track of the sales rank. This field has been declared as *NonSerialized*, therefore it will not be sent through the stream when it is serialized. *BookRecord* now implements the *IDeserializationCallback* interface, and implements the *OnDeserialization()* method. When this method is called the object will retrieve the sales rank information (in this case, a random number, but it could also retrieve it over a network).

Now let's examine some code that uses this new class.

```
using System;
using System.Runtime.Serialization.Formatters.Binary;
using System.IO;

namespace IO
{
    public class StreamObject
    {
        public static void Main()
        {
            BookRecord book = new BookRecord("Building " +
                "Robots with Lego Mindstorms", 1928994679);
            Console.WriteLine(book.title + " " + book.asin);
            Console.WriteLine("Sales rank: " +
                book.sales_rank);

            //Serialize the object to disk.
            FileStream stream = new FileStream(@"book.obj",
                FileMode.Create);
            BinaryFormatter bf = new BinaryFormatter();
            bf.Serialize(stream, book);
            stream.Close();

            //Read the object from disk.
            FileStream streamIn = new FileStream(@"book.obj",
                FileMode.Open);
            BookRecord bookIn = (BookRecord)
                bf.Deserialize(streamIn);
            Console.WriteLine(bookIn.title + " " +
                bookIn.asin);
            Console.WriteLine("Sales rank: " +
```

```
                    bookIn.sales_rank);
        }
    }
}
```

## Output

```
Building Robots with Lego Mindstorms 1928994679
Sales rank: 1621
Building Robots with Lego Mindstorms 1928994679
Sales rank: 1177
```

This program serializes the object to a *FileStream*, then deserializes it and outputs the results. As you can see the sales rank has changed, indicating the CLR executed the *OnDeserialization()* method at some point after the object was deserialized.

# Summary

As we have learned in this chapter, the C# File System differs from Java in two important ways. First, C#'s main platform is Windows; therefore it contains a range of file operations targeting the Windows platform. Second, C# has two separate classes (*FileInfo* and *DirectoryInfo*) to describe files and directories (four, counting the static method classes *File* and *Directory*). This contrasts with Java, which only contains the *File* class to handle both.

C# streams do not separate the input and output streams in two separate classes as Java does. Rather, they contain methods for both reading and writing in one class. The access properties of the streams are set in the constructor for the *Streams*.

The equivalents of Java *DataInputStream* and *DataOutputStream* classes are *BinaryReader* and *BinaryWriter*. *BinaryWriter* contains essentially one method named *Write()* that is overloaded to handle most of the common data types. *BinaryReader()* contains many methods for handling the major data types in C#.

All text is handled by writers in C#. The base classes that all text streams inherit from are *TextReader* and *TextWriter*. These each have two subclasses: *StreamReader/StreamWriter* and *StringReader/StringWriter*.

C# also has built-in methods for *Asynchronous* data streaming. In Java there are only *Stream* methods that block while the transfer occurs, but C# streams have built-in methods to continue the program execution: *BeginRead()* and *BeginWrite()*. A delegate system is used to notify the program when the read/write operation has completed.

Network servers listen for connections with a *TcpListener* object using the *AcceptSocket()* method. From the client side, a *TcpClient* object is used to connect to the server. Streams can also be obtained directly from resources located on Web servers. This is accomplished using the *HttpRequest* and *HttpResponse* classes. These classes handle the protocol transactions with Web servers and allow you to retrieve data easily across the Internet.

Serialization is the process of breaking down the fields of an object so they can be sent across a stream. C# uses methods in the *BinaryFormatter* class to perform serialization and deserialization. Transient data within an object can be defined with the *[NonSerialized]* attribute. If the serialized object uses the *IDeserializationCallback* interface, upon deserialization the *OnDeserialization()* method is called automatically.

# Solutions Fast Track

## File System

- ☑ *File* contains static methods for file operations.
- ☑ *FileInfo* objects are used to handle a designated file.
- ☑ *Directory* contains static methods for directory operations.
- ☑ *DirectoryInfo* objects are used to handle a designated directory.

## Streams

- ☑ *InputStream* and *OutputStream* are amalgamated into a single *Stream* class in C#.
- ☑ *Stream* contains the methods *WriteByte()*, *ReadByte()*, *Flush()*, and *Close()*.
- ☑ There are also four methods for asynchronous data transfer: *BeginRead()*, *BeginWrite()*, *EndRead()*, and *EndWrite()*.

## Encoding Data Types

- ☑ *BinaryReader* is used to read in different data types from a stream.
- ☑ *BinaryWriter* is used to write different data types to a stream.

## Text

- ☑ Use either *StreamReader* or *StreamWriter* for streaming text.
- ☑ Use either *StringReader* or *StringWriter* for streaming from a *String* object.

## Network I/O

- ☑ Create a new *TcpListener* object, specifying a socket number.
- ☑ Call the *Start()* method on the *TcpListener* to begin listening.
- ☑ Call the *AcceptSocket()* method to wait for a client socket.

# Synchronous vs. Asynchronous

☑ Create an *AsyncCallback* object and specify the method name that will act as the delegate.

☑ Write the delegate method to handle notification when the access is complete.

☑ Call *BeginRead()* or *BeginWrite()* to begin asynchronous access. Specify the *AsyncCallback* object in the method call.

# Web Streams

☑ The *System.Net* namespace contains classes for performing transactions with Web servers.

☑ *HttpWebRequest* is used to initiate a request of a file from a Web server.

☑ An *HttpWebResponse* object is received as a response from the *HttpWebRequest* object via the *GetResponse()* method.

☑ A stream may be obtained with the *HttpWebResponse* via the *GetResponseStream()* method.

# Serialization

☑ All objects that are to be sent through streams must have the *[Serializable]* attribute.

☑ *BinaryFormatter.Serialize()* is used to send an object through a stream.

☑ *BinaryFormatter.Deserialize()* is used to retrieve an object from a stream.

☑ The *[NonSerialized]* attribute is used to mark data as transient.

# Frequently Asked Questions

The following Frequently Asked Questions, answered by the authors of this book, are designed to both measure your understanding of the concepts presented in this chapter and to assist you with real-life implementation of these concepts. To have your questions about this chapter answered by the author, browse to **www.syngress.com/solutions** and click on the **"Ask the Author"** form.

**Q:** Why does C# use only one *Stream* class as opposed to *InputStream* and *OutputStream*?

**A:** Probably because most communications are two way. Very rarely does an application only send or only receive data, so it makes it more convenient to contain the read/write operations in one class.

**Q:** Is there really any difference between using asynchronous access vs. creating a separate thread?

**A:** Yes, in C# the *BeginRead()* and *BeginWrite()* methods use a delegate system to notify the program when the IO operation completes. If you were using a thread this would not occur (unless you programmed it yourself).

**Q:** What is a *MemoryStream* store typically used for?

**A:** Often it is used as a buffer for data. Often it is more convenient to start an asynchronous read to transfer large amounts of data over the network, then deal with the data when it has been completely read.

**Q:** Why does C# provide directory and file classes with both static and instance methods?

**A:** When you are performing operations on only a single file or directory it is more convenient to use an object. When doing many functions on many files it is more convenient to use static methods.

**Q:** Once an object is serialized and sent through a stream is it possible to change fields and call methods on the remote object?

**A:** This is not possible with the methods described in this chapter. When an object is shared by more than one machine across a network, it is known as *remoting*. In order for remoting to take place, the object must go through a process of *marshaling*, which prepares the object for remoting. C# provides classes for *remoting* and marshaling in the *System.Runtime.Remoting* namespace.

# Chapter 12

## Creating User Interfaces with Windows Forms

# Introduction

In this book so far, all the example codes you have seen are console-based applications. This might have been great in the good old days of DOS, but for today's programs you might like a richer user interface. In this chapter you will broaden your C# arsenal by learning how to implement a graphical user interface (GUI) using Windows Forms.

Java provided us with the Abstract Windowing Tool (AWT), and then later, with Swing for creating platform-independent GUIs. The .NET Framework followed Java's lead by providing a more unified programming model similar to Swing. However, unlike Swing it is not platform independent. A Windows Form is a tool for building Windows applications, and is built specifically for the Windows platform.

In this chapter we will look at some of the classes found in the *System .Windows.Forms* namespace. You will learn how to create Windows applications by looking at some of the basic controls and event handling. To wrap up the chapter you will learn about rapid application development using Visual Studio.NET.

# Windows Form Classes

Direct, integrated support in Windows classes makes it very easy to create forms in the .NET environment. In Java, GUI forms are often developed using AWT/Swing. In the .NET environment, GUI forms are a part of the *Windows.Forms* class. Thus creating forms in the .NET environment is much more convenient than doing so in Java. In addition, just as What You See Is What You Get (WYSIWYG) Integrated Development Environments (IDEs) (like SUN's Forte) make it easy to develop forms in Java, Visual Studio .NET makes it easy to develop forms in the .NET environment.

The basic Windows programming model consists of three main parts: *forms*, *controls*, and *events*. Forms are windows that enclose the controls, controls are components such as buttons, and events are action notifications such as a pressed key or mouse button down. The .NET environment provides the means for integrating these three parts to enable building of GUIs.

In this chapter we will create a working financial calculator that accepts user inputs for principal and calculates the amount of interest using a particular interest rate. This example will illustrate some of the major GUI concepts and make use of some Windows components.

# Windows Form Class Hierarchy

The *System.Windows.Forms* namespace (also known as the *WinForms* namespace) provides the necessary classes for implementing forms and the various controls that can be placed onto these forms. Figure 12.1 shows some of the major classes within the Windows Form class hierarchy.

**Figure 12.1** Windows Form Class Hierarchy

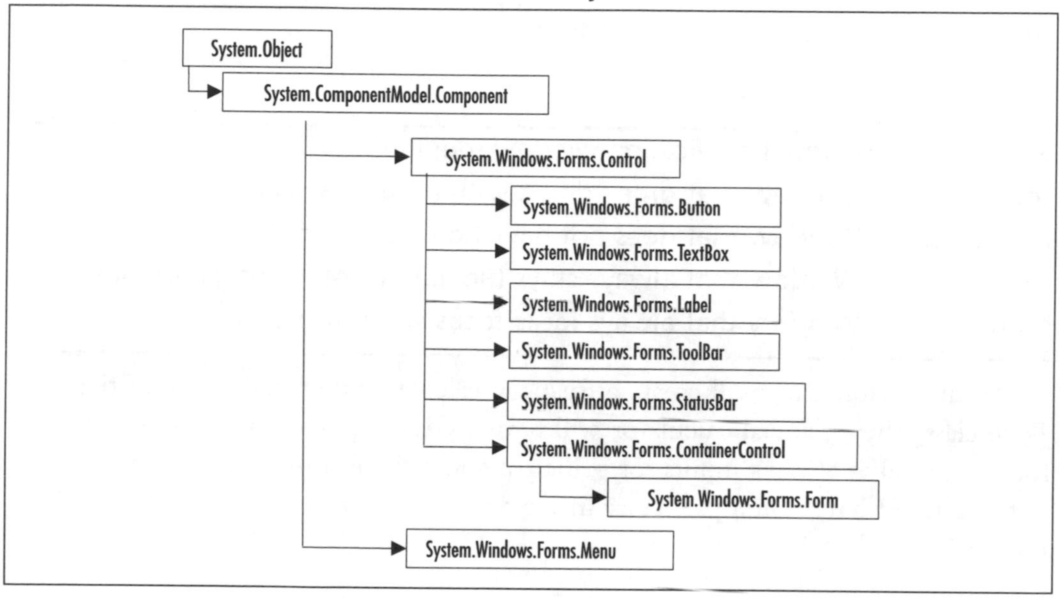

As you can see, this is very similar to Java's AWT/Swing hierarchy where similar objects are derived from *java.lang.Object*. The Form class in C# is similar to the *Applet* class in Java, *Button* class is likewise similar to *Button/JButton*, *TextBox* class is analogous to *TextField* class, and so on. The methods for adding controls to forms are also very similar between C# and Java, as we shall see in the following sections.

> **NOTE**
>
> It is interesting to note that form itself is a special type of control known as a *ContainerControl*. *ContainerControls* can contain other controls (such as *Buttons*, *TextBoxes*, and *Labels*).

# Creating a Windows Form Application

A *form* is a representation of any window in an application. To create a form, simply derive from the *Form* class (i.e., "extending" the *Form* class) within the *Windows.Forms* namespace. The *Form* class can be used to create different types of windows that can interact with the user: standard, tool, borderless, floating, or even modal dialog box (see Table 12.1).

**Table 12.1** Different Types of Windows

| Window | Function |
| --- | --- |
| Standard | Normal application window (default) |
| Tool | Window that drops down with a list of selectable tools |
| Borderless | Window that does not have borders (cannot be resized) |
| Floating | Window that always stays (floats) on top of other windows |
| Modal | Window that always locks focus when it is active |

In this chapter, we will create a financial calculator that makes use of the *Form* class. This financial calculator will have a GUI application window (i.e., a form) that takes a user's inputs for principal and returns an output for the computed interest based on a particular interest rate. The form window will look like Figure 12.2.

**Figure 12.2** Financial Calculator

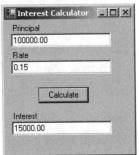

To create a form, three basic steps are involved. First, using the *System.Windows.Forms* namespace, we will derive the form from the *Form* class. Our declaration will look like this:

```
public class InterestCalculator : Form
```

Second, we need to set several of the *Form's* properties. The *Forms* class has several properties that you can set to determine how it is going to look. Some of these properties include:

- **Text** Title text of the form.

- **Size** Size of the form.

- **DesktopLocation** Initial location of the form.

- **ForeColor** Foreground color of the form.

For our calculator we will set only two properties: the *Form.Text* and the *Form.Size*. The declaration looks like this:

```
this.Text = "Interest Calculator"; // Sets title
this.Size = new Size(200,225); // Sets size
```

The only major difference between Java and C# is that C# uses properties, whereas Java uses accessor methods such as *setText()* and *setSize()*.

Finally, to display the form you must provide a *Main()* method to get the ball rolling. Within this we have to call the *Run()* method from the *Application* class and supply it an object instance of form as an argument. The declaration looks like the following:

```
Application.Run(new InterestCalculator());
```

The *Application* class found in the *System.Windows.Forms* namespace provides static methods to manage an application (such as methods to start or stop an application, and to process Windows messages) and properties to get information about an application. This class is sealed and therefore it cannot be inherited.

The following listing illustrates how these three steps are performed for our Financial Calculator example:

```
using System;
using System.Drawing;
using System.Windows.Forms;

public class InterestCalculator : Form
{
  public InterestCalculator()
  {
    this.Text = "Interest Calculator"; // Sets title
    this.Size = new Size(200,225); // Sets size
```

```
    }

    public static void Main(string[] args)
    {
      Application.Run(new InterestCalculator());
    }
}
```

The form class has several member functions that enable the programmer to manipulate the form. Some of the more useful methods of a form are listed in Table 12.2.

**Table 12.2** Form Member Methods

| Method | Function |
|---|---|
| FindForm() | Retrieves the form that the control is on |
| Focus() | Sets input focus to the control |
| Invalidate() | Invalidates the control and causes a paint message to be sent |
| PointToClient() | Computes the location of the specified screen point into client coordinates |
| PointToScreen() | Computes the location of the specified client point into screen coordinates |
| ShowDialog() | Shows the form as a modal dialog box |
| Dispose() | Releases the resources used |
| Close() | Closes the form (calls Dispose() automatically) |

The next steps involve instantiating controls and adding the appropriate event handlers to the controls. The following section illustrates how these two steps are done.

# Using Controls

Once a form is created, *controls* that facilitate user interactions with the form can then be added to it. These user interface controls are managed internally by Windows using special grouping and tabbing logic, thus relieving the programmer of a major burden. Windows provides interface to these controls through the *Control* class. This provides a handle known as the *hWnd* pointer that is established upon the creation of a control and which can obtained by the *Handle()* method.

The *Control* class also implements the functionalities needed for these controls to handle user inputs from devices such as the keyboard and the mouse.

Our Financial Calculator makes use of three common controls: *Buttons*, *TextBoxes*, and *Labels*. *Buttons* allow user interaction through mouse clicking actions. *TextBoxes* can provide information to users and let them input information through the keyboard. *Labels* often are used to display information to the users. In the following sections we will demonstrate how these controls can be added to the form we created in the previous section. Understanding of how these three basic controls are used will provide the basic foundation needed to use any other controls and components provided by the *System.Windows.Forms* namespace. You will also  want to be familiar with the controls *RadioButton*, *CheckBox*, *ListBox*, and *Edit*. Other control-like components like *menus* and *dialogs* exist and can provide you with more sophisticated user interactions.

# Adding Controls

A form (a control itself—a container control as previously mentioned) essentially consists of a collection of controls. This collection of controls is represented by the *Control.Collection* object, which in turn becomes a child of the form. When controls are added to the form, they become members of the form's *Control.Collection* object. Windows then assigns this collection object to the form's *Controls* property through which this collection can be manipulated and managed.

A *Control.Collection* object's members can be managed using the collection object's methods. For example, to add a button control member to a hypothetical collection named *Group*, the *Add()* method can be used as follows:

```
Group.Add(buttonControl);
```

Likewise, the *Contains()* method can be used to determine whether a collection contains a particular control and the *Remove()* method can then be used to remove the intended control from the collection:

```
if (Group.Contains(buttonControl))
{
   Group.Remove(buttonControl);
}
```

Or the *Clear()* method can be used to clear an entire collection:

```
Group.Clear();
```

In the context of the form, the collection group is mapped to the form's *Controls* property as mentioned previously. Thus to add a control to a form, call the form collection object's (i.e., the form's *Controls* property) *Add()* method:

```
Form.Controls.Add(buttonControl);
```

Note the similarity and difference between how controls are added here and how controls are added in Java's AWT/Swing. For example, in Java we would add a button control to an applet by doing the following:

```
Applet.Add(buttonControl);
```

In .NET we are adding to the control's collection group as opposed to adding directly to the control itself as we would in Java.

The following sections illustrate how each type of control can be initialized and added to our financial calculator's form.

# Basic Controls

Three of the most basic controls are buttons, textboxes, and labels. With these three controls, most applications can be built.

To create and use a control, perform the following three steps:

1.  Create and instantiate the control by calling its constructor.
2.  Set its properties as needed (to characterize how it should be displayed, etc.).
3.  Call the form collection's *Add()* method to add the control.

The following section illustrates how these three controls can be utilized to build our financial calculator. Examples will be provided on how these three steps are taken.

# Buttons

Buttons are useful for collecting user inputs through mouse clicks. To add a button, simply instantiate the button and initialize its properties before calling the form collection object's *Add()* method. The following creates a button, sets its location and text properties, and add the control to our Financial Calculator form:

```
Button buttonCalculate = new Button();
buttonCalculate.Location = new Point(50,100);
buttonCalculate.Text = "Calculate";
```

```
this.Controls.Add(buttonCalculate);
```

As you can see, adding controls in C# is fairly similar to how you would do it in Swing. The only major differences are the properties that you would have to set in C# as opposed to calling different accessor methods in Java. Some of the most frequently used properties of button include:

- **Text**  Text of the control.

- **Size**  Size of the control.

- **Width/Height**  Width and height of the control.

- **Left/Right/Top/Bottom**  Distance of the control's edges with respect to the edges of the form window.

- **Location**  Initial location of the control.

- **TabIndex**  Tab order of the control.

In our example, we set the text label and the location of the button. Notice that in order to set the control's location we need to create a *Point* object, which takes in two integers that set the horizontal and vertical positions, respectively, of the control within the form. If desired, the *size, width, height,* edge distances (*left/right/top/bottom*), and the *TabIndex* (which determines the order in which Windows scrolls through each one of the buttons as well as other controls when the user presses the **Tab** key) properties can also be set.

## Developing & Deploying…

### Where Exactly Is the Origin in Device Coordinates?

The origin (0, 0) of the forms window, in device coordinates (i.e., pixels), is located at the top-left corner of the screen. The x-coordinate increases as one moves to the right, and the y-coordinate increases as one moves down. It is important to know the different coordinate systems in Windows.

# Textboxes

Textboxes are useful for collecting user inputs as well as displaying outputs to users. Creation of textboxes is very similar to that of buttons: instantiate, initialize properties, and then add. The following code creates a textbox, sets its location and text properties, and then adds the control to our Financial Calculator form:

```
TextBox textBoxPrincipal = new TextBox();


textBoxPrincipal.Location = new Point(10,20);

textBoxPrincipal.Size = new Size(150,10);

textBoxPrincipal.Text = "100000.00";


this.Controls.Add(textBoxPrincipal);
```

*TextBox* in C# is analogous to *TextField* in Java. Like buttons, we can set the textbox's various properties to control how it should be displayed and managed. Some of the most frequently used properties of textboxes include:

- **Text** Text of the control.
- **Size** Size of the control.
- **Location** Initial location of the control.
- **TabIndex** Tab order of the control.
- **ReadOnly (bool)** Whether the text field is read-only.

Note the similarity of these properties to those of buttons (Text, Size, Location, and TabIndex). In our example we set the text label and location of our textbox. If desired, we can also set the TabIndex (similar to that of button's property). Furthermore, in an application where we do not want the user to alter what is displayed in the textbox, we can set the Boolean *ReadOnly* property to *true*.

# Labels

Labels are useful for displaying information. Adding a label follows the same procedure as that of buttons and textboxes: instantiate, initialize properties, and then add. The following code creates three labels, sets their location and text properties, and adds the controls to our Financial Calculator form:

```
Label labelPrincipal = new Label();


labelPrincipal.Location = new Point(10,5);
```

```
labelPrincipal.Size = new Size(144,15);
labelPrincipal.Text = "Principal";


this.Controls.Add(labelPrincipal);
```

Again, labels in C# are just like labels in Java. We can set the label's properties to control how it should be displayed. Some of the most frequently used properties of labels include:

- **Text**  Text of the control.
- **TextAlign**  Alignment of the text (default is TopLeft).
- **Font**  Font of the text.
- **Size**  Size of the control.
- **Location**  Initial location of the control.
- **TabIndex**  Tab order of the control.

Note once more that these properties are similar to those for buttons and textboxes. In our example we set the text label, location, and size of the label. If desired, the text alignment, the font, and the TabIndex (similar to that of button's and textbox's properties) can also be set.

Now that we have built our controls for our Financial Calculator, we will need to enable them to interact with the users. To do so, we will have to create event handlers and associate them with our controls. Let us now proceed to how event handlers work and how we can make use of them to enable interaction between the user and our application. The following sections describe how this is done.

# Handling Events

To process user inputs, the program must trap user events (such as keyboard and mouse) and handle them accordingly. To handle an event, an event handler must be defined and attached to the corresponding control.

As you may recall from Chapter 8, user events are handled by using delegates and the very common publisher-subscriber model. You can think of the button as the publisher and the main form as the subscriber. So what we need is for the button to define a delegate of type *System.EventHandler*.

The delegated method you define must return *void* and take two parameters: an object (sender) type and a *System.EventArgs* type.

```
void delegateMethod(Object sender, System.EventArgs e) {}
```

For example, to handle the mouse click event on the *Calculate* button, first create an event handler function to take the user inputs (principal and rate), convert them to double, perform the calculation, and finally convert back to string for display:

```
private void buttonCalculate_Click
    (object sender, System.EventArgs e)
{
    double prin = Convert.ToDouble(textBoxPrincipal.Text);
    double rate = Convert.ToDouble(textBoxRate.Text);

    double amt  = prin * rate;
    string ans = amt.ToString("f2");
    textBoxInterest.Text = ans;
}
```

Our *buttonCalculate_Click* event handler takes two parameters and returns *void*, which matches the delegate signature. The sender parameter is a reference to the control that fired the event (the *Calculate* button in this case), and *System.EventArgs* are event objects that will be captured and managed by Windows internally.

Now that our event handler has been created, it needs to be associated with the *Calculate* button to handle the mouse click event (i.e., when the user clicks on this button, the event handler is executed). You do this by creating a *System.EventHandler* delegate, passing in the name of our method *buttonCalculate_Click()*. Then you add it to the button's click event handler list with the += operator. For example:

```
buttonCalculate.Click += new
System.EventHandler(this.buttonCalculate_Click);
```

This will attach the event handling method *buttonCalculate_Click()* to *buttonCalculate*'s click event. Any time this button is clicked, *buttonCalculate_Click()* will be called.

Here is a list of common *Button* events that can take a handler:

- **Button.Click** Mouse click of button.
- **Button.MouseEnter** Mouse entering button area region.
- **Button.MouseLeave** Mouse leaving button area region.

Since a control can generate multiple events, more than one event handler can be attached to a single control. For example, if a second handler function *buttonCalculate_Over()* exists to display a help message when a user's mouse hovers over the button (i.e., a mouseover event), it can be attached with:

```
buttonCalculate.MouseEnter += new System.EventHandler(buttonCalculate_Over);
```

Moreover, more than one event handler can be associated with the *same* event. A program might want to calculate something and at the same time save to file. If the calculate and save to file functions have already been defined and are in separate functions, they can be reused and attached quickly to the control. For example, suppose we have a second handler called *buttonCalculate_Click2()* that performs a save to file. We can add this handler:

```
buttonCalculate.Click += new
System.EventHandler(this.buttonCalculate_Click2);
```

Now both *buttonCalculate_Click()* and *buttonCalculate_Click2()* will get executed upon the mouse click event (i.e., the calculation and saving to file will both happen).

Last but not least, an event handler can be removed from the control in the following manner:

```
buttonCalculate.Click -= new
System.EventHandler(this.buttonCalculate_Click);
```

This is often done when we want to redefine the handler for a particular control: we can just remove the old one and add the new one.

# Using a Text Editor

When creating applications with GUIs, you would want to use an IDE such as Visual Studio.NET, which provides a rich set of drag-and-drop tools. However, now that you know the concepts of how to create a GUI from scratch, you can easily use any text editor to code it by hand. The only downside to this is that the work would probably take longer and be a little more painful because getting the locations of components just right is basically trial and error. But to prove a point, let's look at our Financial Calculator example and first code it using a non-IDE editor (such as Antechinus's C# Editor, or UNIX-originated editors (graphical versions) like EMACS or VI(M). We do not recommend using DOS Edit, NotePad, WordPad, or even Word due to impracticalities with their limited editing capabilities).

Create a file called FinancialCalculator.cs and type in the code. Here is the full source listing:

```csharp
using System;
using System.Drawing;
using System.Windows.Forms;

public class InterestCalculator : Form
{

  Button buttonCalculate;

  TextBox textBoxPrincipal;
  TextBox textBoxRate;
  TextBox textBoxInterest;

  Label labelPrincipal;
  Label labelRate;
  Label labelInterest;

//Constructor
  public InterestCalculator()
  {
    //Set the Form properties.
    this.Text = "Interest Calculator";
    this.Size = new Size(200,225);

    buttonCalculate = new Button();
    buttonCalculate.Location = new Point(50,100);
    buttonCalculate.Text = "Calculate";

    //Add the event handler for the button.
    buttonCalculate.Click += new System.EventHandler
    (this.buttonCalculate_Click);

    //Add the button to the form.
    this.Controls.Add(buttonCalculate);
```

```
//Create the Principal TextBox.
textBoxPrincipal = new TextBox();
textBoxPrincipal.Location = new Point(10,20);
textBoxPrincipal.Size = new Size(150,10);
textBoxPrincipal.Text = "100000.00";
this.Controls.Add(textBoxPrincipal);

//Create the BoxRate TextBox.
textBoxRate = new TextBox();
textBoxRate.Location = new Point(10,60);
textBoxRate.Size = new Size(150,10);
textBoxRate.Text = "0.15";
this.Controls.Add(textBoxRate);

//Create the BoxInterest TextBox.
textBoxInterest = new TextBox();
textBoxInterest.Location = new Point(10,150);
textBoxInterest.Size = new Size(150,10);
textBoxInterest.Text = "15000.00";
this.Controls.Add(textBoxInterest);

//Create the Principal Label.
labelPrincipal = new Label();
labelPrincipal.Location = new Point(10,5);
labelPrincipal.Size = new Size(144,15);
labelPrincipal.Text = "Principal";
this.Controls.Add(labelPrincipal);

//Create the Rate Label.
labelRate = new Label();
labelRate.Location = new Point(10,45);
labelRate.Size = new Size(144,15);
labelRate.Text = "Rate";
this.Controls.Add(labelRate);

//Create the Interest Label.
labelInterest = new Label();
```

```
        labelInterest.Location = new Point(10,135);
        labelInterest.Size = new Size(144,15);
        labelInterest.Text = "Interest";
        this.Controls.Add(labelInterest);
    }


    //This is the event handler for the Calculate button.
    private void buttonCalculate_Click (object sender,
                                        System.EventArgs e)
    {
        double prin =
            Convert.ToDouble (textBoxPrincipal.Text);

        double rate =
            Convert.ToDouble(textBoxRate.Text);

        double amt  = prin * rate;
        string ans = amt.ToString("f2");
        textBoxInterest.Text = ans;
    }


    public static void Main(string[] args)
    {
        Application.Run(new InterestCalculator());
    }
}
```

Note that we added two more textboxes and two more labels: one each for the interest rate and interest amount. Go ahead and compile the code with (*csc FinancialCalculator.cs*) to generate the executable for running.

In the next section, we will use the Visual Studio.NET IDE to create the same Financial Calculator.

# Using Visual Studio.NET

Visual Studio.NET provides a user-friendly, interactive means for creating forms through an effortless drag-and-drop process. Creating forms through Visual Studio.NET is an example of rapid application development (RAD), whereby a significant amount of development time can be reduced. To see how easy it is to create forms in the Visual Studio.NET IDE, we will build the same Financial Calculator using this approach. Let's begin by starting up Visual Studio.NET and performing the following steps:

1. Open **File | New Project | Choose C# Project | Choose Windows Application**. A blank form will automatically pop up. You can resize this form by clicking and dragging any one of the resize handles around the edges of the form. What you have should be the same as what is displayed in Figure 12.3.

**Figure 12.3** Building Windows Forms Via Visual Studio.NET

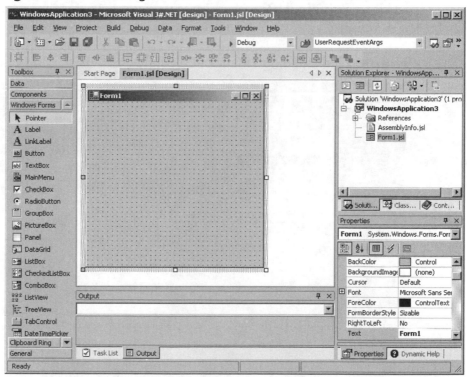

2. Right-click on the form, and then click on the **Properties** in the submenu. Several of the form's properties can be set here. Go ahead and change the text of the form to **Interest Calculator**.

3. Open **View | Toolbox** or left-click on the Toolbox on the left navigation bar to bring up a toolbox menu of controls that can be added to the form. Controls can be dragged and dropped onto the form: try dragging over the following controls for our Financial Calculator:

- One button

- Three textboxes

- Three labels (one for each textbox)

These controls can be moved and resized. Right-click on each one of the controls to enter the Properties form to edit the properties for each of the controls. Set the text of the button to **Calculate**. You may name the button **buttonCalculate** if you want. Name the three textboxes (by setting the *name* property) **textBoxPrincipal**, **textBoxRate**, **textBoxInterest**, and name their respective labels **labelPrincipal**, **labelRate**, **labelInterest**. Also change the texts of the labels to **Principal**, **Rate**, and **Interest**. Figure 12.4 shows where you are currently:

**Figure 12.4** Building Financial Calculator Via Visual Studio .NET

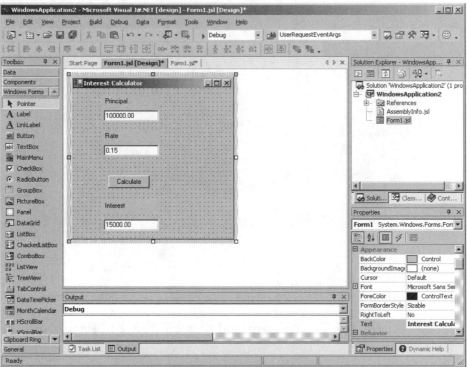

4. Now you are ready to enter the code for our **Calculate** button's event handler. Enter the code section by either double-clicking on the **Calculate** button or right-clicking on the button to select **View Code**

from the submenu. Notice that the IDE already wrote the majority of the code for you: the event handlers have already been attached to the buttons. All there is left to do is to manually type the following five lines into the handler (between the curly bracelets {...}):

```
double prin = Convert.ToDouble(textBoxPrincipal.Text);
double rate = Convert.ToDouble(textBoxRate.Text);
double amt  = prin * rate;
string ans = amt.ToString("f2");
textBoxInterest.Text = ans;
```

5. You are all done—press the **F5** function key to compile and run the application.

As you can see, building Windows applications using Visual Studio.NET's IDE is quick and easy. Being able to quickly put together already-made building blocks and extending them as needed to build an application is one of the strengths of the Visual Studio development environment.

# Creating a File Browser

Let's build one more application: a file browser that can be used to open a text file for reading. In this application we will demonstrate the use of menus and dialogs. Let's begin by starting up Visual Studio.NET and performing the following steps:

1. **Open File | New Project | Choose C# Project | Choose Windows Application**.

2. Rename the form by setting its text property to something meaningful, like **FileBrowser**.

3. Open the Toolbox as before. Drag over two items:

   ■ **RichTextBox**  Resize the box to fill the form and set its text property to blank.

   ■ **MainMenu**  A *Type Here* blank menu will appear. Enter **File** followed by **Open** for the menu items. What you should see is displayed in Figure 12.5.

4. Notice each menu item has several properties. For example, you can add a shortcut to the **Open** menu item by selecting the shortcut property and its key mapping. Select **Ctrl+O** for the shortcut if you want.

**Figure 12.5** Building File Browser Via Visual Studio .NET

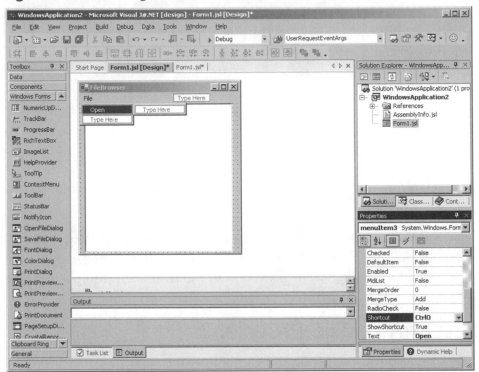

5.  Double-click on the **Open** menu item to go to code. Enter the following code to open a file dialog and read in the file, and to set the Form title when the **Open** menu item is selected:

```
OpenFileDialog dlgOpen = new OpenFileDialog();

if(dlgOpen.ShowDialog() == DialogResult.OK)
{
    richTextBox1.LoadFile(dlgOpen.FileName,
        RichTextBoxStreamType.PlainText);
    this.Text=dlgOpen.FileName;
}
```

6.  Compile and run by pressing **F5**.

Try to open and browse a text file. You can open the FinancialCalculator.cs file we created previously. What you will see is shown in Figure 12.6.

**Figure 12.6** File Browser

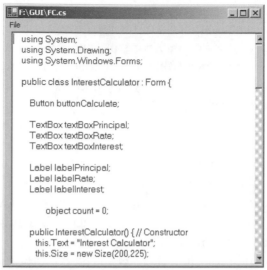

### ShowDialog()

The ShowDialog() method makes a form *modal* (i.e., it freezes all other windows when it is active) and also sets the form's *modal* property. It is usually used in an *if* statement to check whether the user clicks on the button that returns an *OK* result (i.e., *OK*, *Accept*, *Open*, etc.):

```
if (form.ShowDialog() == DialogResult.OK)
{
    ...
}
```

Notice that with the use of a tool such as Visual Studio.NET, creating a graphical user interface for your application is much simpler. The IDE saves you time by eliminating the grunt work of typing in all of the necessary code for adding in your components. This leaves you more time to concentrate on figuring out the actual logic for your application. But if you're the type of programmer that prefers to hand-code everything, you now know the building blocks needed to create a great looking GUI.

# Summary

Forms, controls, and event handlers are essential for creating graphical user interfaces (GUIs). Similar to their counterparts in Java's AWT/Swing, the available classes in the .NET environment offer a rich collection of resources for utilizing forms and controls as well as building event handlers to develop powerful user interfaces and applications.

In this chapter, we created a financial calculator by first building a form, then adding the controls and event handlers for some of those controls. Some of the controls we utilized in our application include buttons (for accepting user inputs from the mouse), textboxes (for accepting user inputs from the keyboard as well as displaying outputs to the user), and labels (for displaying outputs to the user). We also fine-tuned the appearances of our calculator by setting the various properties associated with our forms and controls. To make our controls work, we built event handlers and associated them with the corresponding events produced by user interactions with our various controls. We learned that events can have multiple event handlers associated with each of them.

Lastly, we learned how to employ Visual Studio.NET's rapid application development capability to quickly develop Windows form-based applications. We learned how easy it is to create controls via drag-and-drop and perform on-the-fly modifications to event handlers for our controls' events.

# Solutions Fast Track

## Windows Form Classes

- ☑ A form is the application window that contains the various controls.
- ☑ Controls are components (such as buttons, textboxes, and labels) that can be added to the form.
- ☑ Events are actions monitored by the event handlers. Events include user interactions such as keyboard and mouse actions.

## Creating a Windows Form Application

- ☑ A form is created by extending from the *Form* class.
- ☑ A form has several properties that can be set.

☑ Your opening form is invoked via *Application.Run()* within *Main()*.

## Using Controls

☑ Buttons can be used to take mouse inputs from users.

☑ Textboxes can be used to take keyboard inputs from users or to display text outputs to them.

☑ Labels can be used to display outputs to users.

## Handling Events

☑ User interactions with controls produce events.

☑ Events are captured by Windows and their associated event handlers are executed.

☑ Events can have more than one handler.

## Using a Text Editor

☑ Forms can be coded manually using a text editor.

☑ Coding forms manually takes quite a bit of trial and error as well as time and effort.

☑ Completed codes can be compiled via *csc* at the command line.

## Using Visual Studio.NET

☑ Visual Studio.NET IDE makes it possible to build forms via drag-and-drop.

☑ The Toolbox contains a list of controls that can be dragged into the form.

☑ Manual codes can be added to IDE generated codes.

# Frequently Asked Questions

The following Frequently Asked Questions, answered by the authors of this book, are designed to both measure your understanding of the concepts presented in this chapter and to assist you with real-life implementation of these concepts. To have your questions about this chapter answered by the author, browse to **www.syngress.com/solutions** and click on the **"Ask the Author"** form.

**Q:** Can I define my own controls?

**A:** Yes, to develop your own controls inherit directly from the System.Windows.Forms.UserControl class (which is derived from System.Windows.Forms.Control) and modify/extend the inherited class methods as needed.

**Q:** Which classes do menus use? What about right-click menus?

**A:** Menus use the *Menu* component classes *MainMenu*, *ContextMenu*, and *MenuItem*. *MainMenu* is the menu across the top of the form and *ContextMenu* is the menu displayed upon the right-click of a mouse within the form. *MenuItems* are items in *MainMenu* and *ContextMenu*.

**Q:** How can I add tool icons near the top of a form? How can I display statistics about a certain form (such as page number, and line and word counts) at the bottom of a form?

**A:** Consider using the *ToolBar* control class to add a toolbar to the form, and using the *StatusBar* control class to add a status bar.

**Q:** Where can I find sample Windows Form applications and codes?

**A:** Besides MSDN (msdn.microsoft.com), additional resources can be found on third-party sites such as www.gotdotnet.com, www.codeproject.com, www.c-sharpcorner.com, and www.fawcette.com/dotnetmag/.

# Chapter 13

# Web Development with C#

## Solutions in this chapter:

- Web Services Overview
- Creating Web Services
- Consuming Web Services
- Web Forms Overview
- Using Web Forms Controls
- Creating a Web Forms Application

☑ Summary

☑ Solutions Fast Track

☑ Frequently Asked Questions

# Introduction

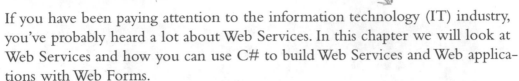

If you have been paying attention to the information technology (IT) industry, you've probably heard a lot about Web Services. In this chapter we will look at Web Services and how you can use C# to build Web Services and Web applications with Web Forms.

For the first part of the chapter we will look at .NET Web Services. A Web service is basically just an application that exposes its application programming interface (API) through the Web. That means you can invoke the application programmatically over the Web. You will learn how to create a Web service and generate proxy files that help publish your Web Service.

The second part of the chapter will look at developing Web applications using Web Forms. Web Forms are similar to Windows Forms from the last chapter, except the applications that you develop with Web Forms are deployed to a Web server, and users interact with the applications through a Web browser. In this section you will learn how to work with Web Forms and how to use the different controls available through the *System.Web* and *System.Web.UI* namespaces.

# Web Services Overview

Web Services can generally be described as a remote method call over the Internet. This means that you can build distributed applications that are made up of components that are distributed across the Web. For example, a car company might have a Web service method that allows you to input a car model and it will return a specific part number. Your application can then use that part number and combine it with another Web service method from a different company, where you can check the price for that specific part. You can see the value in such a system—instead of duplicating the same service that has already been developed, you as the developer can concentrate on adding value to the overall system by stitching together these services.

Web Services have the potential to take the Web to a whole new level. With this technology, you can see how you can have a Web browser in Melbourne act as the user interface for an application that has one component running in a Linux server in London and another from a Windows NT box in New York. It will allow the Internet to be utilized as a medium where methods are invoked and applications are executed.

To realize Web Services, a standard has been developed to facilitate exposing, acquiring, and executing methods over Hypertext Transfer Protocol (HTTP). This standard is called the Simple Object Access Protocol (SOAP).

# Using SOAP

SOAP is an XML-based protocol that uses HTTP for accessing services and objects in a platform-independent manner. The XML structure encapsulates three things: a framework definition for describing what's in the message and how to process it, a set of encoding rules expressing application specific datatypes, and a convention for representing a remote method call.

The SOAP XML structures can be described as *envelopes*. A SOAP envelope will have details about the source, destination, and the query. A typical SOAP envelope will look like this:

```
POST /Books_Web_Service/Book_Details.asmx HTTP/1.1

Host: localhost

Content-Type: text/xml; charset=utf-8

Content-Length: length

SOAPAction: "http://myCompany.com/Books_Web_Service/GetBookTitles"


<?xml version="1.0" encoding="utf-8"?>
<soap:Envelope xmlns:xsi="http://www.w3.org/2001/XMLSchema-
    instance" xmlns:xsd="http://www.w3.org/2001/XMLSchema"
   xmlns:soap="http://schemas.xmlsoap.org/soap/envelope/">
  <soap:Body>
    <GetBookTitles
       xmlns="http://myCompany.com/Books_Web_Service/">
       <Author_Last_Name>Peiris</Author_Last_Name>
    </GetBookTitles>
  </soap:Body>
</soap:Envelope>
```

As you can see, SOAP is based on XML standards. All the remote function call directions are written as XML tags inside a SOAP envelope. The first few lines describe the source, destination, and the implementation details of the SOAP envelope. After the *<soap: Body>* tag the actual query begins. In this query I am trying to access a Web Service SOAP implementation at http://myCompany.com/Books_Web_Service/GetBookTitles by using *Peiris* as an input parameter.

# Creating Web Services

Microsoft has done a great job with the Web Service creation tools in the .NET Framework. Writing Web Services using the SOAP toolkit used to be a very tedious task. Thanks to the .NET Framework the task is relatively simple now.

Most Web Services are built with a three-tier architecture, using separate layers for Presentation, Business Logic, and Database. This is a good design to follow since each layer is not dependent on each other as long as you have a well-defined interface between them. This means that you can create an application with a Presentation layer using a Web browser or a Windows form. Also this wouldn't limit you in terms of which database you would want to use. For example you can start with an MS-Access database and easily scale it up to SQL Server to satisfy the demand without doing a complete rewrite.

Since many real-world applications need to interact with a database, our example will create a Web Service that will allow you to query and interact with one. We'll use a three-tier architecture design so that we can use a Web browser or a simple Windows Forms client to display the result. The Web Service will use an MS-Access database for the database layer and it will use ADO.NET for accessing it. We'll have a simple books database, which has a single table that contains information about books and their authors. We will refer to our *Publication* database as *pubs.mdb*, and the table will be called *tbl_Book_Titles*. Figure 13.1 shows the structure of the database we're trying to access.

## Figure 13.1 Database Table Information

| Title_Id | Title | Au_Lname | Au_Fname | Price | Annual_Sales |
|---|---|---|---|---|---|
| BU1032 | The Busy Executive's Database Guide | Bennet | Abraham | $19.99 | 4095 |
| BU1111 | Cooking with Computers: Surreptitious Balance Sheets | MacFeather | Stearns | $11.95 | 3876 |
| BU2075 | You Can Combat Computer Stress! | Green | Marjorie | $2.99 | 18722 |
| BU7832 | Straight Talk About Computers | Straight | Dean | $19.99 | 4095 |
| MC2222 | Silicon Valley Gastronomic Treats | del Castillo | Innes | $19.99 | 2032 |
| MC3021 | The Gourmet Microwave | Ringer | Anne | $2.99 | 22246 |
| PC1035 | But Is It User Friendly? | Carson | Cheryl | $22.95 | 8780 |
| PC8888 | Secrets of Silicon Valley | Hunter | Sheryl | $20.00 | 4095 |
| PC9999 | Net Etiquette | Locksley | Charlene | $25.00 | 5432 |
| PS1372 | Computer Phobic AND Non-Phobic Individuals | Karsen | Livia | $21.59 | 375 |
| PS2091 | Is Anger the Enemy? | Ringer | Albert | $10.95 | 2045 |
| PS2106 | Life Without Fear | Ringer | Albert | $7.00 | 111 |
| PS3333 | Prolonged Data Deprivation: Four Case Studies | White | Johnson | $19.99 | 4072 |
| PS7777 | Emotional Security: A New Algorithm | Locksley | Charlene | $7.99 | 3336 |
| TC3218 | Onions, Leeks, and Garlic: Cooking Secrets. | Panteley | Sylvia | $20.95 | 375 |
| TC4203 | Fifty Years in Buckingham Palace Kitchens | Blotchet-Halls | Reginald | $11.95 | 15096 |
| TC7777 | Sushi, Anyone? | Gringlesby | Burt | $14.99 | 4095 |

Record: 14 of 17

The *pubs* database is a sample database installed with SQL Server 2000. If you have SQL Server 2000, you can export this database and use it for the example. Or you can download the database from the Syngress Web site at www.syngress.com. Otherwise, you can create the database in MS-Access.

The Web service interface will expose this table data. Our need is to obtain the following information from the table.

- Look up a book title from a given title ID.
- Get a complete list of the books.

We will build a single Web service that exposes two methods to facilitate these needs. We will build this Web service in two steps. First we will build a Web service to look up a book-title functionality. Then we will learn how to handle complex data structures and ADO.NET controls using Visual Studio.NET.

## Connecting to a Database

To start, the first thing we'll look at is how to interact with a database in .NET. The .NET Framework has a rich set of classes for managing and working with databases. These classes are collectively referred to as ADO.NET.

ADO.NET is very similar to, and evolved from, its predecessor ADO. The key difference between the two is that ADO.NET has a *disconnected* data architecture. This means that when you receive the data from the database, the result is stored on your local machine. You can then manipulate the result locally, and only connect to the database when you wish to update it or get new results. This architecture scales very well and it's perfect for using with Web Services.

The following example will show how you can connect to a database and perform a simple query. We'll connect to the *pubs.mdb* MS-Access database and retrieve the book title by supplying a method with the *Title_ID* string.

The first thing we need to do is make a connection to a database. To create a database connection you just need to specify what type of database you're going to use, and the name of the database. You have to supply this to an *OleDbAdapter* object, which is responsible for establishing the connection. This object also takes another string argument for the SQL statement to generate the data you want from the database. The two string declarations are as follows:

```
//Sets up the database connection command
string connectionString =
    "provider=Microsoft.JET.OLEDB.4.0;" +
    "data source= c:\\pubs.mdb";

//Sets up the SQL query
string commandString =
    "SELECT title FROM tbl_Book_Titles WHERE Title_ID='" +
    Title_ID + "'";

OleDbDataAdapter dataAdapter = new
        OleDbDataAdapter(commandString,connectionString);
```

The *OleDbDataAdapter* basically is acting as a bridge between the database and our application. ADO.NET has several data adapters depending on the database you wish to connect to. For example it also has an *SQLDataAdapter* for connecting to an SQL Server database.

Next we declare a *DataSet* object that will contain the result of our SQL select statement. To do this, we use the *Fill()* method in the *DataAdapter* class and supply it with the *DataSet* object and the table name on which we wish to perform the query:

```
DataSet dataSet = new DataSet();
dataAdapter.Fill(dataSet,"tbl_Book_Titles");
```

The result contained in the *dataSet* object is a subset of the entire database. It is disconnected from the actual database and any changes you make to it will not affect the original database. To get the actual result we want, we need to follow several steps. First, we have to create a *DataTable* to get the table from the data set. Then we create a *DataRow* object and extract the row we want from the table. In our example, we can assume that the result will be the first row, since the query will return only one result. Finally, we can extract the *Title* field from the row, which will give us the title of the book. This is shown in the following code snippet:

```
DataTable dataTable = dataSet.Tables[0];
DataRow dataRow = dataTable.Rows[0];
return (String) dataRow["Title"];
```

Let's now put it all together and look at the full source code. The following program has a single method called *GetBookTitleByID()* where you can pass it a string containing a title ID and it will search the database and return the full title of the book.

```csharp
using System;
using System.Data;
using System.Data.OleDb;

public class Book_Details
{
  public Book_Details()
  {
  }

  public String GetBookTitleByID(String Title_ID)
  {
    //Sets up the database connection command
    string connectionString =
      "provider=Microsoft.JET.OLEDB.4.0;" +
      "data source= c:\\pubs.mdb";

    //Sets up the SQL query
    string commandString =
      "SELECT title FROM tbl_Book_Titles WHERE Title_ID='" +
      Title_ID + "'";

    //Make the database connection
    OleDbDataAdapter dataAdapter = new
        OleDbDataAdapter(commandString,connectionString);

  //Fill the dataSet with the result of the query
   DataSet dataSet = new DataSet();
   dataAdapter.Fill(dataSet,"tbl_Book_Titles");

   //Extract the result from the dataset
   DataTable dataTable = dataSet.Tables[0];
   DataRow dataRow = dataTable.Rows[0];
   return (String) dataRow["Title"];
 }
```

```
public static void Main()
{
  Book_Details bookDetails = new Book_Details();

  //Perform the search
  string bookTitle = bookDetails.GetBookTitleByID("BU7832");
  Console.WriteLine("The Book title is: " + bookTitle);
}
}
```

If you've typed the same information shown in Figure 13.1, the program will produce the following output:

```
The book title is: Straight Talk About Computers
```

Now that we have our method for connecting and querying a database, the next section will show you how you can easily turn this into a Web Service.

# Building a Web Service

Declaring your class as a Web service and having certain methods exposed and executed over the Web is fairly easy. In .NET, a Web service is as an ASP.NET file with an .asmx file extension. These files will contain the class and methods of an XML Web service. You can easily expose your program as a Web service by adding several lines and saving it as an .asmx file. For our example, we'll turn our *Book_Details* class into an XML Web service by exposing the *GetBookTitleByID()* method as a Web method. The following code shows how to do this.

```
<%@ WebService Language="C#" Class="Book_Details" %>

using System;
using System.Data;
using System.Data.OleDb;
using System.Web.Services;

[WebService(Name="Book_Details",
            Namespace="http://myCompany.com/Books_Web_Service/")]
public class Book_Details : System.Web.Services.WebService
{
```

```
    public Book_Details()
    {
    }


    [WebMethod (Description="This method will return a Book
        Title for a given Title ID.")]
    public String GetBookTitleByID(String Title_ID)
    {
      //Sets up the database connection command
      string connectionString =
        "provider=Microsoft.JET.OLEDB.4.0;" +
        "data source= c:\\pubs.mdb";


      //Sets up the SQL query
      string commandString =
        "SELECT title FROM tbl_Book_Titles WHERE Title_ID='" +
        Title_ID + "'";


      //Make the database connection
      OleDbDataAdapter dataAdapter = new
          OleDbDataAdapter(commandString,connectionString);


      //Fill the dataSet with the result of the query
      DataSet dataSet = new DataSet();
      dataAdapter.Fill(dataSet,"tbl_Book_Titles");


      //Extract the result from the dataset
      DataTable dataTable = dataSet.Tables[0];
      DataRow dataRow = dataTable.Rows[0];
      return (String) dataRow["Title"];
    }
}
```

The first part in the .asmx file for a Web service is the following:

```
<%@ WebService Language="C#" Class="Book_Details" %>
```

The @ *WebService* directive is used to identify specific attributes of the Web service file. The *Language* parameter specifies the .NET language used to create the Web service and the *Class* parameter specifies the class name being exposed as a Web service. This class can be defined within the .asmx file itself or you can compile this class and have the assembly reside in the \bin subdirectory where you'll be serving your Web service application.

The @ *WebService* directive is the only code required in the .asmx file. If you have the class compiled and located in the \bin directory, then all you need is this line in the .asmx file. For our example we'll have our class definition contained in the .asmx file, which will then be compiled by the JIT compiler just before serving the Web Service page.

The next thing you need to do is declare the *[WebService]* attribute for your class.

```
[WebService(Name="Book_Details",
            Namespace="http://myCompany.com/Books_Web_Service/")]
public class Book_Details : System.Web.Services.WebService
```

This attribute is optional and can take several parameters.

- **Name** specifies the name of your Web service.
- **Description** specifies the description for the Web service.
- **Namespace** specifies the default namespace for the Web service.

It is important to specify the *Namespace* parameter for your Web service, which is used to uniquely identify your Web service. There will be heaps of available Web services on the Internet. There is even a possibility that someone had already built a *Books_Detail* Web service. Therefore, it is important that you define this parameter to distinguish your Web service before deployment. You can set this to any name you like as long as you're positive that it isn't being used by another Web service. A common standard is to use your company Web address as a default name for the Web service. If this parameter is not specified, the .NET Framework supplies the default name *http://tempuri.org*.

The class being defined as a Web service optionally can derive from the *System. Web. Services. WebService* class, as shown:

```
public class Book_Details : System.Web.Services.WebService
```

It is a good idea to derive from this class when creating a Web service to inherit some of the basic functionality provided by the *WebService* class. It allows for some advance features such as state management for a Web service across the lifetime of a particular session.

To expose a method as a Web Service method that can be executed over the Web, all you need to do is attach the *[WebMethod]* attribute to the method you want exposed. You don't need to declare every method in your class as a Web method; however, the Web method you're exposing must have this attribute and it must be declared as *public*. This attribute will indicate to the .NET Framework that the method should be made accessible over the Internet via standard protocols such as SOAP, HTTP GET, and HTTP POST. The declaration follows.

```
[WebMethod (Description="This method will return a Book
        Title for a given Title ID.")]
public String GetBookTitleByID(String Title_ID)
```

This attribute can take several parameters, all of which are optional. The *Description* parameter describes the functionality of the method. The method will have the same declaration as our previous example. By declaring it as a Web method you can interact with this method over the Web through SOAP, HTTP GET, and HTTP POST.

Once you've declared a *[WebMethod]* attribute for your class, you'll have the necessary elements for a Web service. The following section will describe how to build and run your Web service.

## Running and Testing Your Web Service

In order to test and run your Web service, you'll need to have Internet Information Server (IIS) with the Front Page Server extensions installed on your machine. When you install the .NET Framework, it configures IIS to be able to serve the .asmx files for your Web service.

To test the Web service, all you need to do is browse to the .asmx file using a Web browser. Keep in mind that if you have your class file in a separate assembly it must be in the \bin subdirectory. The result will be similar to Figure 13.2.

**Figure 13.2** Books Web Service View

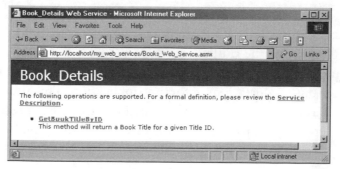

The Web page is generated automatically by the .NET Framework. This is the default implementation of a Web service file. It includes a link to all Web methods for the Web service, which is the *GetBookTitleByID()* method for this example. Below it, you can see the *Description* parameter that we specified in the *[WebMethod]* attribute. Clicking on the *GetBookTitleByID()* hyperlink will open another page where you can test your Web method as shown in Figure 13.3.

**Figure 13.3** Invoking the *GetBookTitleByID* Method

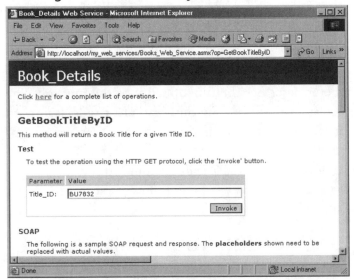

Now you can enter a Title ID as the input parameter and click the *Invoke* button. This will generate the output shown in Figure 13.4.

The Web method returns an XML *String* with the title of the book. We can use this XML output as a data source for any application. This shows the power of a Web Service as it allows you to invoke methods over the Internet, thus allowing you to create an application that is distributed over the Web.

**Figure 13.4** Books Web Service XML Output

# Creating the Books Web Service Using VS.NET

Visual Studio.NET saves you a lot of work when creating Web services. It creates the directories and all the necessary files for your Web service. To show how you can create a Web service using VS.NET, we'll add another Web method to our previous example. We will create a second Web method called *GetBookTitles()*. This method will return the complete list of books in the database by returning a *DataSet* object as opposed to a simple data structure such as a string. To create the Web service in VS.NET, follow these steps:

1. Open Visual Studio.NET and create a new Project (**File | New | Project**).

2. Select **Visual C# Projects** from the *Project Types* pane and select **ASP.NET Web Service** from the *Template* pane. Enter **Books_Web_Service** under location as shown in Figure 13.5. This will create a *Books_Web_Service* virtual directory under IIS and the files will be stored in a subdirectory under *c:\inetpub\wwwroot\*. All the necessary files for the project such as the *Book_Details.asmx* will be stored in this directory.

**Figure 13.5** Creating a C# Web Services Project

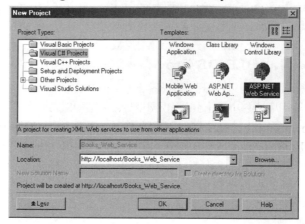

Once you've created the project, you can easily drag and drop controls to it. You can create an ADO.NET connection to the *pubs.mdb* database by using the Data Controls available from the Toolbox. We can manually write code to do this as shown earlier, but utilizing Visual Studio.NET can save a lot of time and debugging headaches. Figure 13.6 shows the Data Controls available.

**Figure 13.6** Data Controls Available in Visual Studio.NET Toolbox

To make a database connection to the *pubs.mdb* database, you'll need to use the following components:

- *OleDbConnection*
- *OleDbDataAdapter*
- *DataSet*

The *OleDbConnection* object is used to make the database connection, and the *OleDbDataAdapter* will be used to handle the SQL query to the database. The result will be stored in a *DataSet* object.

To create the database connection, drag and drop an *OleDbConnection* component on the Web service form and rename it **Pub_Connection**. Then using the properties window of the component, click on the **ConnectionString** property and select **New Connection**. From here you can select the type of database to which you want to connect. For an MS-Access database, we need to select the **Microsoft Jet 4.0 OLE DB Provider** from the **Provider** tab of the **Data Link Properties** as shown in Figure 13.7.

Then click on the **Next** button and it'll bring you to the **Connection** tab. In here you can provide the location of the database you wish to access. You can also specify login information if the database being accessed requires authorization. Then click on the **Test Connection** button to test the connection as shown in Figure 13.8.

**Figure 13.7** Selecting the Provider to the Access Database

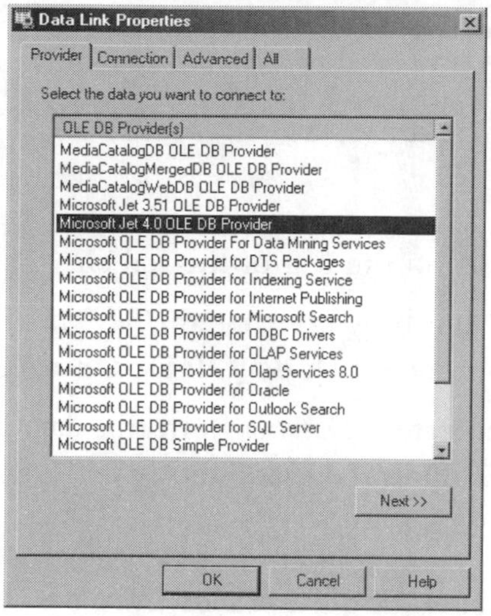

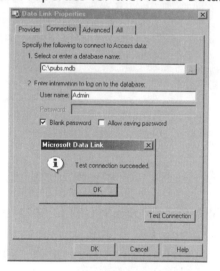

**Figure 13.8** Connection Properties for the Access Database

The next step is to create an *OleDbDataAdapter* to act as a bridge to the database. We can then send our database queries through this object. Dragging and dropping the *OleDbDataAdapter* should bring up the Data Adapter Configuration Wizard. Follow these steps to configure the wizard.

1. Select **Access.c:\Pubs.mdb.Admin** from the **Choose Your Data Connection** screen.

2. Select **Use SQL Statements** form the **Choose a Query Type** screen.

3. In the **Generate the SQL Statements** screen type the following SQL query:

```
SELECT Title_Id, Title, Au_Lname, Au_Fname,
       Price, Annual_Sales FROM tbl_Book_Titles
```

4. Select the defaults on the rest of the screen.

5. The wizard will finish by creating an *OleDbDataAdpater1* component. Rename this component **Pubs_OleDbDataAdapter**.

6. Now we can generate a *DataSet* from this data adapter. Right-click on the **Pubs_OleDbDataAdapter** and select **Generate DataSet** as shown in Figure 13.9.

**Figure 13.9** Generating a *DataSet* from an *OleDbDataAdapter* Object

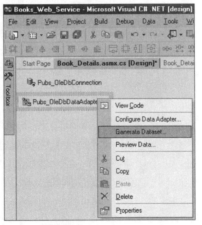

7. Name the DataSet **Pubs_DataSet**. The .NET Framework will also create an XML Schema file to illustrate the structure of the DataSet named **Pubs_DataSet.xsd**. This file is added automatically to the Web Service project.

Once we've created all the components needed to make the database connection, all that is left to do is create our Web methods. The first method we'll add is the *GetBookTitleByID()*, which is similar to the previous example. Therefore, you can just copy and paste the previous code in the Code View of the project. We'll then create another Web method called *GetBookTitles()*, which will return a *DataSet* object that has a complete list of the books in the database. We need to add the following code to our Web service.

```
[WebMethod (Description="This method will return all the books in the
database")]
public DataSet GetBookTitles()
{
    Pubs_OleDbConnection.Open();

    Pubs_OleDbDataAdapter.Fill(Pubs_DataSet,"BookTitles");

    Pubs_OleDbConnection.Close();

    return Pubs_DataSet;
}
```

In this method, the first thing it does is open a connection to the database by calling the *Open()* method of the *Pubs_OleDbConnection*. Next, it invokes the *Fill()* method of the *Pubs_OleDbDataAdapter* component. This executes the SQL query and returns the result in the *Pubs_DataSet* object. Finally, the database connection is closed and the *Pub_DataSet* is returned.

When you run the code in Visual Studio.NET it will automatically open the page for you in a Web browser as shown in Figure 13.10. When this method is invoked it will return a *DataSet* object using SOAP that can be consumed by another application.

**Figure 13.10** Updated Books Web Service

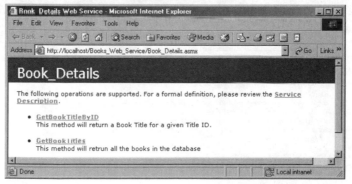

# Consuming Web Services

Before you can create a client application to consume the Web Service, you must first create a proxy object that will be used to interact with the Web Service. The proxy object acts like a middleman between the client application and the Web Service. Its main function is the marshalling of data to execute the Web Service.

You can code this proxy object manually if you like; however, the .NET Framework has a tool that can generate the source code for you. The technical implementation details for creating a proxy object are produced from the Web Service Description Language (WSDL) supplied by the Web Service. Once you have a proxy created, you can then use it in your client application and invoke the methods supplied by the Web Service.

# Web Service Description Language

We need a blueprint or a software contract specification to create our proxy object. This contract specification is referred as a Web Service Description Language file. The WSDL describes the Web Service implementation details to the proxy objects.

You can obtain the contract of a .NET Web Service by appending *?WSDL* to the URL of the Web service you're trying to access. In our previous example the URL will look similar to this.

```
http://localhost/Books_Web_Service/Book_Details.asmx?WSDL
```

You can also click the **Service Description** link in the *.asmx* file. The result of this will be an XML document explaining the structure of the Web Service as shown in Figure 13.11.

**Figure 13.11** WSDL Contract for Books Web Service

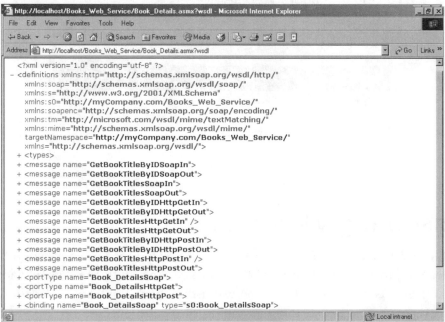

Fortunately, you don't need to fully understand all of this code because there are tools that will generate the WSDL file for you. But just so that you're familiar with it, let's look at what a WSDL file is primarily composed of. WSDL is an XML-based language and it can be broken down to the following elements:

- **XML Namespace Definitions** This could be found at the top of the WSDL file. It lists all the namespaces to which the WSDL file belongs.

- **Messages** This defines the input the client can provide to the Web method and the output the client can expect from the Web method. Most WSDL tools will provide three default implementations for your method: *SOAP, HTTP GET,* and *HTTP POST.* Each one specifies how to handle input and output parameters, through the corresponding port.

- **Port Types and Operations** Operations tie your messages to a corresponding method, which means that it defines the input and output message for a method call. The *portType* (i.e., the class) element is a collection of operations (i.e., the Web methods) exposed by your Web service. In our case *Book_DetailsSoap* will be the *portType* and *GetBookTitles* will be the operations, as shown in Figure 13.12. Since our service is available on three different ports (SOAP, HTTP GET, and HTTP POST), each one will have its own corresponding *portTypes* and *operations* definition.

**Figure 13.12** Books Web Service Port Information

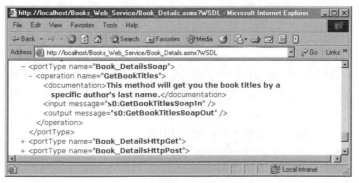

- **Bindings** The bindings will map the client requests to different operations. This client request could either be SOAP, HTTP GET, or HTTP POST. In our example, if we use an HTTP GET request (*Book_DetailsHTTPGet* binding type), the CLR will match the *GetBookTitles* operation name to it. In other words, the *Book_DetailsHTTPGet* binding type will *bind* the HTTP GET request to *GetBookTitles* operation.

- **Service Name**   This is the name of the Web service class. This name is used by the CLR to identify our Web service. In our example the service name is *Book Details*.

Now we understand Web Services and WSDL. Let's learn to create a proxy object—then we can write a client to consume our book's Web service.

# Creating Proxy Objects

To interact with a Web service you will need to create a proxy object that will act as the middleman between your application and the service. The proxy object can be generated from the WSDL file in two ways:

- Using the *wsdl.exe* command line utility
- Using Visual Studio.NET

## Using the *wsdl.exe* Utility

The .NET Framework provides a utility called *wsdl.exe* to create a proxy for command line compilation. To use it, follow these steps:

1. Bring up a command line prompt (**Start | Programs | Microsoft Visual Studio.NET | Visual Studio.NET Tools | Visual Studio.NET Command Prompt**)

2. Execute the following command all in one line:

   ```
   wsdl.exe http://localhost/Books_Web_Service/Book_Details.asmx
   ```

3. The result should be a *Book_Details.cs* file on the current directory as shown in Figure 13.13. This C# file can be compiled to a DLL (using *csc.exe* or Visual Studio.NET) or added to any project as a normal C# class file. Then we can instantiate an object from the class and execute methods on it similar to any local object.

**Figure 13.13** Creating a Proxy Object with WSDL.exe Utility

**NOTE**

Remember that what we're creating in these steps is a *proxy*. All we are doing is mimicking the functionality of the remote Web Service. The actual method execution is done at the remote Web Service end.

# Using Visual Studio.NET

It is very simple to create a proxy object using Visual Studio.NET. We can add a Web reference to any Web Form or Win Form application very easily. When we add a Web reference, a proxy object is generated in the background, which makes it much simpler and more effective to use.

The following example will show you how you can use Visual Studio.NET to create a Windows application that will consume the Web service we've created. We will create a Windows form client that will utilize the Web methods of the Web service and it will have the following components:

- A *DataGrid* control to display the complete list of books in the Pubs database using the *GetBookTitles* Web method

- A *TextBox* to enter a Title ID, which is used to look up a database table and populate a *Label* with the book title using the *GetBookTitleByID* Web method

- A *Button* to initiate the communication between the Web service and the client application

The following steps outline how to create the client application.

1. Open Visual Studio.NET IDE.

2. Create a new C# Windows Application Project (**File | New | Project**). Select **Visual C# Projects** as the project type and select **Windows Application** from the templates.

3. Name the project **Books_WinForm_Client** and save it to a suitable location.

4. To create a Web reference, go in the **Solution Explorer** and right-click on **References** and select **Web Reference** as shown in Figure 13.14.

**Figure 13.14** Adding a Web Reference in Visual Studio.NET

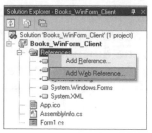

5.  Then, an **Add Web Reference** window will come up. Here you can enter the URL of the Web service with which you wish to work. Enter the URL of the Web service for our example and you can view all the Web methods available. When the Web service is loaded, the left pane will act as a browser interface to run the Web service. You can view the WSDL contract on the right pane. You should see something similar to Figure 13.15.

**Figure 13.15** Add Web Reference Window

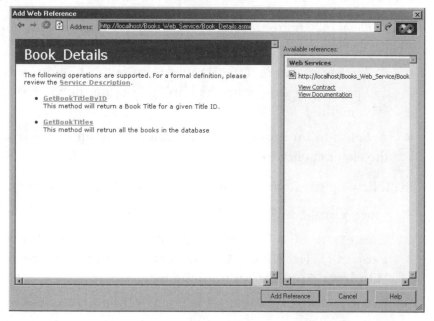

6.  Then click the **Add Reference** button. Your **Solution Explorer** will have an extra **Web Reference** section that will look similar to Figure 13.16.

**Figure 13.16** Updated Solutions Explorer after Adding a Web Reference

7. Next create the interface for the application, which should look similar to Figure 13.17. Our Windows Form will have the following components:

   - A Label (*Lbl_Title*) asking the user to enter the input

   - A Textbox (*Txt_Title_ID*) to enter the Title ID

   - A Button (*Btn_Get_Books*) to initiate the Web service calls

   - A Label (*Lbl_Title_Result*) to display the title of the book as the result from the Title ID search

   - A DataGrid (*Books_DataGrid*) to display the complete list of books

**Figure 13.17** Design View of the Client Win Form

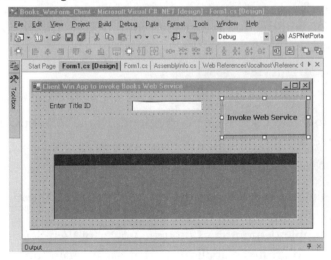

Of course we need to write some code to execute when the button is clicked. First we create the Web Service object. Then we invoke the *GetBookTitles()* and *GetBookTitleByID* Web methods. The *GetBookTitles()* Web method returns a *DataSet* object. This object is used as the data source for the data grid. The *GetBookTitleByID* method accepts the *Txt_Title_ID* textbox value as input. It will return a string, which is used to populate the *Lbl_Title_Result* label. The code will look similar to this:

```
private void Btn_Get_Books_Click(object sender,
    System.EventArgs e)
{
    localhost.Book_Details Books_Service = new
        localhost.Book_Details();
    DataSet Books_DataSet = new DataSet();
    Books_DataSet = Books_Service.GetBookTitles();
    Lbl_Title_Result.Text = "Title :- " +
        Books_Service.GetBookTitleByID(Txt_Title_ID.Text);
    Books_DataGrid.DataSource =
        Books_DataSet.Tables["BookTitles"].DefaultView;
    Books_DataGrid.Visible = true;
}
```

You may ask, how do I know about the *BookTitles* table in the data set? (Remember we do not know any technical implementation of the remote Web Service.) This information is extracted from reading the WSDL description of the Web Service.

```
<BookTitles diffgr:id=" BookTitles1"
    msdata:rowOrder="0">
```

If you look closely, this line corresponds to the following line of the original Web Service file.

```
Pubs_OleDbDataAdapter.Fill(Pubs_DataSet,"BookTitles");
```

After building and running the application the end result should be similar to Figure 13.18.

This example demonstrates the true power of Web Services. As you can see, we were able to create an application that has its main functionality executed remotely from a Web service. As more and more Web services become available on the Web, it is very easy to stitch them together and create very powerful distributed applications.

**Figure 13.18** Win Form Web Service Client

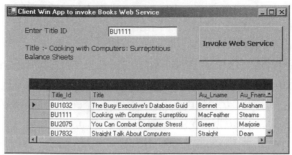

# Web Forms Overview

Web Forms could be described as the presentation layer for Web applications in the .NET Framework. These controls are very similar to Windows Forms. The key difference is the target interface. Web Forms are used to create Web pages, whereas Windows Forms are more focused on Windows applications. Web Forms are also referred to as ASP.NET in the .NET jargon.

The ASP.NET architecture is built on a server model. The primary purpose is to save round trips and increase efficiency between the Web client and the server. The ASP.NET Web Forms are compiled once and cached on the server before they are executed. All subsequent requests to the page emanate from the cache. Compiled code allows for faster execution, especially for post-backs or requests to the same page thereafter, which translates to an application with a noticeably improved performance.

> **NOTE**
>
> The key difference between traditional Active Server Pages (ASP) and ASP.NET is that ASP.NET is compiled (ASP 3.0 and earlier use interpreted code and are slower than ASP.NET).

An ASP.NET Web Forms page is a declarative text file with an *.aspx* filename extension. When a client (either a browser or any Internet-enabled device) requests an *.aspx* resource, the .NET runtime parses and compiles the file into a .NET Framework Page class that is cached on the server. This is then used to dynamically process the incoming request. The same compiled instance will be used on other subsequent requests to the page. The pages are updated in the cache only when the page changes or the caching period expires. We can also programmatically specify the cache time period for a Web form. When the specified time period elapses, the CLR will update the cache with a new version of the ASP.NET page.

A great feature of ASP.NET Web Forms is that it's not targeted towards a particular browser. ASP.NET is smart enough to serve different Hypertext Markup Language (HTML) output for different browser specifications. At the same time, Web Forms applications can be optimized to take advantage of features built into the more recent browsers that support the new standards—such as HTML 4.0, CSS, and client-side scripting support—to enhance performance and responsiveness. In many cases, this optimization is built into the Web Forms components, which can automatically detect browser levels and render pages accordingly.

Another feature of ASP.NET is that it can be written in multiple languages. Currently you can write ASP.NET code in C#, VB.NET, and J#. These are the default languages provided by the Microsoft .NET Framework. You can also utilize any other language that conforms to the CLR to create Web Forms. (e.g., Perl, Eiffel, Python, etc.). C# seems like a natural fit for creating Web Forms, however any other .NET-compliant language can be declared as the default through a directive at the top of the page, like this:

```
<%@ Language = C#%>
```

The language may also be declared within *<script>* blocks:

```
<script language=C# runat=server>
```

# Differences between HTML and Web Controls

Web Forms exist in two types that differ in functionality: *HTML controls* and *Web controls*. Both of these controls render the output in HTML for a Web browser. They also encapsulate the mechanisms for preserving state across server round-trips and for invoking server-side events that are handled on the server. Let's look at some of the key differences between the two types of controls.

1.  Web controls provide a richer functionality than the HTML controls. HTML controls basically are rendered HTML tags. On the other hand, Web controls encapsulate more complex functionality. For example, a *DataGrid* Web control will render text, customize it, bind it to an ADO.NET data source, and then render it in HTML.

2. HTML controls inherit from the *System.Web.UI.HtmlControls* names-pace, and the Web controls inherit from *System.Web.UI.WebControls.*

3. HTML controls are relatively browser neutral, having the output as basic HTML tags. On the other hand, Web controls can detect the browser capabilities and render the HTML in different formats. For example, a Web control can detect older browsers (pre-version 4.0) and serve HTML code to it. If it recognizes a post-version 4.0 browser, it may serve some Dynamic HTML (DHTML) version of the same data.

4. Web controls can be bound to data sources. HTML controls will accept only string arguments.

5. All Web controls starts with the prefix <asp:*>.

There are close to 45 HTML and Web controls available in the Microsoft .NET Framework. Let's look at them in more detail.

# Understanding HTML Controls

HTML controls functionality is very similar to HTML tags. HTML server controls are special HTML interfaces that enable page developers to programmatically manipulate standard HTML elements on the server. By simply converting existing HTML elements to HTML server controls in a Web Forms page, you expose them as elements that you can program on the server, regardless of to which client the page will be exposed. When a Web Forms page is processed on the server, an instance of each HTML server control is created using the information from the underlying HTML element. Attributes recognized by the control class become programmable properties. Any HTML element on a page can be converted to an HTML server control. The conversion is a simple process involving just few attributes. At a minimum, an HTML element is converted to a control by the addition of the attribute *runat="server"*. Here is an example of an HTML control for the *img* HTML tag.

```
<img ID="myImage" src="abc.gif" runat="server"/>
```

There are about 20 HTML controls in .NET released version 1.0; Table 13.1 shows some of the common ones.

**Table 13.1** HTML Controls in .NET

| Component | Description | Syntax and HTML Tag |
|---|---|---|
| HtmlAnchor | To create a hyper link in a Web page | **Syntax:** `<a id= Syngress href= www.syngress.com runat="server">Go To Syngress Publishing </a>`<br>**HTML Tag:** `<a href="www.syngress.com">Go To Syngress </a>` |
| HtmlButton | To create a button in a Web page | **Syntax:** `<button id="myButton" onServerClick=" myButton _OnClick" runat="server"> Click me! </button>`<br>**HTML Tag:** `<input type="button" name="myButton" value="Click Me!" >` |
| HtmlForm | To create a form in a Web page (note that this tag should be present to use the rest of the HTML controls) | **Syntax:** `<form id=myForm runat=server>…</form>`<br>**HTML Tag:** `<Form name="myForm">…</form>` |
| HtmlImage | To display images in a Web page | **Syntax:** `<img ID="myImage" src="abc.gif" runat="server"/>`<br>**HTML Tag:** `<img src="abc.gif">` |
| HtmlInput Button | Normal Button | **Syntax:** `<input type=button value="myButton" onServerClick= "myButton_Click" runat="server">`<br>**HTML Tag:** `<input type="button" value="myButton">` |
| HtmlInput CheckBox | To display a check box in a Web page | **Syntax:** `<input id="my_CheckBox" type=checkbox runat="server" >`<br>**HTML Tag:** `<input type="Checkbox" name = "my_CheckBox">` |
| HtmlInputText | To display a text box in a Web page | **Syntax:** `<input id="myName" type=text size=25 runat=server>`<br>**HTML Tag:** `<input type="text" name="myName" max size="25" >` |
| HtmlTable | To display a table in a Web page | **Syntax:** `<table id="Table1" CellPadding=5 CellSpacing=0 Border="1" runat="server" />`<br>**HTML Tag:** `<table CellPadding=5 CellSpacing=0 Border="1" >`<br>`… </table>` |

# Understanding Web Controls

ASP.NET Web controls are more flexible than HTML controls. They are designed to provide a simplified way to add powerful functionality to a Web page, such as displaying data. Web controls are particularly useful for dynamically generating HTML user interfaces and responding to client requests, as they are designed to work the same no matter what type of browser the user has.

Web controls include the traditional form controls, as well as other higher-level abstractions such as List-bound controls and other controls for special purposes. List-bound controls are used to render the contents of a data source or list with which they are associated. This includes the *Repeater*, *DataList*, and *DataGrid* controls. They offer the ability to create a variety of standard and custom layouts. Special-purpose controls include commonly used page tools such as the *AdRotator* and *Calendar* controls. These controls will be explained in more detail in the following sections.

In addition, the Web controls include a set of validation controls, which are server-side interfaces that incorporate logic to allow evaluation of a user's input. Attached to an input control, validation controls allow testing of what the user enters for that input control. We can match a pattern of the input or we can check whether the field input is of a different data type. For example, a state name can be abbreviated to two characters. We can check the length of a user input and make sure both letters are characters.

# Using Web Form Controls

You can easily add server-side controls to a Web Form by using Visual Studio.NET. The IDE will have a Toolbox window to drag and drop the target Web Form control to a project. This is the same procedure for both HTML controls and Web controls. Figure 13.19 shows some of the available Web controls available in the Toolbox.

Alternatively you can manually write the HTML code directly into the HTML page. For example, suppose you want to use a *Button*. The syntax would be:

```
<asp:Button id="Btn_Submit" runat="server" Text="Submit"> </asp:Button>
```

The general syntax for a Web control is <asp:*ControlName/*>, where *ControlName* would be the control you're going to use. Control names are identified within the HTML markup as namespace tags or declarative tags with a prefix using the format:

```
<asp:ControlName attributes runat="server"/>
```

**Figure 13.19** Web Control Toolbox

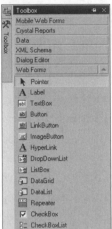

The <asp:> prefix is used to map the tag to the namespace of the runtime component, which in this case is *System.Web.UI.WebControls.* The remainder of the tag is the name of the runtime class itself. The *attributes* in this case are not those of HTML elements; instead, they are properties of the ASP.NET Web control. Like HTML controls, these tags must also contain a *runat="server"* attribute.

When we drag and drop the controls from the Toolbox in Visual Studio, this code will automatically be generated for you.

There are close to 25 Web controls available in the .NET Framework Version 1.0. We will discuss some of the key controls. These controls can be divided into the following categories according to their functionality:

- HTML page access Web controls
- Data enabling controls
- Validation controls
- Complex Web controls

**NOTE**

A sample Web form application will be created at the end of this section. All the components discussed here are used in this application.

# HTML Page Access Web Controls

All of these components are straightforward. These controls, specified in Table 13.2, mainly provide a server API for client HTML tags. The properties of each Web control are very similar to HTML tag properties.

**Table 13.2** HTML Page Access Controls

| Control Name | Description |
| --- | --- |
| Button | Creates a button on a Web Form |
| Checkbox | Creates a check box on a Web Form |
| Hyperlink | Creates a hyperlink on a Web Form |
| Image | Renders an image on a Web Form |
| Textbox | Creates a text box on a Web Form |

# Data Enabling Controls

ASP.NET provides some sophisticated data binding techniques. We're provided with sophisticated controls that allow you to access and bind to different types of data sources. The data sources can be a database or a static data structure like an array or a text file. When connecting to a database, ADO.NET is used to facilitate the communication.

This extremely flexible syntax permits the developer to bind Web control properties not only to data container values such as a database, but also to simple properties, collections, expressions, and even results returned from method calls. To do this you simply enclose the data to which you want to bind the control between <%# and %>. For example, if you have a property called *Student_ID*, you would declare it with <%#Student_ID%>. As another example, say you want to bind a string variable called *Students* to a *ListBox*; you would have the following declaration:

```
<asp:ListBox id="List1" datasource="<%#Students%>"
    runat="server">
```

As you can see, this gives you a lot of flexibility and will allow you to create a very sophisticated Web page with dynamic content. Now let's look at some of the available Data Binding controls.

# DataGrid

The *DataGrid* control is a very important component in Web Forms. This commonly used control has a lot of functionality. We can display, edit, delete, and add data rows using a single *DataGrid*. All these properties can be manipulated using the **Properties** window of the *DataGrid* component in Visual Studio. We can also alter the presentation of the *DataGrid* by right-clicking on the *DataGrid* and selecting the **Property Builder** window in Visual Studio. Figure 13.20 shows an example of a Data Grid.

**Figure 13.20** Data Grid Component

| title | au_ord | au_lname | price | ytd_sales | pub_id |
|-------|--------|----------|-------|-----------|--------|
| The Busy Executive's Database Guide | 2 | Green | 19.99 | 4095 | 1389 |
| You Can Combat Computer Stress! | 1 | Green | 2.99 | 18722 | 0736 |

The code that generates this data set will look similar to this:

```
<asp:DataGrid id="Books_DataGrid" runat="server"
    Width="424px" BorderColor="#CC9966" BorderStyle="None"
    BorderWidth="1px" BackColor="White" CellPadding="4"
    Font-Size="X-Small" Font-Names="Tahoma">
  <SelectedItemStyle Font-Bold="True" ForeColor="#663399"
     BackColor="#FFCC66"></SelectedItemStyle>
  <ItemStyle ForeColor="#330099"
     BackColor="White"></ItemStyle>
  <HeaderStyle Font-Bold="True" ForeColor="#FFFFCC"
     BackColor="#990000"></HeaderStyle>
  <FooterStyle ForeColor="#330099"
     BackColor="#FFFFCC"></FooterStyle>
  <PagerStyle HorizontalAlign="Center" ForeColor="#330099"
     BackColor="#FFFFCC"></PagerStyle>
</asp:DataGrid>
```

# DropDownList

The *DropDownList* control allows a single selection from a number of choices displayed as a drop-down list. Figure 13.21 shows an example of a drop-down list.

**Figure 13.21** DropDownList Component

The code for this looks like this:

```
<asp:DropDownList id="Lst_Last_Name" runat="server">
<asp:ListItem Value="Dull">Dull</asp:ListItem>
<asp:ListItem Value="Green" Selected="True">Green</asp:ListItem>
<asp:ListItem Value="Hunter">Hunter</asp:ListItem>
<asp:ListItem Value="White">White</asp:ListItem>
</asp:DropDownList>
```

The display items in the dropdown list will be specified within the *<asp:ListItem>* and *</asp:ListItem>* tags. We can preselect items by specifying the *Selected* attribute to the value *true*.

# Validation Control

These controls are very handy for form validations. We do not need to spend hours getting client-side Java Script functions to work. These server controls generate the Java Script and push it to the client browser within seconds. We just have to drag and drop them to the Web Form and set the target properties. These controls could facilitate many scenarios. For example, we can use these controls to build an order form for an e-commerce site. A *Required Filed Validator* control can be used to ensure the credit card name field is not blank. And we can use the *Regular Expression Validator* to check for numeric values in the credit card number filed.

## Required Field Validator

This control will check for invalid blank input. If no input is detected, an error message will be displayed. We do not need to make a round trip to the server to get the error message; the error message is a property of the control itself. You can attach a *RequiredFieldValidator* to any Web form control. The following example shows a *Textbox* control named *Txt_Title* with a *RequiredFieldValidator* attached.

```
<asp:RequiredFieldValidator class="NormalRed"
  id="Title_RequiredFieldValidator"
  runat="server"
  ErrorMessage="Please enter a Title"
  ControlToValidate="Txt_Title"> </asp:RequiredFieldValidator>
```

This control validates a blank input for a *Title* field. We display the "Please enter a Title" error message if the user does not enter a value. The control in action is shown in Figure 13.22. You can see the error message in red at the bottom of the image.

**Figure 13.22** Required Field Validator Control

## RegularExpressions Validator

This control will check for a matching pattern in the input. ZIP code, e-mail address, or ISBN number are formatted in a particular pattern. We can use this control to check the validity of the input against these patterns. Visual Studio.NET has wizards to support some common patterns (e.g., US ZIP codes, e-mail address, etc.). Here is a sample to check the validity of an e-mail address.

```
<asp:RegularExpressionValidator class="NormalRed"
    id="Email_RegularExpressionValidator"
    runat="server"
    ErrorMessage="Invalid Author email address"
    ControlToValidate="Txt_Author_Email"
    ValidationExpression=
       "\w+([-+.]\w+)*@\w+([-.]\w+)*\.\w+([-.]\w+)*">
</asp:RegularExpressionValidator>
```

Let's look at the validation rules. The "**\w+([-+.]\w+)\*@\w+([-.]\w+)\*\.\w+([-.]\w+)\***" string will search for a pattern in the input. (In this case the string should have multiple characters before and after the @ sign. These characters could be multiples of letters and ".".) If the input pattern does not follow the string we will see an error message. The code output is shown in Figure 13.23. In this case we are not entering a @ sign in the e-mail field to produce an error.

**Figure 13.23** Regular Expression Validator Control

| Please enter the Book details | |
|---|---|
| Title | C# for Java |
| Author Name | Chris Peiris |
| Author Email | wrong email |
| Available in paper back | ☑ |
| | |
| Select the Publishing day | Invalid Author email address |

# Complex Web Controls

These are special Web controls built into Web Forms. These controls used to be
ActiveX plug-ins under ASP 3.0. Here are some of the important ones.

## Using the AdRotator Control

The *AdRotator* component will behave like an advertisement server. We can enter
our advertisement requirements in a XML file and map the XML file to the
*AdRotator* component as a property. This is a great tool to handle banners in a
small Web site. Again, you can simply drag and drop this control from Visual
Studio and it will automatically generate the following code for you.

```
<asp:AdRotator id="AdRotator_Syngress" runat="server"
  Width="468px" Height="60px"
  AdvertisementFile="Ad_Source.xml">
</asp:AdRotator>
```

You can specify the width and the height of the banners using the *Width* and
*Height* properties. The banner details are read from an XML file. The XML file
should contain elements to describe the image location, navigation URL (when
the banner is clicked), and impression ratios. For our example we will use the following *Ad_Source.xml* file.

```
<?xml version="1.0" encoding="utf-8" ?>
<Advertisements>
     <Ad>
         <ImageUrl>images/banner1.gif</ImageUrl>
         <NavigateUrl>http://www.microsoft.com</NavigateUrl>
         <AlternateText>Microsoft.com</AlternateText>
         <Keyword>MSN</Keyword>
         <Impressions>80</Impressions>
     </Ad>
     <Ad>
```

```
    <ImageUrl>images/banner2.gif</ImageUrl>

    <NavigateUrl>http://www.fuji.com</NavigateUrl>

    <AlternateText>Fuji</AlternateText>

    <Keyword>Fuji</Keyword>

    <Impressions>50</Impressions>

</Ad>

<Ad>

    <ImageUrl>images/banner3.gif</ImageUrl>

    <NavigateUrl>http://www.Monster.com.au</NavigateUrl>

    <AlternateText>Holidays</AlternateText>

    <Keyword>Holidays</Keyword>

    <Impressions>80</Impressions>

</Ad>

</Advertisements>
```

The *AdRotator* will take into account the *<Impressions>* tag to alternate between the three banners. We can also associate key word searches with the *<Keyword>* element. The *<AlternateText>* element will specify some alternative text for the banner.

# Using the Calendar Control

The *Calendar* control provides various ways of date selection, including a range of dates by week or month. This control could be customized to render in different style sheets. The control implements an *OnSelectionChanged* event that could be used to trigger date-specific business logic. Figure 13.24 is an example of a *Calendar* control.

**Figure 13.24** Calendar Web Control

Here is the code behind the image:

```
<asp:Calendar id="Publishing_Date_Calendar" runat="server"
    Font-Names="Verdana" Width="220px" Height="200px"
```

```
BorderWidth="1px" BackColor="White"
DayNameFormat="FirstLetter" ForeColor="#003399" Font-
Size="8pt" BorderColor="#3366CC" CellPadding="1">
 <TodayDayStyle ForeColor="White"
     BackColor=      "#99CCCC"></TodayDayStyle>
 <SelectorStyle ForeColor="#336666"
     BackColor="#99CCCC"></SelectorStyle>
 <NextPrevStyle Font-Size="8pt"
     ForeColor="#CCCCFF"></NextPrevStyle>
 <DayHeaderStyle Height="1px" ForeColor="#336666"
     BackColor="#99CCCC"></DayHeaderStyle>
 <SelectedDayStyle Font-Bold="True" ForeColor="#CCFF99"
     BackColor="#009999"></SelectedDayStyle>
 <TitleStyle Font-Size="10pt" Font-Bold="True" Height="25px"
     BorderWidth="1px" ForeColor="#CCCCFF"
     BorderStyle="Solid" BorderColor="#3366CC"
     BackColor="#003399"></TitleStyle>
 <WeekendDayStyle BackColor="#CCCCFF"></WeekendDayStyle>
 <OtherMonthDayStyle
     ForeColor="#999999"></OtherMonthDayStyle>
</asp:Calendar>
```

# Creating a Web Form Application

We will try to use the existing Books information example from the previous section and use a Web Form as the interface. This will also contrast the difference between a Web Service and a Web Form interface. Probably the greatest lesson is to appreciate the flexibility of .NET. Regardless whether it is a Web Service or Web Form, you will realize that the code is very similar. Here are the steps.

1. Create a new ASP.NET project (**File | New | Project** ).

2. Select **ASP.NET Web Application**.

3. Enter the location of the Web site to be created. Your screen should look similar to Figure 13.25.

4. Press the **OK** button. This will create a Web project for you. In addition it will create a behind-the-scenes virtual directory with the same name as the project name. It will also create a new folder under the *c:\inetpub\ wwwroot* directory.

**Figure 13.25** Creating an ASP.NET Web Application

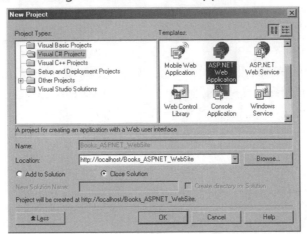

5.  Now you will enter the Visual Studio.NET IDE. There will be a sample Web form called *WebForm1.aspx* created for you. Rename the page **HTML_Form.aspx**. In this Web form we are exploring the Web controls in action. We will create another Web form called **Data_Bindings.aspx** to handle ADO.NET and list bound controls.

6.  Drag and drop HTML and Web controls from the Toolbox to create the Web form shown in Figure 13.26. Our Web form is a *New Book Entry* form for Syngress Publishing. When a new book is published, we enter the book information to our database. We will use *Label* and *Textbox* controls to enter author information. A calendar control is used to select the published day of the book. An *AdRotator* component is used to display multiple banners at the top of the Web form. We will also use some validation controls to stop invalid input.

Table 13.3 lists the controls you need to create this Web form.

**Table 13.3** A List of Web Controls in the Web Form

| Component Name | Type |
| --- | --- |
| AdRotator_Syngress | AdRotator |
| Img_Company_Logo | Image |
| Lbl_Title | Label |
| Lbl_Author_Name | Label |
| Lbl_Author_Email | Label |

**Continued**

**Table 13.3** Continued

| Component Name | Type |
| --- | --- |
| Chk_Paper_Back | CheckBox |
| Title_RequiredFieldValidator | RequiredFieldValidator |
| Email_RegularExpressionValidator | RegularExpressionValidator |
| Publishing_Date_Calendar | Calendar |

**Figure 13.26** Design View for Web Form Application

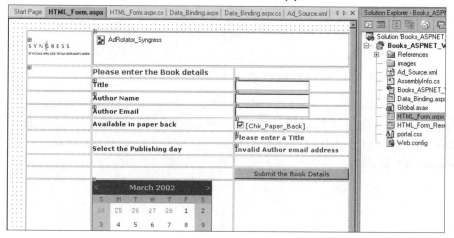

Let's look at the code closely. This is the first line of the Web form.

```
<%@ Page language="c#" Codebehind="HTML_Form.aspx.cs"
    Inherits="Books_ASPNET_WebSite.HTML_Form" %>
```

This line will give instructions to the CLR. The *language* parameter will describe the programming language the code is written. This Web form will consist of several Web controls, with many event handlers. We need to write code to utilize these event handlers. For example, if we have a button on the Web form we need to write code to facilitate the *Click()* event handler. This code is written in a separate C# file. The *Codebehind* attribute will point to this file, which is generated by Visual Studio.NET. The *Inherits* attribute will describe the inheritance structure of the C# code.

```
<form id=HTML_Form name=myForm action=HTML_Form_Result.aspx
    method=get runat="server">
 ...</form>
```

This code segment will describe how a server side *Form* tag is declared. This is very similar to a HTML form tag. The only difference will be the *runat="server"* directive.

```
<asp:image id=Img_Company_Logo runat="server"
    AlternateText="Syngress Logo" Width="112px"
    ImageUrl="images/logo.gif">
</asp:Image>
```

This is how we display an image on a Web form. It is very similar to a HTML *IMG* tag. Let's learn how to use a *AdRotator* component in our Web form.

```
<asp:adrotator id=AdRotator_Syngress runat="server"
    AdvertisementFile="Ad_Source.xml" Height="60px"
    Width="468px">
</asp:AdRotator>
```

We also need a *Required Field Validator* control to stop blank input form the user. We also need to put some pattern validations on the *Email* field. Here is the relevant code for it (please refer to the section, "Validation Controls" to understand this code):

```
<asp:requiredfieldvalidator class=NormalRed
    id=Title_RequiredFieldValidator runat="server" \
    ControlToValidate="Txt_Title" ErrorMessage="Please enter a
    Title">
</asp:RequiredFieldValidator>


<asp:regularexpressionvalidator class=NormalRed
    id=Email_RegularExpressionValidator runat="server"
    ControlToValidate="Txt_Author_Email" ErrorMessage="Invalid
    Author email address" ValidationExpression="\w+([-
    +.]\w+)*@\w+([-.]\w+)*\.\w+([-.]\w+)*">
</asp:RegularExpressionValidator>
```

The combination of all these controls could be viewed in Figure 13.27.

Let's create another Web Form for data bound controls. We are basically going to use the same database layer as our previous Web Services example. We will be accessing the *Pubs* database. You may need to create an *OleDbConnection*, *OleDbDataAdapter*, and a *DataSet* object to handle the ADO.NET queries. These steps are the same as the Web Service example. The only difference is to create a standalone *DataSet*; do not try to create the *DataSet* from the *OleDbDataAdapter*. We need to provide a *Title ID* to get a valid row set from the *Pubs* database. This is done at runtime. Therefore the *DataSet* should be created at runtime; otherwise it will always be empty. Table 13.4 shows the elements in the Web forms.

**Figure 13.27** Sample Web Form in Action

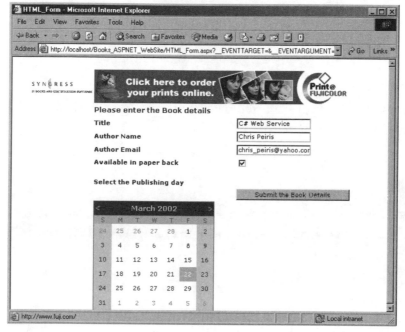

**Table 13.4** Web Controls for Data Access Web Form

| Component Name | Type |
| --- | --- |
| AdRotator_Syngress | AdRotator |
| Img_Company_Logo | Image |
| Lbl_Title_ID | Label |
| Btn_Get_Books | Button |
| Books_DataGrid | DataGrid |
| Lst_Title_ID | Drop-down list box |

The drop-down list box will have a list of the *Title IDs*. A user can pick a *Title ID* and press the *Get Books Titles* button to display the book information in the *DataGrid* control.

We should write some code to enable the data loading to the data grid. First we open the database connection, and then we provide the *Title ID* to make the database query. This *Title ID* is selected from our drop-down list box. Then we fill the *DataSet* and use it to populate the *DataGrid*. First, we will look at the button click event handler.

```
private void Btn_Get_Books_Click(object sender,
    System.EventArgs e)
{
    Render_Data_Grid(Lst_Title_ID.SelectedItem.Value);
}
```

This method passes the selected *Title ID* to the *Render_Data_Grid* function. Let's have a look at this function.

```
private void Render_Data_Grid(String Title_ID)
{
    Pubs_OleDbConnection.Open();
    oleDbSelectCommand1.CommandText = "SELECT Title, Au_Lname,
        Au_Fname, Title_Id FROM tbl_Book_Titles where Title_ID='"
        + Title_ID + "'";
    Pubs_dataSet.Clear();

    Pubs_OleDbDataAdapter.Fill(Pubs_dataSet,"BookTitles");
    Books_DataGrid.DataSource =
        Pubs_dataSet.Tables["BookTitles"].DefaultView;
    Books_DataGrid.DataBind();
    Pubs_OleDbConnection.Close();
}
```

First we open a connection to our *Pubs* database. Then we need to create the correct SQL statement to make the database query. We need to append the selected *Title ID* from the list box to get the correct data row from the table. Then we *Fill* the *DataSet* and bind the *DataSet* to the *DataGrid*. In this example all the data binding is handled by the *DataGrid* control. Finally we close the database connection. Now we can compile and run the Web form. The screen should be similar to Figure 13.28.

**Figure 13.28** Data Bound Web Form Controls in Action

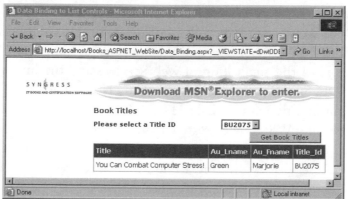

# Summary

In this chapter we have covered two of the most interesting areas in the .NET Framework. Both Web Services and Web Forms are dominant topics in .NET.

First we looked at Web Services and the concepts behind them. You learned about the purpose of the application of Web Services and the importance of SOAP and WSDL. SOAP is the mechanism that lets you bypass firewall security and execute remote function calls over HTTP. A Web service can publish its technical details using WSDL. We created a sample Web service to expose a database query as XML over HTTP. Then we learned how to create a client to consume our Web service by creating a *Proxy* object. A Proxy object can be created using *wsdl.exe* utility or Visual Studio.NET

In the second part of the chapter we learned about Web Forms. We learned that there are two types of Web Form controls, Web controls and HTML controls. There are close to 45 Web and HTML controls in .NET Framework. We also discussed the key difference between Web and HML controls. HTML controls are similar to HTML tags; Web controls can implement functionality on a Web form. We can also bind data sources (database *DataSets*, array of Strings, etc.) to Web controls. We looked into several important HTML and Web controls. Finally we created an ASP.NET application to utilize our knowledge.

# Solutions Fast Track

## Web Services Overview

- ☑ Web Services are remote function calls over HTTP using SOAP envelopes.

- ☑ Since it uses HTTP as the transport protocol, it can bypass firewall restrictions using the default Web port.

- ☑ Web Services deliver data in XML format. Therefore we can build multiple interfaces to consume XML data (Web browsers, PDAs, mobile phones, etc.).

## Creating Web Services

- ☑ Web Services can be created using a text editor or Visual Studio.NET IDE. The Web service files have the .asmx extension.

☑ The methods you like to expose over HTTP should be declared with the *[WebMethod]* attribute.

☑ The .NET Framework will automatically create a runtime implementation for the Web service.

## Consuming Web Services

☑ We need to create a proxy object to consume a Web service. This is done using the *wsdl.exe* command line utility or Visual Studio.NET (using the *Add Web Reference* utility).

☑ The WSDL contract can be obtained by appending the string *?wsdl* to the end of the Web service URL.

☑ The proxy object will be primarily responsible for marshalling of data between the client and Web service.

☑ The clients can be created in multiple interfaces. For example, a Windows application or a Web browser can act as an interface for the Web service.

## Web Forms Overview

☑ Web Forms are the presentation layer for the Web interface .NET.

☑ There are two categories of Web Forms controls: HTML controls and Web controls.

☑ HTML controls are very similar to HTML tags; but they are run at the server end.

☑ Web controls are more sophisticated, and support rapid application development.

## Using Web Forms Controls

☑ There are close to 45 Web controls.

☑ All those controls can be found in the *Toolbox* window of Visual Studio.NET. We need to drag and drop the appropriate control to a Web form and write some code to facilitate the event handlers.

☑ Most of these controls can be bound to data sources. These data sources include strings, array data, and database data (using *DataSet* objects).

## Creating a Web Forms Application

☑ The project type for a Web form application should be *ASP.NET Application*.

☑ The Web form will consist of multiple Web controls and HTML controls. These controls represent the presentation layer of your application. You should use the *Toolbox* window to drag and drop these controls to the Web form.

☑ ADO.NET facilities can easily be accessed from the *Toolbox* controls. These controls represent the database layer in your application. All you have to do is drag and drop them to the Web form and set their appropriate properties.

# Frequently Asked Questions

The following Frequently Asked Questions, answered by the authors of this book, are designed to both measure your understanding of the concepts presented in this chapter and to assist you with real-life implementation of these concepts. To have your questions about this chapter answered by the author, browse to **www.syngress.com/solutions** and click on the **"Ask the Author"** form.

**Q:** Is it necessary to create a proxy object to consume a Web Service?

**A:** No, you do not need a proxy object to obtain the data from a Web Service. The .NET Framework creates HTTP GET, HTTP POST, and SOAP implementations when a .NET Web Service is created. Therefore you can query the Web Service using HTTP GET and POST. In this case you are directly accessing the Web Service, not going through a middleman (proxy object).

**Q:** Is HTTP GET and POST access available on Java and other Web Services architectures?

**A:** To my knowledge, no. The only platform that has a default implementation of POST and GET is MS .NET. You can customize your own SOAP handlers for this in Java implementations.

**Q:** Can we initialize a complete class as a Web Method?

**A:** No, only methods can be initialized as Web Methods.

**Q:** Are HTML controls the same as HTML tags?

**A:** No, they are not. Since HTML controls are processed at the server side they can be optimized to render different tags on the server side (for example, members of the *HTMLGenericControl* class can render multiple tags as *<body>*, *<head>*, *<span>*, etc.).

**Q:** What happens if the client's browser does not support any JavaScript? How do we run the validation controls then?

**A:** The .NET Framework is smart enough to understand this. Therefore the validations are done at the server end and pushed to the client browser. The down side is the increased number of round trips.

# Chapter 14

# Working with ActiveX, COM, and Unmanaged Code

**Solutions in this chapter:**

- **Working with Unmanaged Code**

- **Working with the Platform Invocation Utility**

- **Working with COM Components**

- **Working with ActiveX Controls**

- **Working with Pointers**

☑ Summary

☑ Solutions Fast Track

☑ Frequently Asked Questions

# Introduction

At this point you have learned most of what C# has to offer. This chapter will complete your arsenal by showing you some more advanced programming techniques available in the C# language.

No matter how good a technology is, it just can't come in and replace all of the other existing ones. The designers of the C# language realized this fact and equipped the language with support for old legacy applications. Java provides this functionality through the Java Native Interface (JNI), which allows you to work with code that is written in some other language. This chapter will look at several ways that C# lets you work with objects that are written in another language such as C, C++, or Visual Basic.

Currently, there are several projects, such as the Mono project (www.go-mono.net), which are trying to port the .NET platform to other operating systems like the UNIX–BSD OS. However, Microsoft would probably prefer that you develop most of your C# applications under the Windows environment. Therefore, most of the tools provided by Microsoft are for interacting with existing Windows applications and components such as ActiveX controls, COM DLLs, and the Win32 APIs. You will see some of these tools in action in this chapter.

The first thing you will learn is the difference between managed and unmanaged code in C#. *Unmanaged* codes are methods that are executed outside the .NET Framework's managed environment.

Next, the chapter will show how you can incorporate standard COM dynamic link library (DLL) files with your C# program. You will see how you can easily turn COM components into .NET assemblies that you can use with C#.

Then you will learn how to import ActiveX controls into a C# application. ActiveX controls are objects that support a customizable, programmatic interface that can typically be dropped into a form. Finally, the chapter will talk about unsafe code and how to use pointers within your C# application.

You can access the code files that apply to the examples and demonstrations throughout this chapter at the book's web page at www.syngress.com. This code will be very useful in actively working through the demonstrations and for enhancing your understanding of how to build C# applications.

# Working with Unmanaged Code

COM components and ActiveX controls have contributed to thousands of applications on the Windows platform. Most companies have made a significant investment in these components, and for this reason Microsoft has provided a way to support these legacy applications. The .NET Framework has supplied us with several tools and utilities that allow us to interoperate with these existing components and make it simple to access them. Since COM and ActiveX components run outside the .NET Framework, they've been labeled as *unmanaged code*, which distinguishes them from *managed code* that runs within the framework.

*Managed code* could be defined as code that runs under the control of the Common Language Runtime (CLR). At this point all of the codes that we've looked at are managed code because they're run within the CLR. Managed code has the advantage of utilizing the CLR functionalities about which we don't have to concern ourselves, such as automatic memory management, type checking, and exception handling.

On the other hand, the code that runs outside the runtime is called *unmanaged code*. This includes COM components, ActiveX interfaces, and Win32 API functions. This code is compiled directly into native code, cannot enjoy any benefits that the CLR offers, and is unaware of the existence of the CLR.

In a way, writing unmanaged code is similar to invoking the Java Native Interface API. Just as the JNI API extends the Java virtual machine's horizons to languages like C, C++, or assembly language, the ability to write unmanaged code allows you to extend the boundaries of the Microsoft .NET Framework. Unmanaged code can be written only using a pre-.NET compiler, which means that the .NET compiler can't compile unmanaged code. Since unmanaged code is not compiled as Microsoft Intermediate Language (MSIL) and does not run under the CLR, it has the following limitations:

- Memory management, type checking, exception handling, and garbage collection has to be done within the component.

- The code will not be able to port to another language. (As an example, managed C# programs could be debugged in VB.NET. Unfortunately, an unmanaged VB program will not be accessible to C#.)

- Wrapper components are needed to communicate with managed .NET assemblies. This is also a performance hit under .NET Framework.

# Interoperability with Unmanaged Code

The Component Object Model (COM) is Microsoft's solution to code reusability, binary standardization, language independence, and object-oriented programming. This architecture provides a way for programmers to develop components that can be used by a wide variety of consumers that support its standard. Every COM component written to this standard can easily be updated and reused by other programmers.

This reuse is made possible as COM components are built upon interfaces. As discussed in Chapter 6, an interface is a way for a component to expose its functionality to the caller. As you know, interfaces can be viewed as a binary contract between the server component and its caller. This binary contract establishes how they will communicate with each other, what functions are provided, and the required parameters. Once you know each function and property in an interface, it's simply a case of tying these into your own program to make use of them.

COM is also a binary standard. Therefore COM components can be developed in a wide variety of languages and still obey its rules. Microsoft Visual Basic and Microsoft Visual C++ are two of the most popular languages for developing COM components. You could also use include Microsoft Visual J++, Powerbuilder, Borland Delphi, and Micro Focus Object Cobol. This allows project teams to take advantage of a variety of skill sets (C++, Delphi, VB, Java, etc.) for a wide variety of needs.

> **NOTE**
>
> ActiveX controls are COM components that follow the COM binary standard.

The .NET base class library has specialized classes to support interoperability with unmanaged COM components. These classes could be found under the *System.Runtime.InteropServices* namespace. The interoperability services in .NET could be categorized into the following scenarios:

- .NET assembly (managed) calling a single COM DLL (unmanaged)
- .NET assembly (managed) calling a COM object or an ActiveX control (unmanaged)
- COM DLL (unmanaged) calling a .NET assembly (managed)

# Managed Code Calling an Unmanaged COM DLL Function

In C# you can easily invoke a function from any native dynamic link library (DLL). If you've done some Windows development and you are familiar with certain COM components or with Win32 DLL, it is still possible to utilize them under .NET. To access any function in a DLL, all you need to know is the function name you wish to call, the DLL that contains the function, and how to marshal or handle the function parameters. This can be done using the *Platform Invocation Services* with the .NET Framework. This topic will be discussed in greater detail later in this chapter.

# Managed Code Calling an Unmanaged COM Object or an ActiveX Control

In this case we want our .NET assembly to have access to the complete COM DLL. We need to convert the COM DLL into a structure that the CLR can recognize. The major difference between a COM DLL and a .NET assembly is the lack of metadata. The .NET Framework provides a tool called the *Type Library Importer (TlbImp.exe)* that will create a wrapper for COM components and make them accessible to .NET assemblies. This *Runtime Callable Wrapper (RCW)* acts as a proxy object between the COM DLL and the .NET assembly.

A similar tool, called the ActiveX Control Importer (*AxImp.exe*), is provided for creating wrappers for ActiveX objects. ActiveX objects are prepackaged COM components working to build a functional unit of software. We will discuss both utilities and how to work with RCWs later in this chapter.

# Unmanaged COM DLL Calling Managed .NET Code

We can also call a .NET assembly from *unmanaged* code, such as a COM component or a Windows program not written in .NET. To do this, we must make our .NET assembly behave like an ordinary COM DLL. Typically, to access a COM DLL you have to refer to the Windows registry to get information about that component. Therefore we need to create a registry entry for our .NET assembly if we want it to be accessed by another COM component or program. The .NET Framework provides a utility called the *Register Assembly (RegAsm.exe)* for this purpose. This utility will generate a GUID for the .NET assembly and will register it in the system registry. This allows a .NET assembly to behave like a typical COM object and can be accessed by any program, or by another COM DLL.

Figure 14.1 summarizes the interoperability options available in the .NET Framework.

**Figure 14.1** Interoperability Options in .NET

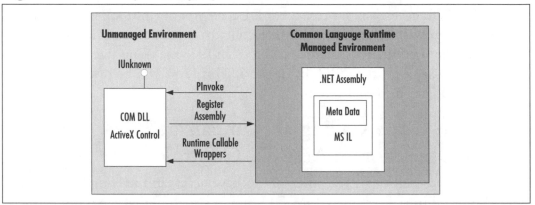

Figure 14.1 illustrates the communication between unmanaged and managed code in a Windows environment. The unmanaged environment is composed of COM components and ActiveX controls. COM components can be defined as a component that implements the *IUnknown* interface. As you can see, the managed environment is composed of code that runs within the CLR or, basically, .NET assemblies. There are two ways we can access unmanaged code from .NET assemblies: by using the *PInvoke* and by using Runtime Callable Wrappers (RCW). You can also make your managed code available to COM components by using the Register Assembly utility (*regasm.exe*). However, this is beyond the scope of this book and will not be discussed.

# Working with the Platform Invocation Utility

The Platform Invocation Service (*PInvoke*) allows you to access unmanaged public functions residing in a Win32 DLL component. This could be very useful as it allows you to work with the Windows API and to expose functions in any DLL. This is helpful for software developers that are very familiar with a particular COM object or Win32 API and would like to continue using it. For example, with *PInvoke* you can easily invoke the *MessageBox* function in the *user32.dll* COM object. This is not advisable; I would suggest using its .NET equivalent instead because accessing unmanaged code incurs some overhead and you loose the benefits of the CLR. However, we have to acknowledge the fact that there will be third-party COM components out there we might still need to use, and for this situation, *PInvoke* can be very useful.

To expose functions in any DLL, you have to attach the [*DllImport*] attribute to the method and declare it with the *static* and *extern* keywords. The [*DllImport*] attribute allows you to specify the name of the DLL that contains the DLL function that your method will use. For example, if you want to access the *puts()* function in the *msvcrt.dll*, you will have to code the following line:

```
[DllImport("msvcrt.dll", EntryPoint="puts")]
public static extern int puts(string c);
```

The common practice is to name the C# method the same as the exported function, but you can use any name you like as long as you specify in the *EntryPoint* parameter which function you would like to use. The *static* keyword means there is only one instance of this method in the class, and the *extern* keyword instructs the compiler that the method is implemented using an external unmanaged source and will be invoked through *PInvoke*.

## Developing & Deploying…

### The EntryPoint Parameter

The *EntryPoint* attribute parameter is optional. However, if you don't declare this parameter, then your method name *must* be similar to the function name you wish to invoke. By specifying the *EntryPoint* parameter, you could have a different name from the method name. But for convention, it's typically a good idea to use the same function name you wish to invoke.

Optionally, you can specify custom marshaling information for the method's parameters and return a value, which will override the .NET Framework default marshaling. This is implemented by the *[MarshalAs]* attribute. The CLR needs to marshal the input and output parameters of unmanaged code invocation. It has default types to match every unmanaged type. For an example, a C# *String* is equal to a *LPTSTR* (pointer to a *TCHAR* char buffer) in unmanaged code. If we do not specify any marshalling instructions the CLR will use these default marshalling values. In some cases we need to marshal data to a specific type, which you can do by using *[MarshalAs]* attribute. For example, let's look at the following code:

```
[DllImport("msvcrt.dll")]
[return : MarshalAs(UnmanagedType.I4)]
public static extern int puts(string c);
```

In the preceding example we are instructing the runtime to override the default marshalling with an *Integer 4* type for the *puts()* function return value. All the marshalling information could be found under *System.Runtime.InteropService .Marshal* and *System.Runtime.InteropService.MarshalAs* attribute classes.

Let's take a complete example to witness *Platform Invocation* in action. We will create a small application to bring up a message box and display some text. From experience I am aware of the *user32.dll* library that implements this functionality. It contains the *MessageBox* function, which displays a message box on the screen. The following is the C# code listing:

```
// PInvoke_Test.cs
using System;
using System.Runtime.InteropServices;

public class DisplayText
{
    [DllImport("user32.dll", EntryPoint="MessageBox",
             CharSet=CharSet.Auto)]
    public static extern int MessageBox(int hWnd, String
        text, String caption, uint type);
}

public class Display_MessageBox
{
    public static void Main()
    {
        DisplayText.MessageBox(0, "This text is displayed
            using user32.dll", "Display Text", 0);
    }
}
```

Let's try to understand this sample code. First we create a *DisplayText* class that acts as a wrapper for the *MessageBox* function in the *user32.dll* library. The main part that we want to look at is the *DllImport* attribute declaration:

```
[DllImport("user32.dll", EntryPoint="MessageBox",
        CharSet=CharSet.Auto)]
```

The first parameter specifies that we're going to use the *user32.dll* library. The next parameter specifies that the *EntryPoint* for our method is the *MessageBox* function. Finally, the *CharSet = CharSet.Auto* attribute parameter is just a compiler directive informing the runtime to marshal the string automatically. The default marshalling pattern will be ANSI strings.

We then declare our method as *static extern* to instruct the compiler that the method is residing on a separate DLL. Then we create another class called the *Display_MessageBox* to act as the driver program to test the *DisplayText* class. Figure 14.2 displays the output of the program, and as you can see, a message box pops up with our message.

**Figure 14.2** Executing the *PInvoke* Test Program

# Working with COM Components

In general terms, a COM component is any object that conforms to the binary standards that COM enforces, and that supports the *IUnknown* interface. The *IUnknown* interface allows clients to invoke the COM object and also controls the object lifetime. The underlying principle behind COM specifies that interfaces are immutable, and once published, they cannot be changed. Each interface and object is uniquely identified by a *Globally Unique Identifier* (GUID), which has a 128-bit value and is stored in the registry.

The COM runtime maps COM object calls to a GUID, which points it to the location of the COM object. This information is stored in the registry under the *HKEY_CLASSES_ROOT\CLSID* key. All registered classes are stored here and usually have an *InprocServer32* or *LocalServer* key that point to the location of the object. A client uses this information to locate a COM object and to utilize its services. Further, COM components generate type libraries that can be used by calling clients to obtain information about the COM object and its exposed interfaces and types.

The component model in .NET is represented by assemblies. COM and .NET assemblies are similar but, at the same time, very different technologies in their own ways. The following are differences between COM components and .NET assemblies:

- .NET managed components behave very differently from COM components. Managed components do not interact with the registry to store and locate information. Instead, the metadata is self-contained in the assembly and the runtime looks for the assembly in the local or global cache.

- .NET Assemblies do not utilize GUIDs to identify objects, and they do not support the *IUnknown* interface. Object lifetime is managed by the .NET runtime via garbage collection. The .NET assemblies do not explicitly call methods to create *AddRef()* method and destroy object references via the *Release()* method. (We will discuss these methods later in the chapter.) A managed component is identified by its namespace and object name and it does not need to be registered with any runtimes (like the registry). The .NET runtime will look into the global assembly cache or the application cache to locate the assembly; this information is not obtained from the registry.

- Every assembly has embedded metadata that completely describe the assembly and its types. Unlike COM, managed components do not generate type libraries.

# Creating a Simple COM Component

To demonstrate how we can use COM components with our C# application, we'll first create a sample COM component. Later we will convert this COM object to a .NET assembly and investigate the differences in detail. In the first part we will create a COM component using MS Visual Basic 6.0. This is a simple component, which will take two numbers as input and multiply them. Then we will use a Web client to test the component to make sure that it's functional. If you don't have Visual Basic 6.0, you can download the precompiled

DLL from the Syngress Web site at www.syngress.com. To create the component, follow these steps:

1. Open Visual Basic 6.0 (this is a part of Visual Studio 6.0).

2. Select **ActiveX DLL** from the **New Project** menu in VB 6.0 (see Figure 14.3).

**Figure 14.3** Select ActiveX DLL as the New Project Type

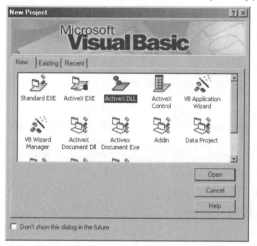

3. Name the project **COM_Example**.

4. Add a Form called **Multiply** and type the following code:

```
Function MultiplyNumbers(ByVal Number1 As Integer, ByVal
    Number2 As Integer)
    Multiply = Number1 * Number2
End Function
```

5. Compile the project by selecting **File | Make COM_Example.dll**. Now you have a very simple COM object. The next step is to create a client to consume it. Let's use a Web interface as our client. Here is the code for our sample Active Server Page. The ASP page is called *test_COM.asp*.

```
<html>

<head>
<meta http-equiv="Content-Language" content="en-us">
```

```
<meta name="GENERATOR" content="Microsoft FrontPage 5.0">
<meta name="ProgId" content="FrontPage.Editor.Document">
<meta http-equiv="Content-Type" content="text/html;
    charset=windows-1252">
<title>COM Test Page</title>
</head>

<body>
<%
Dim obj, result
Set obj = Server.CreateObject("COM_Example.Multiply")
result = obj.MultiplyNumbers(2,2)
%>
<p><b><font face="Verdana">The Product of  2 
    x  2 is <%=result%></font></b></p>

</body>

</html>
```

6. Create a virtual directory called **Simple_COM_Example** in Internet Information Server (IIS) and map the location of the file.

7. Send a HTTP request to the IIS Web server. To do so, load a Web browser and invoke the Web page http://localhost/Simple_COM_Example/test_COM.asp.

IIS will try to load the ASP file. IIS needs to create an instance of the COM object to load the Web page. IIS looks up the registry with the keyword *COM_Example.Multiply* and creates an instance of our simple COM component. The instance would have been assigned a GUID when it was created. The COM component takes the two integers as the arguments and returns the product to IIS. Then IIS renders HTML and sends it back to the client. The end result is shown in Figure 14.4.

From this example you can see the flexibility of a COM object. In this example, an ASP page made use of the component. You easily could have written a Windows application to use the COM object. Now let's see how we can use this COM component under the .NET Framework.

**Figure 14.4** Web Client for the COM Component

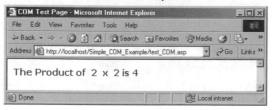

# Runtime Callable Wrappers

The semantics of object creation and maintenance are very different under COM and .NET. In order to invoke a COM component we need to know the class IDs and interface IDs of the component. We also need to call the *AddRef()* and *Release()* methods on the COM component to maintain its lifetime. The *AddRef()* method allocates memory for a COM component and the *Release()* method will release the memory resources. Unfortunately *managed* components are not aware of the *IUnknown* interface and it is not practical for the managed components to explicitly support this interface solely to support legacy COM components.

What we need is seamless support from the .NET runtime that allows managed components to transparently invoke COM components in the exact manner as it would invoke a managed component. This is done by creating a managed wrapper around the COM object, called the *Runtime Callable Wrapper (RCW)*. The RCW takes care of the incompatibilities between .NET and COM and acts as a proxy that makes the COM component accessible to managed components. Essentially the RCW is the bridge between COM and .NET assemblies, acting as a COM component on one side and as a managed component on the other. Since there is now an extra layer, there will be a performance hit while using wrappers. Figure 14.5 shows where RCWs fit into the .NET Framework.

**Figure 14.5** Runtime Callable Wrapper Architecture

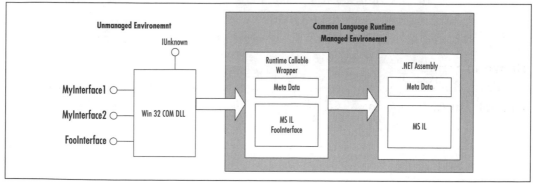

As you can see in Figure 14.5, RCW acts as a middleman between the COM component and the .NET assembly. The runtime will create one RCW for each COM component regardless of the number of references to that COM component. If there are 50 references to the COM object, all of them will be channeled through one RCW. The managed single .NET client can access multiple RCWs to reach different COM objects. The following lists the major tasks carried out by the RCW:

- **Marshalling** This is the most important functionality of the RCW. The RCW marshals the calls from the managed component to the COM component. This involves converting types into those recognized by the managed and unmanaged worlds, handling errors in the COM component and handling return values and output parameters. Further, this ensures that all threading and apartment issues are resolved.

- **Map Underlying Interfaces** The RCW maps calls to the underlying COM interfaces. Every time a new interface is requested, the RCW performs a *QueryInterface* on the underlying COM component and caches the returned interface. On subsequent calls, the cached interface is made available to the managed component. There is a single RCW for each COM component that is being accessed.

- **Maintain Object Lifetime** COM requires using *AddRef()* and *Release()* to maintain object lifetime. However, since the managed components do not explicitly call *AddRef()* and *Release()*, the RCW has to maintain a reference on the COM object to ensure that it is not released while a managed object is still connected to it. The RCW maintains a reference on each interface pointer it wraps, and calls *Release()* on these interfaces when it itself is being freed by the garbage collector.

- **Consume Interfaces** A COM component supports multiple interfaces such as *IUnknown*, *IDispatch*, and *IErrorInfo* that provide the plumbing necessary for COM to work. These have no parallels and are not required in the .NET Framework. The RCW consumes these interfaces and does not expose them to the managed object. If you look closely at Figure 14.5, you will view three interfaces in the COM component (*MyInterface1*, *MyInterface2*, and *FooInterface*). The RCW has consumed the *MyInterface1* and *MyInterface2* interfaces and made the *FooInterface* available in the RCW. You can think of *MyInterface1* and *MyInterface2* as similar to *IDispatch*; therefore their only purpose is to provide the plumbing for the COM object. In other words, the RCW hides certain interfaces that handle the COM object lifecycle and expose only the interfaces that provide functionality.

# Creating a Runtime Callable Wrapper for a COM Component

Creating a Runtime Callable Wrapper for a COM component is fairly straight-forward. There are two ways we can create a RCW:

- Using the Type Library Importer (TibImp.exe) command line utility
- Using Visual Studio .NET

We will learn both methods by creating a RCW for the simple COM object that we created previously. It is important to note that both of these methods use *early binding*. This means we have the *ProgID* or COM Registry information available at compile time for us. In other words, we know the name of the component, function name, and types that we're going to use. In our example the COM DLL name is *COM_Example.dll*, and we're going to use the *Multiply* function. With this information, we can bind to the component at compile time.

In some cases we do not have this information available to us and therefore we need to dynamically bind to a COM object at runtime. This mechanism is referred to as *late binding*. Both these methods have their merits and each will be examined.

## *Early Binding Using the TlbImp.exe Utility*

The purpose of the Type Library Importer (*TlbImp.exe*) utility is to add metadata information to COM components in order to make them behave like a .NET assembly. The key difference between COM components and .NET assemblies is the lack of metadata. By utilizing the *TlbImp.exe* utility it will import the COM type library to run under the .NET Framework by wrapping it in a .NET assembly. For an example, let's import our *COM_Example.dll* that we created earlier and import it to a .NET assembly that we will call *Managed_NET_Assembly.dll*. The following steps will outline how to do this:

1. Bring up a command line window.
2. Use the *TlbImp.exe* utility.

   ```
   Syntax: TlbImp.exe TypeLibName [Options]
   c:\TlbImp.exe COM_Example.dll /out:Managed_NET_Assembly.dll
   ```

**NOTE**

You can use the command prompt that comes with Visual Studio.NET by clicking on **MS Visual Studio .NET | Visual Studio .NET Tools | .NET Command Prompt** from the programs menu. Otherwise you need to set the PATH variables for the *TlbImp.exe* utility manually.

This command will create a new .NET assembly called *Managed_NET_Assembly.dll* in the current directory. The */out:* keyword is used to name the target DLL. Figure 14.6 shows the output of running the *TlbImp.exe* utility.

**Figure 14.6** Using the TlbImp.exe Utility

Once you've imported the COM component to a .NET assembly, it will now be available for you to use in your C# programs. The *Managed_Net_Assembly.dll* will behave identically to a native managed component. Table 14.1 shows some of the important parameters used in the *TlbImp.exe* utility.

**Table 14.1** Available Options for the *TlbImp.exe* Utility

| Parameter | Description |
| --- | --- |
| /asmversion:versionNumber | Specifies the version number of the assembly to produce. |
| /keyfile:filename | Signs the resulting assembly with a strong name using the publisher's official public/private key pair found in filename. |
| /namespace:namespace | Specifies the namespace in which to produce the assembly. |
| /out:filename | Specifies the name of the output file, assembly, and namespace in which to write the metadata definitions. The /out option has no effect on the assembly's namespace if the type library specifies the Interface Definition Language (IDL) custom attribute that explicitly controls the assembly's namespace. |

*Continued*

**Table 14.1** Continued

| Parameter | Description |
| --- | --- |
| /unsafe | Produces interfaces without .NET Framework security checks. Calling a method that is exposed in this way might pose a security risk. You should not use this option unless you are aware of the risks of exposing such code. We will look into unsafe code later in the chapter. |
| /? | Displays command syntax and options for the tool. |

Since we did not specify a namespace, the runtime will create a default namespace using the DLL name. In this case *Managed_NET_Assembly.dll* will belong to a .NET namespace called *COM_Example*. Remember, *Managed_NET_Assembly.dll* is a RCW and functions as a native component, but it acts as an intermediary between the runtime and the *Com_Example.dll* object.

## *Early Binding Using Visual Studio .NET to Create a RCW*

You can also use Visual Studio.NET to create the RCW, which is much simpler than using the *TlbImp.exe* utility. All the plumbing work is done for you by Visual Studio .NET and all you have to do is to add the COM DLL as a reference to an existing project. Here are the steps.

1. Right click on the **Solutions Explorer** of the project and select **Add Reference**.

2. Browse to the COM Component location you want to add. For our example, you can browse to the location of the *COM_Example.dll*. Please make sure you select the **COM** tab. The default tab is **.NET**. You can also navigate through the list to find the *COM_Example.dll*. It should appear in the component list under the **COM** tab. You should have something similar to that shown in Figure 14.7.

The .NET Framework will recognize the COM component and will create a managed assembly wrapper. It will also add the wrapper to the local cache of the project. The name of the Wrapper will be *interop* plus the DLL name. So for our example it will be called as *Interop.COM_Example*. This DLL could be found in the *bin* directory under either the *Release* or *Debug* subdirectories, depending whether you have released it or debugged it. You will be able to call this object as an assembly like any other inside the project scope.

**Figure 14.7** Adding a COM Component to Your Visual Studio .NET Project

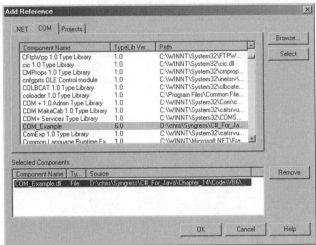

## Building a Client for the RCW

Now that we know how to early bind a COM component in the .NET Framework, let's build a sample client to invoke these RCWs. We'll create a Windows application to use our existing *COM_Example.dll*. The application will let you enter two integers and it will invoke the multiply function in the *COM_Example.dll* using our RCW. The RCW will pass the two integers to the COM component and then it will pass the result of the multiplication back from the COM component to the Windows Form to be displayed. Here are the steps to build the application.

1. Create a Windows Application project called **Simple_Net_Assembly** in Visual Studio .NET.

2. Add a reference to our *COM_Example.dll* by right-clicking on **Solutions Explorer** and selecting **Add Reference** as shown in Figure 14.7. We can also add the *Managed_Net_Assembly.dll* we created under the *TlbImp.exe* tool. However, there is no point in adding the RCW generated by the *TlbImp.exe* when Visual Studio will generate a RCW and add it for you.

3. Drag and drop the Windows controls from the **ToolBox** to the Web form design view. The list of Windows controls can be found in Table 14.2. These controls will build an interface to enter the input parameters (two integers).

**Table 14.2** Design Properties for RCW Windows Application

| Control Name | Type | Description |
|---|---|---|
| Lbl_Number1 | Label | The caption for first number input |
| Txt_Number1 | Text Box | The text box to enter the first number |
| Lbl_Number2 | Label | The caption for the second number input |
| Txt_Number2 | Text Box | The text box to enter the second number |
| Btn_Get_Result | Button | To initiate the method call to the COM component |
| Lbl_Result | Label | The caption for the result from the binding |
| Txt_Result | Text Box | The text box to display the result from multiplying number 1 and number 2 |

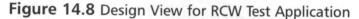

4. Use the components listed from Table 14.2 to create the user interface for the application. The Windows form should be similar to Figure 14.8.

**Figure 14.8** Design View for RCW Test Application

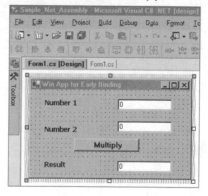

5. The next thing we need to do is write some code to call the COM component when the button is clicked. We'll add this code in the button's click event:

```
private void Btn_Get_Result_Click(object sender, System.EventArgs e)
{
    COM_Example.Multiply myMultiply = new
        COM_Example.Multiply();
    Txt_Result.Text = myMultiply.MultiplyNumbers(
        System.Convert.ToInt16(Txt_Number1.Text),
```

```
              System.Convert.ToInt16(Txt_Number2.Text)).ToString();
}
```

First we create a *myMultiply* variable and we invoke the *MultiplyNumbers* method in the COM component. The *number1* and *number2* text box arguments have to be converted to integers from a String type using the *System.Convert* class. The result will be displayed in the *Txt_result* text box.

6.  Now let's debug and run the application. The user will enter the two numbers as integers and press the **Multiply** button. We have not created any new methods or interfaces in our old COM_Example.dll. The same *Multiply()* method is used to produce the product for two given integers. The output will be similar to Figure 14.9.

**Figure 14.9** RCW Win Application in Action

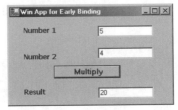

## Examining Runtime Callable Wrapper Properties

Let's look at our RCW in more detail. There is a tool called the Intermediate Disassembler (ILDASM.exe) in the .NET Framework. This is great tool to explore .NET assembly data structure.

### Debugging…

### ILADSM .NET Utility

ILDASM allows you to investigate the methods, properties, and classes of an assembly. Any managed component can be loaded to the ILDASM viewer. The data in the ILADSM is displayed as MSIL code. We can also convert our C# file to MSIL code using the Dump menu option from the ILDASM menu.

Let's look at our wrapper class in the *ILDASM.exe* utility. Start the utility by typing in *ildasm.exe* at the .NET command prompt. To open an assembly that you wish to view, simply click on **File | Open** in the menu.

Our assembly will look like Figure 14.9 when it has been loaded to the *ILDASM*. Remember you can use either *Interop.COM_Example.dll* created by Visual Studio .NET or the *Managed_NET_Assembly.dll* that we created using the *TlbImp.exe* utility. It is important to note that both RCWs are the same. I have used the latter in Figure 14.10.

**Figure 14.10** Using Intermediate Language Disassembler to Investigate RCW Properties

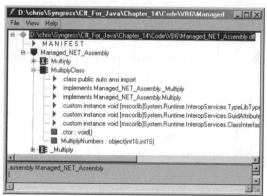

If you are familiar with COM objects, you'll find that there are no *IUtility* or *IDispatch* interfaces in the assembly. These interfaces were essential in the COM world to force components to have a specified structure. If the interface or the structure of the component is modified, it could not communicate with another component. The structure of these components (which includes the interfaces that the components implement) is recorded in the registry. In the .NET world we do not need these rigid structured interfaces any more because of the meta-data information contained in the assemblies. Therefore the *IDispatch* and *IUtility* interfaces have been filtered out by *TlbImp.exe* utility.

Furthermore, there are no *AddRef()* and *Release()* methods. All of these methods are still available in the COM object, however. Remember that the RCW is just a vehicle that the .NET Framework uses to get to the COM component, and doesn't actually modify the COM component itself. It relies on the System Registry to locate the COM object. To illustrate this point, let's unregister the COM component.

```
c:\regsvr32 COM_Example.dll -u
```

Now if you try to execute our sample Windows application, it will result in an error. Therefore, we can conclude that the RCW is just a vehicle to get to COM components. Now let's try to move the *COM_Example.dll* to another directory and try to execute our Windows application. Again, you'll find that it will result in an error.

The reason for this is because the RCW relies on the registry data to locate the COM component. Since we change the location of the *COM_Example.dll*, the registry values are invalid. If you unregister the *COM_Example.dll* from its original location, then copying it to a new location and registering it again will result in a successful execution.

## Using Late Binding RCWs

The previous methods we discussed relate to early binding to RCWs. We knew exactly what the COM registry name was (*COM_Example.Multiply*) before we executed our applications. The COM registry name was hard-coded into the source code as a reference in the projects. Sometimes we need to use late binding when we develop code. Late binding is a mechanism where at runtime we read a *ProgID* of an object and create an instance of it on the fly. The difference with early binding is that in late binding we do not know the target COM registry name. The name is provided when the application is executing during runtime.

In the COM world we used to implement the *IDispatch* interface specifically to support late binding for COM components. The .NET Framework's support for late binding to COM components is a little bit more difficult. With late binding we do not know about the target object type, so first we need to get an idea of the object type. Then we have to come up with a way to pass the input parameters to the object and then invoke the COM DLL. Let's try to learn all these steps using a sample Windows application in Visual Studio .NET.

Let's create a small Visual Studio .NET project to explain late binding. The specification for the project is the same for the early binding project. We will create a small Windows application that takes in two integers and displays the result of them. But we do not know that the component we are creating is of type *COM_example.Multiply*; type information is provided by the user at runtime. Here are the steps to create the project.

1. Create a Windows application and call it *COM_Late_Binding*.

2. Create the following controls on a Form. (Remember we are not adding any references to this project. This is late binding, and the binding is done at runtime.) Add the Windows controls from the **ToolBox** to the Windows Form. The list of controls can be found in Table 14.3. After adding the controls the Windows Form will look similar to Figure 14.11.

**Table 14.3** Design Properties for Late Binding Windows Application

| Control Name | Type | Description |
| --- | --- | --- |
| Lbl_Caption | Label | To display the top caption. |
| Lbl_COM_Name | Label | The caption for the COM registry name text box. |
| Txt_COM_Name | Text Box | The text box to enter COM registry name. This name is used to look up the registry when late binding is activated. |
| Lbl_Header | Label | The caption for the header for the input parameters. |
| Lbl_Number1 | Label | The caption for first number input. |
| Txt_Number1 | Text Box | The text box to enter the first number. |
| Lbl_Number2 | Label | The caption for the second number input. |
| Txt_Number2 | Text Box | The text box to enter the second number. |
| Btn_Invoke | Button | To initiate the late binding process. |
| Lbl_Result | Label | The caption for the result from the binding. |
| Txt_Result | Text Box | The text box to display the result from multiplying number 1 and number 2. |

3. Now we need to write some code. Let's populate the *Btn_Invoke_Click* event for this application. Here is the complete code.

```
private void Btn_Invoke_Click(object sender,
    System.EventArgs e)
{
    Type myType = Type.GetTypeFromProgID(Txt_COM_Name.Text);
    object myObject = Activator.CreateInstance(myType);
```

```
    object [] inputParameters = new object []
        {Txt_Number1.Text,Txt_Number2.Text};
    Txt_Result.Text = myType.InvokeMember("MultiplyNumbers",
        System.Reflection.BindingFlags.InvokeMethod,
        null,myObject,inputParameters).ToString();
}
```

**Figure 14.11** Form Design for COM Late Binding

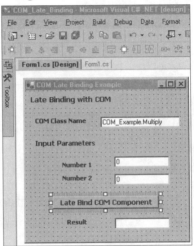

Let's take a look at this code. The top line will get the COM registry name or *ProgID* (in our case it will be *COM_Example.Multiply*) from the input box and query its type. Then using the *Activator* class we will create an instance of that type. The *Activator* and the *Type* classes are used to query the data type of the binding object. Using the *Type* class we can extract the data type information at runtime for a given object reference. The *Activator* class has a method called *CreateInstance()*, used to instantiate an object for a given type. Then we create an array of objects to store the input parameters for a method invocation. At runtime we do not know what types these input parameters are going to be; therefore we create objects type of *System.Object*. Since *System.Object* is the super class of every .NET class, we will not have a type compatibility issue.

The next line will use the *InvokeMember* method of the *Type* class to communicate with the COM component. We specify the function name *MultiplyNumbers*, the target object (*myObject*), and the input parameters (*inputParameters*) to invoke method. Note that we are not using Reflection on this project. The *System.Reflection.BindingFlags.InvokeMethod* is a compiler directive to facilitate late binding.

4. Now let's debug and compile the code. The user needs to enter the COM registry class name (*COM_Example.Multipy*), number1, and number2 inputs, and press the button. The result of the late bound COM query could be displayed in the result text box. The output should be similar to Figure 14.12.

**Figure 14.12** COM Late Binding Application

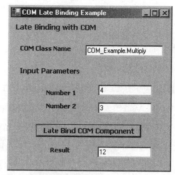

## Limitations of Using RCWs

Finally, the last thing we'll look at is the limitations you need to take into account when using RCWs:

- If you are using COM components in a .NET application you still need to register the COM components. This will unfortunately take away the xcopy philosophy in .NET architecture. Just copying the files across will not result in a successful deployment. (You also need to register the COM components.)

- A Runtime Callable Wrapper only channels the instructions to the COM components. The actual code is still executed at the COM level. Therefore we are still getting unmanaged code, and running unmanaged code under the .NET Runtime incurs a performance hit.

- The data access in a COM component is done by using Active Data Objects (ADO). ADO uses COM-based marshalling. If we were using .NET assemblies we could have used ADO.NET to leverage XML based marshalling to increase performance.

# Working with ActiveX Controls

ActiveX controls could generally be described as prepackaged COM components that are small and easy to work with. They're typically dropped into a form, and they might or might not have a user interface. ActiveX controls are a perfect example of binary reuse; for example, you can create a control in Visual Basic and use it in a C++ application. There are thousands of ActiveX controls developed, sold, and used over the past few years. For this reason, Microsoft made it easy to import ActiveX controls into .NET.

Most user interface programming in the Windows environment makes use of prepackaged controls. The notion of distributing reusable software containing user interface elements, methods, properties, and events in a convenient package that plugs into a smart environment for rapid development has been fantastically successful in the software marketplace. It started with 16-bit VBX controls and moved to ActiveX controls when Windows moved to a 32-bit environment. The ActiveX controls are usually a dynamic link library (DLL) or an .OCX file.

The user interface portion of .NET, called Windows Forms, provides support for developing your own Windows Forms controls. Think of them as conceptually doing the same thing as ActiveX controls, except they're written for .NET. Therefore we need to convert these ActiveX components to new Windows Forms controls to run under the .NET Framework. The following sections will show you how to do this. First we will try to understand a bit about ActiveX controls and how they differ form Windows Forms controls. Then we will investigate the methods available to import existing ActiveX components into the .NET domain.

## Differences between ActiveX Controls and Windows Forms Controls

ActiveX controls are built on Component Object Model (COM) architecture, which is limited to the Windows platform. On the other hand, Windows Forms controls are built for the .NET Framework, which is the key difference between the two. The traditional COM components have to be imported to run under the .NET Framework. ActiveX components are prepackaged COM components working together to ease software development. Therefore we need to import ActiveX components to run under the .NET environment.

You might be wondering whether we can run Windows Forms controls on other platforms. Windows Forms controls are tightly integrated to use the Win 32 APIs. Therefore, it will not be very efficient on other platforms. But it does extend the reach to other platforms compared to ActiveX components.

Most of the prepackaged ActiveX controls were written in Visual Basic (VB). Inheritance is a very important concept in OO programming. Unfortunately Microsoft did not implement the Inheritance concept well in VB. Having multiple interfaces basically confused the developers and added more complexity to the code. Microsoft has taken measures to rectify this problem with VB.NET. Windows Forms controls that are written in VB.NET, C#, or any other CLR-compliant language will truly inherit from the basic classes in the Windows Forms controls. Specifically the controls can directly inherit from *System.Windows.Forms.Control* class and extend their functionality. Therefore developers can use Inheritance to build complex software components under Windows Forms controls. This feature wasn't available for VB ActiveX controls.

These are some of the critical differences between ActiveX controls and Windows Forms controls. There are many applications that are built on ActiveX controls. Especially most of Microsoft's Web technologies were dominated with ActiveX controls in the past few years. You can still make use of these controls by importing them to .NET. There are two ways of doing this:

- Use ActiveX Control Importer utility (*AxImp.exe*)
- Use Visual Studio .NET

## Using the ActiveX Control Importer Utility (*AxImp.exe*)

The Microsoft .NET Framework comes with a set of command line utilities; one of them is the *AxImp.exe* utility. You can use this utility to create a wrapper class for any ActiveX control that you can use under the Windows Forms environment. The wrapper control is derived from the class called *System.Windows.Forms.AxHost*. This wrapper class will act as a proxy between the ActiveX control and .Net runtime. The following is the syntax for using the utility:

```
Aximp.exe [options]{file.dll | file.ocx}
```

The filename should be a valid ActiveX DLL or .OCX file. Table 14.4 lists some of the important options available for this utility.

**Table 14.4** Options Available for the *AxImp.exe* Utility

| Options | Description |
| --- | --- |
| /help | Displays command syntax and options for the tool. |

**Continued**

**Table 14.4** Continued

| Options | Description |
| --- | --- |
| /out:*filename* | Specifies the name of the assembly to create. |
| /source | Generates C# source code for the Windows Forms wrapper. |
| /? | Displays command syntax and options for the tool. |

Let's look at an example on how to use this tool. We are going to pick an existing ActiveX control and create a wrapper class for it. Let's utilize the Microsoft Date and Time Picker control, which is one that is regularly used. The filename for the control is *mscomct2.ocx*, and it should be located in the *system32* subdirectory under your main Windows directory. So for example, if you are running Windows 2000, the file will be located at *C:\winnt\system32\mscomct2.ocx*. By creating a wrapper for this control we'll be able to use it in our C# application. To create the wrapper:

1.  Bring up a .NET command prompt window. Use **MS Visual Studio. NET | Visual Studio .NET Tools | .NET Command Prompt** from the Programs menu. Otherwise you need to manually set the PATH variables for the *AxImp.exe* utility.

2.  Navigate to the c:\winnt\system32\ directory.

3.  Type the following command:

```
AxImp.exe mscomct2.ocx /out:ActiveX_Date_Time_Wrapper.dll /source
```

This will create an ActiveX Importer wrapper for the *mscomct2.ocx* control called *ActiveX_Date_Time_Wrapper.dll*. The *AxImp.exe* utility will result in multiple DLL in most cases. Remember that an ActiveX control is a combination of COM DLLs that work in harmony for a common goal. Therefore the runtime will create a wrapper for each COM DLL. Figure 14.13 shows the output for using the *AxImp.exe* utility.

**Figure 14.13** Executing Commands with the *AxImp.exe* Utility

As you can see this will generate a set of assemblies. The .NET runtime will create an implementation module called *MSComCtl2.dll* and a proxy class called

*ActiveX_Date_Time_Wrapper.dll.* We can use the *ActiveX_Date_Time_Wrapper.dll* as a vehicle to execute methods and properties on *MSComCtl2.dll.* The .NET runtime will execute method calls through the *ActiveX_Date_Time_Wrapper.dll.* Then this DLL will communicate with the *MSComCTl2.dll* to produce the desired output. The developer interacts only with the wrapper DLL and the runtime is responsible for invoking, marshalling, and reallocating memory for the wrapper. The bridging concept will be much clearer if we can look into the structure of the wrapper class. Figure 14.14 shows the properties of the ActiveX wrapper using the *ILDASM* utility.

**Figure 14.14** Investigating the Properties of the ActiveX Wrapper

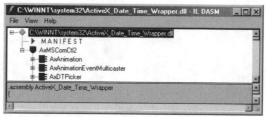

Observe that the *AxImp.exe* utility has prefixed *Ax* in front of all the interfaces available. It had renamed *MSComCtl2* to *AxMSComCtl2* and *Animation* to *AxAnimation.* In theory the *Animation* method in *MSComCtl2.dll* will match to the *AxAnimation* method of the *ActiveX_Date_Time_Wrapper.dll.*

Now you can use this wrapper class in your C# applications. This wrapper is treated the same as a native .NET assembly by the .NET runtime.

# Using Visual Studio .NET to Import ActiveX Controls

The Visual Studio.NET IDE makes the conversion process seamless and hides the complexity from the developer. This method is relatively easier than using the *AxImp.exe* command line utility. Let's use the same ActiveX control we used in the previous scenario to highlight the effectiveness of the Visual Studio .NET IDE. Here is a sample application to convert ActiveX controls using Visual Studio .NET. To import the ActiveX control:

1. Open Visual Studio .NET and create a new project: **File | New | Project Menu items**.

2. Select **Windows Project** from the **New Project** window.

3. Name the project **Simple_ActiveX_Control**.

4. Select **Tools** from the Menu bar and then click on **Customize ToolBox**. Figure 14.15 is a screen shot of the window that appears.

**Figure 14.15** Creating an ActiveX Wrapper Using Visual Studio .NET

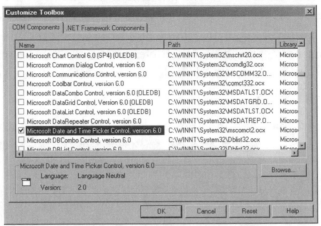

5. We can toggle between the *COM Components* and the *Windows Forms Components* in the toolbox. Select the **COM Components** tab.

6. Select **Microsoft Date and Time Picker Control, version 6.0** from the component list. This ActiveX control will be added to the available Windows Forms control list now. When you click on the **ToolBox** menu you will see this control (short name *DTPicker*) added to the list, as shown on Figure 14.16.

**Figure 14.16** DTPicker Control in the Toolbox List

Now we can create a sample application using this ActiveX control. We can simply drag and drop the control from the toolbox to our Windows Forms. Let's create a Windows application that will display a Date and Time Picker control and ask the user to select a date. Then the user can enter a value for *number of days*. The application will add the amount of days to the selected day and display the new date. As an example, if I select today as the date and enter **1** as the *number of days* value, the application will add one day to the current day and return tomorrow's date as the result. Table 14.5 is a list of controls we are embedding to the form. Now create the form to look like Figure 4.17.

**Table 14.5** Design Properties for ActiveX Test Application

| Control Name | Type | Description |
| --- | --- | --- |
| Lbl_Caption | Label | To display the top caption. |
| axDTPicker1 | Date Time Picker (DTPicker) | The ActiveX control to pick the date and time. We drag this control from the toolbox (DTPicker control—refer to Figure 14.17). |
| Lbl_Days | Label | Caption to enter number of days. |
| Txt_Days | Text Box | The text box to enter number of days. |
| Btn_Get_New_Date | Button | The button to initiate the call to the ActiveX wrapper. |
| Lbl_Result | Label | The caption for the result of the new date. |
| Lbl_New_Date | Label | The label to display the result of the new date. Alternatively you can use a text box control. |

**Figure 14.17** Adding the DTPicker to a Win Form

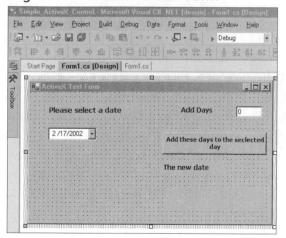

Now we need to write a bit of code to initiate the process with the button click. The following code is for our button click event:

```
private void Btn_Get_New_Date_Click(object sender,
    System.EventArgs e)
{
    int day =0;
    int month = 0;
    int year = 0;
    int interval = 0;
    day = System.Convert.ToInt16(axDTPicker1.Day);
    month = System.Convert.ToInt16(axDTPicker1.Month);
    year = System.Convert.ToInt16(axDTPicker1.Year);
    interval = System.Convert.ToInt16(Txt_Days.Text);
    DateTime selectedDate = new DateTime(year,month,day);
    DateTime newDate = selectedDate.AddDays(interval);
    Lbl_New_Date.Text = newDate.ToLongDateString();
}
```

**NOTE**

When you convert an ActiveX control to run under the .NET Framework, Visual Studio puts the prefix "Ax" in front of the object's name. In our example, the default name given to our date time control when it is dragged and dropped to a form will be *axDTPicker1*.

Let's have a look at the code. First we get the selected *day*, *month*, and *year* value from the *Date and Time Picker ActiveX* control. As you can see it is behaving very similarly to a native .NET assembly in Visual Studio .NET. The developer is actually unaware of the wrappers that are created to access these ActiveX controls. Then we basically create a new *Date* object with these values and invoke the *AddDay()* method to produce the target date, which we will display to the user. Figure 14.18 displays the output of our program.

If you check the references of the project, you will notice a reference to *AxMSComCtl2*. Visual Studio seamlessly does all this work, by loading the ActiveX component into the *ToolBox*. If we were using the *AxImp.exe* utility we need to add a reference and declare the variable manually. Therefore Visual Studio .NET makes our life much simpler in this way.

**Figure 14.18** Win Form Client Program for the ActiveX Wrapper

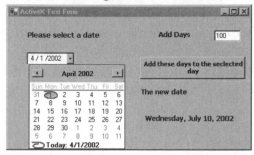

# Working with Pointers

Under certain situations, developers need the ability to use pointers to write performance critical code by manually manipulating the system memory. Pointer support is available only in C# and Managed C++ under the .NET Framework. Pointers by their nature are dangerous and should be handled with great care. When pointers directly access memory location it creates an *unsafe* environment under the .NET Framework. Therefore pointer code is referred to as *unsafe code*. We make an unsafe environment by using pointers because we give up some of the protection that the CLR provides by default, such as garbage collection, protection against uninitialized variables, dangling pointers, and accessing memory beyond the bounds of an array. As most of you know, Java doesn't support pointers because of their unsafe nature. But pointers do serve a purpose, so let us continue and try to understand what *unsafe code* is.

## Unsafe Code

We should make a clear distinction between *unsafe code* and *unmanaged code*. Unmanaged code does not run under the CLR. On the other hand, unsafe code will run under the CLR but will not benefit from any CLR advantages. One of those advantages is the memory management by CLR. Unsafe code will be able to access memory locations *directly* using pointers. Therefore the CLR will not be able to manage memory for unsafe code. The rest of the CLR functionalities are still available for unsafe code. Hence, any unrelated memory errors will still raise an exception. Unsafe code is indeed managed code with a few exceptions. C# allows you to write unsafe code, but unmanaged code cannot be written in C#, or for that matter, by any .NET language.

As you've learned in Chapter 5 the CLR handles memory management. As you know, when objects are instantiated they are allocated memory from the heap. When the object is destroyed and all references to the memory are freed up, the garbage collector steps in to reclaim the memory space. When the garbage collector runs, it can move chunks of memory around in order to compress them and free up some memory space to maximize heap storage. Since managed code does not have direct memory access, it doesn't get affected when the garbage collector move objects around in memory. It will still retain its object references because the CLR is in charge of the memory management.

Unfortunately, with pointers this causes an issue because pointers have direct access to memory. Pointers contain the memory address of an object and they always expect the object to be present at that location. If the garbage collector moves the object from that address to another, it can cause unexpected behavior and may even cause the program to crash. Therefore, we need a mechanism to let the garbage collector know that we are using pointers and that it should not move the contents of the memory block that is being accessed via pointers.

C# implements pointer functionality with the *unsafe* and *fixed* keywords. The ability of C# to hold the contents of memory fixed is called *pinning*. When an object is pinned, it is guaranteed that the object will remain in memory while there are outstanding pointers to it.

# The *unsafe* Keyword

The *unsafe* keyword signifies an unsafe context. This keyword acts as the foundation to implement pointers in your code. Once a block of code is marked as unsafe, the C# compiler will allow you to write code that will perform the following functions:

- Use pointers
- Dereference pointers
- Use the & operator to obtain the address of the object to which you want to point

If we do not use the *unsafe* keyword, the compiler will result in an error. Therefore the compiler forces us to declare this keyword before we write any pointer code. The *unsafe* keyword can be applied to any block of code within a class. The block of code may be an entire method, a property, a single line, or any other code block.

> **NOTE**
>
> An *unsafe* keyword cannot be applied to an entire class.

For example, the following code will instruct the compiler to treat the whole *Person_In_Line* data structure as unsafe:

```
public unsafe struct Person_In_Line
{
    public int Current_Position;
    public Person_In_Line* Back;
    public Person_In_Line* Front;
}
```

We can also make the individual variables to be declared as *unsafe*:

```
public struct Person_In_Line
{
    public int Current_Position;
    public unsafe Person_In_Line* Back;
    public unsafe Person_In_Line* Front;
}
```

In this case we are instructing the compiler that the *Back* and *Front* variable is unsafe code. These variables are a pointer to a *Person_In_Line* structure and pinned to a memory location. The ★ operator is the compiler directive to recognize a pointer in a data structure.

## The *fixed* Keyword

The *fixed* keyword pins an object down to a fixed memory location when the code is being executed. This allows the garbage collector to recognize the pinned object so it will not relocate it.

It is your responsibility to ensure that pointers created by *fixed* statements do not survive beyond execution of those statements. For example, when pointers created by *fixed* statements are passed to external APIs, it is your responsibility to ensure that the APIs retain no memory of these pointers.

Using fixed objects may cause heap fragmentation because they cannot be reallocated or deleted by the garbage collector. Therefore objects should be fixed only when absolutely necessary and then only for the shortest amount of time possible. The *fixed* keyword cannot be used on managed types. However, if the managed type has value types, you can declare pointers to these value types. Doing so requires the runtime to pin the entire managed object to a fixed location in memory. Let's try to illustrate these points in an example.

In this example, we will try to directly manipulate memory using pointers. Our small C# program will display the text *Syngress Media Ltd* on the screen. We will display each of the three strings using different methods using pointers. Lets look at the complete code.

```
using System;
class Unsafe
{
   static string testString = "Syngress";
   unsafe static void DisplayString(char* pointerToChar)
   {
      for (int i = 0; pointerToChar[i] != '\0'; ++i)
      {
         System.Console.Write(pointerToChar[i]+" ");
      }
   }

   unsafe static void Main()
   {
      char[] text = new char [3];
      text[0] = 'L';
      text[1] = 't';
      text[2] = 'd';
fixed (char* pointer = testString) DisplayString(pointer);
fixed (char* pointer = "Media") DisplayString(pointer);
fixed (char* pointer = &text[0]) DisplayString(pointer);
   }
}
```

Let's look at the code closely. First we declared a class variable called *testString* with the value *Syngress*:

```
static string testString = "Syngress";
```

Then we create a function called *DisplayString* that takes a pointer to a character and displays the contents till the *null* value is found, which is represented by *\0*. As you know, a string could be described as an *array of chars*. Therefore this function will navigate through the memory space and display each memory location's content until it finds *null*.

Then we have the *Main()* method that declares an array of characters to hold the value *Ltd*. Let's see how we can display the different strings using pointers.

```
fixed (char* pointer = testString) DisplayString(pointer);
```

This line will declare a pointer to a character, and that pointer will point at the *testString* variable, which is fixed to a memory location. Then the *DisplayString* function is invoked.

```
fixed (char* pointer = "Media") DisplayString(pointer);
```

This line will declare a pointer to a character and will point at the string *Media*:

```
fixed (char* pointer = &text[0]) DisplayString(pointer);
```

We will also declare a pointer to a character that will have the memory address of the *text* array. The memory address of the array is obtained by using the & operator.

It is important to note that in all instances of the pointer, the variable is fixed or pinned to a memory location by the .NET runtime. This is done by using the *fixed* keyword. Let's name this file *unsafe.cs* and compile it using the command line C# compiler (*csc.exe*). To compile this you will need to add the */unsafe* compiler directive because it contains unsafe code. It should look something like this:

```
C:\csc Unsafe.cs /unsafe
```

The output of the program follows.

```
S y n g r e s s M e d i a L t d
```

The last thing to remember about pointers is that if a type is passed by reference to a method, then that object will have to be pinned before its address can be assigned to a pointer type. This makes sense because we do not want the garbage collector to delete any references to the address. Trying to access an object passed by reference outside a fixed block will also raise a compiler error. A single fixed block can pin objects only of a certain type. If you need to pin objects of different types, you will have to use nested fixed blocks.

# Summary

This chapter concentrates on accessing legacy and pre-.NET code. We have to be realistic and acknowledge that no organization is going to dump all their systems and embrace pure .NET architecture. Therefore it is essential that the .NET Framework consists of good interoperability tools. The .NET Framework uses command line utilities and the Visual Studio .NET IDE to implement these tools. Visual Studio .NET provides a user-friendly and seamless integration environment for the developers. It hides most of the underlying complexities of the framework.

Previous Microsoft software architecture such as COM and ActiveX components are widely used around the world. Visual Studio .NET or command line tools are used to import these components into .NET space. This is achieved by using wrappers around COM components. We can use the *TblImp.exe* command line utility to create a wrapper around a COM component. An ActiveX control wrapper is created using the *AxImp.exe* command line utility. These COM and ActiveX wrappers can be generated alternatively by adding a reference to a Visual Studio .NET project. These wrappers are necessary to supply the metadata to the .NET runtime. This metadata is the key difference between these wrapper assemblies and the COM or ActiveX components. We can build wrappers at compile time (*early binding*) or at runtime (*late binding*).

The .NET Framework also allows runtime communication with other DLLs using the Platform Invocation Services (*PInvoke*). This will let the developer access the Win32 DLLs at runtime. This is implemented by using the *DllImport* attribute in C#. On top of all these features, pointer manipulation is also available in C# to accommodate mission critical scenarios. It is implemented by using *unsafe* and *fixed* keywords.

# Solutions Fast Track

## Working with Unmanaged Code

- ☑ Unmanaged code is defined as code that runs outside of the CLR. This includes COM components, ActiveX components, and Win32 DLL calls.

- ☑ Unmanaged code could be accessed either through a wrapper class or through Platform Invocation Service at runtime.

# Working with the Platform Invocation Utility

☑ *PInvoke* is used to invoke functions in Win32 DLLs.

☑ You need to know the name of the DLL you want to access (e.g., user32.dll).

☑ You need the method name of the DLL function (*MessageBox()*).

☑ Attach the *DllImport* attribute before the function name.

☑ Add the *EntryPoint* parameter of the *DllImport* attribute to change the function name.

☑ You can also use the *MarshalAs* attribute to alter default marshalling of data.

# Working with COM Components

☑ COM components can be run under the .NET Framework.

☑ There are utilities that will create a Runtime Callable Wrapper (RCW) class around the COM component. This wrapper class will act as a proxy to the CLR.

☑ We can use either Type Library Importer (*TlbImp.exe*) or Visual Studio .NET to build wrappers around COM objects.

☑ There is a performance hit with using these wrappers.

# Working with ActiveX Controls

☑ ActiveX components can also be run under the .NET Framework.

☑ Like COM, we need to create wrapper classes to communicate with the CLR. These wrapper classes can be created by the *AxImp.exe* utility or Visual Studio .NET.

☑ Most ActiveX components will result in multiple assemblies after conversion.

☑ You can add these components to the Visual Studio toolbox and drag and drop them to your Windows Forms.

## Working with Pointers

- ☑ Pointer syntax is available in C# to access memory directly. This is implemented using the *unsafe* and *fixed* keywords.

- ☑ The *unsafe* keyword instructs CLR to suspend memory management on the specified code block.

- ☑ The *unsafe* keyword can be applied to any block of code within a class. The block of code may be an entire method, a property, a single line, or any other code block.

- ☑ The *fixed* keyword pins an object down to a fixed memory location.

- ☑ If a type is passed by reference to a method, then that object will have to be pinned before its address can be assigned to a pointer type.

# Frequently Asked Questions

The following Frequently Asked Questions, answered by the authors of this book, are designed to both measure your understanding of the concepts presented in this chapter and to assist you with real-life implementation of these concepts. To have your questions about this chapter answered by the author, browse to **www.syngress.com/solutions** and click on the **"Ask the Author"** form.

**Q:** If a COM component has 100 references to it how many Runtime Callable Wrappers does the runtime need to track the COM Component?

**A:** Just one. There is one RCW for each COM component regardless of the references to the object.

**Q:** What is the difference between *PInvoke* and COM wrappers?

**A:** Platform Invocation Service (*PInvoke*) is used at runtime to communicate with Win32 DLL. COM wrappers are proxy objects that could be early bound to C# code.

**Q:** How does the garbage collector treat a managed component, which has an unsafe pointer as a class?

**A:** From the garbage collector's point of view the whole managed object is treated differently for memory management. Therefore memory will not be reallocated for this managed object. The whole object is pinned to the memory location and not just the pointer class variable.

**Q:** What is the difference between the treatment for managed code and unsafe code by the .NET runtime?

**A:** Memory management. All the other CLR utilities (such as Type checking) are available for unsafe code.

# Chapter 15

# Microsoft Says JUMP—Java User Migration Path

## Solutions in this chapter:

# Introduction

Now that you have learned the C# language exhaustively, you are equipped with enough skills to develop full-fledged Windows or Web applications. With your new knowledge about the features and the capabilities of the C# language, you are in a position to assess its suitability against that of the Java language as a platform for developing applications, and to choose between the two.

One thing for sure is that the .NET platform is very much here, and here to stay. As a developer, it is a platform you want to get familiar with and have as part of your repertoire. With the aid of this book and the leverage provided by your Java experience, you have learned C# quite easily and quite thoroughly. However, if you still prefer sticking to the Java syntax but want to use the .NET platform, Microsoft has the solution you need.

The .NET platform originally was designed with the primary objective of enabling as many developers using different languages as possible to avail the .NET Framework. To encourage Java developers to use the .NET platform, Microsoft formulated a scheme called JUMP (Java User Migration Path) to .NET. As the name suggests, JUMP to .NET offers developers a number of paths for migrating to the .NET platform. These include tools for converting Visual J++ applications for .NET, a tool for migrating existing code entirely to the C# language, and a new language, J# (pronounced J-Sharp), that uses the Java language syntax for creating new .NET applications. As the product documentation states, "Microsoft Visual J# .NET is a development tool that developers who are familiar with the Java-language syntax can use to build applications and services on the .NET Framework. It integrates the Java language syntax into the Visual Studio .NET shell. Microsoft Visual J# .NET also supports the functionality found in Visual J++ 6.0 including Microsoft extensions. However, Microsoft Visual J# .NET is not a tool for developing applications intended to be run on a Java Virtual Machine. Applications and services built with Visual J# .NET will run only in the .NET Framework. Visual J# .NET has been independently developed by Microsoft. It is not endorsed or approved by Sun Microsystems, Inc." Thus, J# uses only the Java language syntax and not the Java Foundation classes. Besides, as mentioned, applications created with J# will not run on any Java Virtual Machine (JVM).

At the time of this writing, Microsoft has just released the Java Conversion Language Assistant (JCLA), which is part of their JUMP to .NET strategy. According to the documentations, the purpose of the JCLA is to help move Visual J++ 6.0 projects to C# and the .NET Framework. The JCLA tool will convert

Java-language code to the C# syntax, and Java code that accesses most JDK 1.1.4 level classes to use the .NET framework directly. The tool is currently available for download and Microsoft is planning to include it in the future versions of Visual Studio.NET. This tool is beyond the scope of this book and will not be discussed. Latest information in this regard is available from the MSDN Web site.

# What Is J#?

J# is a complete implementation of the Java language specification. J# allows the majority of existing Java applications to run after recompilation or after binary conversion. However, J# code is different from Java code and does not use the Java Foundation classes. J# code is not compiled into a byte code as is Java code. Therefore, J# cannot be compiled using a JDK or any other development environment for Java, nor can it be run by a JVM. This means that a Java *.class* file cannot be used within a J# project and vice versa. However, Microsoft's byte code converter can be used to convert Java *.class* files into Microsoft Intermediate Language (MSIL). The byte code converter also allows batch conversion of a collection of Java class files and hence is quite fast. This converted code is compatible with the .NET platform and can be called from within a J# application. Nevertheless, this byte code conversion needs to be done during development process, not at runtime.

J# was developed by Microsoft to encourage Java developers to migrate to the .NET platform. Naturally, with J# code being compiled into MSIL, J# is designed to work on the .NET platform only.

J# is quite compatible with Visual J++ and implements its extensions to Java. This includes Component Object Model (COM) support and the J/Direct native code interface. This allows for migration of VJ++ projects to J#. However, J# functionality is restricted to the JDK1.1.4 level and as per indications from Microsoft, later versions of the JDK will not be emulated. This is primarily because Microsoft feels that JDK compatibility is irrelevant to them. The .NET framework makes up for the lack of compatibility of J# with the JDK libraries.

The J# interface blends with the .NET framework, although not as smoothly as C# does. Specifically speaking, J# code cannot define new .NET properties, events, value types, or delegates. If these are already defined in code written in another language, J# can make use of them. Still, the inability of J# to define these limits its scope and interoperability as compared to other .NET languages. Thus, J# is meant primarily for those Java developers who seek to move to the .NET platform but need to preserve or enhance their Java language projects.

Such developers can use their existing skills in Java to write J# code to move on to the .NET platform before making the full leap to C#.

Visual J# is the development tool Microsoft offers for developing J# applications. Visual J# not only provides the transition to the .NET platform, but also enables the use of Java syntax (as explained earlier, J# follows the Java syntax, but is not Java by any means, and hence, use of the term "Java syntax") to create XML (extensible markup language)-based Web services.

Visual J# technology enables developers and users to make Java code operable on the .NET platform. It also allows existing applications developed with Visual J++ to be modified to execute on the .NET framework. This means that such applications can now interoperate with other .NET-based languages and applications.

# Features of Visual J#

Visual J# has the following features:

- Visual J# applications and services will run only on the .NET platform. They are not understood by any JVM and hence will not compile or run on any JVM. Visual J# is neither endorsed, nor approved by Sun Microsystems. It is an independent endeavor on the part of Microsoft that targets Java developers.

- Visual J# tools support complete integration with the integrated development environment (IDE) of Visual Studio.NET. A Visual J# developer can easily access all the features of the IDE.

- Visual J# has been designed to target the .NET framework. Thus, it provides full integration with the .NET functionality available as XML-based Web services, ASP.NET, ADO.NET etc. It also allows integration with other .NET languages.

- Visual J# includes tools to convert (and automatically upgrade, if required) existing Visual J++ 6.0 projects to the new Visual Studio .NET format. It provides existing Visual J++ developers with tools to migrate to Visual J# and develop .NET applications and components.

# Using Visual J#

To reiterate, you can install and hence, use, Visual J# only on the .NET platform. To install Visual J#, simply download and run the setup file available from the MSDN Web site http://msdn.microsoft.com/visualj/jsharp/beta.asp.

As of this writing, Visual J# is available only as a Beta 1.0 version. However, Microsoft is slated to release the Beta 2 version shortly. Note that the Beta 2 version would require Visual Studio 7.0 to be installed on your computer.

Once you have installed the Visual J# application on your system, use the **Start | Programs | Microsoft Visual Studio.NET | Visual J#.NET** path to run Visual J#.NET. To start a J# application, follow these steps:

1. On the Visual J#.NET application window, choose **File | New Project** as shown in Figure 15.1. This will open a new project window as shown in Figure 15.2.

**Figure 15.1** The Visual J#.NET Application Window

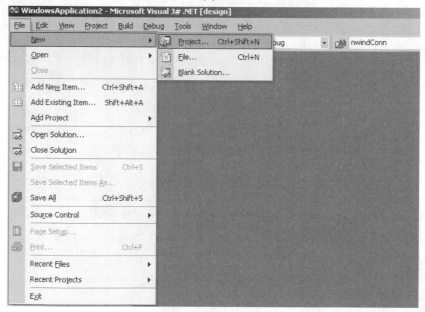

2. Choose **Visual J# Projects** from the **Project Types** option as shown in Figure 15.2. The upper right frame of the **New Project** window shows the templates that can be chosen for the project. For example, your project could be a windows application or an ASP.NET Web application. Choose the appropriate template. In Figure 15.2, we have chosen

the **Windows Application** (This is the template on which the code in Figure 15.5, to be discussed in the next section, is built).

**Figure 15.2** Starting a New Visual J# Project

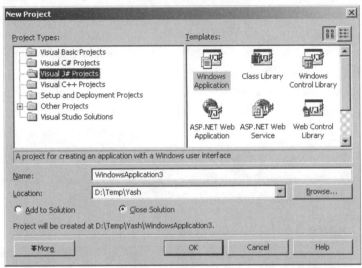

3.  In the **Name** option, enter the name you propose for your project.

4.  In the **Path** option, provide the physical path of the directory/folder where you wish to save your J# project.

5.  Click the **OK** button. You will now be presented with a Visual J# project window as shown in Figure 15.3.

When you open a new project, by default, it starts with a *Form* interface that can, in turn, be used to create a user interface consisting of buttons, text field, and so forth. If you need to write your code, choose the **View | Code** option from the Visual J# project window, and you will be presented a skeleton code (see Figure 15.4) that is built automatically by the Microsoft Visual J# development environment when you start a new project.

**Figure 15.3** The Visual J# Project Window

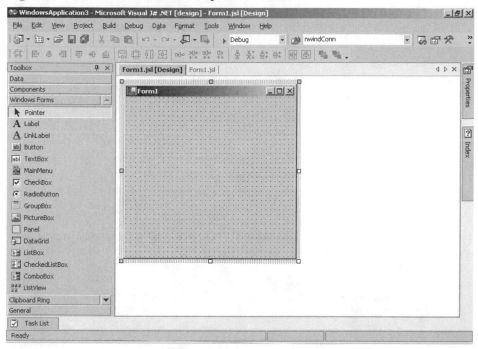

**Figure 15.4** The Skeleton Code for a New Visual J# Project

```
import System.Drawing.*;

import System.Collections.*;

import System.ComponentModel.*;

import System.Windows.Forms.*;

import System.Data.*;


//Summary description for Form1

public class Form1 extends System.Windows.Forms.Form

{

  //Required designer variable

  private System.ComponentModel.Container components = null;


  public Form1()

  {

    //

    // Required for Windows Form Designer support
```

**Continued**

**Figure 15.4** Continued

```
  //
  InitializeComponent();
  //
  // TODO: Add any constructor code after
  //InitializeComponent call.

}
// Clean up any resources being used.
protected void Dispose(boolean disposing)
{
  if (disposing)
  {
    if (components != null)
    {
      components.Dispose();
    }
  }
  super.Dispose(disposing);
}

//Region Windows Form Designer generated code
//Required method for Designer support - do not modify
//the contents of this method with the code editor.
private void InitializeComponent()
{
  // Form1
  this.set_AutoScaleBaseSize(new
      System.Drawing.Size(((int)5), ((int)13)));
  this.set_ClientSize(new System.Drawing.Size(((int)292),
      ((int)273)));
  this.set_Name("Form1");
  this.set_Text("Form1");
}
//Endregion
```

**Continued**

**Figure 15.4** Continued

```
// The main entry point for the application
/** @attribute System.STAThreadAttribute() */
public static void main(String[] args)
{
  Application.Run(new Form1());
}
}
```

The code in Figure 15.4 begins with certain default *import* statements. Java programmers should note that the *import* statements in a Visual J# project do *not* import packages from the Java class library. Instead, they specify namespaces that are part of the .NET Framework. For example, *Drawing, Collections, ComponentModel, Forms*, and *Data* in Figure 15.4 are all namespaces. Each one of these namespaces contains classes that provide certain basic functionality to a Visual J# project, just as the imported packages do in a Java application. These namespaces are the same ones used by C# (and in fact all languages that support .NET), and the functionality provided by these five *namespaces* is as follows:

- The *System.Drawing* namespace provides classes that provide graphics functionality, namely drawing bitmaps, setting fonts, and so on.

- The *System.Collections* namespace provides classes that define various collections of objects, such as arrays, hash tables, and so on.

- The *System.ComponentModel* namespace provides classes that implement runtime and design-time behavior of components.

- The *System.Windows.Forms* namespace provides classes for creating windows-based applications that can fully utilize the GUI features provided by the Windows operating system.

- The *System.Data* namespace provides ADO.NET support to manage data from data sources.

Note that the code body of Figure 15.4 declares a class, *Form1* (this is the default name—you may specify any name that is descriptive of your project), and its constructor (if you change the class name, remember to rename the constructor). The code starts at the *main()* method similar to Java. The points of difference will be clarified in the next section, where we will build a sample Visual

J# application as shown in Figure 15.5, and compare the code with its relevant counterpart code in Java.

# Creating a Simple Visual J# Application

We will now build a very simple Visual J# application that is meant solely to give you an idea of what a Visual J# application looks like. You are encouraged to change and manipulate its graphical user interface and methods to build code that is of some practical use to you, or to improve upon the code.

The Visual J# application we're going to build is an image previewer program that displays Bitmap images from a specified directory. Figure 15.5 shows the graphical user interface (GUI) for the application.

**Figure 15.5** The GUI for the Visual J# Application

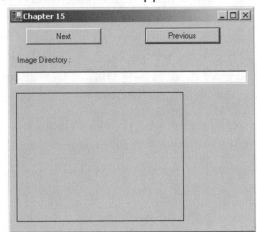

The application's GUI contains a text box where you can specify an image directory on your local computer. Each time the **Next** button is pressed, subsequent images from the directory (in the order that they are present in the directory) are shown in the picture box. The **Previous** button shows the previous image in the directory. If you intend to test the code as it is, ensure that the directory you specify contains no files of a format other than *.bmp*. This code is not designed to handle any data other than Bitmap images. If a file format other than *.bmp* is encountered, the code throws an exception. The code for the Visual J# application is listed in Figure 15.6. In this code listing, the code you want to focus on is shown in **bold** typeface. The rest of the code is automatically generated by Microsoft Visual J# development environment when various elements (buttons, text boxes, etc.) are placed on the form.

## Figure 15.6 The Visual J# Code

```
package Chapter15;

import System.Collections.*;
import System.ComponentModel.*;
import System.Windows.Forms.*;
import System.Data.*;
import System.IO.*;

//      Summary description for Form1
public class Form1 extends System.Windows.Forms.Form
{
  private System.Windows.Forms.Button btnPrevious;
  private System.Windows.Forms.Button btnNext;
  private System.Windows.Forms.PictureBox ptrBox;
  private System.Windows.Forms.TextBox txtImageDirectory;
  private System.Windows.Forms.Label Lable;
  //      Required designer variable
  private System.ComponentModel.Container components = null;
  private int ImageFile = -1;

  public Form1()
  {
   //
   // Required for Windows Form Designer support
   //
   InitializeComponent();

   //
   // TODO: Add any constructor code after
   //InitializeComponent call
   //
  }

// Clean up any resources being used.
protected void Dispose(boolean disposing)
```

**Continued**

**Figure 15.6** Continued

```
{
 if (disposing)
 {
  if (components != null)
  {
   components.Dispose();
  }
 }
 super.Dispose(disposing);
}


#region Windows Form Designer generated code
//     Required method for Designer support - do not modify
//     the contents of this method with the code editor.
private void InitializeComponent()
{
 this.btnPrevious = new System.Windows.Forms.Button();
 this.btnNext = new System.Windows.Forms.Button();
 this.ptrBox = new System.Windows.Forms.PictureBox();
 this.txtImageDirectory = new System.Windows.Forms.TextBox();
 this.Lable = new System.Windows.Forms.Label();
 this.SuspendLayout();
 //
 // btnPrevious
 //
 this.btnPrevious.set_Location(new
   System.Drawing.Point(((int)200), ((int)8)));
 this.btnPrevious.set_Name("btnPrevious");
 this.btnPrevious.set_Size(new
   System.Drawing.Size(((int)112), ((int)24)));
 this.btnPrevious.set_TabIndex(((int)0));
 this.btnPrevious.set_Text("Previous");
 this.btnPrevious.add_Click( new
   System.EventHandler(this.btnPrevious_Click) );
 //
 // btnNext
```

**Continued**

**Figure 15.6** Continued

```
//
this.btnNext.set_Location(new
   System.Drawing.Point(((int)24), ((int)8)));
this.btnNext.set_Name("btnNext");
this.btnNext.set_Size(new System.Drawing.Size(((int)112),
    ((int)24)));
this.btnNext.set_TabIndex(((int)1));
this.btnNext.set_Text("Next");
this.btnNext.add_Click( new
   System.EventHandler(this.btnNext_Click) );
//
// ptrBox
//
this.ptrBox.set_BorderStyle(System.Windows.Forms
   .BorderStyle.FixedSingle);
this.ptrBox.set_Location(new
   System.Drawing.Point(((int)8), ((int)104)));
this.ptrBox.set_Name("ptrBox");
this.ptrBox.set_Size(new System.Drawing.Size(((int)248),
   ((int)192)));
this.ptrBox.set_SizeMode(System.Windows.Forms
   .PictureBoxSizeMode.AutoSize);
this.ptrBox.set_TabIndex(((int)2));
this.ptrBox.set_TabStop(false);
//
// txtImageDirectory
//
this.txtImageDirectory.set_Location(new
   System.Drawing.Point(((int)8), ((int)72)));
this.txtImageDirectory.set_Name("txtImageDirectory");
this.txtImageDirectory.set_Size(new
   System.Drawing.Size(((int)344), ((int)20)));
this.txtImageDirectory.set_TabIndex(((int)3));
this.txtImageDirectory.set_Text("");
//
```

**Continued**

**Figure 15.6** Continued

```
// Lable
//
this.Lable.set_Location(new
  System.Drawing.Point(((int)8), ((int)48)));
this.Lable.set_Name("Lable");
this.Lable.set_Size(new System.Drawing.Size(((int)104), ((int)16)));
this.Lable.set_TabIndex(((int)4));
this.Lable.set_Text("Image Directory :");
//
// Form1
//
this.set_AutoScaleBaseSize(new
  System.Drawing.Size(((int)5), ((int)13)));
this.set_ClientSize(new System.Drawing.Size(((int)360), ((int)309)));
this.get_Controls().AddRange(new
  System.Windows.Forms.Control[] {this.Lable,
                   this.txtImageDirectory,this.ptrBox,this.btnNext,
                   this.btnPrevious});
 this.set_Name("Form1");
 this.set_Text("Chapter 15");
 this.ResumeLayout(false);

}
#endregion

// The main entry point for the application
/** @attribute System.STAThreadAttribute() */
public static void main(String[] args)
{
  Application.Run(new Form1());
}

private void btnNext_Click (System.Object sender, System.EventArgs e)
{
 if( txtImageDirectory.get_Text().get_Length()!= 0 )
```

**Continued**

**Figure 15.6** Continued

```
{
 try
 {
  if(Directory.Exists(txtImageDirectory.get_Text()))
  {
   System.String [] files = Directory.GetFiles(txtImageDirectory.
      get_Text());
   Bitmap image = new Bitmap(files[++ImageFile]);
   ptrBox.set_Image(image);
  }
  else
   MessageBox.Show("Directory doesn't exist.","Image Viewer");
 }
 catch(Exception ex)
 {
  MessageBox.Show("No more images in the Directory.","Image Viewer");
  --ImageFile;
  return;
 }
 }
 else
  MessageBox.Show("Please specify the image directory.","Image Viewer");
}


private void btnPrevious_Click (System.Object sender,
   System.EventArgs e)
{
 if( txtImageDirectory.get_Text().get_Length()!= 0 )
 {
  try
  {
   if(Directory.Exists(txtImageDirectory.get_Text()))
   {
    System.String [] files = Directory.GetFiles(txtImageDirectory.
       get_Text());
```

**Continued**

**Figure 15.6** Continued

```
    Bitmap image = new Bitmap(files[--ImageFile]);

    ptrBox.set_Image(image);

  }

  else

    MessageBox.Show("Directory doesn't exist.","Image Viewer");

  }

  catch(Exception ex)

  {

   MessageBox.Show("No more images in the Directory.","Image Viewer");

   ImageFile = -1;

   return;

  }

 }

 else

   MessageBox.Show("Please specify the image directory.","Image Viewer");

 }

}
```

The code listing of Figure 15.6 contains a new import statement, apart from the five import statements whose namespaces have already been discussed (see explanations for the skeleton code of Figure 15.4). This new import statement is as follows:

```
import System.IO.*;
```

The *System.IO* namespace, discussed in Chapter 11, enables reading and writing of data from data streams or files. Here, this namespace is required to read the image data from the image files. Let's now dissect the J# code and compare it to its Java counterpart.

The Visual J# application declares a class, *Form1*, that extends the *Form* class in the *System.Windows.Forms* namespace. It then declares two buttons, a picture box, a text box, and a label to be used in creating the application's GUI. The constructor of the class calls the *InitiallizeComponent()* method that instantiates the GUI elements and sets their size, location, and label. Note that the code generated for creating the GUI elements and setting their properties is quite similar to Java in syntax but differs in the classes being used. For example, the *Previous* button is created using the *System.Windows.Forms.Button()* class and its label is set as given in the following code snippet:

```
private void InitializeComponent()
{
  this.btnPrevious = new System.Windows.Forms.Button();
  this.btnPrevious.set_Text("Previous");
  ...
}
```

For comparison, in Java you would use the *JButton()* class from the *javax.swing* package to create a button as well as to set its label, in a single code line as follows:

## Java

```
JButton btnPrevious = new JButton("Previous");
```

The *InitiallizeComponent()* method also adds event handlers to the two buttons and sets the controls for various GUI elements within the context of the current form. Note that the event handling mechanism in J# is different than in Java. For example, to recognize a click event on the **Previous** button, the *btnPrevious_Click()* method is passed as a parameter to the *System.EventHandler()* class as shown in the following code line:

## J#

```
this.btnPrevious.add_Click( new
    System.EventHandler(this.btnPrevious_Click) );
```

The *btnPrevious_Click()* method defines actions to be taken in the event of the *Previous* button being clicked. In Java, you would use the *ActionListener* interface to add an action listener to the *Previous* button as given in the following code line:

## Java

```
BtnPrevious.addActionListener(this);
```

Also, the J# application defines separate methods to handle the events generated upon clicking different buttons. For example, our J# application contains two event handling methods, the *btnNext_Click()* and the *btnPrevious_Click()* as shown by the following code snippet:

## J#

```
private void btnNext_Click (System.Object sender,
    System.EventArgs e)


private void btnPrevious_Click (System.Object sender,
    System.EventArgs e)
```

However, in Java you can achieve the same by defining a single *action Performed()* method and checking the source of the event as shown by the following code snippet:

## Java

```
public void actionPerformed(ActionEvent ae)
{
  if (ae.getSource() == btnPrevious)
  {
   // Actions to be taken if the Previous button is clicked
  }

  if (ae.getSource() == btnNext)
  {
    // Actions to be taken if the Next button is clicked
  }
}
```

The J# application uses the *PictureBox* control to display the picture, using its *set_Image()* method. The *PictureBox* element is created in the *InitiallizeComponents()* method, using the *System.Windows.Forms.PictureBox()* class as shown in the following code line:

```
this.ptrBox = new System.Windows.Forms.PictureBox();
```

The image is set within the *btnPrevious_Click()* and *btnNext_Click()* methods using the following code line:

```
ptrBox.set_Image(image);
```

Java does not have a picture box element; instead, you can use the *JLabel* class from the *javax.swing* package to display an image. This will require passing an object of type *ImageIcon* to the *setIcon()* method of the *JLabel* class. Assuming that the physical paths for the images in the specified directory are stored in the *files[]* array and *ImageFile* contains the index of the current image, the following Java code lines will serve the purpose:

## Java

```
JLabel imageLabel;
ImageIcon img;


imageLabel = new JLabel();


img = new ImageIcon(files[++ImageFile]);
imageLabel.setIcon(img);
```

The program execution for the J# application begins at the *main()* method (just as it does in Java) where the constructor function *Form1()* is called. The *Dispose()* method disposes the application; that is, it takes its components off the screen. This method is called when the project is closed. Now let's look at what the method *btnNext_Click()* does. First, the *btnNext_Click()* method checks whether or not a directory is specified in the text box named *txtImageDirectory*, and whether the specified directory exists. If a directory has not been specified, a message box pops up displaying the message "Please specify the image directory." If the specified directory does not exist, the message displayed in the message box is "Directory doesn't exist." These two message box codes are enclosed in the *else* clause of an *if/else* statement. If the last image in the directory has been displayed, then clicking the **Next** button will display a message box saying "No more images in the Directory." This message box code is specified within the *catch* block of the *try-catch* statement. The following code listing displays the *if/else* and *try-catch* statements that perform the checks and display the respective message boxes:

```
if( txtImageDirectory.get_Text().get_Length()!= 0 )
{
  try
  {
    if(Directory.Exists(txtImageDirectory.get_Text()))
    {
      // Code to obtain image files
```

```
        }
      else
       MessageBox.Show("Directory doesn't exist.","Image
                       Viewer");
      }
    catch(Exception ex)
    {
      MessageBox.Show("No more images in the
                      Directory.","Image Viewer");
    }
  }
else
   MessageBox.Show("Please specify the image
                   directory.","Image Viewer");
 }
```

If the specified directory exists, the names of the files in that directory are stored in the array named *files[]*. The image data is stored using the Bitmap variable *(image)* that is derived from the *Bitmap* class as given in the following code:

```
if(Directory.Exists(txtImageDirectory.get_Text()))
{
  System.String [] files = Directory.GetFiles(txtImageDirectory.
     get_Text());

  Bitmap image = new Bitmap(files[++ImageFile]);
  ptrBox.set_Image(image);
}
```

The variable, *ImageFile* serves as a counter that carries the index of the current image in the *files[]* array. Quoting from what was said at the beginning of the application, this Visual J# application is designed to handle Bitmap data only. If the specified directory contains a file other than a Bitmap image, an exception will be thrown.

The method *btnPrevious_Click()* is the same as *btnNext_Click()* except that it uses the decremented value of the *ImageFile* variable to obtain the previous image in the directory.

Let's now look at the process of saving our J# project, compiling it, and running it. When you save the project, it is saved with the extension *.jshproj*. The source code files are saved with the extension *.jsl* in the same folder as the *.jshproj* file. To run this Visual J# application, perform the following steps:

1. Use the **Build** menu on your Visual J# application window and choose the **Build Solution** option as shown in Figure 15.7. This will compile your Visual J# project and generate a compilation report at the bottom right frame of the window. Errors, if any, will be listed. If the compilation is successful, an *.exe* file of your project will be created at the location *<yourProjectFolder>\bin\debug*. Here, *yourProjectFolder* indicates the directory/Folder where your Visual J# Project file is saved.

**Figure 15.7** Building the .exe File for the Visual J# Application

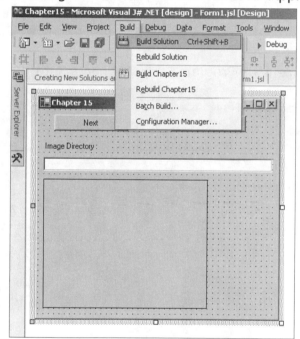

2. Double-click on the *.exe* file to run your Visual J# application. When you run this Visual J# application, it displays two buttons, a text box, and a picture box as shown in Figure 15.8.

3. Put the physical path of your image-directory in the text box and click the **Next** button. You will be presented with the first image in your directory as shown in Figure 15.9.

**Figure 15.8** The GUI for the Visual J# Application

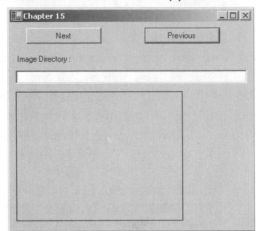

**Figure 15.9** Program Output When a Button Is Clicked

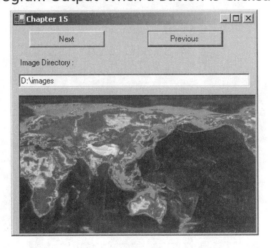

Note that the code syntax for the Visual J# project (see the code listing of Figure 15.6) is just as it would be for a Java program (declares a class, defines its constructor, defines the *main()* method, etc), but the similarity ends right here. An experienced Java programmer will readily notice that none of the Java packages are being used. Instead, the base .NET classes are being used. There are other points of difference, too. The major differences are the following:

- The first and most important difference is that you are required to save your Java code file with the class name itself. The filename has to be *Form1.java* for the code to compile, whereas, in the case of Visual J# you may save your project with any name you like.

- Java classes extend the *Frame* (or *JFrame* if you're using Swing) class from the Java class library to present their GUIs, whereas the Visual J# class extends the *Form* class in the *System.Windows.Forms* namespace.

- In Java, a call to the class constructor using the *new* keyword automatically will instantiate the class (*new Form1()*). On the other hand, the Visual J# class passes this instantiation code to the *Run()* method of the *Application* class that starts an application in the current thread. This is similar to how you would start a C# windows application.

- A Java code explicitly states that the components are shown, using the *show()* method. However, in case of a Visual J# application, a call to the *Run()* method of the Application class in itself includes the option to show the form and its components by default.

- The Java class implements the *ActionListener* interface to handle button-click events, whereas in the Visual J# application these events are handled through controls provided within the *System.Windows.Forms.Form* class itself.

- Java defines a single method *actionPerformed()* that takes an action event as a parameter. The source of this action event is determined using the *getSource()* method, which identifies every button clicked to generate the corresponding output. On the other hand, the Visual J# project defines separate methods for each of the buttons. These methods take two parameters, the object that sends the event and the event itself. This event handling mechanism is the similar to the C# event handling model.

As mentioned in the beginning of the chapter, a Visual J# code cannot be run using any JVM other than the Microsoft JVM on the .NET platform. Copy the code in Figure 15.5 to any text editor and save it with a *.java* extension (just as you would save a Java program). Now try compiling the code using the *javac* command at the command prompt (you need to have JDK/J2SE installed on your system to compile a Java program). You will find that the compiler generates multiple errors (I got 20 of them when I tried to compile the code of Figure 15.5 using JDK 1.3). This is because the J# code in Figure 15.5 is *not* a valid Java program. Its syntax resembles the syntax of Java, but the basic classes are not valid classes from the Java class library. Hence, the classes and their respective method properties are not recognized or supported by Java's development or runtime environment.

# Summary

In this chapter, you were introduced to the concept of J#. You learned how Microsoft's Visual J# development environment can be used to develop J# applications. The emphasis in this chapter was on the fact that though J# is syntactically similar to Java, it is not compatible with any JVM, and will only run on the .NET platform. To clarify this point, the sample Visual J# application of this chapter was also built in Java and the points of differences were highlighted. The main goal of the chapter is to present Visual J# to you, in order to help you migrate to the .Net platform. Thus, most of the Visual J# concepts and codes in the chapter have been presented in relation to Java concepts and codes.

# Solutions Fast Track

## What Is J#?

☑ J# is a complete implementation of the Java language specification. J# allows the majority of existing Java applications to run after recompilation or after binary conversion.

☑ J# is *not* Java. It follows Java's syntax but none of Java's Foundation classes can be used in a J# project, nor can a J# project be run on any JVM other than Microsoft's JVM on the .NET platform.

☑ J# code is not compiled into a byte code as happens with Java code. Therefore, J# cannot be compiled using a JDK or any other development environment for Java.

## Using Visual J#

☑ Install the Visual J# development environment and use it to create a new J# project.

☑ Visual J# allows access to all the features of the integrated development environment of Visual Studio.NET.

☑ Visual J# allows integration with .NET services (ASP.NET, ADO.NET, etc.).

## Creating a Simple Visual J# Application

☑ This Visual J# application we've built is an image previewer program that displays Bitmap images from a specified directory.

☑ The program execution for our simple Visual J# application begins at the *main()* method (just as it does in Java) where the constructor function *Form1()* is called.

# Frequently Asked Questions

The following Frequently Asked Questions, answered by the authors of this book, are designed to both measure your understanding of the concepts presented in this chapter and to assist you with real-life implementation of these concepts. To have your questions about this chapter answered by the author, browse to **www.syngress.com/solutions** and click on the **"Ask the Author"** form.

**Q:** How is J# similar to Java?

**A:** J# is syntactically similar to Java. J# is Microsoft's implementation of the Java language specification. Nevertheless, Sun Microsystems has not contributed to the development of J#, nor does Sun approve or endorse J#.

**Q:** Can I use my Java *.class* file (created using JDK) in a J# project?

**A:** No, you cannot use a Java *.class* file in a J# project. However, you can use Microsoft's byte code converter to convert Java *.class* files into Microsoft Intermediate Language (MSIL) and then use them in your J# project.

**Q:** Can I run my Visual J# project on any JVM?

**A:** No, you cannot run your Visual J# project on a JVM other than the Microsoft runtime available on the .NET platform.

**Q:** How do I convert my Visual J++ applications to Visual J#.NET?

**A:** You can convert Visual J++ applications to Visual J#.NET by using Java Language Conversion Assistance.

# C# Keywords and Java Equivalents

| C# | Java | Description |
|---|---|---|
| abstract | abstract | A class modifier that specifies that the class can't be instantiated but only derived by another class. |
| as | N/A | An operator used to perform casts conversion between compatible types. It casts the left operand to the type specified by the right operand and it returns *null* rather than throwing an exception if the cast fails. |
| base | super | A keyword used to access members of a base class from within a derived class. |
| bool | boolean | Used to declare *System.Boolean* variables. Boolean variables contain either *true* or *false* as their values. |
| break | break | Terminates the innermost loop in which it occurs. Transfers program flow to the statement immediately following the loop. |
| byte | N/A | Used to declare *System.Byte* variables. A byte is an 8-bit unsigned integer value between 0 – 255. (Note: A byte in Java is signed) |
| case | case | A keyword to define a labeled value within a switch statement. |
| catch | catch | A catch block specifies an exception to catch. They can only be used when coupled with a try block. |
| char | char | Used to declare a Unicode character variable of data type *System.Char*. Unicode characters are 16 bit integer values capable of representing most of the world's languages. |
| checked | N/A | A keyword used to control overflow checking on integral type arithmetic operations and conversions. |
| class | class | A keyword used to declare a class. |
| const | const | A field or local variable modifier that specifies the field cannot be modified. The const keyword is reserved in Java, but is not implemented. |
| continue | continue | The continue statement transfers program flow to the next iteration of the innermost enclosing loop. |
| decimal | N/A | A keyword used to declare a variable of the *System.Decimal* data type. The *decimal* data type is a 128-bit value with a precision of 28-29 significant digits. |

**Continued**

| C# | Java | Description |
| --- | --- | --- |
| default | default | A keyword used to designate a "catch all" case in a switch statement. |
| delegate | N/A | The delegate keyword permits you to pass a method as a parameter in a type-safe manner. |
| do | do | The do statement executes a block of code until a control expression evaluates to false. They are coupled with a while statement to form the do-while iteration loops. |
| double | double | A keyword used to declare a variable of type *System.Double*. A double is a 64-bit floating-point number. |
| else | else | A partner statement for the *if* keyword. The else expression executes if the partnered *if* statement evaluates to false. |
| enum | N/A | A keyword used to declare an enumeration. |
| event | N/A | A keyword used to specify an event. |
| explicit | N/A | A keyword used to declare a user-defined explicit type conversion. |
| extern | native | A keyword used to declare that a method implementation is declared externally. |
| false | false | A keyword that evaluates to the boolean value of false. |
| finally | finally | A code segment label used to designate code that executes after a try block regardless if an exception has occurred. |
| fixed | N/A | Use in pointer operations to prevent the garbage collector from moving the address of a variable in memory. |
| float | float | Used to declare a variable of type *System.Single*. *System.Single* contains a 32-bit floating-point value. |
| for | for | Creates a *for loop* which will execute a code segment until its control expression evaluates to false. |
| foreach | N/A | Creates a *foreach loop* for iterating through an Array or object collection. |
| goto | goto | Transfers program execution to the target label. This is a reserved keyword in Java but is not implemented. |

**Continued**

| C# | Java | Description |
| --- | --- | --- |
| if | if | The *if statement* executes a block of code, if a control expression evaluates to true. |
| implicit | N/A | A keyword used to declare a user-defined implicit type conversion. |
| in | N/A | Used with a foreach statement to specify the name of the collection that you are iterating through. |
| int | int | Used to declare a variable of type *System.Int32*. An int contains a 32 bit signed value. |
| interface | interface | Used to define a reference type that has abstract members. |
| internal | protected | An access modifier used to specify that members are only accessible from within the same assembly. |
| is | instanceof | Used to determine if an object is an instance of an object class. |
| lock | synchronized | Specifies that a code segment is a critical section. |
| long | long | Used to declare a variable of type *System.Int64*. A long contains a 64 bit signed integer value. |
| namespace | package | Specifies a scope that contains your classes. Permits you to organize your code. |
| new | new | Creates an instance of a class and calls its constructor. The keyword is overloaded and it's also used as a method modifier to hide inherited methods. |
| null | null | The *null* keyword represents a *null* object. The default value for all reference types is *null*. |
| object | N/A | An alias for *System.Object*. You can assign values of any type to variables of object. |
| operator | N/A | Declares an operator in a class or struct. Used for overloading operators. |
| out | N/A | This keyword on a method parameter causes the method to refer to the same variable that was passed into the method. |
| override | N/A | Used to override inherited methods. |
| params | N/A | This keyword on a method parameter lets the method take a variable number of arguments. |

**Continued**

| C# | Java | Description |
|---|---|---|
| private | private | An access modifier that restricts access to a member to the body of the class in which they are declared. |
| protected | N/A | An access modifier that restricts access to a member to the class in which it is declared, or to any class derived from it. |
| public | public | An access modifier specifying no restrictions on access to a member. |
| readonly | N/A | A modifier specifying that a field's value may only be set during construction, or at declaration. |
| ref | N/A | This keyword on a method parameter causes the method to refer to the same variable that was passed into the method. The difference between the ref keyword and the out keyword is that the argument specified by the ref keyword must be initialized prior to using it. |
| return | return | This keyword terminates the function in which it is used and returns program flow to the calling code. It may also be used to return a value to the calling code. |
| sbyte | byte | Used to declare *System.SByte* variables. A sbyte is an 8-bit signed integer value between −128 and 127. |
| sealed | final | A class modifier that specifies that a class can't be derived by another class. |
| short | short | Used to declare a variable of type System.Int16. A short contains a 16 bit signed value. |
| sizeof | N/A | Used to obtain the size in bytes of a type. |
| stackalloc | N/A | Allocates a block of memory on the stack. |
| static | static | Designates that a member belongs to the class itself, and not to an instance of the class. |
| string | N/A | Used to declare *System.String* variables. A string is a string of Unicode characters. |
| struct | N/A | Used to define a value type that can contain fields, methods, properties, indexers, operators, and nested types. |
| switch | switch | Used to specify a control statement which that has multiple selections indicated by case statements. |

**Continued**

| C# | Java | Description |
|---|---|---|
| this | this | Used to refer to the current instance object. |
| throw | throw | Used to throw an exception. |
| true | true | A keyword that evaluates to the Boolean value of true. |
| try | try | Specifies a code segment, which might throw an exception. When coupled with catch blocks, it provides the base mechanism for C# exception handling. |
| typeof | N/A | Used to obtain the *System.Type* object for a type. |
| uint | N/A | Used to declare a variable of type *System.UInt32*. A uint contains a 32 bit unsigned value. |
| ulong | N/A | Used to declare a variable of *System.UInt64*. A ulong contains a 64 bit unsigned integer value. |
| unchecked | N/A | A keyword used to control overflow checking on arithmetic operations and conversions. |
| unsafe | N/A | Declares code is run under an "unsafe context". Indicates the code might involve pointers. |
| ushort | N/A | Used to declare a variable of type System.UInt16. A ushort contains a 16 bit unsigned value. |
| using | import | Creates an alias for a namespace. |
| virtual | N/A | Indicates a virtual member. A virtual member can be overridden. |
| volatile | volatile | Indicates a field can be modified by something outside of the current thread. |
| void | void | Indicates a method does not return a value. |
| while | while | Creates a *while* loop which will execute a code segment until its control expression evaluates to false. |
| : | implements | Indicates a class is derived from another class. |
| : | extends | Indicates a class implements an interface. |
| N/A | strictfp | No C# equivalent. |
| N/A | throws | No C# equivalent. |
| N/A | transient | No C# equivalent, however the [NonSerialized] attribute is available. |

# Index

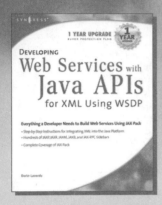